Pubblicazione realizzata con il contributo di:
Università degli Studi della Campania "Luigi Vanvitelli"
Dipartimento di Scienze Politiche

Andrea Russo

THE GARNISHMENT

A COMPARATIVE LAW STUDY

L'Harmattan Italia
via Degli Artisti 15
10124 Torino

L'Harmattan
5-7 rue de l'École Polytechnique
75005 Paris

Structures éditoriales du groupe L'Harmattan

L'Harmattan Italie
Via degli Artisti, 15
10124 Torino
harmattan.italia@gmail.com

L'Harmattan Hongrie
Kossuth l. u. 14-16.
1053 Budapest
harmattan@harmattan.hu

L'Harmattan Sénégal
10 VDN en face Mermoz
BP 45034 Dakar-Fann
senharmattan@gmail.com

L'Harmattan Cameroun
TSINGA/FECAFOOT
BP 11486 Yaoundé
inkoukam@gmail.com

L'Harmattan Burkina Faso
Achille Somé
tengnule@hotmail.fr

L'Harmattan Guinée
Almamya, rue KA 028 OKB Agency
BP 3470 Conakry
harmattanguinee@yahoo.fr

L'Harmattan RDC
185, avenue Nyangwe Commune
de Lingwala – Kinshasa
matangilamusadila@yahoo.fr

L'Harmattan Congo
67, boulevard Denis-Sassou-N'Guesso
BP 2874 Brazzaville
harmattan.congo@yahoo.fr

L'Harmattan Mali
ACI 2000 - Immeuble Mgr Jean Marie Cissé
Bureau 10
BP 145 Bamako-Mali
mali@harmattan.fr

L'Harmattan Togo
Djidjole – Lomé
Maison Amela
face EPP BATOME
ddamela@aol.com

L'Harmattan Côte d'Ivoire
Résidence Karl – Cité des Arts
Abidjan-Cocody
03 BP 1588 Abidjan
espace_harmattan.ci@hotmail.fr

Nos librairies en France

Librairie internationale
16, rue des Écoles
75005 Paris
librairie.internationale@harmattan.fr
01 40 46 79 11
www.librairieharmattan.com

Librairie des savoirs
21, rue des Écoles
75005 Paris
librairie.sh@harmattan.fr
01 46 34 13 71
www.librairieharmattansh.com

Librairie Le Lucernaire
53, rue Notre-Dame-des-Champs
75006 Paris
librairie@lucernaire.fr
01 42 22 67 13

---

www.editions-harmattan.fr / harmattan.italia@gmail.com

ISBN (Italia) 978-88-7892-484-0 / ISBN (France) 978-2-336-46085-7

CONTENTS

PART I
THE GARNISHMENT: ORIGINS AND STRUCTURE OF THE INSTITUTION

*****

1. The common law origin of garnishment

The custom of pursuing a debtor's property that is in the possession of a third party most likely originated in England's trading centers, specifically the "Custom of London"[1].

A London resident could use the foreign attachment to pursue the assets and liabilities of a nonresident debtor that were held by a third party. By the late 1800s, property attachment on mesne process had completely vanished in England due to the disfigurement of practice caused by the desire to extend the jurisdiction of this institution[2]. The early colonies, however, found the foreign attachment principles especially appealing because it was simple for a local debtor to flee to another English-speaking jurisdiction and avoid his creditors[3]. The American procedural systems became so ingrained with foreign attachment that it was taken for granted as standard business procedure[4].

The origin of the English word "garnishment" comes from the French term *garnissement*, meaning «a warning to a person not to pay money or deliver property to another, but appear and answer to plaintiff's suit»[5].

A garnishment is a notice given by the plaintiff to a third party who owes the defendant money or has property that belongs to him, allowing that person to retain the debt or bring the property into Court to enforce the suit's outcome. In a nutshell, it's the attachment of assets held by an unknown party to the lawsuit[6]. The stranger is referred to as a garnishee[7].

The remedy most likely originated from London custom, which allowed a citizen London to pursue the rights and assets of a non-resident debtor held by a third party[8]. Since the remedy is not one of the more traditional common law remedies, it would not exist in the absence of a statute[9].

A common law procedure[10], this attachment of chattels to force the appearance of a defaulting defendant had likely been used in kings' Courts as well as manorial Courts since ancient times[11]. Presumably, at least during the colonial era, its usage was much more widespread in England than we typically realize[12]. To be sure, writs of attachment were granted by colonial Courts to an astonishing degree[13]. Subsequent colonial legislation regulated and refined the processes[14], while early charters and statutes approved their use[15].

In fact, since garnishment is a statutory proceeding, strict adherence to the statutory forms is required[16]. As *quasi-in rem* proceeding, garnishment necessitates two services: a summons to bring the property before the Court and an application for the garnishment[17]. As a result, the garnishee cannot assist or hasten the process[18]. The garnishee cannot waive service of the proceedings required by law to make a seizure of effects or property in his hands, and if the garnishee is not legally served, nothing is attached in his hands[19]. A defendant's voluntary appearance and submission to questioning does not excuse a defect in the affidavit or grant jurisdiction[20].

According to the statutes, garnishment is a suit[21]. The plaintiff may end it and has all the rights of any other plaintiff[22]. Legal notice can be given to the garnishee without informing the primary defendant[23]. There is no legal requirement for the defendant in the initial lawsuit to stand up for the garnishee. The garnishee's responsibility is to ensure that he is not ordered to pay in a way that deviates from the law[24]. The judgment against the garnishee is not nullified by the plaintiff's death prior to its rendering[25]. The garnishee will be executed in substantial compliance with the judgment form, which will be recited by the executioner and presented to the constable. An additional directive should specify that, should the goods and assets under the garnishment be sold for a higher price than that for which the execution was issued, the excess, less the selling expenses, shall be given back to the garnishee[26].

Many times, it is claimed that when a garnishment is used, the plaintiff obtains a lien on the debt owed to the defendant by the garnishee[27]. It is preferable to argue that there isn't a real lien and that the plaintiff is only granted the authority to personally hold the garnishee liable for the debt or its value and to prevent them from paying the defendant[28].

In Ohio, a garnishee who is called before a justice of the peace is not considered a party to the case, and the justice's order for him to pay a certain amount on a note when it's due isn't a judgment against him or a determination of the parties' ultimate rights[29]. Essentially, it merely transfers the defendant's claim rights to the plaintiff, enabling the latter to pursue legal action in the event that the order is not followed[30].

The garnishee cannot use his payment of money under an execution as a defense after the garnishment is served. He ought to have requested a halt to the execution[31]. However, when informed later that the other party's creditors want to garnish him, a person who has entered into a contract to purchase land in good faith and is unaware of any claims made against him or his ability to pay them, need not wait for legal action to take place. Instead, they can proceed with the purchase and pay the consideration in full without consulting the other party's creditors[32].

If the garnishee is not charged but the lower Court's judgment is overturned due to a writ of error, the garnishee's payment to his creditor will remain unaltered in the interim[33].

After being served as garnishee in an initial attachment proceeding and having money belonging to the attachment defendant in his possession at the time of service, the garnishee is not allowed to deliver the money to the defendant's attorney after learning from the plaintiff's attorney that the proceedings have been compromised and dismissed. By doing so, the garnishee will be released from his liability as garnishee to another creditor of the defendant who has filed under the original suit, even though the garnishee has not received actual notice of the filing[34].

The garnishee finds themselves in the unfortunate situation of accruing obligations with no prospect of compensation. In order to protect himself, a garnishee should fully answer the writ, offer third party exemptions and claims, determine whether the judgment upon which the garnishment is sought is void, and pay any money he owes the defendant into Court after answering in order to prevent interest from accruing[35].

If he wants to avoid liability, he must respond completely, unequivocally, and fairly to all parties. In certain instances, he is considered a "stakeholder", and he has an obligation to always act in a way that respects the rights of others[36].

The goal of this book is, therefore, to present the old institution of garnishment diachronically in the legal system where it originates, compare to its civilian answer (the *saisine* institution) and, then, describe how the garnishment circulate globally in different contexts showing its capability to resist also after the de-colonization, the changing of time, and even if not perfectly adjacent to the legal culture of the transplanted legal system.

Notes

[1] R. W. MILLAR, *Civil procedure of the trial Court in historical perspective,* New Jersey, 1952, pp. 481-487. Professor Millar notes that earlier authors thought that this practice in London was a holdover from the legal system in place during the Roman occupation of Britain. This «may be dismissed as something out of the realm of legend», the speaker says. *Ivi*, p. 482.

[2] *Ivi*, p. 483. See also, M. ASHLEY, *England in the seventeenth sentury*, London, 1974; M. CIAN, *Le antiche leggi del commercio*, Bologna, 2016; C. M. CIPOLLA, *Storia economica dell'Europa pre-industriale,* Bologna, 1974.

[3] R. W. MILLAR, *cit.*, p. 485.

[4] *Ivi*, p. 486.

[5] K. A. CROSS, *Pleading in Courts of ordinary jurisdiction,* United States, 1885, p. 335. Moreover, the garnishment process was incorporated into Louisiana law by the Code of Practice of 1825's redactors, drawing inspiration from English jurisprudence. See, also Monroe Grocery Co. v. J. A. Perdue & Co., 123 La. 375, 48 So. 1002 (1909). Nonetheless, there is little more than a passing similarity between the Louisiana garnishment process and the common law jurisdictions of England at the time. A. WOOD RENTON, *Encyclopaedia of the laws of England*, ed. 3, vol. 5, London, 1940, p. 810 ss.; *Halsbury's laws of England,* ed. 2, 1934, p. 106 ss. It should be mentioned that England still allows garnishment under a writ of *fieri facias. Ibid.* Interestingly, despite having French roots, the term *garnissement* is not used in France to refer to the Louisiana-corresponding remedy. In fact, more in detail, the term *saisie-arrêt* refers to the French equivalent of the Louisiana garnishment procedure. It is established that common law jurisdictions jurisprudence, not French law, should be consulted when attempting to determine the origins of the garnishment process. See, again, Monroe Grocery Co. v. J. A. Perdue & Co., 123 La. 375, 48 So. 1002 (1909). For further details on garnishment in Louisiana see J. D. MCDONALD, J. B. CARTER, *Garnishment in Louisiana*, in *Lou. L. Rev.,* vol. 18, no. 3, 1957, pp. 446-508.

[6] R. WAPLES, *A treatise on attachment and garnishment*, United States, 2010, p. 341.

[7] The stranger is called a trustee in Massachusetts, where the procedure is

known as the trustee process. In Connecticut, instead, the procedure is known as factorizing and the stranger a factor. There is no authority for an equity Court to support the garnishment See, C. D. DRAKE, *A treatise on the law of suits by attachment in the United States,* Boston, 2010, § 451.

[8] Conventionally, the institution of garnishment has its roots in English common law. The practice was first introduced in the 12th century as a means for creditors to recover what their debtors had not spontaneously fulfilled. In fact, the etymology of the term garnishment comes from the Norman French "garnir" meaning to warn. C. J. NABIT, *Garnishment in Virginia,* in *William & Mary law review*, vol. 21, n. 3, 1980, p. 793, nt. 2. In medieval Europe, the garnishment afferent in particular to the concept of "foreign attachment" (a legal mechanism that is comparable to both contemporary attachment and garnishment practices. See, C. D. DRAKE, *cit.,* § 1-4.) widely used in the practice of medieval boroughs in England and on the continent. W. S. HOLDSWORTH, *A history of English law,* United Kingdom, vol. 3, 2012, p. 387; *ex multis,* the most meticulous research is done by R. B. MORRIS, *Select cases of the mayor's Court of New York City 1674-1784*, Washington, 1935, p. 14. This practice was commonly used in the early days of international trade to ensure that foreign merchants could be held accountable for their debts to local merchants. It provided a means for plaintiffs to secure their claims against non-resident defendants who may have fled the jurisdiction or had no assets within reach. W. E. MUSSMAN, S. A. RIESENFELD, *Garnishment and bankruptcy,* in *Minn. L. Rev.,* vol. 17, no. 1, 1942, p. 8. See, also, M. LUPOI, *Sistemi giuridici comparati. Traccia di un corso*, Naples, 2000; P.G. MONATERI, *Il precedente in Inghilterra*, in M. L. VACCA, *Lo stile delle sentenze e l'utilizzazione dei precedenti. Profili storico-comparatistici*, Turin, 2000; A. NEGRI, *Sistemi giuridici nel mondo*, Turin, 2010.

[9] This practice was brought from England to American shores during the early colonial era, giving it greater authority by virtue of enforcement by Court and statutes. See, Ownbey v. Morgan et al., 256 U.S. 94, 41 S. Ct. 433, 65 L. Ed. 837, 1921. See, also, P. GALLO, *I rimedi restitutori in diritto comparato, Trattato di diritto comparato*, R. SACCO (edited by), Turin, 1997; A. GUARNERI, *Lineamenti di diritto comparato,* ed. 2, Padova, 2004. On the formants of the legal norms, the references go to R. SACCO, *Legal formants: a dynamic approach to comparative law (Installment II of II)*, in *American journal comparative law*, vol. 39, no. 2, 1991; R. SACCO, P. G. MONATERI, *Legal formants*, in *2 The new palgrave dictionary of economics and the Law*, 1998; A. WATSON, *Comparative law and legal change*, in *Camb. L.J.*, vol. 37, no. 2, 1978, pp. 313-336.

[10] W. BLACKSTONE, *Commentaries on the laws of England*, vol. 1, Philadelphia, 1893, p. 280. Noteworthy is the statement made by Chief Justice Gilbert (1726) regarding attachment as the «great process in Courts of judicature...which lies as well in inferior Courts, not of record, as in superior Courts…». G. GILBERT, *Law and practice of distress and replevin*, London, 2018, p. 18. Gilbert underlined that the process is against the defendant's goods and chattels rather than his body. At first, attachment was a physical outburst of disdain. Among the

many scholars dealing with the Common law system, references are due to See, also, V. BARSOTTI, *La tradizione giuridica occidentale. Testo e materiali per un confronto civil law common law*, Turin, 2018; P. GALLO, *Introduzione al diritto comparato. Analisi economica del diritto*, vol. 3, Turin, 1998; O.W. HOLMES, *The Common law*, Boston, 1881; S. LITVINOFF, *Materials for an introduction to common law legal methodologies,* Baton Rouge, 2005; U. MATTEI, E. ARIANO, *Il modello di common law*, ed. 5, Turin, 2018; U. MATTEI, *Common law*, in *Trattato di diritto comparato,* R. SACCO (edited by), Turin, 1992; H. ZWEIGERT, H. KOTZ, *Introduzione al diritto comparato*, vol. 1, Milan, 1992; R. DAVID, C. J. SPINOSI, *I grandi sistemi giuridici contemporanei*, ed. 5, R. SACCO (edited by), Padova, 2004.

[11] A in earlier times, an example, the attachment was, often, physical. In fact, Wakefield's manorial Court mandated that two defendants "be attached by one cow" in order to respond to an agreement plea in 1316, see J. LISTER, *Court rolls of the manor of wakefield*, vol. 4, Cambridge, 2013, p. 132.

[12] Looking to the past, the attachment process is traced back to the time of Bracton, approximately 1256. In his renowned work, Bracton discusses the "solemnity of attachments", which is a method used in civil suits to compel attendance. In comparison to distress for services, which was established through the seizure of property, sureties established the attachment in civil lawsuits. Distress by land and chattels in different degrees of severity could only be made after multiple defaults. H. BRACTON, *De legibvs et consuetudinibus angliae,* vol. 6, Cambridge, 2012, pp. 439-441. However, Bracton was not enthusiastic with the cumbersome process and proposed, in the most progressive passion, that in money-related civil suits, chattels equal to the debt's value should be attached and given to the plaintiff in the event that the plaintiff defaulted. In fact, in a document signed 25 years later, Britton states that chattels could be attached immediately in cases of trespass against the peace in suits in the king's Court. In addition, chattels could be attached after the first default in suits for debts and smaller trespasses without a royal writ in county Courts. See F. M. NICHOLS, *Britton*, vol. 1, London, 2016, p. 105. Subsequently, it appears that the use of the later attachment increased over time. For additional mentions of attachment cases, especially during Queen Elizabeth's and her successors' reigns, see J. COMYNS, *A digest of the laws of England*, vol. 5, Hampshire, 2010.

[13] For instance, consider the numerous arrest warrants issued by the Provincial Court of Maryland, Maryland Archives, vols. 4, 10, 41, 49, 57, encompassing the years 1637 through 1670, available at: https://msa.maryland.gov/megafile/ msa/speccol/sc2900/sc2908/html/volumes.html; and by the Maine Courts, mentioned in C. T. Libby, *Province and Court records of Maine*, Portland, vol. 1, 1928, and vol. 2, 1931. Furthermore, all of the attachments there became "foreign attachment" when the Maryland Assembly decided to only allow attachments from non-residents.

[14] According to London customs, common law attachment, as opposed to foreign attachment, did not allow the plaintiff to receive any satisfaction from the attached chattels; instead, they were forfeited to the king. Even in

cases of "domestic" attachment, the colonies laws and, presumably in some cases, customs allowed the plaintiff to have execution over the attached assets. Massachusetts passed the first legislation to this effect in 1650. N. DANE, *The charters and general laws of the colony and province of Massachusetts Bay,* Detroit, 2012, p. 50.

[15] It emerges that a Massachusetts statute from October 1644 was the ancient act. In this regard, see N. DANE, *cit.,* p. 49. A March, 1658, statute in Virginia allowing attachments against the defendants' estates following a return *non est inventus* allowed a judgment to be rendered in this type of situation. W. W. HENING, *Statutes at large,* vol. 1, p. 466. Available at: https://vagenweb.org/hening/. Later laws specifically authorized execution.

[16] See, Illinois Cont. R. R. Co. v. Weavor, 54 III. 319; Shoody v. Second Nat. Bank. 62 Mo. 17.

[17] See, Epstein v. Salorgne, 6 Mo. App. 352; and Mosher v. Bartholow, 6 Mo. App. 598. Consequently, it is widely acknowledged that, in the event that the defendant is not served with legal papers and does not make an appearance, the proceeding is *in rem.* This is because the only outcome is that the defendant's property held by the garnishee, or the debt owed by the defendant, is subject to the payment of any sum decided in the plaintiff's favor against the defendant. The process is directed towards the garnishee directly, with the goal of forcing him to answer for the amount of any debt he may have owed the defendant or the worth of any property the defendant may have. See, R. P. SUGG, *Writ of garnishment*, in *Miss. L. J.*, vol. 24, no. 1, 1952, pp. 48-57.

[18] See, Schindler v. Smith, 18 La. Ann. 476; and in Hebel D. Amazon Ins. Co., 33 Mich. 400, the Court say: «Many things may a plain take place in the course of such [garnishment] proceedings which the garnishee on the one hand, or the garnishor on the other, may be bound or estopped by, as between themselves, but which the garnishee may not be able to urge as matter of defense against the suit of the principal defendant. Still there is no question of the right of one prosecuted as garnishee to make many admissions and waivers without endangering his protection. He need not wait to be led by the shoulder into the Court. He need not wage battle at every step. The law itself not only recognizes his right to suffer default, but provides what the practice shall be in such case, and invests the judgment with the same protective force as it does one awarded after vigorous contest».

[19] Phelps v. Boughton, 47 In. Ann. 592. The writ may be served by reading it to the garnishee: Pilor. Lytle, 6 Ark. 212. It is not necessary that the notice served on the garnishee should be signed by any one: Moore v. Stainton, 22 Ala. 831.

[20] See, Steen v. Norton, 45 Wis. 412; Rasmussen v. McCabe, 46 Wis. 600.

[21] See, Tunstall v. Worthington, Hemp. 602 And the summons there in is "process": Middleton Paper here Co. 19 Fed. Rep. 252.

[22] See, Griel v. Loftin, 65 Ala 591.

[23] See, Phillips a Germon, 13 Towz, 101.

[24] See, Pounds v. Hamner, 57 Ala. 342.

[25] See, Coleman v. McAnulty, 16 Mo. 173.

[26] See, Masters v. Turner, 10 Phila. 482.
[27] C. D. DRAKE, *cit.*, § 453 s.
[28] Bigelow v. Andress, 31 III. 322. In Cottrell v. Varnum, 5 Ala, 229, 3. Am. Dec. 323, the Court say: «By the service of a garnishment on a debtor of a defendant, the plaintiff acquires a lien on the debt for the satisfaction of his demand, which cannot be divested by any arrangement between the defendant and garnishee; and the judgment only consummates the legal transfer of so much of the garnishee's indebtedness as is condemned thereby to the payment of the plaintiff's demand. In this view, the argument that he rendition of the judgment previous to the maturity of the debt would prevent a rescission of the contract between the defendant and garnish out of which the liability of the latter arose, can have no influence, since a rescission as against the plaintiff could have no effect. If anything should occur subsequent to the garnishee's examination which would furnish a legal defense to a notion against him by the defendant, if remediless at law, he might resort to a Court of equity, and there have the benefit of that defense by perpetually enjoining the plaintiff's judgment against him. And this would be the garnishee's only mode of redress if the proceedings against him were to be stayed until the debt matures, unless the Court in its discretion were to permit an amendment of his answer. So that, whatever practice be adopted in a case like the present, the garnishee is not foreclosed from any defense arising after his answer, which he could have successfully urged against the defendant».
[29] T. S. MOORE, R. PFEIFFER, *Garnishment in Ohio: where is it now*, in *Ohio St. L.J. 856*, 1971, p. 856 ss.
[30] See, Secor v. Witter, 39 Ohio St. 218.
[31] See, Skipper v. Foster, 29 Ala. 330; 65 Am. Dec. 405.
[32] See, Fisher v. Ball, 44 Mich, 493.
[33] See, Webb v. Miller, 24 Mise 635; 57 Am. Deo. 189.
[34] See, Ryan v. Barkham, 42 Ind. 507.
[35] Red v. Powers, 69 Miss. 242, 13 So. 586 (1891).
[36] R. P. SUGG, *cit.*, pp. 48-57.

2. AVAILABLE EXECUTION TYPES

2.1. *The purpose and applicability of monetary enforcement*

All legal systems distinguish between different types of enforcement, notwithstanding, practically the victorious party typically receives financial compensation from the defeated party[1]. In general, these distinctions are warranted. First off, in some cases – such as when a specific item or plot of land is forcibly reclaimed – enforcement may not even require payment of money. Even if the winner receives only money in the end, there are a number of ways to get there, which calls for a variety of enforcement strategies under various sets of regulations[2].

It is theoretically possible to differentiate between the modes of enforcement based on five criteria. The elements of an execution strategy include: (i) the nature of the claim to be satisfied by execution; (ii) the object upon which execution is imposed; (iii) the specific means of enforcement (specific enforcement or enforcement by direct or indirect coercion); (iv) the type of enforceable instrument (judgment or extrajudicial document) that provides the means for execution; and, finally, (v) the type of Court that issued the judgment in the case of a judgment[3].

Actually, countries in Central Europe have a tendency to follow the claim's nature[4]. Although they allow for nonmonetary enforcement as well, the Romanic legal systems are primarily focused on the different ways to recover money; that is, they are more focused on the goal of enforcement than on the type of claim that needs to be satisfied through execution. Even when considering enforcement in its entirety, its different modes can be distinguished by the purpose of the object to which they are applied: enforcement against individuals, particular performance (*exécution en nature*), and asset enforcement[5].

By focusing on the different ways to collect money from the debtor, English law makes a distinction between them based on the specific types of assets that must be attached[6].

Today's enforcement methods are generally categorized as claim-oriented. This means that the criteria used to differentiate between different types of enforcement are based on the nature of the claim that needs to be satisfied by execution, not on the characteristics of the object of enforcement or its specific means, the kind of enforceable instruments, or the type of Court from which they originated. Consequently, the satisfaction of any enforceable instruments expressed in terms of claims for money is referred to as monetary enforcement.

On the other hand, since every mode in monetary enforcement involves a money claim, the further development of each mode must take a different approach. Nonetheless, levying the debtor's property in the broadest sense of the word is the typical method of enforcing a money judgment in the great majority of cases.

There are two reasons why monetary enforcement is more important today than any other kind of enforcement. Firstly, the predominant monetary nature of contemporary economic transactions provides restricted opportunities for alternative forms of enforcement to be implemented. Second, the idea and purpose of the debtor's property in relation to the satisfaction of prospective creditors become important since monetary enforcement primarily deals with the debtor's assets[7].

Generally speaking, the statutory exemptions serve as the sole exception to the general rule that the debtor's entire estate is subject to monetary enforcement against him.

2.2. *Different approaches to monetary enforcement*

As far as England is concerned, it is customary to use a range of financial enforcement methods. Four main approaches can be identified: (i) execution of debtor's assets; (ii) garnishment of debt (garnishee orders); (iii) garnishment of profits; and (iv) charging orders. The latter allows assets such as stocks, securities and land to be treated as collateral for judgment debts by placing a charge on the asset in an amount equal to the judgment debt. Its strategic decisions are often referred to because it is the creditor's responsibility to determine the best means of enforcement[8].

The garnishment of earnings differs from the garnishment of debts in general, just as in French Law[9]. The distinction is based on the idea that the latter type of garnishment applies only to existing obligations (even if collectible in the future), whereas an employee's earnings are not due or collectible until the entire service has been rendered[10].

In addition, there are three more things that should be brought up. First, in certain situations, alternative enforcement options are also available. For example, administration orders allow a debtor with several debts to pay off all of their obligations in installments, which are then divided equally among their creditors[11]. Second, where other means of enforcement are unavailable or ineffective, R.S.C.O. 51 allows the Court to designate a receiver who will subsequently gather funds that are anticipated to be paid to the debtor in the future[12]. Third, the High Court and the county Courts have different methods of enforcement, especially when it comes to the execution of goods. The primary distinction is that enforcement in the county Court is handled by Court employees, specifically the bailiffs, whereas in the High Court it is under the control of sheriffs, a private company[13].

Confronted with an enforcement that was «unduly cumbersome, inefficient, and expensive», coupled with a «bewildering multiplicity and choice of Courts and procedures», the Payne Committee attempted to simplify and consolidate the numerous options available in 1969[14]. These recommendations have not yet been put into practice.

In a comparative perspective, the types of execution in the United States deviate both from the distinction between execution at law and execution in equity and from the Common Law model[15]. As the Federal Rules of Civil Procedure were enacted in 1938, more state jurisdictions modernized and streamlined their enforcement remedies[16]. Three distinct methods of enforcement are now apparent in all cases: execution (i) against interests in land, where a judgment typically establishes a lien on the debtor's real estate; execution (ii) against interests in chattels; and execution (iii) against interests in choses in action, primarily through garnishment[17].

2.3. *Committing to and giving up all assets*

It is now evident that two additional forms of monetary enforcement that were somewhat prevalent in the past are no typically exist. The legislative evolution in England has been typical in this regard[18]. In spite of its name, the Debtors Act 1869[19] limited the use of imprisonment for debt, with the debtor's deliberate actions serving as the primary groundwork for this restriction[20]. In accordance with the Payne Committee's recommendations[21], the Administration of Justice Act of 1970 further limited this remedy.

Accordingly, committal to prison is limited to nonpayment of taxes, maintenance orders, and amounts owed to the government[22]. A committal order would be obtained in conjunction with a writ of sequestration, a harsh procedure that is rarely used - except on occasion against corporate bodies - even in cases of contempt of Court[23]. Furthermore, there are now voices advocating for the complete abolition of imprisonment for any type of civil debt, including debts to the Crown and maintenance orders[24]. In summary, the debtor's committal is currently the most widely used method of enforcing money judgments in a very small number of legal systems[25]. In any case, the parties cannot stipulate or use enforcement methods other than those stipulated by law, regardless of how easier, quicker, or self-executing they may be. This is because the enforcement rules are mandatory.

2.4. *Competition and cumulation of different types of enforcement*

The question of whether using one type of enforcement prevents the creditor from using other types later if it proves unsuccessful and whether the contemporaneous cumulative use of multiple types is permitted have emerged due to the variety of enforcement methods. Both of these issues are primarily relevant to monetary enforcement because, depending on the specifics of the nonmoney claim, nonmoney judgments and orders are typically enforceable through different means. The question of whether the creditor's choice of one form of execution precludes him from subsequently using another determines whether or not different types of monetary execution can be used consecutively. Since there is no recognized preclusive effect, it seems clear that consecutive employment should be answered in the affirmative[26].

In contrast, there has been a great deal of discussion throughout history and in certain real systems regarding the second issue, which is the cumulative use of various forms of monetary enforcement. Prior to the major codifications in the 19th century, the common European law of procedure adopted a system of predetermined sequential resort to the various forms of monetary enforcement (*gradus executionis*)[27]. Through legislative silence that is subsequently interpreted in favor of the creditor, as in England[28] or France, or by expressly allowing the creditor to resort to more than one type of execution at the same time, as in Italy[29], Austria[30], Germany[31], even Japan[32], most modern legal systems have abandoned this rigid sequence. Additionally, a few US jurisdictions have decided to execute movables first rather than immovables first. But even in most legal systems, where the creditor must collectively use multiple enforcement strategies, he cannot always move forward "all guns blazing"[33]. First, proportionality concerns under the constitution might prohibit him from doing so. More importantly, and in a second instance, many systems implement particular regulations that are essentially required in order[34]. Second, and perhaps more importantly, many systems adopt certain rules that are essentially mandatory in a number of specific cases[35].

2.5. *Brief considerations*

In light of what has been analyzed, there appears to be a genuine and commonly acknowledged tendency towards a decrease in the various forms of financial enforcement. The majority of systems appear to distinguish between three different sorts of execution: garnishment, execution on immovable property, and execution on movable property. The third type, garnishment, has a technical basis because it involves a third party, but the distinction between the first and second types is based on a lengthy legal tradition and has significant technical implications as a result. But in the midst of the differentiation, a convergence feature has emerged with respect to the requirements for monetary execution. These days, an enforceable title is necessary for all three forms of financial enforcement, including garnishment.

One last observation concerns the current trend of permitting the combined use of multiple enforcement strategies, at least in theory. While most modern systems have moved away from the antiquated rules of formal sequence, they have expanded the creditor's rights without freeing him from certain restrictions in certain situations. This development can also be seen as a move away from earlier, more broad approaches to enforcement and toward more specific regulations.

2.6. *The value of money and monetary enforcement*

The purpose of monetary enforcement is to pay a money claim. As a result, variations in the value of money could cause problems for enforcement procedures. This problem occurs more frequently it comes to the value of domestic currency in some systems (*i.e.,* France, Spain, China) and much more often it comes to enforceable instruments expressed in foreign currency.

In the latter case, three separate but related issues are important: (i) what kind of enforcement is necessary to recover such claims; (ii) whether a pecuniary enforcement judgment can be issued in terms of foreign currency; and (iii) when is the appropriate time to convert foreign currency into domestic currency.

The first query appears to be answered in the great majority of legal systems today, despite early skepticism or even obstinate insistence on the distinction between local and foreign currency[36]. Unless the parties have agreed otherwise, an obligation to pay foreign money is a monetary debt and should be enforced as such, rather than as a claim for the performance of a specific act or the delivery of goods[37]. Such equal treatment of claims in domestic and foreign currency for the purposes of enforcement has been brought about by decisions of the respective supreme Courts in a number of countries, including England[38].

The second query concerns the more technical question of whether the judgment granting effect to a foreign money claim may also be expressed in the foreign currency, even if the claim is to be enforced like any other money claim. Although this seems obvious in most legal systems[39], the House of Lords in England explicitly adopted this principle in 1976, ruling that English Courts had the right and obligation to render judgment in the foreign currency that was contracted for in cases involving foreign money obligations[40]. Other Commonwealth nations adopted similar measures[41].

The third query, which asks when it is appropriate to convert foreign currency into domestic currency, is still up for debate and has varying answers depending on the system. First of all, not even the most liberal system would use its enforcement tools to recover a foreign money claim in this manner. Monetary policy considerations deeply ingrained national sentiments, and the requirement for a uniform unit of account for distribution purposes have mandated the conversion of all funds into the local currency everywhere.

On the other hand, the lengthening of enforcement proceedings and the rise in monetary fluctuations make the relevant time for the conversion a crucial consideration. Theoretically, four points in time could be considered: the date the obligation becomes due, the date of the judgment, the date the enforcement proceedings are started, or the date the money is actually paid[42].

The fourth option took the place of the first alternative, which had long been a part of English law, in 1975[43].

Since 1988, the judgment-date rule has been in effect in the federal system of the United States as well as in New York. However, some states appear to have adhered to the breach-day conversion rule even earlier[44].

2.7. *Levy*

Even though the High Court and County Court have different enforcement procedures, the primary means of monetary enforcement in both cases is still execution on the judgment debtor's goods[45]. This procedure involves the execution warrant in the county Court and the writ of *fieri facias* (writ of *fi.fa.*) in the High Court. In any event, the creditor must select the proper enforcement method and open the Court[46]. On the question of whether prior notice to the debtor is required, there is a difference based on where the writ originated: in the High Court[47], it is not required, but in the county Court, it is[48].

When a sheriff receives a writ of *fi.fa.* or another type of execution against goods, it binds the debtor's property as of the moment it is delivered for execution[49]. But without notice of that or any other unexecuted writ, no writ will impair the title of a buyer acting in good faith and for a fair price[50]. There may not be a forced entry by the sheriff[51]. Title to the goods remains with the debtor until they are sold, and the sheriff may allow the debtor[52] to deal with the seized goods to a limited extent. Rather than acting as the charging creditor's agent, the sheriff is a civil servant[53]. As a result, in order to fulfill the claim stated in the writ, the sheriff, not the charging creditor, obtains a legal right in the goods[54].

When multiple creditors have issued writs of *fi.fa.* against the same property, they do not need to proceed with separate seizures; instead, one seizure ensures for the benefit of all[55]. However, the creditor may make a second levy for the remaining amount after being partially satisfied[56]. A third party must notify the sheriff of any claims they may have made regarding money, property, or other items that have been taken or are planned to be taken in execution. The sheriff is then required to bring "inter-pleader proceedings" before the Court[57].

In summary, enforcement of movables for money claims in England functions more as a warning than as a means of achieving a sale, which happens very infrequently[58]. The frequency of monetary enforcement on immovables is not notably higher. The "charging order" is the proper mode to use. The Administration of Justice Act, 1956 introduced it, and the Court may impose it not only on the judgment debtor's land but also on his stocks and shares, as well as on funds in Court that are standing to his credit[59].

The Court will first issue a charging order nisi on the creditor's application, which is backed by an affidavit. The debtor will then be invited to provide justification for why a charging order absolute should not be issued. The Court will make the order absolute, implying the imposition of a charge akin to a mortgage on the debtor's property, if the application is not contested, as is customary[60].

A joint proprietor may also obtain the charging order on their individual share[61]. The writ of execution in the United States is sent to the sheriff of the county where the assets to be levied upon are located and is issued by the clerk of the Court where the judgment is entered. A writ's typical maximum duration is substantially shorter than it is in England: thirty to sixty days, as opposed to twelve[62]. On the designated date, the writ must be returned to the clerk; otherwise, new writs may be issued as long as the judgment is not satisfied. Most jurisdictions allow the sale of real or personal property sold after the writ of execution's return date, provided that the property was seized prior to that date.

The judgment itself establishes an independent lien in the majority of American jurisdictions in addition to the execution lien, which is obtained by the issuance or levy of a writ of execution; this lien, however, only applies to real property. A levy on real estate can take many different forms, such as being recorded in certain offices, posted with notice, or even just being an endorsement of the levy on the writ, or "paper levy"[63].

Lastly, it must be remembered that the use of monetary enforcement through the levy and sale of either immovables or movables has become progressively less common in recent years throughout all systems. This outcome could be explained by the debtor's concealment strategies as well as the evolving range of exemptions[64]. In fact, different forms of garnishment are now frequently used in place of tangible property levy.

2.8. *Sale or collection of assets levied upon*

The three steps of monetary enforcement – levy, sale, and distribution of the proceeds – generally apply to both movable and immovable assets. Instead of actually resulting in a sale, the levy on goods in England functions as a threat or sanction of a potential sale and typically leads to some sort of agreement between the creditor and the debtor. According to reports, only one out of every 200 warrants truly lead to a seizure and sale[65].

In the case of immovables, the process of enforcing a charging order on the debtor's land results in an indirect rather than a direct method of enforcement because it has the effect of imposing a kind of mortgage on the land[66].

It is not shocking that there are no explicit guidelines governing the actual conduct of sales given these pragmatic considerations. As an alternative to a public auction, the Committee on the Enforcement of Judgment Debts suggested selling the goods through a private contract[67]. For the remainder, it states that the

Court may postpone execution in the event that unique circumstances make it impractical to carry out the judgment or order or in the event that the debtor applicant is unable to make payment for any reason[68].

The forced sale of a levied asset is more common in the United States, where the debtor's protection against an unfair or insufficient price at the execution sale is the main concern. In general, if there are no additional procedural irregularities, an inadequate price does not result in the sale being canceled. Particularly when it comes to real estate, a number of jurisdictions either allow for a subsequent public sale at higher bids or give the debtor the statutory right to redeem, which allows him to buy back the land from the buyer at the execution or foreclosure sale for the amount he bid[69].

The laws governing forced sales have relaxed recently. A growing number of legal systems allow the Court to choose a different, less formal method of sale in lieu of holding a public auction. The most recent laws pertaining to enforcement have expanded the Court's discretionary authority, even beyond this specific matter. Nonetheless, there are still a number of matters that divide the different legal systems, especially in relation to the execution of real estate. The question of whether mortgages and other lien rights survive after the real estate is sold to the highest bidder is the most crucial one in this case. These distinctions significantly impact the corresponding real estate laws and demonstrate that a key issue in this field is the peaceful coexistence of property law and law enforcement.

Notes

[1] For a systematic framework, see G. J. POSTEMA, *Common law e sistema*, Naples, 2019; R. DAVID, C. Jauffret-Spinosi, *I grandi sistemi giuridici contemporanei*, ed. 5, R. SACCO (edited by), Padua, 2004; G. ALPA, R. DELFINO, *Il contratto nel common law inglese*, ed. 2, Padua, 1997; P. GLENN, *Legal traditions of the world: Sustainable diversity in law,* Oxford, 2014; U. MATTEI, P.G. MONATERI, *Introduzione breve al diritto comparato*, Padua, 1997.

[2] Even if in this book we resort to different legal system whose nature is catalogued in predetermined legal families, their traits are not so clean. Indeed, all our national private laws in Europe today can be described as mixed legal systems. None of them has remained "pure" in its development since the

Middle Ages. They all constitute a mixture of many different elements: Roman Law, indigenous customary law, canon law, mercantile custom, and Natural Law theory, to name the most important ones in the history of the law of obligations. R. ZIMMERMANN, *Roman law, contemporary law, European law*, Oxford, 2001, p. 159.

[3] The first three criteria are mentioned by Rosenberg, Gaul, and Schilken § 9, the first two by the Stalev Report 2, the fourth is insisted upon by Latin-American doctrine (refer to the Vescovi Report 8-10), and the last is well-known in English law. See K. D. KERAMEUS, *Enforcement proceedings*, in K. ZWEIGERT, U. DROBNIG, *International encyclopedia of comparative law online, vol. XVI: Civil procedure*, Leida, 2002, ch. 10.

[4] For instance, German law makes a distinction between enforcement for money payments, property deliveries, acts of any kind, and abstentions from acts of any kind. See Code of Civil Procedure, § 803-882a; § 883-886; § 887-889, 894-898; § 890. Moreover, the Austrian law on enforcement follows a similar, albeit more thorough, classification. See Execution Code §87-369. In contrast, Switzerland's federal law on debt collection and bankruptcy distinguishes between monetary enforcement - which includes attachment, mortgage enforcement, and bankruptcy applications - and nonmonetary enforcement, which is left to cantonal legislation. See, Federal law on execution and bankruptcy, 1889. Available at: https://www.fedlex.admin.ch/eli/cc/11/529_488_529/de. The last, and major, amendment of 16 Dec. 1994 came into force on 1 Jan. 1997. See, *Message concernant la révision de la loi fédérale sur la poursuite pour dettes et la faillite* of 8 May 1991: FF 1991 III no. 27 of 16 July 1991. Federal law on execution and bankruptcy, Articles 89-150; Articles 151-158; Articles 159-196.

[5] In Italy, M. CAPPELLETTI, J. M. PERILLO, *Enforcement proceedings*, in *Civil procedure in Italy*, Netherlands, 2013, p. 323, introducing the use of a Court-appointed substitute for the enforcement of compulsory and restrictive measures. The Italian Civil Code makes a distinction between specific forms of enforcement (Articles. 2930-2933) and forced liquidation (Article 2910). In Spanish-speaking countries some doctrine makes a distinction between the execution of an extrajudicial act or a judgment.

[6] C. OSBORNE, *Civil litigation*, ed. 8, London, 2000, p. 409; see, also, C. M. SCHMITTHOFF, *The English conflict of laws,* London, 1954.

[7] Regarding this, Romanic legal systems have enacted a clear provision requiring the debtor to submit all of his assets to measures of enforcement by or on behalf of his creditors. According to the *Code civil français*, Article 2093: « Les biens d'un débiteur sont le gage commun de ses créanciers […] ». See also S. GUINCHARD, *L'affectation des biens en droit privé français*, Paris, 1976, pp. 22-26. Numerous Latino-American legal systems have also embraced this French rule. See E. J. COUTURE, *Fundamentes del derecho procesal civil*, Buenos Aires, 1958, pp. 465-466. In Italy the Civil Code, Article 2740 par. 1 and in Spain Civil Code, Article 1911 provide that «the debtor is liable for the performance of his obligations with all his assets, present and future». See S. SATTA, *Diritto processuale civile*, ed. 9, Padua, 1981, pp. 35-37. The same idea

is widely accepted in Central European nations without official backing. See, for example in Switzerland, G. Scyboz, P. R. Gilliéron, *Code civil suisse et code des obligations annotés,* Lausanne, 2016, pp. 22-23.

[8] Gatenby, *Recovery of money*, ed. 7, London, 1989, p. 120.

[9] See Loi n° 91-650 du 9 juillet 1991, Articles 42, 48, 50.

[10] J. I. H. Jacob, *The Supreme Court Practice 1973,* vol. 2, London, 1972, p. 292. The Attachment of Earnings Act of 1971 completed the introduction of the attachment of earnings, which had begun in part in 1958.

[11] *Ivi*, p. 293.

[12] See G. Gilmore, C. L. Black, *The law of admiralty*, ed. 2, New York, 1975, pp. 112-118; R. J. Walker, *English legal system,* ed. 5, London, 1980, p. 395.

[13] See Gatenby, *cit.,* pp. 126-127.

[14] *Payne* Report par. 287, 293, 295, 314 (a), 316.

[15] S. A. Riesenfeld, W. J. Pakter, *Comparative law casebook,* vol. 4, Leida, 2001, Cases 6-11.

[16] *Ivi,* Cases 11.

[17] *Ivi,* Cases 89-91, 149-151, 204-207, 221-224.

[18] See, A. Watson, *The Evolution of law,* Baltimore, 1985; *Id.*, *Society and Legal Change*, Edinburgh, 1978.

[19] Act for the Abolition of Imprisonment for Debt, 1869. Available at: https://www.legislation.gov.uk/ukpga/Vict/32-33/62/part/I/crossheading/abolition-of-imprisonment-for-debt/enacted

[20] W. Thoday, *Imprisonment by Justices for nonpayment of money*, London, 1936, pp. 3-11, who claims that more than 23.000 imprisonments for failure to pay money were imposed in 1933, meaning that this accounted for nearly half of all imprisonment sentences issued. By 1965, there were only 7.500, and by 1976, there were only 2.617.

[21] *Payne* Report par. 952-1007.

[22] R. M. Jackson, *The machinery of justice in England*, ed. 6, Cambridge, 1972, pp. 91-93.

[23] Which should be separated from incarceration due to civil debt. See H. Cecil, *The English judge,* London, 1970, p. 99.

[24] R. M. Jackson, *cit.*, p. 93.

[25] For instance, in India the Code of Civil Procedure 1908, Order XXI, Rule 30 providing for the debtor's «detention in the civil prison». See, B. N. Banerjee, *Law of civil appeals and revisions,* ed. 2, Allahabad, 1963, p. 440.

[26] H. Jacob, *Courts, law, and politics in comparative perspective,* Connecticut, 1996, p. 290.

[27] R. C. Van Caenegem, *History of European civil procedure*, Tübingen, 1973, pp. 64-79. Since this system was designed to be based on roman law sources, it was necessary to try the previous type before employing any other. The order was claims *(mobilia, immobilia, nomina),* movables, and immovables.

[28] J. O' Hare, R. N. Hill, *Civil litigation*, ed. 5, London, 1990, p. 546.

[29] Code Civil Procedure, Article 483. See, also, A. Saletti, *Cumulo ed eccesso dei mezzi di espropriazione forzata*, in *Riv. dir. proc.* 1984, pp. 506-559.

[30] Execution Code § 14.

[31] Even though Code Civil Procedure § 866 par. 2 only applies to enforcement on immovables, cumulative enforcement for the remaining provisions is based on the legislator's silence, taking into account the opposing stance taken by earlier legislation.
[32] Law on Civil Execution, Article 43 par. 1, 2.
[33] The phrase originates from J. O' HARE, R. N. HILL, *cit.*, p. 546.
[34] This is characteristic for France: Court Orléans 29 Nov. 1973, J.C.P. 1974. IV.6414 p. 174-176 note J.A. (one does not kill a fly with a canon): a creditor may not levy upon the debtor's immovable property for the purpose of a claim of Fr. 1600 (approximately US $218) as long as the debtor has other disposable assets.
[35] See Code Civil Français, Article 2209; German Code of Civil Procedure § 777; Italian Civil Procedure Code, Articles 496-558.
[36] F. A. MANN, *The legal aspects of money*, ed. 2, London, 1953, p. 198.
[37] With additional comparative remarks see, *Ivi*, pp. 190-199.
[38] See Miliangos v. George Frank (Textiles) Ltd., [1975] 3 W.L.R. 758 (767), 3 All E.R. 801 (810) (H.L.); already in the earlier case *In re* United Railways of Havana and Regla Warehouses Ltd., [1961] A.C. 1007 the House of Lords had departed from the "commodity" theory of foreign money.
[39] The ability to issue judgments in foreign currencies is especially taken for granted in Romanic legal systems, as evidenced by the way they handle the issue of when it is appropriate to convert foreign currency into domestic currency.
[40] See F. A MANN, *cit.*, p. 198.
[41] B. C. CAIRNS, *Australian civil procedure,* ed. 2, Sidney, 1985, p. 520.
[42] For a summary of comparisons, see G. VAN HECKE, *Currency*, in K. ZWEIGERT, U. DROBNIG, *International encyclopedia of comparative law online,* vol. III, 1972, ch. 36, p. 14.
[43] See Schorsch Meier G.m.b.H. v. Hennin, [1975] Q.B. 416 (C.A.); also, Miliangos v. George Frank (Textiles) Ltd. (supra n. 35) W.L.R. 772. See also F. A. Mann, *cit.*, pp. 351-357.
[44] F. A. MANN, *cit.,* p. 346-351. See, also, E. A. FARNSWORTH, *Contracts, cases and materials*, ed. 6, New York, 2001.
[45] GATENBY, *cit.*, p. 120.
[46] R.S.C.O. 45 r. 1 (1). Civil Procedure Rules, 1999, p. 102, R. 45.02 p. 883 state that the word "writ" is only used in relation to enforcement.
[47] See Land Credit Company of Ireland v. Lord Fermoy, *Ex parte* Munster (1870) L.R. 5 Ch. 323 (325); Hopton v. Robertson (1884), W.N. 77, 23 Q.B.D. 126 n. (127).
[48] See J. I. H. JACOB, *The Supreme Court Practice, cit.,* p. 291.
[49] Supreme Court Act 1981 s. 138 (1).
[50] *Ivi*, s. 138 (2).
[51] Civil Procedure Rules 1999, R. 45.1.11, part 888.
[52] Civil Procedure Rules 1999, R. 45.1.7, part 887.
[53] See per Lord Cranworth, L.C. in Hooper v. Lane (1857), 6 H.L. Cas. 443 (549–550), cited: In re a Debtor (No. 2) of 1977, Ex parte the Debtor v.

Goacher, [1979] 1 W.L.R. 956 (961), [1979] 1 All E.R. 870 (874) (Ch. D.).
[54] See Samuel v. Duke (1838), 3 M.&W. 622, 150 E.R. 1294, cited: Civil Procedure Rules, 1999, R. 45. 1.7, part 887.
[55] Jordan v. Binckes (1849), 13 Q.B. 757 (758–760), 116 E.R. 1453–1454.
[56] *Ex parte* Shaw in re Henderson, [1884] W.N. 60 (C.A.); Re Hille India Rubber Co. (no. 2), [1897] W.N. 20 (C.A.).
[57] R.S.C. O. 17.
[58] J. I. H. JACOB, *The Supreme Court practice,* cit., p. 291; R. J. WALKER, *cit.,* p. 392.
[59] Charging Orders Act 1979 s. 2(2); R.S.C. O. 50.
[60] Charging Orders Act 1979 s. 1(1). See, J. I. H. JACOB, *The Supreme Court practice, cit.,* p. 294-295.
[61] Charging Orders Act 1979 s. 2 (2) (a), as understood in National Westminster Bank v. Stockman, [1981] 1 All E.R. 800 (801) (Q.B.).
[62] R.S.C. O. 46 r. 8 (1).
[63] Riesenfeld, *Regional Report 72*, Cases 125, no. 3.
[64] F. SCHAUER, *Civil law, common law, and the data of jurisprudence,* in N. BERSIER, C. BEZEMEK, F. SCHAUER (edited by), *Common law - Civil law,* Berlin, 2022, pp. 5-15.
[65] J. I. H. JACOB, *The Supreme Court practice, cit.,* p. 291.
[66] *Ivi*, p. 295; Civil procedure rules, 1999, R. 50.1.17, part 952.
[67] *Payne* Report par. 698-699. See, also, J. CHITTY, *On contracts, vol. II, Specific contracts*, London, 1983; G. CRISCUOLI, *Il contratto nel diritto inglese*, Padua, 1990.
[68] R.S.C. O. 47 r. 1 (1).
[69] Riesenfeld, *Regional Report 72*, Cases 138-144.

3. The institution of garnishment

3.1. *Introduction*

A significant portion of transactions in the modern economy end in financial claims. They become part of the creditor's assets, the realization of which is contingent upon the debtor's performance, as long as they remain unfulfilled. Therefore, if this creditor also has other creditors, those creditors have the right to view their debtor's money claims as part of their assets and may attempt to enforce their own money claims against a third debtor[1]. The practical significance of garnishee proceedings can be explained by the predominant monetary nature of modern transactions. They become even more significant because, in many cases, enforcement is used against people whose only source of income is from their job; attachment of earnings is the second stream that enters the wide field of garnishment[2]. In this field, numerous persistent issues have existed spanning national boundaries. They deal with the unity or multiplicity of garnishee proceedings, whether earnings or other civil debts are attached, whether money claims or tangible property in the possession of the third debtor are targeted, and, finally, the primary formal requirement of garnishment: whether garnishment may be initiated by an enforceable instrument, as in all other methods of enforcement, a judicial order, or even the garnishor's sole private initiative. The consequences of garnishment, the position of the garnishee, and the interactions between different creditors attempting to garnish the same claim of their shared debtor are further common issues. Within legal families, responses to these and related questions frequently differ. Thus, it would seem prudent to take a functional approach in this case, focusing on the problems rather than the legal families per se.

3.2. *Object of garnishment*

There are differences amongst common law[3] jurisdictions concerning the method of attaching choses in action. While foreign attachment of debtor's goods in the hands of bailee quickly evolved into garnishment in medieval England[4], the matter does not appear to attract actual interest at this time and, in any case, is covered by the application of a *fi.fa.* writ[5]. This also applies to the Committee on the Enforcement of Judgment Debts' recommendations[6].

The United States, on the other hand, presents a convoluted and unclear image. While some jurisdictions, like those in Kansas, Minnesota, North Dakota, and South Dakota, have chosen to use both options, most jurisdictions alternate between regular levy proceedings and garnishment[7].

In England, garnishment was first used in 1854 as a way to help the business community work toward efficient enforcement[8]. However, it wasn't until the Maintenance Orders Act, 1958 (s. 6-15) that earnings were subject to garnishment in order to enforce affiliation and maintenance orders. In 1969, the Committee on the Enforcement of Judgment Debts recommended expanding the use of earnings attachment for the enforcement of civil debts (also known as monetary claims) generally, in part because it served as a substitute for the elimination of incarceration.

The recommendation was implemented by Parliament via the Attachment of Earnings Act 1971. As a result, the gradual and hesitating equalization of earnings to other monetary claims as a garnishment object characterizes English law.

Two matters – the conditions under which checks and bills of exchange may be seized and the possibility of future claims being garnished – present a particular comparative interest among the many attributes that may be associated with the claim to be garnished. Checks and bills of exchange must be in free commercial circulation, and the corresponding instrument must be delivered at the same time in order for them to be transferred. Consequently, in order to avoid impeding the debtor's ability to transfer these instruments freely or severing the claim from the actual possession of the instrument, claims arising from such instruments should not be garnished. English law attempts to achieve a similar outcome by prohibiting the debtor from handling the bill during the interim through an injunction[9].

Moreover, garnishment is a technique that attaches debtor's claims against a third debtor, so it depends on the existence of these claims; if they don't, garnishment loses its purpose and becomes meaningless. But whether future claims may be garnished is a more pressing issue that is crucial in real life. As long as the fundamental legal relationship that gives rise to potential future claims already exists, the majority of legal systems typically provide an affirmative response. In contrast, English law under R.S.C.O. 49 r. 1 (1) state that «Any debt due or accruing due to the judgment debtor from the garnishee» is subject to garnishment. This has been interpreted to include debts that are currently outstanding but will become due *in future* (*debitum in praesenti, solvendum in futuro*)[10]. However, since wages are not considered a debt "due or accruing due" to the debtor until the entirety of the relevant service has been rendered, there is actually no grace period within which the judgment creditor can treat wages[11].

It has been decided that a garnishee order cannot shorten the period of time needed to pay a debt; if the debt is not owed, nothing can be attached[12]. Thus, except in relation to a maintenance order, future earnings are not subject to garnishment in the High Court; they are, however, attachable in county Courts[13]. Even the Committee on the Enforcement of Judgment Debts only suggested an interim order, not extending the ability to garnish future earnings generally[14]. For the remainder, and to the extent that future earnings may be garnished, as in county Courts, the debtor shall notify the Court upon terminating his first employment and taking up a new position so that the order may be transferred to the new employer[15].

3.3. *Parties to Garnishment*

For the most part, legal systems only require that there be a relationship of creditor and debtor between the first debtor and the third debtor (garnishee)[16]. In order for the garnishment to be finalized, notice must be given to both the first debtor and the garnishee, as the latter is a third party who has not yet been involved in the previous proceedings and against whom no enforceable instrument is asserted[17]. The key query then becomes which procedural actions are required of the garnishee and what legal ramifications follow from them.

The English legal system provides that the Court must issue an order inviting the garnishee "to show cause" at the outset of the garnishee proceedings, in accordance with the standard procedure for English enforcement remedies[18].

The Court has the authority to convert its initial order nisi into an order absolute if he fails to appear or does not contest the amount owed[19]. Otherwise, the Court may decide the matter at hand summarily or order that it be tried in the proper way if the garnishee contests his liability[20].

The most common type of garnishment is the attachment of a bank account. Specifically, banks, like any other garnishee, are generally required to provide information regarding the existence and scope of the garnished claim, even though their relationship with their client is confidential. The Committee on the Enforcement of Judgment Debts in England recommended that garnishment be extended to all bank accounts[21]. However, parliament only partially acted on this recommendation, allowing garnishment of any deposit account or withdrawable share account with any deposit taking institution, regardless of whether any previously stipulated conditions had been met[22].

Notes

[1] See, A. Hamilton, *Garnishment*, in *The American law register (1852-1891)*, vol. 33, no. 10, New Series vol. 24, 1885, pp. 625-634.
[2] J. I. H. Jacob, *The Supreme Court practice, cit.*, p. 294.
[3] G. Romeo, *L'argomentazione costituzionale di common law,* Turin, 2020.
[4] Riesenfeld, *Regional Report 72,* Cases 205.
[5] Civil Procedure Rules, 1999, R. 45.1.20, part 889.
[6] *Payne* Report par. 564, 566, 574, 579 ; also, par. 712, 713.
[7] Riesenfeld, *Regional Report 72,* Cases 205-207.
[8] A bill to amend the procedure, practice, and mode of pleading in the Superior Courts of Common Law at Westminster and the Superior Courts of Common Law of the Palatine Counties of Lancaster and Durham, as well as to expand their jurisdiction. See, The Common Law Procedure Act, 1854, s. 60-67.
[9] Hyam v. Freeman, 35 Sol. J.87 (1890) (Q.B.).
[10] J. I. H. Jacob, *The Supreme Court practice, cit.,* p. 292.
[11] *Ibid.*
[12] Webb v. Stenton (1883), 11 Q.B.D. 518 (522–531) (C.A.); Re Greenwood, [1901] 1 Ch. 887 (890-891, 893).
[13] R. J. Walker, *cit.*, pp. 392-393; J. O' Hare, R. N. Hill, *cit.*, pp. 552-555.

[14] *Payne* Report par 723, 726 no. 4, p. 565.
[15] Attachment of Earnings Act 1971 s. 15 (a), (b).
[16] See, for instance, S. SATTA, C. PUNZI, *Diritto processuale civile,* Milan, 2000, pp. 788-789.
[17] It's possible that the garnished claim has a judgment debt attached to it as well, but in that case, the judgment is against the garnishor and in favor of the first debtor. See Holtby v. Hodgson (1889), 24 Q.B.D. 103).
[18] R.S.C. O. 49 r. 1 par. 1, 2.
[19] R.S.C. O. 49 r. 4.
[20] R.S.C. O. 49 r. 5. Strangely enough, the English model is similar to the Romanic one - more specifically, to its second alternative - because the garnishee is also required to appear before the judge and provide a justification. Furthermore, as opposed to the garnishor, who challenges the garnishee's incomplete or inaccurate declaration under the third alternative of the Romanic systems, it is the garnishee who contests his liability. Still, there is a distinction in that the Romanic systems leave it up to the garnishor's initiative to initiate a garnishment; this, it is argued, is a divergence characteristic of the entire English system of enforcement rather than one particular to garnishment.
[21] *Payne* Report par. 314 (b), 712, 713, 716-720, 736 (3).
[22] Supreme Court Act 1981, s. 40, par. 4 permits the Lord Chancellor to include or exclude accounts by order, of any kind mentioned in the order. See also R.S.C. O. 49 r. 1 par. 3.

4. The *Saisie-Arrêt* in France

4.1. *The enforcement of French Court judgments*

The fundamental result of the reform brought about by a *Loi n° 91-650 du 9 juillet 1991,* is the framework for French law that governs the channels of enforcement. According to Article 1 of the Law, a creditor may, under certain conditions, compel a noncompliant debtor to fulfill his debts to the creditor[1].

A creditor who has an enforceable right establishing a claim for a debt that is fixed and due may, in accordance with the requirements for each enforcement action, execute the enforcement on the debtor's assets, as stated in article 2 of that legislation[2]. Certain requirements must be met before using legal action to force a debtor or the person against whom a judgment has been issued to fulfill his obligations under a contract or judgment. An enforceable right establishing a claim for a debt that is fixed and due and declared enforceable is required in order to carry out an enforcement order[3]. When it's a judgment, it's also important to make sure that the debtor has been informed[4] and that the decision is not appealable unless there is provisional enforcement[5]. Lastly, there is a deadline for implementing the enforcement order[6]. That said, while waiting to obtain an enforcement order from the Court, it is possible to make the debtor's assets unavailable through a so-called precautionary measure. This means of preserving the debtor's property ensures the effectiveness of enforcement, which the creditor is entitled to implement upon fulfillment of the conditions necessary for such implementation. To obtain the implementation of a precautionary measure, the creditor must file an application with a judicial officer[7]. However, the creditor is dispensed from the obligation to obtain prior authorization from the Court where he or she has already obtained one of the acts specified in Article 68 of the *Loi du 9 juillet, 1991*[8].

The document enabling the judicial officer to impose a protective measure must be given by the creditor to him; this document may be a judicial order authorizing the protective measure or it may be one of the rights listed in Article 68 of the *Loi du 9 juillet 1991*. In the latter *scenario*, there is no time limit on implementing the preventive intervention. Conversely, if the protective measure is implemented through the application of Court authorization, it needs to be completed within three months starting from the day the order was issued. According to Articles 70 of the *Loi du 9 juillet 1991*, and 215 of the *Décret du 31 juillet 1992*, a creditor who lacks the authority to impose a protective measure must initiate, prosecute, or establish a procedure, or complete the requisite formalities, within one month after the protective measure's implementation.

4.2. *Types of precautionary measures*

Depending on the assets that need to be safeguarded, two different kinds of protective procedures exist: protective attachments and judgments. There are notable differences between the two types of measures' impact. Specifically, the debtor may not sell or otherwise transfer property seized for precautionary purposes. Assets subject to attachment are: (i) the tangible assets where they are held by the debtor or a third party. A creditor who obtains or is already the holder of an enforceable title establishing the right of claim has the right to convert the precautionary attachment into an attachment and subsequent sale of the attached property to be satisfied from the price obtained from the sale; (ii) the debts, that is, the creditor may hold a claim that the garnishee debtor, in turn, holds with third parties. The bailiff orders service of the attachment on the third parties and notifies the debtor of said service within eight days. As specified above, a creditor who obtains or already holds an enforceable title establishing the claim is entitled to convert the attachment into a garnishment. As for the other hand, the assets subject to a judgment are nonetheless transferable and alienable. As a result, they are marketable. A judgment's particular objective is to guarantee the creditor's retention of certain rights. Because of the dual registration, they provide the creditor a favorable rank. There is a provisional registration, which is the date the final inscription will be rated retrospectively, after the creditor's rights have been confirmed[9].

Two categories of rights are advantageous to the creditor: 1. right of priority, the asset's forced sale will be permitted by the creditor. The creditor holding the judgment has the right to share in the selling price distribution based on his ranking even if he does not start the forced sale; 2. resale right, regardless of who owns the asset – even if the debtor has sold it to a third party, for example – the creditor is still able to exercise his rights over it. The following assets are susceptible to a judgment: (i) immovable property that belongs to the debtor may be subject to the registration of a provisional mortgage, by submitting paperwork to the mortgage register; (ii) a company can apply for temporary security by submitting paperwork to the commercial Court registry; (iii) shares of a corporation may be used as a temporary security by serving a document on the issuing company; (iv) securities can also be used as interim security, by serving a document on the ethical person who issued the securities or, in some cases, the portfolio manager. In any event, the debtor needs to get notification of the judgment by a document from the judicial authority within eight days of it being actual. Furthermore, definitive advertising needs to be used to validate provisional advertising. The judicial officer will handle this in compliance with the legally prescribed requirements. Regarding the total amounts safeguarded by the latter, this advertisement assigns weight to the ruling made on the day of the first formality[10].

4.3. *The enforcement actors*

The judge of enforcement and the judicial officers[11] are the two primary players in enforcement in France. The creditor can request the enforcement measure be implemented by contacting the authorized judicial official if they have an enforceable title that meets the requirements for enforcement. The enforcement judge will intervene in the event that there are any issues or disputes during the execution of this mandatory enforcement action.

The first article of the Nov. 2, 1945 *Décret* states that the following duties may be performed only by bailiffs: service of documents; execution of judgments. Notifying the receiver of a document is the service rendered by a procedure via a Court authority, also known as "signification". The law stipulates that the signification must be made personally, that is, directly in the hands of the addressee. Only in the event that in-person service is impossible, the law provides for other methods of service: at the domicile or residence by means of a copy delivered to anyone present at the place-the person present must have accepted such delivery (Article 655 *Code des procédures civiles*); if no person is present who can or wishes to receive the document at the domicile, the bailiff leaves a delivery notice in the mailbox indicating that the document can be picked up at his office within three months (Article 656 *Code des procédures civiles*); by unsuccessful search report, in the event that neither domicile nor residence nor place of work of the addressee of the document is known, the judicial officer sends the signification to the last known address (Article 659 *Code des procédures civiles*). If the receiver consented to this mode of delivery, Court authorities can now serve papers electronically.

In addition, with regard to enforcement of judgments only bailiffs are permitted to use any coercive means permitted by law to collect money or seize a debtor's property, as stated in Article 18 of the July 9, 1991 statute. The judicial officer is expected to help in the collection of the debt for which he has been appointed as soon as a creditor requests it. He may, however, challenge this in two situations, subject to having the enforcement Court consider the matter: (i) if the measure appears to be illegal; or (ii) if the charges are likely to exceed the amount claimed.

The creditor is free to select any and all methods of securing the repayment of the obligation, provided that he adheres to the requirements of need and proportionality. He may choose to use enforcement or protective measures, as well as moveable or immovable property. These actions cannot be taken in excess of what is required to get the debt paid off. The execution actions are carried out by the Court official in charge of enforcement.

The judicial officer can reclaim and enforce the enforceable title through a variety of means, including: the debtor may have their furniture seized for sale, their debts seized, premises seized, evicted, etc. Lastly, the Court officer can issue an enforceable title in the event that the check is not paid. Then, this enforceable title will be worth the same as a judgment and enable enforcement of it[12].

In France, the Chairman of the *Tribunal de Grande Instance* performs the functions of an enforcement judge and may, in certain circumstances, assign this role to another judge[13]. The enforcement judge is capable of: (i) interpret the contested title that gave rise to the proceedings; (ii) fix the serious mistakes in the title that caused the measures; (iii) rule on the demand made by the debtor; (iv) impose restrictions (the judge of enforcement may add a decision from another judge to a restriction if the plaintiff's circumstances warrant it); (v) the judge of enforcement is also aware of the expiration of a restriction that he has declared or that another judge has declared (the latter only in the event that the judge has explicitly claimed knowledge of the restriction or if he remains the sequester); (vi) announce the acquisition of the resolutory clause; (vii) offer grace periods; (viii) determine the cost and quantity of mandatory enforcement costs; (ix) order the payment of a sum of money that he will specify; (x) order the removal of the motorized land vehicle immobilization measures; (xi) order the payment or sequestration of certain amounts of money. However, the enforcement judge is not allowed to alter, revoke, or postpone the decision measure that forms the basis of the proceedings (except from situations where a grace period or expulsion are granted)[14]. Moreover, the enforcement judge has the authority to grant protection orders and to be informed of any legal action resulting from the implementation of a protection order. The enforcement judge is aware of the process for seizing real estate, any disagreements that may arise, and any requests that may result from this process. As soon as the demands for compensation are filed in accordance with the protective or mandatory enforcement measures, he may be able to handle them. This pertains to: (i) a claim for damages resulting from improper execution by the creditor; (ii) a claim for damages resulting from the debtor's abusive resistance; (iii) a claim for liability against a third party that is obligated to contribute their expertise to the execution measures; (iv) a claim for liability against execution agents, namely the judicial officer who is selected by the debtor[15].

The enforcement judge is often called upon via summons. The general guidelines pertaining to the introduction of an instance are relevant. The summons writ must be supported by both legal and factual evidence. Three situations allow the judge of enforcement to issue orders upon request: (i) when the law specifically permits it (for example, when a creditor without an enforceable title requests permission from the judge to impose a protective measure); (ii) when the situation necessitates taking an emergency action in a non-contradictory way; and (iii) when the judicial officer overseeing the execution of the title needs the judge of enforcement's authorization to carry out a specific act (for example, when the judicial officer plans to seize a debtor's property that is kept in a third party's residential area)[16].

4.4. *Garnishment of tangible movable property*

Loi n° 91-650 du 9 juillet 1991, and *Décret 97-755 du 31 juillet 1992*, control the civil processes for enforcement, namely for carrying out the attachment of tangible movables.

An action for the attachment of the debtor's moveable physical property may be taken by a creditor who has an enforceable title and wants to recoup the money owed to him. After then, the attached property may be sold, and using the sale profits, the creditor may use the processes particular to that kind of attachment to recoup the amount he is owing. There are many methods in which moveable tangible property can be taken in France: (i) the *saisie-vente, i.e.*, the sale and garnishment of movable property[17]; (ii) the *saisie-appréhension, i.e.,* the garnishment of material goods by a recipient who is entitled to receive them[18]; (iii) the garnishment of motor vehicles[19]; (iv) the garnishment of assets placed in a safe[20]; (v) the garnishment of standing crops[21]. The process to be followed may vary according on the goal (being paid a certain amount of money or getting things delivered), the item being stretched (a car, a television), and the place (the debtor's house, a safe). In addition to the requirements unique to each civil procedure for the enforcement of debt against movables, there are a few requirements that apply to all enforcement actions. As a result, the creditor needs an enforceable title that acknowledges a known obligation with a set sum and an execution clause[22].

4.5. *The incorporeal movables' garnishment*

An asset without a material presence is called an incorporeal moveable asset. It is an intangible asset, similar to money or stock in a business.

In France, there are several methods for attaching incorporeal moveable property. The measure that is chosen mostly depends on the attachment point (pay, rights of shareholders, etc.).

The attachment containing third-party money is below: (i) attaching securities and short-term investments[23]; (ii) attaching monies held by third parties; (iii) recovering subsistence pensions; (iv) attaching wages; (v) notifying third party holders. Specifically, with regard to the attachment of sums of money held by third parties is an enforcement method under civil law that is limited to amounts owing. It permits the attaching creditor, who holds a writ of execution verifying a debt that is due and payment, to attach receivables related to amounts held by an attached third party, who will act as his debtor (the attached debtor). To put it another way, it gives the creditor access to the money-related receivable that his debtor (the attached debtor) possesses against his own debtor (the attached third party).

This procedure can be carried out only where the following conditions are met: (i) a warrant of execution attesting to an established debt that is due and payment must be in the creditor's possession. This debt is the attachment's underlying receivable (the receivable that gave birth to the attachment); (ii) a receivable against a third party (the attached third party) must be held by the creditor's debtor (the attached debtor); (iii) by virtue of established, independent power, the debtor (the third party connected) must due a certain amount of money. The third party attached is expected to disclose to the process-server the amount of his responsibilities towards the debtor attached after receiving an attachment order. The attached debtor is then told about the attachment, primarily so that he may raise a defense. The linked third party will handle payment when these procedures are finished. The amount paid will vary based on whether or not an objection is filed[24].

The attachment of monies in third-party custody in bank accounts is unique in that it pertains to a bank rather than the debtor (the attached third party) of the creditor's debtor. Attached here are any amounts that are currently owed on the debtor's account. This process is applicable to all accounts displaying amounts of money opened at a location permitted by law to maintain deposit accounts, as well as deposit accounts. All cash, current, and deposit accounts – regardless of whether they bear interest or not – are eligible for it. The debtor's bank is served with a writ of attachment, which requires the bank to notify the process-server on the amount owed on the debtor's account. Afterwards, the process-server will attach the debtor's account based on whether it has a credit or debit balance. The attachment will be subject to a sum equal to the non-disposable bank balance (SBI) that is left on it if the account displays a credit balance. The protected actual income (RSA) is equal to the non-disposable bank balance[25].

In actuality, the creditor will request that the bank continue with attaching the debtor's account using his process-server. After that, the bank will inform the creditor if the account balance is debited or credit. If there is a debt balance, the bailiff will let the creditor know that foreclosure cannot be carried out. A 15-day deadline will follow the foreclosure notification. This window of time is required to settle any transactions that may have occurred before the garnishment and restore the debtor's account to its previous state.

Within fifteen days, the bailiff will notify the creditor that there could be an excess in the account. In this situation, garnishment could be considered. Nonetheless, the bailiff will notify the creditor that, in any event, the debtor will get an amount equal to the protected actual income (RSA) of 466.99 euros for a beneficiary who is not a caregiver for a kid and lives alone in 2011. If there is a credit balance, the protected actual income (RSA) balance specified in Article 47 of the 1992 decree cannot be attached.

Fifteen days are given so that any surgeries performed prior to the attachment can be considered. Any operations performed after the attachment are not considered. This is where it's important to distinguish between non-attachable debts of a non-periodical character (like repayment of medical bills) and non-attachable obligations of a periodic form (like wage, retirement pension, unemployment benefit, family allowances, etc.)[26].

Nevertheless, there may be exceptions to these guidelines. Put differently, under certain conditions, the non-attachable debt might be attached (for example, the debtor's non-attachable receivables could be attached by a subsistence creditor). The debtor will still be in possession of the non-accessible bank balance (which is equivalent to the RSA) notwithstanding these exclusions, and it is never attachable[27].

The debtor's account balance must be disclosed by the business (head office or branch) holding the account at the attachment date. The establishment is required to disclose the amounts recorded as of the attachment date in addition to the balance on the debtor's account at that time. The receivable under the attachment is made up of these amounts. Nonetheless, the bank is not required to disclose any changes made to the debtor's account following the attachment. In theory, the bank is required to disclose the balance of each individual account when there are many accounts. The third party is not limited to using the deposit account that just displays the amount of money. It must give the debtor any form of account statement as of the attachment date. Any adjustments made to ongoing activities afterward may have an impact on the amount displayed on the attachment date.

According to Article 74 of the decree, the action of attachment essentially renders all of the debtor's accounts with the attached third party inaccessible. However, by putting up a guarantee, in particular, the attached creditor may restrict the non-availability to specific accounts.

For joint accounts or accounts formed in the name of just one spouse, specific provisions are made: (i) when it comes to joint accounts, the joint account holder who is not participating in the attachment has to demonstrate that it is the rightful owner of all or a portion of the money placed into the account; (ii) when an account is formed in the name of only one spouse, the situation is different and depends on the relevant marital arrangement[28].

In addition, regarding the process for recovering subsistence pensions enables any creditor of a person receiving a subsistence pension to demand that third parties pay them the amount they owe him directly. Only with third-party support – the third-party debtor for payment or other income – can this process be implemented (typically the employer). The linked debtor (the debtor of the creditor who first implemented the procedure) or the creditor might receive the amount due by the third-party debtor immediately through the procedure. That's what a process-server does. The process-server in question is located at the residence of the subsistence pension creditor. The amounts will subsequently be paid to the creditor directly by the third-party debtor. Like any process, some issues could come up. They are within the district Court's jurisdiction in the location where the subsistence pension debtor resides. The attachment procedure may come to an end if the pension is no longer due or if the attachment is lifted.

Moving forward, wage garnishment is a process that enables a creditor to seize money owing to him by his debtor "at source". This technique only applies to sums in the kind of compensation. They only pay the attachable portion of salary or compensation[29]. The execution Court does not have authority over this operation; rather, the local Court does. Prior to the rigorous attachment of wages, there is a waiting period known as conciliation. The Court tries to bring the parties together. If that doesn't work, the Court will look up the whole debt – principal, interest, and costs – to see if attachment may be pursued. By serving the employer with an attachment document, the chief clerk initiates the attachment process. A copy is eventually given to the debtor. After that, the employer must pay the withholdings for which the attachment is made each month. The clerk receives payment for these amounts and transfers them to the creditor.

In conclusion, third-party notice isn't strictly speaking a civil enforcement process. The process actually comes under tax legislation. It permits monetary claims made by taxpayers against third parties to be garnished by the public treasury. This process is applicable to all tax-related debts. It starts when the third-party related to it receives a registered letter with a receipt advise from the public accountant. All of the debtor's creditors are in the same position under the terms of this procedure: none of them is a privileged creditor. If a disagreement arises over the appropriateness of the process, the competent Court will be the one to carry out the decision. However, when it comes to disagreements pertaining to the receivable underlying processes, the administrative Court has authority[30].

4.6. *Garnishment of immovable property*

Enforcement against property is the process by which a creditor gets the Court to take possession of the debtor's belongings so they may be sold and the proceeds paid to him.

In France according to the provisions of Article R. 523-5 of the *Code des procédures civiles d'exécution*: «*Le tiers saisi qui, sans motif légitime, ne fournit pas les renseignements prévus, s'expose à devoir payer les sommes pour lesquelles la saisie a été pratiquée si le débiteur est condamné et sauf son recours contre ce dernier. Il peut être condamné à des dommages-intérêts en cas de négligence fautive ou de déclaration inexacte ou mensongère*».

First and foremost, domestic legal sources are available for enforcement. Historically, laws passed by Parliament have governed enforcement nearly entirely. Nonetheless, the French Constitution of 1958 created the opportunity for the executive branch to enact laws by decree. This area of the law saw its first contemporary change in 1991[31] thanks to a legislation and 1992[32] application decree. The statute's goal was to ensure that legitimate debtors would get "humane" treatment while also modernizing the enforcement order to increase the effectiveness of the legislation. On the other hand, immovables enforcement practices were not changed until 2006. Two more instruments were enacted with the intention of ensuring a balance between the interests of the creditors and the rights of the debtor: application decree n° 2006-936, July 27, 2006, and decree (*ordonnance*) n° 2006-461, April 21, 2006 (which amended Title XIX of Livre III of the Civil Code to read «*De la saisie et de la division du prix de vente de l'immeuble*»).

Later, on December 19, 2011, decree n° 2011-1895 was passed, adopting a *Code des procédures civiles d'exécution*. It becomes operative on June 1, 2012. Naturally, constitutional principles must be respected in the application of the law. Because each judgment is, in theory, enforceable and may result in enforcement actions, it should be highlighted that the *Conseil Constitutionnel* places a high value on the prospect of enforcement[33].

The goal of enforcement legislation is to strike a balance between the rights of the debtor and the interests of the creditor, or between the humanity and effectiveness of the enforcement actions. On the one hand, the creditor's interest presupposes quick and affordable enforcement measures. Efficiency, in the eyes of the creditor, is found in diversifying methods and tailoring them to the debtor's legacy. Special protocols are specifically required with regard to securities and shares. Help is also required for the creditor to look for the debtor's residence, place of employment, and bank accounts. However, it is also in the debtor's best interest to consider other imperatives. It should be possible for the debtor to refute the creditor's claim. Furthermore, consideration should be given to his right to privacy and dignity. A further expression of the need for efficiency is the inclination to prioritize extra-judicial proceedings. The 1991 Act does, in fact, have the feature of introducing processes without a formal judicial oversight structure. The creditor does not have to take over the Court in a methodical manner if he has an enforcement title.

4.7. *"Juge de l'exécution"*

In front of the *juge de l'exécution*, or specialized enforcement judge, the standard approach is an adversarial one[34]. The first hearing that is available is when the claim should be made. Nonetheless, even on weekends or holidays, a claimant may be permitted to submit his case in an emergency at a time appointed by the judge[35]. There is no requirement for legal representation for the parties throughout the oral procedure. The parties are notified by the registrar of the judgments of the *juge de l'exécution* (a registered letter is used). Within fifteen days of notification, an appeal may be filed. A unique method is established for in some statutory scenarios where it is justified to take an urgent step *ex parte* (unilaterally) based on the circumstances[36]. The *ordonnance sur requête* is this. When the enforcement authority, or *huissier de justice*, encounters challenges when enforcing an enforcement title, there is an additional protocol in place[37].

The 1991 change was designed to support extrajudicial processes and strengthen enforcement titles. Therefore, a Court is not usually required to approve enforcement when the creditor possesses an enforcement title. However, prior to using coercion, the creditor must submit a letter of demand, sometimes known as «a commandement to pay», that has been delivered by the enforcement authority. Nonetheless, under French law, a judge's order can be enforced; this is required for temporary measures in cases where the creditor lacks an enforceable title.

The *juge de l'exécution*, or enforcement judge, has substantive authority. The *Tribunal de Grande Instance* president is this person (first instance Court that has broad jurisdiction). He has obligatory and exclusive jurisdiction. Any other Court that is called upon must independently proclaim itself unfit. As an exception, the issue of compensation seizure falls under the jurisdiction of the *Tribunal d'Instance*, another Court. The *juge de l'exécution* normally sits alone, but he has the authority to assign the case to a panel of three judges. However, his jurisdiction is limited to matters concerning enforcement titles and enforcement. He can't change the decision. Distinguishing between change and interpretation might be challenging at times.

The president of the *Tribunal de Grande Instance* – the first instance Court with universal jurisdiction – performs the role of enforcement judge, or *juge de l'exécution*, in accordance with article 213-5 of the *Code de l'organisation judiciaire.* He has obligatory and exclusive jurisdiction. The concentration of litigation before the enforcement judge with the intention of streamlining enforcement operations is precisely one of the features of enforcement procedures in France. There are several specifics to the enforcement judge's procedure. First off, parties may get assistance or legal representation under Article R 121-5.

Legal representation is not required. Parties may have other representatives or helpers, such as a spouse, partner, or parents; a list of them is provided in Article R121-7 of *Code des procédures civiles d'exécution.*

Generally speaking, the process is oral. Nonetheless, the legislation further arranges for the opportunity to present written arguments through certified letters addressed to the judge. The Enforcement Judge's rulings are final and binding. The parties are advised of them by registered letter. The Court has the authority to rule that service is not required in certain situations. One may file an appeal against the enforcement judge's rulings. After serving, the appeal must be filed within 15 days. Legal representation is required. The Court of Appeals has to make a decision "shortly after". An appeal has no suspenseful impact. Nonetheless, under specific conditions, an application for a suspension of the enforcement judge's ruling may be made to the Court of appeals' first president.

French law allows for "judicial securities" (*sûretés judiciaires*) in addition to protective seizure (*saisie conservatoire*), which prevents the debtor from disposing of assets. Generally speaking, the Court will approve the establishment of a security interest in specific categories of assets, mostly securities and immovables, without influencing the debtor's disposition of the assets.

The list of assets is not all-inclusive; for instance, a commitment on a moveable item cannot be fulfilled. As a general rule, every protective measure requires previous judicial authorization. On the other hand, a Court's authorization is not always required. This is especially true in situations when the applicant possesses a judgment, even if it isn't legally binding.

The same is usually acknowledged to apply to decisions made abroad (the *Cour de Cassation* specifically acknowledged this resolution for an arbitral judgment). Since it is an *ex parte* (unilateral) application, the debtor must be notified within eight days.

4.8. *The "astreinte"*

The debate[38] regarding the enforcement of obligations arising from the need for specific performance does not go back to the present day. Indeed, when a party owes a specific performance of doing or not doing, the problem arises (goes) of identifying a valid means of enforcing the performance of the infungible obligation[39].

It is not uncommon, in fact, for the activity of the holder of the right asserted at trial to be frustrated by the uncooperative attitude of the losing party. It is well known that one of the most serious shortcomings of the enforcement procedure was (or perhaps will continue to be) constituted by the inadequacy of imposing on the enforcer the exact performance of the obligation that has as its object obligations to do of an infungible character or not to do, which at most could find its satisfaction only through forms of induction to cooperation through compulsory measures imposed by the Court, after ascertaining the legal reality claimed by the aggrieved creditor[40], since *nemo ad factum praecisum cogi potest*[41]. In such cases, the civil process is in fact in danger of becoming a sterile tool for implementing substantive law. Therefore, it seems useful to briefly dwell on the French procedural institution of *astreinte*[42], since it is an instrument of indirect coercion and deterrence suitable for reinforcing the judge's command, since it constitutes an effective means of pressure (including psychological pressure[43]), and thus would have the effect of making the losing party cooperate in a specific doing or continued non-doing.

The main purpose of *astreinte* is to compel the debtor to execute a Court decision, which for his counterpart – the creditor – is an integral part, subsumed also under Article 6 § 1 of the European Convention on Human Rights[44], of the right to a fair trial. The institution of *astreinte*[45] dates back to the time of *Le Code Napoléon*[46] as a pecuniary penalty proportional to the delay in complying with what the judge ordered in a judgment of conviction.

Of praetorian creation, intended to remedy the imperfections of Article 1142 of the *Code Civil* of 1804, it made its appearance in

France in the 19th century through jurisprudence[47]. Its nature allowed it to evolve jurisprudentially[48] until it took the shape of a true means of coercion of judicial measures[49]. Today the institution in question finds in the modern French procedural system an autonomous discipline, regulated among the rules relating to the process of execution. The *astreinte* in civil matters was first regulated by *Loi n° 91-650 du 9 juillet 1991*, now codified in Articles L131-1 to L131-4 and Articles R131-1 to R131-4 of the *Code des procédures civiles d'exécution*[50], and aims to persuade debtors to fulfill their obligations in a timely manner.

The particularity and efficiency of *astreinte* are due to the (gradual) increase in its perception by the defaulting party, as it moves from a merely hypothetical stage – where the institution in question only performs an intimidating function – to a concrete stage with legal effects, where instead *astreinte* acquires an almost punitive value, in addition to the fact that it goes to affect not only the position of creditors, but also the judiciary since: it *mantaint* (or at least seeks) the fundamental supremacy of the law[51]. *Astreinte* is thus a coactive sanction, and it is directed at the party to whom the condemnation order is addressed to comply to behave in a certain manner[52]. The unsuccessful debtor's coactive cooperation-and thus the satisfaction of the plaintiff/creditor-is induced by the fact that the cost related to the protracted default is devolved to the party who will derive greater convenience in complying in a timely manner with the Court's order[53]. It is obvious that the total amount of the *astreinte* will be determined according to the speed with which the condemned party decides to comply with what the judge ordered[54]: in this manner, uncooperative behavior thus becomes rationally inconvenient.

It must be pointed out that the sanction of *astreinte* in France can be applied not only to an obligation to do or not to do, but also to pecuniary obligations without the sum attained going in any way to substitute for legal interest, thus going to cumulate with the latter, being independent of each other[55], since the prejudice suffered by the creditor due to the delay in payment is compensated by the interest on arrears paid by the debtor, while the purpose of *astreinte* is of a compulsive nature[56].

4.9. *Self-defense*

French law authorizes the creditor to take certain precautionary measures that can often force the debtor to deal or pay.

The precautionary procedures available to the creditor are, for example, the garnishment of bank accounts, the attachment of debts owed to third parties, and the mortgaging of real estate; the creditor may proceed immediately with these procedures without prior Court authorization if he or she is in possession of a security such as a check or promissory note. The Court always summons the parties to attempt conciliation; in the absence of conciliation, ordinary action is taken, i.e., a writ of summons served by bailiff.

Up to this point, the procedure for debt collection in France does not require the assistance of lawyers. The parties crystallize their positions in a memorandum, and the terms of the judgment are never peremptory: extensions and postponements in France are quite common. Having obtained a favorable judgment, the creditor has 10 years to start the enforcement phase, while the debtor has two months to voluntarily fulfill the obligation imposed by the judgment.

4.10. *The last developments*

The French legal system launched a robust and organic program of justice reform with *Loi n° 2019-222 de programmation 2018-2022 et de réforme pour la justice*[57], directed at a comprehensive rethinking of judicial organization with a view to improving the time and quality of justice. The project is driven by the awareness that the albeit numerous innovations introduced in recent years have not led to the hoped-for improvements, although they too, it should be recalled, had been organized according to a method that has become customary in France, based on the organic and programmatic identification of areas of intervention through rapports often entrusted to authoritative jurists, and carried out according to a precise political-legislative planning[58].

The need felt was, therefore, to adopt an instrument of even broader scope and time horizon, moved by the realization that the last guidance and planning law for justice dated back to *Loi n° 2002-1138 du 9 septembre 2002.*

The major areas of intervention are articulated on a few main fronts, consisting of the simplification of civil procedure, lightening the load of administrative jurisdictions and strengthening them, simplifying and enhancing the effectiveness of criminal justice, including juvenile justice, reviewing the efficiency and purpose of punishment, and reorganizing the justice system in various respects.

Within each of these areas, numerous interventions are envisaged that can redesign, in their own right, the face of French justice. The symbolic measure of this reform is, in fact, the establishment of a new body, the *Tribunal judiciaire* (in operation as of January 1, 2020), born out of the amalgamation of the offices of first instance, namely the *Tribunal d'Instance* and the *Tribunal de Grande Instance.*

The *Tribunal judiciaire* is today, as was the *Tribunal de Grande Instance*, the jurisdiction of common law, thus competent for all matters, without prejudice to those deferred to the Courts of exception[59], although planning provides for the possibility of grouping at the new body also the matter of labor, today in the cognizance of the *Tribunal des Prud'hommes*[60], and the competences of the *Tribunal commercial.* It has absorbed the powers of the former *Tribunal d'Instance*, currently devolved to specialized chambers which, while being integral parts of the *Tribunal judiciaire*, may be constituted in branch offices, as Article L212-8, c.o.j., expressly provides, and are called *Tribunaux de proximité.* This is a revision that is part of a broader organizational operation, aimed at the creation of "poles", susceptible to different territorial reference to be determined by means of subsequent decrees, e.g., city or departmental, including highly specialized chambers. The old *Tribunals d'Instance* constitute an example of this new organizational vision of absorption and reconversion: in Paris, the *Tribunal de Grande Istance* was merged with the *Tribunalsd'Instance* and the attributions of the latter were grouped into a single pole, called *Pôle civil de proximité du Tribunal judiciaire.*

Newly minted Article L211-9-3 ff., c.o.j., provides that when more than one *Tribunal judiciaire* exists in the same department, they may be, by decree, vested with special jurisdiction within the department. This could be for particular criminal violations, as reported in the same Article L211-9-3, or for specific matters, indicated in the rules that follow that one, such as literary and artistic property, industrial law (Article L211-10, c.o.j.), EU trademarks, Community designs (Articles L211-11, L211-11-1, c.o.j.), international child abduction also Community (Article L211-12, c.o.j.)[61].

The revisitation of the organization also provides for the establishment of the new *Contentieux de la protection du judge* (Article L 213-4-1 ff, c.o.j.) destined to hear a number of heterogeneous matters, united by a lack of complexity, such as the protections of the most incapacitated (devolved today to the tutelary judge, who disappears), some actions related to leases including commercial and squatting, actions concerning consumer credit, registrations and cancellations to the risk central, over-indebtedness, disputes up to the value of 10.000.00 and, as judge of first and last instance, those up to € 5,000.00. It is normally a single judge, with the possibility of *passerelles* to the collegial formation of the *Tribunal judiciaire* as the judge of the *Contentieux de la protection* (Article L213-4-8, c.o.j.).

Provision is made for the initiation of a jurisdiction (included in new rules that will become Articles L211-17 and L211-18, c.o.j.), dedicated to *injonction de payer*[62], domestic and international, with total dematerialization of the monitory phase of the proceedings. The latter, in a first version of the reform project, was proposable, due to its complete computerization, before a single authority at the national level, therefore, without any criterion of competence to preside over the territorial distribution of the relevant petitions; for the opposition, on the other hand, the treatment before the territorially competent jurisdiction according to the rules of common law was maintained, to which the file would have to be transmitted. In the course of the drafting of the law there was a turn in favor of the applicability of the ordinary criteria of jurisdiction for the monitory phase as well, subject to the dematerialization of the procedure and centralized processing in a special organizational unit at the competent Court, which is still being studied to entrust to the clerk of the Court[63].

The operation of this institution, which in the past has suffered from the presence of the more rapid and deformalized *référé-provision*, has been significantly enhanced and deformalized in a direction clearly marked by the EU injunction. The operability of this institution, which in the past suffered from the presence of the more rapid and deformalized *référé-provision*[64], has been significantly enhanced and deformalized in a direction clearly geared toward the EU injunction. Evidence of this is the way in which dematerialization has been implemented through the en ligne compilation of the application for an injunction directly on the website of the competent Court on which a form is prepared to be filled out in a guided manner[65]; even the payment of costs is executable electronically. The *injonction de payer* is structured according to an original reinterpretation of the pure model of the *monitorio* procedure, in which the influence of the mechanisms proper to the documentary process has manifested itself much more tenuously than in the choices implemented in our system[66]. This characteristic, coeval with its establishment and not the result of the innovations under discussion, gives it a not excessively formal and easy-to-manage nature that has made it possible to keep the institution excluded from the general extension of the mandatory nature of technical defense implemented by the planning law.

As part of the modernization of the system through the use of IT tools, the *Service d'accueil unique du justiciable* (SAUJ) is also organized, which constitutes a kind of telematic chancery set up for each *Tribunal judiciaire*, also including the litigation of the *Conseil de prud'hommes*, and the new Justiciable portal for online consultation of files. This is a wide-ranging and ambitious reform, of which it is only possible here to offer a few glimpses, but which deserves further study. It should be emphasized that, with this project, France is setting itself up for modernization in which it is easy to discern the goal of offering itself as a European center for attracting and managing litigation of significant economic and commercial significance.

Notes

[1] *Code des procédures civiles d'exécution*, Article L111-1.
[2] *Ivi*, Article L111-2.
[3] According to the provisions of Article 3, of the *loi du 9 juillet 1991*, they are only enforceable titles: (i) «*Les décisions judiciaires ou administratives rendues par les autorités compétentes ainsi que les transactions présentées au président du Tribunal de Grande instance si elles sont exécutoires; (ii) les actes étrangers et les condamnations étrangères ainsi que les sentences arbitrales rendues exécutoires par une décision sans appel de manière irrévocable visant à suspendre leur force exécutoire; (iii) copies certifiées conformes du procès-verbal de conciliation signées par le juge et les parties; (iv) documents légalisés s'ils sont exécutoires; (v) les preuves présentées par l'huissier en cas de non-paiement d'un chèque; (vi) les preuves présentées par une personne morale de droit public et constituant par la loi un titre exécutoire, ou les décisions qui sont considérées comme des condamnations par la loi*».
[4] Article 503, alinéa 1: «*Le défaut de notification de la sentence empêche son exécution à l'encontre des condamnés, sauf en cas d'exécution volontaire*».
[5] A decision that has been issued by default - that is, when one of the parties failed to show up - may be appealed to an appellate Court for reformation or cancellation, or it may be the subject of an opposing appeal to have it revoked before the same Court. The defendant has a deadline for filing the appeal or opposition. The Court where the decision was rendered or the judicial person serving the judgment will provide the deadline for the appeal or challenge. Until this time runs out, the judgment's execution will be halted. Article 500 *du Code de procédure civile*: «*La peine non susceptible de réexamen qui suspend son exécution acquiert force de chose jugée. La peine faisant l'objet d'une procédure de révision a la même efficacité à l'expiration des termes de ladite procédure si la procédure de révision n'a pas lieu dans les délais prescrits*». Nonetheless, in some circumstances, the law or the Court may permit the party who has been served with the judgment to begin enforcement even prior to the expiration of the appeal term or the resolution of the filed appeal. This execution is preliminary in this instance. Enforcement of the right will be achievable even prior to the appeal's deadline expiring. Article 501 du *Code de procédure civile*: «*La sentence est exécutée, dans les conditions fixées ci-après, à compter du moment où elle devient juridiquement contraignante, sans préjudice du cas où le débiteur bénéficie d'un délai de grâce ou le créancier bénéficie d'une exécution provisoire*». The execution of a decision is not, in general, suspended by "exceptional" appeal processes (like cassation appeal), unless there are certain instances involving nationality (Article 1045 *Code de procédure*

civile), divorce (Article 1086 and 1087 *Code de procédure civile*), adoption (Article 1178-1 *Code de procédure civile*), or filiation (Article 1150 *Code de procédure civile*).

[6] Article 3, *loi 91-650*: «*L'exécution des titres exécutifs mentionnés aux points 1 et 3 de l'article 3 doit intervenir dans un délai de dix ans, sauf dans le cas où une prolongation desdits délais pour les actions en recouvrement est convenue de manière documentée credit*».

[7] Pursuant to Article 67 of the *Loi du 9 July, 1991*: «*la personne titulaire d'un droit au crédit apparemment fondé a, en principe, le droit de présenter au juge une demande d'autorisation pour obtenir l'application d'une mesure conservatoire sur le patrimoine de au débiteur, sans injonction préalable, si cette personne est en mesure de démontrer qu'il existe des risques réels de préjudice pour le recouvrement du credit*».

[8] They are: (i) an enforceable right (although a payment order is usually required before any action is taken, in theory the creditor might proceed with execution. The creditor may continue with a protective measure without informing the debtor beforehand in order to maintain the "effect of surprise"); (ii) a Court decision that is still not enforceable; (iii) an accepted bill of exchange; (iv) a promissory note; (v) a check; (vi) a written lease.

[9] H. Michelin-Brachet, L. Veyre, M. Guez, O. Sabard, *Cours de procédure civile 2024. Modes alternatifs de résolution des différends, voies d'exécution,* ed. 6, Paris, 2024, *passim.*

[10] M. L. Guinamant, S. Hafi, S. Aparisi, *La procédure civile et les procédures civiles d'exécution en cas pratiques*, ed. 2, Paris, 2024 *passim.*

[11] A series of legislative and regulatory documents that together form a law and specify the duties and responsibilities of the profession place tight restrictions on the performance of the judicial officer's profession. The November 2, 1945, order No. 45-2592 serves as the primary source that outlines the profession's legislation.

[12] M. Barba, *Procédure civile*, Paris, 2024.

[13] *Code de l'organisation judiciaire, Article L213-6* states: «*Le juge de l'exécution connaît, de manière exclusive, des difficultés relatives aux titres exécutoires et des contestations qui s'élèvent à l'occasion de l'exécution forcée, même si elles portent sur le fond du droit à moins qu'elles n'échappent à la compétence des juridictions de l'ordre judiciaire. Dans les mêmes conditions, il autorise les mesures conservatoires et connaît des contestations relatives à leur mise en œuvre. Le juge de l'exécution connaît, sous la même réserve, de la procédure de saisie immobilière, des contestations qui s'élèvent à l'occasion de celle-ci et des demandes nées de cette procédure ou s'y rapportant directement, même si elles portent sur le fond du droit ainsi que de la procédure de distribution qui en découle. Il connaît, sous la même réserve, des demandes en réparation fondées sur l'exécution ou l'inexécution dommageables des mesures d'exécution forcée ou des mesures conservatoires. Il connaît de la saisie des rémunérations, à l'exception des demandes ou moyens de défense échappant à la compétence des juridictions de l'ordre judiciaire. Le juge de l'exécution exerce également les compé-*

tences particulières qui lui sont dévolues par le code des procédures civiles d'exécution».

[14] S. GUINCHARD, M. MOUSSA, *Droit et pratique des voies d'exécution*, Paris, 2009.

[15] P. THERY, R. PERROT, *Procédures civiles d'exécution*, ed. 3, Paris, 2013, *passim*.

[16] G. COUCHEZ, J.P. LANGLADE, D. LEBEAU, *Procédure civile*, Paris, 1998.

[17] A creditor may choose to have his debtor's assets attached so that they can be sold and the creditor can recover the costs incurred through a process known as *saisie-vente*. Both tangible movable property and attachable property must be attached to the garnishment. A list of assets that cannot be attached is outlined in Article 14 of the *Loi du 9 juillet, 1991* and Article 39 of the *Décret du juillet 31, 1992*.

[18] Through the seizure of moveable assets based on an enforceable title or a Court order, the creditor may utilize this legal procedure to enforce the debtor's execution of its duty to produce or restore such assets. *Code des procédures civiles d'exécution*, Articles R222-1-R222-25; see, also, E. BLANC, *Les nouvelles procédures d'exécution: commentaire article par article de la loi n °91-150 du 9 juillet 1991 et du décret n °92-755 du 31 juillet 1992 suivi d'un formulaire,* Paris, 1994, p. 235 ss; B. NICOD, *Les voies d'exécution*, deuxieme partie, ch. 4, partie 2, Paris, 1994,

[19] This execution action is meant to rob the debtor of his ability to get rid of his car and, more specifically, to keep him from selling it. In the event that finding the car is not feasible, it is helpful. A. LEBORGNE, O. SALATI, L. DARGENT, *Code des procédures civiles d'exécution*, Paris, 2013, *passim*.

[20] A unique type of attachment known as the attachment for sale of assets kept in a safe enables a creditor to arrange for the removal of his debtor's assets from a safe, sell them, and collect payment from the sale price. *Ivi*.

[21] A unique type of attachment of moveable property is standing crops, which allows a creditor to evict the owner of the debtor's crops so that they may be sold and the earnings used to pay the debtor's outstanding balance. The *Décret du 31 juillet, 1992*, specifically articles 134 through 138, address this method.

[22] *Code des procédures civiles d'exécution*, Articles R222-1- R222-25.

[23] The process by which a creditor can have his debtor's transferable securities and shareholder rights seized and sold in order to recoup the amount owed to him from the sale's profits is known as attachment of transferable securities and shareholder rights. See, *Code des procédures civiles d'exécution*, Articles R232-1 - R232-8.

[24] G. COUCHEZ, D. LEBEAU, O. SALATI, *Procédures civiles d'exécution*, ed. 13, Paris, 2022, p. 33.

[25] Articles 55 to 68 of the *décret* and Article 47 of the Act of July 9, 1991, as well as the additional provisions provided under Articles 44 to 49 and Articles 73 to 79 of the decree of July 31, 1992, control this civil law enforcement procedure under ordinary law. It relates to deposit accounts, but it also applies to any account that displays amounts owed and is opened in a loca-

tion that is legally permitted to hold deposit accounts (banks, postal giro centers, and savings banks). All cash accounts, current accounts, and deposit accounts - regardless of whether they yield interest or not - may have money held by third parties attached to them. It cannot, however, be made for the entire amount indicated on the debtor's account.

[26] Periodically payable non-attachable debts: the debtor may request that these amounts be made available to him right now. Since alimony is typically involved, these debts are subject to prompt disposal rather than being paid off at the conclusion of the fifteen-day term. However, these non-attachable debts of a recurring character will not include operations charged to the debtor's account as of the date of the last payment of the non-attachable sum. Under no circumstances will the amount of these payments be added to the so-called non-attachable bank balance (SBI), which is equivalent to the protected real income (€ 466.99 in 2011) in practice. Non-periodic non-attachable debts: the debtor may demand that these amounts be made available to him. But in this instance, they are delayed rather than made available right away. In order to give operations completed prior to the attachment time to be considered, there is a 15-day delay. Again, accumulation using the SBI bank amount that is not available is not feasible in this case. A. LEBORGNE, C. BRENNER, C. GIJSBERS, *Droit de l'exécution. Voies d'exécution et procédures de distribution*, ed. 3, Paris, 2019.

[27] *Ibid.*

[28] *Code Civil*, Article 1402 governs the system of joint property ownership: *«Tout bien, meuble ou immeuble, est réputé acquêt de communauté si l'on ne prouve qu'il est propre à l'un des époux par application d'une disposition de la loi. Si le bien est de ceux qui ne portent pas en eux-mêmes preuve ou marque de leur origine, la propriété personnelle de l'époux, si elle est contestée, devra être établie par écrit. À défaut d'inventaire ou autre preuve préconstituée, le juge pourra prendre en considération tous écrits, notamment titres de famille, registres et papiers domestiques, ainsi que documents de banque et factures. Il pourra même admettre la preuve par témoignage ou présomption, s'il constate qu'un époux a été dans l'impossibilité matérielle ou morale de se procurer un écrit»*. Ownership documentation for the funds is required. Whereas Article 1538 (3) of the *Code Civil* covers the separate property system: *«Les biens dont aucun des époux ne peut justifier la propriété exclusive sont considérés comme leur appartenant indivisément, moitié-moitié»*. Consequently, attachment may be completed without issue if the ownership of the money is determined. If not, the joint holder of the monies will have to demonstrate that they are his.

[29] See, *Code du Travail Français*, Article R3252-2.

[30] *Code de procédure fiscale*, Article L. 263 A.

[31] *Loi n° 91-650, 9 juillet 1991 portant réforme des procédures civiles d'exécution.*

[32] *Décret d'application n°92-755 du 31 juillet 1992.*

[33] *Cons. Constit.*, 29 *juill.* 1998, n° 98-403, JCP G1999, I, 141, Mathieu et Verpeaux.

[34] *Code des procédures civiles d'exécution*, Article R. 121-11.
[35] *Code des procédures civiles d'exécution*, Article R. 121-12.
[36] *Code des procédures civiles d'exécution*, Article R. 121-23.
[37] *Code des procédures civiles d'exécution*, Article R. 151-1.
[38] About the doctrinal debate *ex plurimis* A. PROTO PISANI, *L'attuazione dei provvedimenti di condanna*, in *Foro Italiano*, vol. 111, 1988, pp. 177-188. The author highlights how the debate of injunctive relief intensified in the 1970s, a period when perhaps, "for the first time", civilists and proceduralists ceased ignoring each other to discuss together the topic of techniques and forms of rights protection. Hence an inseparable link was created between the emerging need for protection at the level of substantive law and the forms of procedural protections.
[39] Enforceable protection, as is well known, serves to ensure the concrete realization of the interest of the right holder, that is, everything and precisely that which has been granted to him or her by the substantive law upstream and by the Court in its assessment, by means of enforcement forms doing without the cooperation of the obligor; this implies that this activity is of a substitutive and subrogation type. G. BALENA, *Elementi di diritto processuale civile*, Bari, 2007, pp. 27- 28 and 38.
[40] It is common ground that for orders to do of an in fungible nature and for orders not to do, the question arises as to the possibility of coercive execution. A. FRIGNANI, *La penalità di mora e le astreintes nei diritti che si ispirano al modello francese*, in *Riv. dir. civ.*, 1981, pp. 506 ss.
[41] F. VASSALLI, *Il diritto alla libertà morale*, in *Studi giuridici in memoria di F. Vassalli*, vol. 2, Torino, 1960, pp. 1682 ss.; D. AMADEI, *Tutela esecutiva ed azione inibitoria delle associazioni dei consumatori*, in *Riv. esec. forz.*, 2003, pp. 326 ss.; *Id.*, *La tutela degli interessi collettivi e le modifiche al procedimento d'ingiunzione (seconda parte)*, in *Resp. civ. e prev.*, 2003, pp. 897 ss.
[42] There is an initial observation about the current propensity for comparison in Italian trial studies: comparison is liked and can be done, supposedly very easily. V. ANSANELLI, *Comparazione e ricomparazione in tema di expert whithes testimony,* in *Riv. dir. proc.*, n. 3, 2009, p. 713 ss.
[43] M.B. DE BOER, *Osservazioni sull'astreinte nel diritto processuale olandese*, in *Dir. proc. civ.*, 1996, p. 790 ss. *in species* p. 793.
[44] CEDU 19 marzo 1997, Hornsby c. Grecia, CEDU, p. 495; AJDA 1997. 977.
[45] F. CHABAS, *Astreinte*, in *Encyclopédie dalloz de procédure civile*, 1993; S. CIMAMONTI, *Astreinte judiciaire. Formulaire analytique de procédure.*
[46] Article 1412 C.C.N. provides that every obligation to do or not to do is resolved in *dommages-intets*: «*Toute obligation de faire ou de ne pas faire se résout en dommages et intérêts, en cas d'inexécution de la part du débiteur*». The *dommages interets* constitute the financial compensation to the damage suffered both in terms of loss of profit and emergent damage. On the point V. TARIOL, *L'Evaluation des dommages-intérêts en contrefaçon de marques*, Paris, 1990, pp. 23-26. The distinction between *astreinte* and damages for default is not always clear, but as early as the 1972 law, the *astreinte* was given (by defining it) a compulsive character in such a way as to distinguish

it from the codified provision in question. Any doubt would then be resolved the moment the judge indicated the definitive *astreinte* ex Article 34 L. 91-650: in this way, any possible admixture with *dommages interest.* In this sense, F. CHABAS, *La pena privata in Francia*, in *Riv. dir. proc.*, 1999, p. 349 ss; M. TARUFFO, *L'attuazione esecutiva dei diritti: profili comparatistici*, in *Riv. trim. dir. proc. civ.*, 1988, p. 142 ss. *Astreinte* is in fact an instrument of duress to be distinguished from damages, and its purpose is not to compensate for the harm that arose from the delay in compliance, but rather the failure to comply with what the Court ordered. F. CHABAS, *La pena privata in Francia, cit.*, p. 356.

[47] See, Civ. 28 dic. 1824, DP 1825. 1. 141; S. 1825. 1. 166.

[48] The most recalled historical pronouncement of *astreinte* can be found in a judgment of the Paris Court of Appeals dated August 7, 1878, when the Princess of Bauffremont was ordered by the Court, following her divorce with her husband, to hand over her children to the latter. The Court ruled that as long as the Princess did not hand over the children, she would be forced to pay 500 French francs for each day of delay (for the first month) and 1,000 francs during the second month (*astreinte* defined as 1,000 francs). The cause célèbre indicated actually ended with the Princess fleeing to Belgium with her children. See, AA.VV., *International & Comparative Law Quarterly*, vol. 5, Cambridge, 1956, pp. 378- 394.

[49] In the French process, *astreinte* can also apply as a means of endo procedural coercion to fulfill investigative duties. A. FRIGNANI, *cit.*, p. 506. Pursuant to Article 10 *Code des procédures*, *«Le juge a le pouvoir d'ordonner d'office toutes les mesures d'instruction légalement admissibles»*. See, A. GIUSSANI, *L'esibizione di documenti situati nello spazio giuridico europeo*, in *Riv. trim. dir. proc. civ.*, no. 3, 2002, p. 867, note 419 e 420; J. VINCENT, S. GUINCHARD, *Procédure civile,* Paris, 1994, p. 614 ss., p. 620 ss.; G. COUCHEZ, *Procédure civile*, Paris, 1998, p. 298 ss.; J. Mestre, *De quelques difficultés concernant les conditions d'obtention des modes de preuve*, in *Rev. trim. dr. civ.*, 1996, p. 166 ss.

[50] Although it should be pointed out that it is not properly a means of enforcement since only when the debtor fails to comply with the Court's command can the creditor have recourse to traditional enforcement measures. F. CHABAS, *La pena privata in Francia, cit.*, p. 559. *Loi n° 91-650 9/7 1991* and Implementing *Décret n° 92-755 du 31 juillet 1992* (subsequently novated by *Décret n° 96-1130 of Dec. 18, 1996)* made noticeable changes to the *astreinte* scheme.

[51] J. JACOB, *Trends in the enforcement of non-money judgments and orders. The first international colloqium on the law of civil procedure,* Berlin, 1988, p. 44.

[52] The regulatory provision under Article 33 *Loi* 91-650 is clear in this regard: *«Tout juge (by each judge is meant both the judge of first and second instance and the judges – du provisoire référés – of the precautionary) peut [...] ordonner une astreinte pour assurer l'exécution de sa decision»*. Paragraph 2 of Article 33 of this law further provides that in case of neces-

sity, the Court hearing the case may issue an *astreinte* on a decision issued by another Court. The execution judge also may not only order an *astreinte*, but may also modify it. In this sense, J. BASTIA, *16 Avril 1993*, in *Rev. Huissiers*, 1994, p. 934.

[53] It seems to me that the teachings of Coase, in predicting that in order to achieve a high degree of efficiency, responsibility must be allocated to the party that can most successfully contain it. R. COASE, *The Problem of social cost*, in *Journal of law and economics*, vol. 3, 1960, pp. 1-44; see, also, G. CALABRESI, D. MELAMED, *Property rules, liability rules and inalienability: one view of the cathedral*, in *Harv. Law Rev.*, vol. 85, 1972 p. 1089; *Id*, *Regole di proprietà, responsabilità e inalienabilità: un'istantanea della cattedrale*, in *Riv. dir. civ.*, 2020, p. 497 ss.

[54] It should be pointed out that *astreintes* is independent of damages and has, by its very nature, the sole purpose of forcing the party to execute a judicial decision, since the claim for *astreinte* is not a citation for damages but merely a coercive measure. In this sense, the *Cour de Cassation*, 2éme Civ. 17 *Avril* 2008, BICC: «[…] *L'astreinte est indépendante des dommages-intérêts et a, par sa nature même, pour but de contraindre la partie à exécuter une décision judiciaire […]. Dès lors, la Cour d'Appel (N° 07-10.065. – CA Chambéry, 29 août 2006) qui a constaté que l'astreinte ne figurait pas dans la définition des risques garantis par le contrat d'assurance responsabilité en a à bon droit déduit que l'assureur n'avait pas à prendre en charge la condamnation à une astreinte et n'avait pas à supporter les conséquences de la résistance de son assuré* […] ».

[55] Cf. soc. 29 May 1990, Bull. Civ. C. Cas. 1990, V, n. 244, p. 145. With this ruling, the Court ordered an employer to pay a former employee an indemnity plus damages for wrongful dismissal by adding an *astreinte* of 50 French francs for each day of delay. This jurisprudential approach abandoned previous (well-established) case law by positing the principle that *astreinte* can also be pronounced as an accessory to a pecuniary sentence. A. FRIGNANI, *L'injunction nella common law e l'inibitoria nel diritto italiano*, Milano, 1974.

[56] In Italy, on the other hand, the impossibility of applying the measure of indirect coercion even for pecuniary obligations would not be admissible by virtue of the function that interest performs: corresponding (*ex* Article 1282 c.c.), therefore remunerative, or compensatory (*ex* Article 1499 c.c.) or default (*ex* Article 1224 c.c.) that serve a compensatory function in the event of non-performance of this type of obligation, avoiding an unjustified duplication of measures aimed at reducing the extent of the prejudice caused by the violation, non-observance or delay in the execution of the judgment, as well as of the unjustified enrichment of the party already a creditor of the main and ancillary performance, consequently cumulating a model of subrogatory execution with one of a compulsive nature.

[57] See the entire text at https://www.legifrance.gouv.fr/affichTexte.do?cidTexte=JORFTEXT000038261631&categorieLien=id.

[58] The reports involved civil justice in different aspects; first and second

instance judgeships were affected, respectively, by the rapport, *L'ambition raisonnées d'une justice apaisée, della Commission sur la répartition des contentieux*, chaired by S. Guinchard, 2008, at http://www.justice.gouv.fr/publications-10047/rapports-thematiques-10049/commission-sur-la-repartition-des-contentieux-15546.html; the report *Magendie, Célérité et qualité de la justice devant la cour d'appel. La géstion du temps dans le procès,* of the 2008, is available at http://www.justice.gouv.fr/art_pix/1_rapport_magendie_20080625.pdf. Commenting the said reports, Y. Picod, J. Villaceque, *Les rapports guinchard et magendie: vers quelle réforme de la procédure civile?,* in *Rev. Huissiers,* no. 6, 2010. The subsequent rapport P. Delmas-Goyon, *Le juge du 21 siècle-Un citoyen acteur, une équipe de justice*, 2013, is available at http://www.justice.gouv.fr/publication/rapport_dg_2013.pdf. On this S. Amrani-Mekki, L. Raschel, in *Gaz. Pal.*, 9-11 mars 2014. During 2017 have been launched five further projects to «*transformer en profondeur la justice et de répondre efficacement aux attentes des justiciables*» (see the official vie publique, at https://www.vie-publique.fr/rapport/37123-chantiers-de-la-justice). On the topic, see S. Guinchard, *Prolégomènes pour réformer la procédure civile*, Paris, 2017, p. 2488.

[59] The nature of common-law jurisdiction is enshrined in Article L211-3, *Code de l'organisation judiciaire*, which states: «*Le tribunal judiciaire connaît de toutes les affaires civiles et commerciales pour lesquelles compétence n'est pas attribuée, en raison de la nature de la demande, à une autre juridiction*». The change from the previous version concerns the name of the body and the removal of the reference to the value of the litigation, as a consequence of the uniqueness of the Court of first instance. The other competences are indicated in the subsequent rules and correspond to those.

[60] See on the historical evolution of the French legal tradition, C. Silvestri, *Il foro lavoristico nell'Unione Europea*, Naples, 2016, p. 31 ss.

[61] *Amplius* see *Étude d'impact*, *cit.*, p. 453 ss.

[62] H. Boularbah, *Requête unilatérale et inversion du contentieux, Bruxelles*, 2010; P. Estoup, *La pratique des procédures rapides*, Paris, 1990; R. Perrot, *L'inversion du contentieux ou les prouesses de l'ordonnance sur requête, de Justice et droits fondamentaux, Mélanges offerts à Jacques Normand*, Paris, 2003, pp. 387-399.

[63] *Étude d'impact*, *cit.*, p. 114 ss.

[64] J. Vuitton, X. Vuitton, *Les référés*, Paris, 2018; C. Silvestri, *Il référé nell'esperienza giuridica francese*, Turin, 2005.

[65] It is the site Service-Public.fr, available at https://www.service-public.fr/particuliers/vosdroits/F1746.

[66] See C. Silvestri, *Il référé nell'esperienza giuridica francese*, *cit.*, p. 254 where are made references to the institutions under examination. On the *injonction de payer*: R. Perrot, *Il procedimento di ingiunzione* (*studio di diritto comparato*), in *Riv. dir. proc.*, 1986, p. 715; J. Taisne, *La réforme de la procédure d'injonction de payer*, Paris, 1981, p. 319 ss.; P. Estoup, *cit.*, p. 279 ss.; P. Hebraud, *Le recouvrement des petites créances commerciales,* in *La semaine juridique*, 1938; D. Martin, *Recouvrement simplifié des*

créances commerciales, in *Rev. trim. dr. comm.*, 1954, p. 769; J. DIETSCH, *La procédure de recouvrement simplifié de certaines créances*, in *Thèse*, Paris, 1959; P. JULIEN, *Les injonctions de payer*, Paris, 1963, p. 157; B. LE COURT, *La procédure d'injonction de payer,* Paris, 1984; D. MAS, *Injonction de payer*, in *Enc. Dalloz, Rép. proc. civ.*, vol. 3, Paris, 1997.

PART II
CIRCULATION OF THE INSTITUTION OF GARNISHMENT

*****

5. Garnishment in the United States

5.1. *Federal law on garnishment in the United States*

Once solely governed by federal, state, or municipal laws, garnishment has lately seen a number of necessary but debatable adjustments. These modifications affect every state in the union, not just one. Federal regulations were placed on this area of law on July 1, 1970, with the implementation of Title III of the Consumer Credit Protection Act[1].

The goals and legal bases of the Act itself provide insight into the reasons the federal government has been interested in this area for just a short time. The Act lists two interstate commerce interruptions that Congress deems adequate justification for using the Constitution's Commerce Clause to provide permission to join this industry[2].

The first is that more predatory credit extensions are being made as a result of unfettered garnishment[3]. The second interruption that has been seen is the frequent termination of employees due to wage garnishment[4]. The legislators assert that the bankruptcy laws' consistency has been threatened by the several state garnishment statutes[5]. Congress created a second justification for becoming involved in garnishment by using the constitutional authority to enact and limit universal bankruptcy rules[6].

The limitations outlined in the Act seem more like a baseline need than a rigid legal guideline on the limiting of garnishment. Upon a comprehensive reading of the legislation, it appears that Congress aimed to create a framework for state garnishment laws and to incentivize the states to enact local rules that will restrict garnishment and provide debtors with even greater benefits than those provided by federal regulations.

This view is based on the application of Section 1677 of the Federal Act, which states that in the event of a disagreement between the Federal Act and state garnishment legislation, the law that provides debtors with the most protection and the greatest restrictions on creditors shall take precedence[7].This clause has the effect of superseding the federal prohibitions and keeping in place the portions of state law that restrict garnishments more than do comparable provisions of federal legislation. The implementation of Section 1675 is another decisive aspect in this view. This portion of the Act addresses the exemption of state garnishment laws from Section 1673's requirements (a).

The amount of a debtor's salary that can be garnished is decided using Section 1673(a). According to this Section, the Secretary of Labor may exclude a state from the federal laws if the Secretary finds that the state's garnishment limits are essentially the same as those in Section 1673(a)[8].

One of the most significant provisions of the new Federal Act is Section 1673. What percentage of an employee's disposable income may be spared from garnishment procedures depends on how this clause is applied.

In accordance with this provision, the maximum amount that can be taken from a debtor's disposable earnings is the lesser of (a) 25% of the employee's earnings for that particular week, or (b) the amount that makes the debtor's earnings for that particular week exceed 30 times the federal minimum wage as set out in Section 6 of the Fair Labor Standards Act[9]. The latter amount would be $48 as the federal minimum wage as of right now is $1.60.

Under these limitations, the debtor-employee's salary cannot be garnished if he has earned less than $48 in disposable earnings for that particular week. The only amount that will be garnished if the debtor's weekly disposable income is more than $48 but less than $64 is the amount that will surpass $48. On the other hand, 25% of the debtor's disposable income will be subject to garnishment if it exceeds $64[10]. When calculating the amount of a debtor's salary that will be garnished, it is crucial to keep in mind that the Act mandates using disposable earnings rather than the employee's take-home pay. The Act defines disposable earnings as the amount of an employee's wages that remains after legally mandated deductions have been made[11].

Nevertheless, things like union dues and charity contribution – which are frequently subtracted from an employee's salary – are not covered by these mandated deductions. The limitations outlined in Section 1673(a) apply in all circumstances, with the exception of those in where there is a Court order requiring payment of child support, a bankruptcy Court order under Chapter XIII of the Bankruptcy Act, or a debt pertaining to any federal or state tax[12].

Additionally, the Federal Deposit Insurance Corporation (FDIC) has policies regarding the garnishment of accounts holding Federal benefit payments. These payments are shielded from access or garnishment by creditors – aside from the federal government and specific state agencies – under Federal law.

The overall goal of American federal legislation regarding garnishment is to strike a balance between the preservation of government benefit payments and employee earnings, and the rights of creditors to collect debts.

5.2. *States regulation*

The purpose of garnishment is to bring the garnishee before the Court; it is a process, not a pleading[13]. If there are flaws in the procedure, they cannot be addressed by a demurrer[14] and are instead the focus of a move to quash[15] or a plea in abatement.

As seen earlier, a garnishment is a type of proceeding in *rem* because its goal is to give the plaintiff the authority to seize defendant property held by the garnishee or a debt owed by the garnishee to the defendant in order to satisfy his claim against the defendant[16].

A garnishment is an effective attachment of the defendant's effects in the hands of the garnishee[17]. It is not fundamentally different from an attachment by levy, save from the fact that the plaintiff only obtains a lien that entitles him to hold the garnishee personally accountable for the property in question or its value[18], and to prevent the garnishee from using the property to satisfy his obligation to the defendant[19]. The defendant's rights to the property held by the garnishee are so completely eliminated as to prohibit the defendant from disposing of it in a way that would conflict with the plaintiff's claim being paid after it has been legally perfected[20]. However, the defendant's rights are unaffected by the pending garnishment and can still be used to fix the garnishee's liability to him, secure it via legal actions, or in any other way. Of course, these rights can only be used in subordination to the lien thus formed[21].

According to the US Supreme Court, the effects in the garnishee's possession are deemed to be in *custodia legis* as of the time of the garnishment; as such, the garnishee is required to keep them secure and is not free to alter, exchange for cash, or otherwise exercise any kind of ownership over them[22]. As the Court's agent[23], he gains a special property interest in them and is permitted to hold them until his liability is established against the defendant and any subsequent purchaser or pledgee[24]. This is true even if the attachment is made against someone other than the purported owner who gave the garnishee the items[25]. If the attachment legally binds effects later received by him, he has no right to surrender any of the defendant's things that were in his possession when he was garnished or that came into his possession thereafter[26]. Nor may he legitimately levie on and remove any of the defendant's goods from his possession[27]; if that is the case, the officer seizing must retain them subject to the lien of the creditor who carried out the garnishment[28]. If so, or if seized from him by a wrongdoer, it will not release the garnishee from culpability[29]; nevertheless, it may provide justification for postponing proceedings until the party who took them may recover damages[30]. However, the garnishing plaintiff cannot then hold the garnishee liable for the property if he causes a levy and sale under execution to occur[31].

The following Section above outlines the Supreme Court of the United States' stance that the garnishee must retain the effects safely in his possession and cannot alter, cash, or otherwise exert ownership over them. This ruling must be interpreted in light of the particular facts of the case that the Court was asked to decide. The item that was in the garnishee's possession was goods, and in that specific instance, the decision made was definitely the right one. However, that rule cannot be applied everywhere.

Thus, the question arose as to how much the consignor should charge him when items were committed to a factor for sale on which he had paid advances and was later called upon as the consignor's garnishee. The commodities were valued at $1,856 at the time of the garnishment, but he later sold them for $1,260. In the transaction, no fraud was reported. The plaintiff argued that the amount that should determine the garnishee's responsibility was the former sum. This raised the question of whether the factor's capacity to sell the products was suspended by the garnishment. If it did, the garnishee was liable for the greater amount; if not, they were liable for the lesser amount. It was decided that the selling power remained intact[32].

Furthermore, it is unlikely that the US Supreme Court's ruling could be strictly enforced in cases where statutes enable the attachment of choses in action. This is permitted in Missouri, and a garnishee may be held accountable for any defendant owned choses in action that are in his possession. In a specific case, a bank was called as a garnishee and had a bill of exchange belonging to the defendant in its custody for collection. The bank then sued the acceptor, who claimed that the bank's garnishment had taken away its ability to pursue a claim based on the bill. However, the Court determined that the bank's right to pursue the claim had not been forfeited[33].

The scope of garnishment cannot be expanded beyond the point at which the garnishee obtains the defendant's belongings. It leaves the garnishee's real or personal property unencumbered. Consequently, a judgment rendered against the personal representatives of a garnishee who passed away during the course of the proceedings does not attach to the garnishee's estate, nor does it bind it[34]. Nor does it grant the attaching creditor priority over other creditors[35].

Expectations and contingent interests are foreign concepts to garnishment[36]. As a result, in cases where a devisee's interest in a testator's estate was attempted to be reached by garnishment - even if the testator may never have legal ownership of the estate during her lifetime - the Court declined to uphold the attempt to get the devisee's interest through that method, even while it held that anything with a present and certain existence might be obtained through garnishment – despite the fact that possession and enjoyment may be temporarily delayed[37]. An injunction or other equity proceeding cannot be used to supplement a garnishment, and no separate legal action not permitted by statute may be based on a garnishment to obtain security for the payment of a judgment that may be recovered against the garnishee[38].

In a chancery case, for example, certain parties were garnished. Later, the complainant filed an additional bill claiming that the garnishees were bankrupt and that they had shipped substantial quantities of their assets to other parties for auction. If the profits of the sale of the goods were given to the garnishees, the complainant would lose the benefit of the decree. The Court then placed a restraining order on the auctioneers, and when they answered and showed that the remaining balance was in their possession, they were ruled to pay the complainant. Consequently, it was decided that the proceeding was unlawful[39]. Therefore, in a case where C. was garnished in a suit in which A. was the plaintiff against B. in a Circuit Court of the United States; B. was then the defendant in a suit that was pending in a state Court, in which judgment was later rendered and execution was issued against C. Consequently, A. requested an injunction to stop the execution until C. answered in the United States Court and the matter of his liability as garnishee was considered by that Court. The injunction was denied, not only because the State Court's jurisdiction had first attached, but also because there was no basis for equitable interposition in support of the garnishment[40]. Furthermore, it has been decided that a garnishment will not be upheld in an equity bill to prevent the garnishee from selling the defendant's property while it is in his possession, pending the plaintiff's ability to achieve a judgment and execution against the garnishee[41]. Even less, a Court of Chancery has no jurisdiction to seize a debt owed by one of the defendant's debtors and use the money to settle the defendant's debt[42]. Additionally, under a judgment against a garnishee, from whom nothing can be obtained upon execution, it is decided in Illinois that unless the law specifically permits it, no action by garnishment of the defendant's debtors may be taken; the action must terminate with the defendant's debtor[43].

A garnishment cannot be used retroactively to change already completed transactions between the defendant and the garnishee or hold the former party liable for the latter's property that was in his possession before the garnishment but not at the time of it. Therefore, it was decided that the garnishee could not be charged in cases where, prior to the garnishment, he had been in possession of defendant property under a secret trust, which would have been invalid against creditors. However, since the garnishee had given the defendant the property before being garnished, the defendant could not have been held accountable[44].

Furthermore, in cases where an execution permitted a garnishment and the execution constituted a lien on the defendant's personal property as of the time of its issuance, it was decided that the garnishment did not apply to that period of time but rather began on the day of its service and was unable to override any intervening attachments that had been filed between the execution's issuance and the garnishment under it[45].

Garnishment cannot be used to undermine trusts in order to get funds that are believed to be the debtors. Any funds or property that the debtor seeks to get via this process must be entirely his, free and clear of any trusts established in his or anybody else's name. In this case, the Court determined that the money was a trust fund under the will, and the son did not have the absolute right to allow its attachment for his obligations, either before or after it got into his hands. The testator had left his son a large sum of money, «for the sustenance of himself and family, and for no other reason». A portion of the bequest had been recovered and handed to the son's attorney. The Court declared that «the will should be carried out according to the intent of the testator. And we can have no possible doubt that it was his object to create the money in the hands of his son a trust fund for the use specified in the will. The testator not only used affirmative words, appropriate to create a trust fund, but he saw fit at the same time to add a negative. The words are, "for the support of himself and family, and for no other purpose". To hold that under this will the son took the money absolutely as his own, and not as a trust fund, would be to pervert the use of language, and the obvious intent of the testator»[46].

A widow left her husband the whole value of her property, «to be prudently used if needed by him for his support during the remainder of his life; and should it not be used or should there be any left after paying the expenses of sickness and funeral charges, to be divided among my children» according to her will.

To cover the outstanding amount of the purchase money, the farm was sold and payment was made in part with cash and in part with a mortgage. The wife's executor was garnished in a lawsuit against the hug-band for the cash and note he obtained from the farm's sale. The judge ruled that he was not charged and stated: «The intention of the testatrix was, to provide a fund for her husband's support during life, and that to be prudently appropriated according to his necessities. To effect the object of the bequest it must be regarded as a trust...and the money and note in the hands of the executor cannot be taken by process of foreign attachment to pay the general indebtedness of the defendant»[47]. Therefore, upon the trust, when lands were devised to trustees: «to pay over all remaining rents and income in cash into the hands of my daughter J., in person, and not upon any written or verbal order, nor upon any assignment or transfer by the said J.»; it was decided that the trustees would not be permitted to collect the estate's net income to pay off her obligations[48]. Thus, in cases when bequests made to one were handed to her: «expressly upon condition that they shall not be liable to be attached or seized for her debts, but that the whole amount shall be paid directly to her by my executor, without diminution», it could not be attached to satisfy the legatee's debts as it was considered a trust in the executor's hands until it was really paid to her[49].

Thereby, when a trustee received property by devise, «to hold upon trust, to collect and receive the rents and income… and to pay the said rents and income...to and for the support and maintenance of my son C., during the term of his natural life, with the intent and purpose, that the said trustee may either pay the said income, or such portion thereof as he may think proper, into the hands of my said son, or disburse the same in such way as to the trustee may seem best for his comfortable maintenance; such payments and disbursements to be at all times at the sole and absolute discretion of the said trustee». Upon the trustee's summons as C's garnishee, the Court determined that charging him would completely undermine the testator's intention when establishing the trust. As a result, the trustee was released along with other grounds[50]. Thus, a railroad corporation, acting via its assistant treasurer, deposited a certain amount of money with a New York City brokerage business and obtained a receipt from them that stated the following: «Received from J. M. C. R. 825,000 in trust, to apply the same to an equal amount of the coupons of the first mortgage bonds and consolidated mortgage bonds of the M. C. R. Co., in the order in which such coupons shall be presented to us for payment, after having been duly identified for payment at our office by stamp impressed thereon; the said money not to be subject to the control of said company, otherwise than for the payment of said coupons as above described». This money was a portion of a bigger sum that the railroad business obtained specifically to pay the coupons on the bonds that were stated. The brokers recorded this money on their records to the credit of "Coupon trust account" after receiving it. An attachment was placed in the hands of the M. C. R. Co. after a portion of the money had been paid out. However, it was decided that the transaction constituted an absolute and irreversible appropriation of the funds invested in trust for the purposes specified in the receipt, and that the attachment was secondary to the rights of the coupon holders under the trust[51].

While it is certain that a garnishment cannot be used to dissolve trusts in order to get funds intended for a debtor, there is no way to prevent a garnishment from reaching funds held by a trustee as income to be given to a *cestui que trust* in cases where the trust's creation document does not forbid alienation, does not shield the trustee from accountability for the obligations of the trustee, or restrict the use of the proceeds to certain purposes. In the event that the trust is unrestricted, the trustee might be held liable as a garnishee of the *cestui que trust* for any income owed to him at the time of the garnishment and, should the legislation permit, for any income that accrues thereafter[52].

Similar to a levy, attachments are served first in the order of priority in a garnishment. Strict law governs the right of several attaching creditors, as between themselves, to receive the effects of their common debtor in the hands of a garnishee through their consecutive processes. If a creditor in a previous process does not perfect his claim against the garnishee by getting a final decision that can be enforced legally, his process will not be able to prevent or delay the future attaches from receiving the same effects. In such a scenario, the garnishee was still due to a later attaching creditor, whose judgment was executed and whose process was issued prior to the agreement, even if the garnishee had paid his obligation to the first of numerous attaching creditors and the defendant under the terms of that arrangement, and the latter had not pursued his action to judgment against the garnishee and the defendant[53]. Therefore, if a junior attachment matures into a judgment before a writ has been filed, it does not grant priority of action against the garnishee[54].

Garnishments against the same person for the same sum often originate from Courts in various jurisdictions. In this instance, there is no question that the Court granting the first garnishment has complete authority over the fund in order to use it to satisfy the plaintiff's claim. However, this power does not extend beyond that point, nor does it prevent a separate Court from recognizing a second garnishment, which will bind the fund susceptible to challenge if the first one calls for the entire amount[55]. In addition, if a person has been garnished in more than one jurisdiction and notifies the Court where he was last served about the prior garnishment, that Court will take any appropriate action to shield him from double liability while also retaining his obligation to it in the event that he is released from the Court where he was previously garnished. The Supreme Court of Louisiana ruled in this case that either the procedures should be halted for a reasonable amount of time or that the plaintiff should provide the garnishee with adequate security to protect him from any losses resulting from the prior attachment[56].

Through garnishment, the Court can obtain property that cannot be seized and compel the defendant to pay back any debts owed to him. The latter is what makes garnishment under the London custom special and unique, and it is this that gave rise to the garnishment laws systems in the United States. The unusual method by which the defendant's assets that are not able to be apprehended or seized may nevertheless be subject to payment of his debts has been designated as a garnishment[57], or warning.

The person to whom these assets are attached is referred to as the garnishee because he has been warned not to give the plaintiff the money or turn over the defendant's assets to him, but rather to appear and respond to the plaintiff's lawsuit[58].

This arrangement is found in every state, with the exception of a few in New England, where the person who receives, the warning is referred to as a trustee and the procedure used to warn him as a trustee process[59].

Garnishment is exclusively a statutory procedure in the United States and cannot be used for purposes other than those for which it is authorized by law. Therefore, unless the statute specifically states otherwise, no assets belonging to the defendant that the garnishee obtains or debt that the garnishee accrues after the garnishment are bound by it[60]. Thus, absent a specific statute, the administrator of a garnishee who passes away before responding to the plaintiff's interrogatories cannot be forced to do so[61].

The Court was asked to order the garnishee to open the safe and file an inventory of its contents when a Safe Deposit Company was summoned as the garnishee of a person who rented a safe in one of its vaults, but the contents of the safe did not appear. The order was denied because the Court lacked the authority to hold such a proceeding[62]. Therefore, in a case where a bank was garnished and there was a small trunk that the defendant had deposited there, the contents of which no bank officer knew, it was decided that the garnishee could not be charged because there was no indication that the trunk contained attachable effects. The Court acknowledged the English doctrine, which states that an officer may break open a defendant's private trunk in the course of an execution if the contents are subject to execution but stated that the officer must first obtain lawful possession of the trunk, and that the Court could not assist him in the ongoing case[63].

The entire basis of garnishment is the legal system, and it is contingent upon following the legal procedures in order to be prosecuted. It cannot rely on the garnishee's voluntary actions for assistance. When such acts infringe upon the rights of third parties, they will be deemed null and void. Therefore, it was decided that the person who acknowledged and accepted service by writing on the petition under a law that required the garnishment process to be personally served on the garnishee had no right to do so and that doing so rendered the acceptance or waiver of service void against other attaching creditors[64] as well as against the assignee of the debt that the garnishee was charged with[65]. Therefore, an admission of service of garnishment by the corporation's attorney was deemed insufficient to grant the Court jurisdiction over the corporation in cases where the statute stipulated that process should be served on the corporation by serving the president, any director, or manager thereof[66]. Consequently, it was decided that no judgment could be made against a corporation in cases where no formal process had been served to the corporation as garnishee, but the secretary of the corporation still showed up, answered, and did not object to the sufficiency of the service[67].

One of the basic tenets of garnishment is that the plaintiff does not get any additional rights against the garnishee beyond those of the defendant. Because of this, the attachment plaintiff's capacity to use the defendant's rights against the garnishee is constrained by the degree of the garnishee's obligation to the defendant[68]. There is one exception to this rule, though, and that is in cases when the garnishee obtained the defendant's belongings through a false transfer from the latter. Even though the defendant would not have any rights against the garnishee in that situation, a defendant's creditor might nevertheless attach the garnishee's possessions[69].

As long as the plaintiff has the ability to pursue his claim against the defendant in the Court in which the garnishment occurs, he is entitled to hold a garnishee. His recourse against the garnishee ends when his remedy against the latter does. It is undeniable that the latter may demonstrate that the plaintiff's claim against him has been therefore terminated. As a result, if a garnishee is called under an ancillary attachment – one that is issued after the initiation of an action by summons and in aid thereof – and the original action is dismissed, the garnishee is discharged and the ancillary attachment drops along with it.

The plaintiff is thus unable to challenge the judgment discharging him if the main action's dismissal is not appealed against[70]. Therefore, in cases when someone was garnished during an execution, they were allowed to demonstrate that the defendant had met the judgment through a prior execution in the same case[71]. In cases where a defendant's passing and the probate Court's declaration of his estate's bankruptcy resulted in the removal of an attachment placed on his property, it was also decided that the lien obtained through a garnishment was eliminated[72].

The garnishee is released with the termination of the attachment, but the defendant is still legally entitled to face legal action in Court[73].

There were no particular constitutional requirements obtained in the United States regarding enforcement proceedings prior to 1969. There was no need for a rule stating that «after a judgment has been rendered against him, a defendant who has been granted an opportunity to be heard and has had his day in Court should have a further notice and hearing before supplemental proceedings are taken to reach his property in satisfaction of the judgment»[74]. Similarly, garnishment proceedings were true[75].

However, the due process and equal protection clauses of the US Constitution have been used to challenge local law in four significant rulings by the US Supreme Court since 1969[76].

In Sniadach v. Family Finance Corp[77] the Court held that prejudgment wage garnishments are «a specialized type of property presenting distinct problems in our economic system»[78] – «a taking of property without that procedural due process that is required by the Fourteenth Amendment»[79] – without first holding a hearing on the merits of the underlying claim; the debtor must be given more than just advance notice in order for him to raise any defenses. Three years later, the same requirement was extended to all prejudgment property seizures in Fuentes v. Shevin[80], a four-to-three decision. This was done because the Court «has not... embraced the general proposition that a wrong may be done if it can be undone», even in cases where the defendant may be able to reclaim possession of the property by posting a security bond double its value[81].

It is unconstitutional to have a statute that permits garnishment upon the creditor's conclusory allegations and without allowing for an early hearing by order of the Court clerk[82]. However, no procedural due process or other constitutional rule is violated if the prejudgment seizure is ordered by a judge instead of a clerk of the Court pendente lite and with the expectation of an imminent hearing, upon a showing by verified petition or affidavit of specific facts that justify the sequestration[83].

American law, purposefully shield the defendant in enforcement from the danger of excessive or unfounded enforcement, rather than the problem of ensuring that the judgment creditor has the fullest possible enforcement of his claim[84].

Regarding the issuance and levy of a writ of execution or post-judgment garnishment, American case law does not bother with constitutional requirements, even after Sniadach v. Family Finance Corp. and its progeny. Rather, the majority of cases deal with prejudgment attachment and demand that the defendant has the opportunity to refute the underlying claim.

Even the seminal Shaffer v. Heitner[85] ruling was subject to a prejudgment sequestration and quasi in rem jurisdiction to the minimum contacts test required by conventional ideas of substantial justice and fair play[86]. Consequently, American constitutional concerns generally forbid an attachment prior to the defendant being heard regarding the merits of the claim, but they do not grant him the right «to notice prior to the issue of an execution..., in satisfaction of the judgment»[87].

The entirety of the outlined doctrines would seem to clearly show that a garnishment is a proceeding against third parties, or those whose relationship to the defendant is such that their garnishment is actually the defendant's garnishment. And this is undoubtedly the goal of the London customary procedure, which states that «if the plaintiff will assume that another individual in the city owes the defendant any money, he will have a garnishment against him»[88]. Thus, it is completely inadmissible to summon one defendant in a case involving multiple defendants and use them as garnishees of the others. However, attempts have been made to garnish individuals when doing so would have actually garnished the defendant; examples of such individuals include ticket agents and turnpike gate keepers. It has been questioned whether such a proceeding can be maintained. It would appear that it cannot in theory.

Insofar as their relationship with the defendant is concerned, they are the defendant and not third parties. The money that the defendant has with them is his property. Until he demands the money from them, and they refuse to pay, he cannot take legal action against them. They are merely the defendant's money custodians, working under his direct supervision and control. They hold the same position toward him as a cashier does toward a bank, a cash clerk does toward a merchant, and a treasurer does toward a municipal corporation.

5.3. *Virginia*

Historically, a creditor has been able to use the garnishment procedure to achieve two different goals at two different points in the judicial process. In order to provide security for debts or expenses, the defendant's property that is in the possession of a third party may be placed under legal custody prior to judgment. In order to get property held by a third party and fulfill the lien formed by the judgment, the procedure may also be utilized to assist in the execution of a judgment in favor of the creditor.

In Virginia, the term garnishment refers only to the post judgment procedures that support execution; garnishment prior to judgment is referred to as "attachment" in general[89]. The method by which a judgment creditor in Virginia executes the lien of a writ of *fieri facias* against any debt or property owed to the judgment debtor and in the custody of a third party, the garnishee, is known as garnishment[90]. In essence, it's a legal proceeding where the judgment debtor's rights against his garnishee are subrogated to the judgment creditor[91].

A sheriff was required by common law to seize the specified sum of money from the defendant's tangible personal property in order to satisfy the judgment. This was known as the writ of *facias*[92]. This common law heritage was reflected in Virginia's laws prior to July 1, 1850. As a result, intangible personal property – often referred to as "choses in action"[93] – could not be accessed to fulfill a creditor's judgment since it was not a lien on it and could not be subject to collection and public auction under a writ of *fieri facias*[94].

A significant overhaul of the Virginia Code was started in 1849. The writ of *fieri facias* was authorized to constitute a lien on all of the debtor's intangible personal property as of July 1, 1850[95].

Since the lien was neither inchoate or conditional, it just needed to be presented to the sheriff in order to be enforceable[96]. This fresh and comprehensive lien was put to use against the intangible property as soon as the writ was submitted to the sheriff for execution[97]. Moreover, the new lien persisted until the judgment creditor's ability to levy a fresh execution stopped, not ending with the passage of the return date[98]. The process of garnishment was developed as a way to allow the creditor to get the debtor's intangible personal property, which was formerly subject to the all-encompassing lien of the writ of *fieri facias*, in fulfillment of the judgment[99]. To guarantee that the lien of execution was properly executed, garnishment just gave the judgment creditor a direct recourse against a third party that was somehow obligated to the judgment debtor.

The garnishment procedure supplemental character as a proceeding in assistance of execution was established by the precedent-setting decision of Charron & Co. v. Boswell[100]. Despite the fact that their judgment was delivered later than that of certain other creditors, some creditors in Boswell were able to serve their garnishment summons on the garnishee first. They argued that they were entitled to precedence over other creditors since the garnishment procedure gave them a unique lien on the disputed cash. The Court rejected this argument and said: «Now this view is wholly inconsistent with the purpose and effect of the [garnishment] proceedings [they] do not give any lien at all, general or specific. They are merely a means provided by law for the enforcement of a legal lien which already exists»[101].

By giving the writ of *fieri facias* the authority to bind simple choses in action, the Court completed the framework of Virginia's contemporary execution of judgment legislation and rendered the garnishment remedy a more humane substitute for the debtor's jail. Since its establishment in 1850, Virginia's garnishment procedure has mostly not altered.

5.3.1. *Nature of garnishment and its effect*

It is crucial to first comprehend the nature and implications of the garnishment procedure. It has been observed that the word "garnishment" in Virginia solely pertains to the use of this remedy in support of execution; hence, the presence of an earlier, legally sound decision is assumed[102]. A judgment creditor may garnish someone, known as the garnishee, to enforce the lien created by the writ of *fieri facias* arising out of that judgment against any debt or other chose in action due his judgment debtor[103]. Garnishment is a procedure that can only be implemented in accordance with law enactment[104]; it cannot be expanded upon to meet the specific requirements of a certain situation[105]. Since the process is typically viewed as violating common law, the judgment creditor is required to adhere closely to the statute's prescribed method[106]. Similarly, in order to avoid responsibility, the garnishee cannot safely forgo compliance with any of the core provisions of the legislation or uphold a decision in an unapproved garnishment procedure. To the extent that the garnishee's voluntary actions infringe upon the rights of other parties, they shall be deemed null and void[107].

In Virginia, a garnishment procedure is not a summary execution process; rather, it is a separate civil action[108] that is taken in support of and additional to a judgment. In Tunstall v. Worthington[109], decided in 1853, the Court said: «The proceeding must be regarded as a civil suit, and not as a process of execution to enforce a judgment already rendered. In this proceeding the parties have a day in Court; an issue of fact may be tried by a jury, evidence adduced, judgment rendered, costs adjudged, and execution issued on the judgment»[110]. As a result, a garnishment process is essentially an action at law brought by the judgment debtor against the garnishee on behalf of the judgment creditor[111]. In these processes, the judgment creditor asserts that the judgment debtor is responsible for a debt owed to the garnishee or property held by the latter. As a result, the main goal is to determine whether or if there is, and if so, how much of it there is[112]. Without a formal pleading, the Court must investigate the garnishee's liability if he disputes any debt to the judgment debtor or if the judgment creditor claims the garnishee has not completely revealed his liability[113]; the judgment creditor bears the affirmative burden of proof when determining the existence and scope of such responsibility. The Court may, upon request from either party, appoint a jury to decide this matter[114]. Furthermore, in the event that there is an adverse claim about the purported indebtedness, the opposing claimant may be joined by Court order at any point during the proceedings, and the veracity of his claim may be determined[115].

The basic tenet of garnishment law is that the judgment debtor retains all rights against the garnishee, and the judgment creditor does not obtain any additional ones[116]. As a result, in order to hold the garnishee accountable in the garnishment process, he must have a current, fixed responsibility[117].

Until the judgment debtor is able to recoup the amount the creditor is trying to get through garnishment, the garnishee is not subject to charges. The creditor must demonstrate that the legal duty for the debt is absolute and not contingent upon any unfulfilled condition precedent or future eventuality in order to hold the garnishee responsible[118]. Nonetheless, Courts have determined that even when a debt is due at a later time, it is enforceable by garnishment and is susceptible to a writ of *fieri facias* lien[119].

In Virginia, there has been a great deal of litigation surrounding the question of whether there is a current, fixed responsibility that a creditor may satisfy his judgment[120]. The Virginia case providing the most in-depth analysis of this problem is Boisseau v. Bass Administrator[121]. By arguing that her writ of *fieri facias* formed a subsisting and ongoing lien on all of the debtor's personal assets, including the insurance policy, the judgment creditor in Boisseau attempted to make an insurance company accountable as garnishee for the proceeds of a life insurance policy on the life of one R.T. Bass[122]. The Court rejected the creditor's request for the funds, noting that the insured's ability to make a claim under the policy depended on the insured making premium payments, which were completely voluntary[123]. The insurance arrangement did not generate any current obligation that the insured may demand, the Court said, nor did it impose a present fixed responsibility upon the corporation to pay anything[124]. It was debatable whether the firm would ever be required to pay anything because of the policy because it was subject to forfeiture for nonpayment of premiums up to the insured's death[125]. Similarly, the Court determined that if the judgment debtor had no authority to seek payment in full or in part from the insurance company for his personal benefit, then his creditor also had no right to garnish the proceeds in Lynch v. Johnson[126], a case involving a disagreement over the proceeds of a fire insurance policy. The proof showed that the judgment debtor had received the damaged property, while the grantor had retained a life estate for herself. For the benefit of everyone with an interest in the property, the policy covered its full worth. The debtor's creditor was unable to obtain the proceeds of the policy because the Court determined that the debtor lacked a personal claim to them[127].

In conclusion, a judgment creditor must follow the proper legal processes in order to garnish any debt owed by the judgment debtor from any source. In order to get a writ of garnishment issued, he must first allege - and be ready to prove - that the garnishee has a current, definite obligation to the debtor.

5.3.2. *Parties involved in the garnishment proceedings*

Until the creditor has obtained a legitimate judgment against his debtor, no judgment against the garnishee may be made[128].

The lien placed on the debtor's intangible personal property that is held by a third party is effective for a year from the date of the final determination of the amount owed, provided that the creditor has received a valid judgment[129]. The judgment creditor may file an unlimited number of garnishment writs to get satisfaction during this time, and doing so will not affect his lien[130]. The creditor may also take advantage of other statutory remedies[131]. One other tool at the judgment creditor's disposal is the interrogatory process, which allows them to force anybody to respond to questions posed by the Court or creditor in order to ascertain whether the debtor has any personal property[132]. However, the Act stipulates that in order to provide the debtor with the greatest possible advantage of the protections and exemptions that come with the procedure, a judgment creditor seeking to have an employer withhold payment of a debtor's wages or salary must initiate a garnishment case[133].

Subject to any legislative exemptions provided for his protection, the judgment debtor's whole personal estate, including all obligations from whatever source, is available for the creditor to satisfy after being proven responsible to the creditor[134]. It is possible for an assignee who pays a valuable payment and gets possession of the debtor's intangible property to challenge the creditor's claim[135], even if the debtor meant to commit fraud while making the assignment[136].

It has been stated that the garnishee's role in the procedure is that of a "mere stakeholder" or "custodian" of the debtor's belongings that are in his possession[137]. However, if the garnishment procedure is seen as a distinct civil action, this description is not entirely correct[138]. The defendant in the separate process is really the garnishee once they have been issued with a notice of garnishment. In addition to being forced to appear in Court or face contempt proceedings, he may also face a direct lawsuit from the creditor for any costs the creditor incurred as a result of the garnishee's refusal to comply[139]. By turning over the money or other assets owed to the debtor to the Court, the garnishee can avoid any personal obligation[140]. Anybody who holds property belonging to the judgment debtor or who owes money to them may be held liable as a garnishee and ordered to make a mandatory assignment for the creditor's advantage. In a wide sense, "person" refers to "corporation"[141], "partnerships"[142], unincorporated groups[143], and any other body that is recognized by law.

Virginia is also one of the few states that allows a municipality to be sued as a garnishee in cases other than those that are specifically allowed by legislation[144]. In the Virginia case of Portsmouth Gas Co. v. Sanford[145] (1899), the then-recent repeal of sovereign immunity was seen as signaling a change in public policy that permitted the garnishment of debts due by municipal corporations, particularly with regard to the ability to garnish wages and salaries of municipal and state workers[146].

Portsmouth has recently been read more narrowly, with its holding limited to «an ordinary obligation to a third person» in situations when the city will experience «little difficulty and no discrimination»[147].

Lastly, it is well-established that a Court cannot decide on a nonparty's rights[148]. As a result, unless a third-party claimant is a party to the garnishment case, his rights to the assets sought to be garnished cannot be decided[149]. The Virginia Code allows for the broad addition of additional parties at any point throughout the proceedings as needed by the interests of justice[150].

5.3.3. *Beginning of garnishment procedure*

The judgment creditor must submit an oral or written request to the Court, in order for the issuing of a garnishment summons, indicating that the lien of his writ of *fieri facias*[151] has rendered someone other than the judgment debtor accountable or that someone else has the authority to act as the personal representative of a deceased person[152] and possess an amount of money to which the judgment debtor is or may be entitled as a creditor or distribute of such decedent[153].

The amount of interest owed on the judgment and any credits provided toward fulfillment of the judgment must also be specified by the judgment creditor in his proposal[154]. Furthermore, if the judgment debtor raises any of the six charges listed in the legislation, no summons will be issued at his suggestion of guilt when the judgment creditor attempts to garnish the judgment debtor's earnings or pay[155]. This clause frequently has the overall effect of preventing the issuing of a second garnishment summons on a separate judgment secured by the judgment creditor against the same judgment debtor for eighteen months[156]. A summons[157] may be served out of the clerk's office of the Court where the judgment was given, or to which an execution thereon has been returned against such person, in response to the judgment creditor's suggestion of culpability[158].

In Virginia, the procedures cannot commence until the summons has been served on the judgment debtor and the garnishee. This notification is required[159]. However, the Act stipulates[160] that the clerk may send a copy of the summons to the debtor's last known address by first class mail if the judgment debtor cannot be served in the usual manner[161].

The garnishment legislation stipulates that an officer or management employee of the corporation is the only person to receive a summons when the garnishee is a corporation[162].

If the judgment creditor produces a certificate certifying that he has exercised reasonable diligence and that no such official or management employee could be discovered inside the state, only then may the summons be served on the registered agent or the clerk of the State Corporation Commission[163]. If the United States government is the garnishee, the summons must be served on the managing employee of the agency that is allegedly at fault. Alternatively, if the judgment debtor is an active-duty member of the armed services, the summons must be served on the senior financial officer of the military base where the debtor is stationed[164]. When any the individuals listed in the statute are unable to accept the summons, it may be served upon the United States Attorney or another agency[165]. The fact that government employees' income and salaries, including those of soldiers, may only be garnished in order to fulfill legal responsibilities to pay alimony and child support, is also significant[166].

5.3.4. *Analyzing of the garnishee, judgment and costs*

Following receipt of the summons, the garnishee is required to either attend in person and undergo an oath examination or make a statement, substantiated by an affidavit, outlining the property he possesses that is entitled to the judgment debtor or the amount of his obligation to the debtor[167]. In the case of a corporation, the garnishee must appear via an authorized agent or have that agent write a statement, substantiated by an affidavit[168]. In the event that the judgment debtor or judgment creditor disputes the veracity of the declaration, the garnishee may be obliged to attend and show the relevant records and documents[169]. A written response explaining whether or whether the garnishee has any money in his possession in his fiduciary role that is owed to the judgment debtor, and if so, how much, must be filed when the garnishee appears in Court as the personal representative of a decedent[170]. The garnishee must notify the Court when the amount is determined and paid to the debtor, and the Court must continue the case if the amount has not been decided upon[171].

If the Court receives a suggestion that the garnishee has not completely revealed his responsibility in his answer, it will investigate the debt without requiring a formal pleading[172]. If the case is in circuit Court, a jury will be seated to conduct the investigation upon demand from any side[173]. It is imperative that the proof presented by the judgment creditor prove the existence of the debt or the property held by the garnishee. Even while the garnishee may be questioned as an opposition witness, this won't invalidate his testimony or support a decision to find him not guilty if the evidence isn't strong enough[174].

The Court may issue judgment against the garnishee for the amount owed and direct its delivery to the judgment creditor, a designated officer, or have the money paid into Court when the verified statement or inspection of the garnishee reveals his duty to the judgment debtor[175]. A cost judgment will be rendered against the party the Court finds appropriate[176]; however, the garnishee cannot be subject to a cost judgment until he appears or does not fully reveal his liability[177]. The Court may either compel the garnishee to attend or, in his absence, hear proof of any obligation on his side and issue appropriate orders as if the proof had presented by his examination in the event that the garnishee fails to appear or file a statement[178].

5.4. *Louisiana*

Compared to the laws of the other 49 states in the union, Louisiana's legal system draws from a wider range of sources. With certain common law influences, private law has a civil law character and is founded on French and Spanish codes and eventually Roman law. Private law is substantive law between private sector parties, primarily contracts and torts. The only state where the common law of the United States is not the foundation of the private legal system is Louisiana[179].

Attorneys James Brown, Louis Moreau-Lislet, and Edward Livingston wrote the first Louisiana civil code, Digeste de la Loi Civile, which was later translated into English as The Digest of the Civil Laws presently in Force in the Territory of Orleans, or more often known as the Digest of 1808. Louis Moreau-Lislet, the principal drafter, was a French colonial who was born in

Saint-Domingue (present-day Haiti) and earned his legal degree in Paris shortly before the French Revolution of 1789[180].

Attorneys in the state worked very hard over many years to make sure that the two versions were in agreement. Notwithstanding these attempts, several clauses were limited to one translation or the other. The original French and the English translations are now largely of historical relevance because of contemporary legislative enactments that repeal and recreate Louisiana's civil code articles as any other set of legislation[181].

Contrary to popular perception, the Napoleonic Code and the Louisiana Civil Code are not directly related. Instead, their common ancestor is the 1800 Draft of the Napoleonic Code. France did not adopt the Napoleonic Code until 1804, a year following the Louisiana Purchase. The actual notes of the 1808 Digest drafters, who claimed their objective was to model Louisiana law on Spanish law and made no reference of the Napoleonic Code, were found by historians in 1941 and 1965. French law, however, became the primary foundation of Louisiana jurisprudence with the 1825 Code, which was specifically designed to overturn previous Spanish law[182].

Louisianan common law differs greatly from common law in every other state in the union. The "civilian" heritage is still strongly ingrained in Louisiana private law and certain areas of criminal law, despite the fact that many disparities have been overcome as a result of common law's powerful impact[183]. One frequently mentioned difference is that judges in Louisiana make decisions based on their own understanding of the law, but common law Courts are constrained by stare decisis and typically base their decisions on precedents[184]. However, this distinction is not unqualified. Established precedent is respected differently in civil law, according to the jurisprudence constante theory. The main distinction between the two legal theories, according to the Louisiana Supreme Court, is that while a single Court ruling might serve as a sufficient basis for *stare decisis*, «a series of adjudicated cases, all in accord, form the basis for jurisprudence constante». Furthermore, the Louisiana Courts of Appeals have made it clear that stare decisis does not apply to jurisprudence constante; rather, it is only a secondary source of law that is not authoritative[185]. The Louisiana Revised Statutes grant the right to a jury trial in civil proceedings, but the state constitution does not grant this right because of the civil law heritage. Furthermore, the discretion of appellate Courts to examine factual conclusions made by juries in civil matters is even more expansive. Additionally, particular performance is nearly always possible, damages are allocated differently than in common law nations, and juries may hear instances that would be deemed fair in other jurisdictions[186].

The Uniform Commercial Code (UCC) has been fully embraced by the other 49 states in the area of commercial law, simplifying the regulations governing business dealings. With the exception of Articles 2 and 2A, which are at odds with civil law customs governing the sale and lease of commodities, Louisiana enacted the majority of the UCC's provisions. Nonetheless, the Civil Code now has a number of provisions pertaining to the insertion of words into contracts[187].

The states that make up the Union are not autonomous branches of government. Conversely, every state possesses independent authority over all subjects, with the exception of those for which the US Constitution grants the federal government specific authority. This is significant for private law since, in theory, each state chooses what its own private law will be. Examples of specific federal private law laws that are applicable in every state are those pertaining to bankruptcy, maritime affairs, and other specific subjects to the extent that they are related to interstate or international commerce, such as labor, communications, and securities regulation. These laws are made possible by the federal government's grant of legislative jurisdiction under Article 1, Section 8 of the US Constitution, which is frequently interpreted broadly. Federal legislation will not, in theory, alter civil law that is solely the province of the states, albeit it occasionally will indirectly supplant it[188]. These displacements have been uncommon overall. State Courts have the authority to create and interpret state law, and each state has its own judiciary. The United States Supreme Court may examine decisions made by state Courts if one of the parties to the litigation argues that the judgment - or the statute upon which it is based - violates the Constitution, federal laws, or international treaties[189].

It is also true that federal Courts do interpret and construe state statutes in cases that would otherwise rightfully come before them, but in these cases, they typically follow the interpretations and constructions that the state Courts have made or ought to make. Therefore, the construction and interpretation of state statutes are often left to the Louisiana Courts. The structure of Louisiana's state Courts is quite similar to that of Anglo-American Courts. Serving at the bar for a number of years is one of the requirements for election as one of the judges. The fact that judges are chosen may have contributed to their widespread perception as popular representatives of the people rather than just legal translators and implementers[190].

In Louisiana, Anglo-American common law pleading was never practiced. The territory Legislature established a very basic civil procedure the year the Territory of Orleans was established, requiring the judge to apply the law to the alleged and proved facts[191]. The litigant did not have to develop the legal arguments. In contrast to the "issue pleading" allowed by the common law suit forms then in use in the other states, this was "fact pleading". Based on the same structure, the codes of civil process from 1825, 1870, and 1960 were arranged[192].

5.4.1. *The garnishment in Louisiana*

In order to protect the defendant's property and ensure that there are assets available to satisfy the judgment when it is acquired, the plaintiff may decide that it is wise to get conservatory writs prior to the suit's conclusion. Therefore, whether the property is in the defendant's custody or in the hands of a third party, plaintiff may order the seizure of defendant's property or credits[193] under a writ of attachment or sequestration without resorting to garnishment procedures[194].

In a similar vein, in the event that a money judgment is obtained and not paid, the judgment creditor will be obliged to demand the issuing of a writ of *fieri facias*, which permits the seizure of the defendant's property at any location and use it to satisfy the judgment[195].

Even if the use of writs of attachment, sequestration, or *fieri facias* may effectively take the defendant's property and credits in the hands of a third party without further action required, this practice still leaves much to be desired. For instance, under this procedure, the plaintiff frequently needs to wait more than a month to find out if the defendant's property has been effectively taken and if the quantity of property that has been successfully confiscated is enough to fulfill a judgment that has been delivered or is being considered[196]. In addition, because of this method, plaintiff cannot be sure that the credits and property he has ordered to be seized actually belong to defendant. As a result, plaintiff has the danger of being held liable for unlawful seizure should it turn out that the property actually belongs to someone else[197].

The Code of Practice provides for the employment of the garnishment procedure to implement the efficacy of writs of attachment or *fieri facias* in order to overcome the drawbacks of relying only on these writs to achieve a seizure of the defendant's property and credits that are in the hands of a third party. Plaintiff may direct third parties to respond under oath to thorough interrogations about any assets or credits in their possession or under their control that belong to defendant by using garnishment procedures in conjunction with a writ of attachment or *fieri facias*[198].

The garnishee, who is the third party thus listed, is required to provide a clear and definitive response to the interrogatories posed within the allotted time frame for replying in regular suits[199]. The garnishee may be held liable to the plaintiff for the entire amount that the plaintiff is attempting to recover from the defendant if he chooses not to respond or ignores questions[200]. The plaintiff may review the garnishee's replies if he has reason to suspect that they are fraudulent and demonstrate that the garnishee actually has defendant-owned property[201]. Therefore, via the employment of garnishment procedures in conjunction with a *fieri facias* or writ of attachment, the plaintiff is often informed of the status of his seizures within a week. Furthermore, the plaintiff often does not run the danger of being held liable for damages for unlawfully seizing another person's property during garnishment proceedings. Even if the defendant's property that is in the garnishee's custody can be seized as of the interrogatories' delivery, no seizure has occurred if the garnishee really has no defendant property. We shall go into further detail about these and other garnishment process concepts in the following Sections[202].

The employment of garnishment procedures in conjunction with the various writs is optional, and plaintiff may, under one of numerous writs, place defendant's property seizure in the hands of a third party without using the garnishment process[203]. Nonetheless, this is rarely carried out due to the benefits of using the garnishment procedure.

5.4.2. *Writs that could be issued in a garnishment process*

The Code of Practice of 1870 states that garnishment procedures may only be used in conjunction with *fieri facias* and writs of attachment; they may not be used as a writ of sequestration's accessory[204].

The Louisiana Law Institute has allowed for garnishment under the writ of sequestration in the Code of Practice[205], acknowledging that there is no justification to deny a plaintiff the benefits of the procedure in this particular case[206]. The availability of this action in turn depends on the plaintiff's capacity to obtain the issue of one of these writs, as the garnishment process is now only possible as an accessory to the writ of attachment or *fieri facias*[207].

Garnishment cannot occur and any action performed is void if no writ is acquired, on which to base the garnishment proceeding[208], or if an incorrect writ is obtained[209]. However, if the sheriff has a valid and enforceable writ in his possession when he summons[210] the third party to respond to the interrogations, then the defendant's property will be garnished[211]. However, if the writ has expired[212] or been returned by the sheriff before the third party is cited, garnishment cannot be issued[213]. Similarly, in the event that the writ is subsequently dissolved, the proceedings will be void even if a legitimate garnishment is issued[214]. Almost the same process is used to garnish the defendant's property regardless of whether the proceedings are based on a writ of *fieri facias* or a writ of attachment[215]. However, the few procedural distinctions that do occur in this context are significant and clearly defined. The location of the garnishment proceedings[216], the timing of the decision directing the garnishee to turn over the defendant's property to the sheriff, the parties authorized to post bond to secure the release of the seized property, the maximum length of time allotted for filing responses to the interrogatories, and whether the amount confiscated would be sufficient to settle the plaintiff's claim alone or the plaintiff's unpaid judgment plus fees are among the issues that give rise to these disparities[217]. But there are other variables in the garnishment procedure besides the kind of writ that serves as its foundation. There are procedural changes based on whether the property sought to be garnished is property owned by the defendant or property held by a third party. These variances occur regardless of whether the garnishment procedure is based on a writ of attachment or *fieri facias*. These latter distinctions will be discussed in a later Section[218].

5.4.3. *Venue*

Depending on the type of writ the garnishment case is based upon, the relationships between the plaintiff, defendant, and garnishee vary. If plaintiff uses a writ of attachment to garnish during the course of the lawsuit against the defendant, the garnishment procedure is just an incident to the pursuit of the primary claim against defendant. The primary dispute in this case is between the plaintiff and the defendant, and the Court with jurisdiction over the main demand is the appropriate venue[219] for filing a petition to cite the third party as garnishee, regardless of the parish in which the third party may reside[220]. There are, however, specific situations in which the plaintiff uses a writ of *fieri facias* to initiate garnishment proceedings after obtaining a money judgment against the defendant. The only matters before the Court now are those between the garnishee and the plaintiff, as the dispute between the defendant and the plaintiff has come to a conclusion[221].

The garnishee is eligible to be sued under the venue rules for lawsuits against defendants since, under certain circumstances, their standing is similar to that of a defendant[222]. Therefore, in most cases, the Court of the garnishee's residence receives a petition for the issuing of garnishment procedure under a writ of *fieri facias*[223]. In most cases, the plaintiff must start separate garnishment procedures in each of the parishes if two or more people who reside there are to be made garnishees. In cases when a nonresident individual is the target of a money judgment and personal citation is not an option, the plaintiff may be compelled to seek jurisdiction by attaching the nonresident's property located inside the state[224]. In this sense, one crucial method of establishing jurisdiction is the employment of garnishment procedures under a writ of attachment to locate and take property held by third parties that belongs to the nonresident. The eligible forum for filing a lawsuit against the nonresident and initiating garnishment procedures against the third parties will be determined by the parish in which it is known or believed that one or more third people may be located in possession of the nonresident's property or credits[225]. Since jurisdiction is conditioned on the nonresident's property being attached, the plaintiff's complaint against the defendant will be dismissed if it turns out that none of the third parties listed as garnishees own any property or credits that belong to the nonresident[226].

The Court's jurisdiction is established and the primary demand may be addressed on the merits[227] if any of the defendant's assets or credits are attached by a garnishee[228], or if a garnishee is found in default of the money that the plaintiff has claimed and is rendered in judgment[229]. Plaintiff is not need to depend only on the property that has been attached in order to satisfy the judgment he expects to collect against defendant once jurisdiction has been established. As a necessary concomitant to this jurisdiction, the Court has the authority to extend its process to defendant's property situated anywhere in the state. This gives the Court jurisdiction over the entirety of the claim made by the plaintiff[230]. As a result, in nonresident attachment lawsuits as well as lawsuits based on the defendant's personal citation, the Court that has jurisdiction over the primary demand is the appropriate Court to file a petition to begin garnishment procedures through a writ of attachment.

5.4.4. *People who may be subject to garnishment*

For the party that is designated the garnishee, garnishment procedures can be costly as well as frustrating. Plaintiff is given considerable latitude in choosing which parties to name as garnishees, even though it would seem that sufficient protections should be in place to prevent abuse of the power to employ the garnishment procedure. As to the terms of the Proposed Code[231] and the Code of Practice of 1870[232], the plaintiff has the right to request the garnishment of any "third party". Certain people cannot be considered garnishees, even though all parties save the plaintiff and defendant are typically viewed as strangers or "third persons" with relation to the main litigants. In certain cases, the third party's legal relationship with the defendant is so strong that designating the party as the garnishee is tantamount to garnishing the defendant directly. As a result, they cannot be garnished since the parties thus linked with the defendants are not "third persons" under the Code[233]. Because the curator acts as the interdict's substitute in all aspects relating to the ownership and management of the interdict's estate, the defendant's property cannot be garnished when the defendant is under an interdict[234].

Depending on how they obtain the defendant's property, a person may or may not be considered a third party liable to citation as a garnishee. Therefore, corporate executives who own corporate property in their role as officers are not third parties liable to citation as garnishees in situations where the defendant is a company[235]. It would not be disputed, nevertheless, that the same executives may be garnished for the unpaid subscriptions on the stock they owned in the company in their position as debtors of the company[236].

There is at least one exception to the rule that any party who may be regarded as a "third person" for the purposes of the Code may be designated a garnishee. Even though a wife is legally a "third person" in relation to the community in her role as a debtor, it has been decided that the wife is immune from garnishment by community creditors[237]. Plaintiff is allowed to choose any party or parties that he wants the Court to name as garnishee after it has been shown that different parties are members of the class of individuals susceptible to citation as garnishee. The plaintiff is not limited to designating as garnishees just those people that it is conceivable that they might be in possession of defendant property[238].

Despite the slim chance that any of the defendant's assets would be discovered, the Courts have approved the garnishment of parties[239]. Moreover, the plaintiff has no restrictions on how many persons he can make citations to. In one instance, the plaintiff believed that the defendant may have possessed some property that was damaged in a fire, and if so, the defendant may have had fire insurance, therefore the Court allowed the garnishment of forty-nine insurance companies[240].

5.4.5. *Property subject to garnishment*

Plaintiff may be barred from garnishing all or part of the defendant's property because the property itself is of a type that is immune from seizure by legislation, even though a third party may possess defendant property or credits and even though such party belongs to the class of individuals subject to citation as garnishee[241]. Generally, the plaintiff has the right to seize any kind of defendant property that is under the garnishee's jurisdiction, regardless of whether the property is made up of the defendant's physical belongings or an incorporeal right like a debt that the garnishee owes the defendant[242].However, some goods cannot be seized through the garnishment procedure due to specific legislation[243]. Generally, garnishment of the defendant's pay is only partially permitted due to his employer's debt to him[244]. However, in some situations when the primary demand against the defendant is predicated on a cause of action that arises outside of the state, or in situations where the defendant's wages are derived from work with the federal government, they are completely excluded[245]. In all other cases[246], 80% of the defendant's earnings are immune from garnishment with the additional caveat that the defendant may never lose more than $60 of his monthly income this amount is always exempt[247].

It should be emphasized that if plaintiff obtains an assignment of income from defendant, this exemption for defendant's profits can be efficiently avoided[248]. Given that plaintiff has the right to receive all of defendant's wages through an assignment, this outcome seems to go against the intent of the earnings exemption. The idea, however, is that no wages are ever payable to defendant to which the earnings' exemption may apply because the assignment functions automatically to vest the earnings in plaintiff as they accumulate[249]. Plaintiff may be precluded from taking the property or credits even if they are of a kind that can be seized via the garnishment procedure because defendant's ownership of the property or credits in question is so shaky as to not be deemed to belong to defendant. The circumstances that exist at the time the interrogatories and other pleadings are filed on the garnishee[250] – since this is the point at which seizure is effected – single out whether the defendant's ownership of the property or credits is sufficient to justify a seizure under the garnishment procedure. According to the Code of Practice, if the defendant is fully entitled to ownership of the property or credits or if the only flaw in his ownership is that the time for payment or delivery has not yet arrived, then his claim to the property and credits held by a third party is sufficient to warrant seizure under the garnishment procedure[251]. Therefore, a non-negotiable promissory notes future due amount to the defendant may be garnished before to the note's maturity[252]. However, if the defendant's claim to ownership of the disputed property or credit is dependent, then there is no foundation for garnishment under this general rule[253]. As such, it is not possible to garnish an heir's residual interest in a succession that is under administration[254].

In a similar vein, a defendant's claims for personal injury against a tortfeasor cannot have their damages garnished prior to the defendant receiving a judgment from the Court[255]. The garnishee's responsibility is not dependent simply because the defendant and garnishee cannot agree on the exact amount of money owing to the defendant[256]. There are at least two exceptions[257] to the basic rule that states that the defendant must either be fully entitled to possession of the property or credits in issue or have just the unfulfilled condition of payment or delivery pending in order for there to be a cause for seizure under the garnishment procedure.

The first exemption stems from jurisprudence and allows for the seizure of the defendant's assets and credits that are deemed to be *in esse* at the moment the garnishee receives the interrogatories and other pleadings[258]. According to this rule, even if the defendant's future right to obtain the property and credits depends on the fulfillment of one or more contingent events, the Courts appear to be inclined to allow their seizure at the time of the interrogatories and other pleadings. Because of this, plaintiff is allowed to take any funds that may subsequently belong to defendant under an executory contract that involves the defendant lumber firm and the garnishee for the purpose of milling and selling timber. However, defendant's claim to these proceeds is subject to his execution of his responsibility to saw the logs that he supplies, and the amount of such proceeds depends on the quantity of logs given and the price at which the lumber is sold[259].

The minimal legal claim that a defendant must possess in terms of property or credits in order to be classified as being *in esse* has not been specified by the Courts. Because there aren't many instances on the issue, it's impossible to develop a reliable guide that would say, for example, if a defendant's claim to property and credits would be deemed contingent and hence exempt from seizure, or if seizure will be allowed on the grounds that the defendant owns the property and credits[260]. It should be emphasized that, in a limited sense, the Code of Practice of 1870's rules allow the seizure of property and credits that are *in esse* by enabling seizure, even in cases where the relevant items and credits have not yet been delivered or paid for. Presumably, the authors of the Code of Practice of 1870 intended for it to provide the parameters that would allow for the seizure of assets and credits *in esse* through a garnishment procedure. There is no contingency and the Court can safely decide on the property and credits without impairing the garnishee's rights or making a pointless attempt to take something that may never come to pass when the defendant's right to claim the property or credits from the garnishee is hampered only by the passage of time.

A statutory legislation gives birth to the second exception to the general rule about the type of claim the defendant must have to the property and credits held by the garnishee in order to justify seizure under the garnishment procedure. By Act 181 of 1932[261] garnishment of wages, salaries, and commissions in the hands of defendant's employer were exempted from the operation of the general rule[262].

Under this statute seizure is made under a single garnishment proceeding not only of the accrued earnings due defendant for the work he has performed, but also of so much of defendant's future earnings as is necessary to satisfy plaintiff's claim. When evaluating property that is subject to garnishment, it should be remembered that, although the plaintiff's rights against the property or credits in issue are often determined by the defendant's rights against the garnishee, there are situations in which the plaintiff gets rights that are larger than those to which the defendant is entitled[263].The plaintiff retains the right to regard the property as belonging to the defendant even if the defendant gives up possession of the property or credits. This might occur in transactions involving the assignment of a debt without providing the debtor with notice of the assignment, or the sale of a moveable item without the item being delivered[264]. In such a case, even if the defendant was unable to assert any ownership claims against the vendee or assignee, the plaintiff might nonetheless seize the amount owing the defendant as well as the item sold[265].

5.4.6. *Process*

The Code of Practice contains the fundamental procedural guidelines that control garnishment procedures. When an employer was designated a garnishee in order to confiscate the defendant's earnings, the demands put upon the garnishee under the requirements of the Code of Practice of 1870 had unfavorable outcomes. In 1932, the Legislature enacted special rules to address this issue. These regulations essentially replaced the Code of Practice's provisions about the employer's right to garnish the defendant's earnings, salaries, and commissions[266].

The 1950 Revised Statutes contain these clauses[267]. Certain features of the process authorized to garnish the defendant's wages differ from the process used to garnish other types of property because of this particular law. Therefore, the process by which garnishment is carried out depends on the kind of property that is being sought to be garnished.

The technique for garnishing property other than the defendant's earnings will be discussed first since the variations between the two procedures are not very significant. The procedure for garnishing wages, salaries, and commissions will be addressed separately by highlighting the places at which these particular regulations deviate from the approach that is outlined in the Code of Practice. Garnishment procedures are frequently used to take control of a defendant's bank account or a debt that a third party owes the defendant. Garnishment procedures can also be used to confiscate the defendant's tangible assets, such as goods kept in another person's warehouse or vehicles and animals that may have been given to another person. However, they are rarely used for other purposes.

5.4.7. *Petition*

Proceedings for garnishment must be initiated by petition[268]. Typically, when a plaintiff requests garnishment under a writ of attachment, he includes the request in the petition he files to start a lawsuit against the defendant. However, these procedures may be requested by additional petition at any point before to the case's verdict[269]. The amount of money or property that the plaintiff claims against defendant[270] and the fact that the plaintiff thinks a specified third party is either owed to defendant or in possession of his property are the sole accusations necessary to obtain a writ of attachment[271].

Plaintiff does not have to specify the conditions under which the garnishee owes the defendant anything[272]. The petition's prayer requests that a writ of attachment be granted, that the named third party be named and garnished, and that he be required to respond to the interrogatories that are attached. The plaintiff lacks the authority to order the garnishee to respond to the interrogatories in public; the Court has discretion over this subject[273]. In his petition, the plaintiff must expressly request for the garnishee to respond in open Court[274]. The petition's claims and plea are essentially the same when garnishment is carried out in accordance with a writ of *fieri facias*[275]. A follow-up petition to the Court that delivered the verdict may initiate the garnishment process if the Court has personal jurisdiction over the third party[276]. Nonetheless, these procedures must often be started at the residence of the third party if they are not within the Court's jurisdiction and they are the target of a garnishment. Here, the plaintiff is required to submit an original petition requesting both the institution of garnishment proceedings against the third party and the recognition and execution of his decision[277]. The plaintiff may name two or more garnishees in the same petition in matters of garnishment under the writ of attachment or *fieri facias*, provided that the venue requirements are followed[278]. This is a convenience pleading, and although though there is only one petition submitted, unique and individual garnishment procedures are initiated against each of the garnishees listed[279].

5.4.8. *Sheriff's serving of a Court order initiating the garnishment procedure*

After reviewing the plaintiff's petition, the majority of Courts issue an official order initiating the garnishment procedure. Neither the 1870 Code of Practice nor the proposed Code of Practice mandate the issuing of such an order. The Supreme Court has ruled that there is no need for an order to initiate the garnishment procedure if the interrogatories are included in the petition's text[280].

The underlying theory behind these instances is that the garnishee has adequate notice of the requirement to respond from the copy of the petition with the interrogatories and the citation as garnishee. It's unclear if an order is required if the interrogatories are just appended to the petition, as is the situation when they are typewritten using a template. However, it would seem that the garnishee would have adequate notice and that no order for the garnishment procedure to be issued would be required if the plaintiff explicitly states in the petition text that he wants the attached interrogatories to be regarded as a part of the petition itself[281]. Issuing the order is, in any case, the safe course of action.

The selected person must be cited by the sheriff as the garnishee, and he must get a copy of the petition and the interrogatories as well as a notice of seizure[282]. This service must be personal in accordance with both the proposed Code and the Code of Practice from 1870[283]. The necessity of providing personal service has been strictly enforced and is not negotiable[284]. The ordinary methods of citation service are permitted if the garnishee has hidden or absconded from personal service[285]. There are specific guidelines for garnishing a local or international corporation as well as a partnership[286]. It is not necessary for the defendant to receive notification from the garnishee that the property has been seized[287].

5.4.9. *Seizure*

The Code of Practice of 1870 and the proposed Code provide that the garnishee may seize the defendant's property and credits[288]. This process is known as constructive seizure, and it is accomplished by serving the garnishee with the petition, citation, and interrogatories[289].

Property and credits are subject to seizure via the garnishment procedure, as opposed to the way of effecting seizure under a writ of attachment or *fieri facias* without more. This is because the property and credits do not need to be specifically chosen and recognized by the sheriff as the assets which he causes to be taken. By operation of law, even when the plaintiff and the sheriff are not aware of the defendant's property and credits in the garnishee's possession, and in certain instances even while the garnishee does not think he is owing to defendant, may be susceptible to seizure[290]. A cap must be imposed on the quantity of property and credits taken in order to prevent unwarranted meddling in the defendant's business, as the constructive seizure effectively seizes any asset of the defendant in the garnishee's possession that is legally subject to seizure under the garnishment process[291]. Article 256 and other articles of the Code of Practice of 1870 provide that the total value of the assets taken in the garnishee's possession cannot exceed the amount of the plaintiff's claim against the defendant plus an anticipated sum to cover Court expenses, interest, and costs of seizure and sale when such goods may be incurred, even though the proposed Code is quiet on the subject[292].

This regulation allows the same amount of the defendant's assets to be taken through the garnishment procedure as it does when the assets are seized by *fieri facias* or a simple writ of attachment, both of which do not require the use of the garnishment process. Thus, the garnishee bank should be legally allowed to accept withdrawals from the defendant's account as long as the account never falls below the amount required to pay the judgment and any interest that may accrue thereon. This is because the plaintiff has won a $250 judgment against the defendant and is seeking to execute that judgment against the defendant's $1000 bank account through the garnishment procedure. The garnishee bank should be legally permitted to honor withdrawals from the defendant's account if the garnishment procedure was initiated in addition to a writ of attachment, provided that the defendant's account balance falls short of the amount demanded in the lawsuit against the defendant by the deadline[293].

When property and credits are confiscated from the garnishee's hands, the sheriff does not take them[294]. Following the occurrence of a seizure, the garnishee assumes the role of the assets' legal custodian and is required to keep them in accordance with the Court's orders[295]. Unless they are released from seizure earlier for various reasons that will be mentioned later, these assets are under seizure until the Court makes a final decision on them[296]. The act of seizure functions to grant the plaintiff a privilege over the property and credits seized, much like in the event of seizure according to a writ of attachment or *fieri facias* without the need for a garnishment procedure[297]. With the exception of one legislative exemption[298], the established norm in the law is that only those assets and credits that are subject to seizure under the garnishment procedure at the time the garnishee is served with interrogatories and other pleadings, may be seized[299].

Regarding the specific garnishee, neither the Code of Practice of 1870 nor the proposed Code grant the right of attachment or *fieri facias* ability to seize property and credit after this period[300].

The rule of jurisprudence limiting the grabbing power of these writs is sound in the absence of such authority and considering the severity of devices that allow the seizure of another person's property[301]. It should be emphasized that this rule simply determines whose property and credits are seized in the hands of a specific garnishee and does not conflict with rule, which states that plaintiff may make many parties garnishees for the duration of a single writ of attachment or *fieri facias,* so effectively seizing defendant property and credits in the hands of each. As a result, assets and credits that are acquired by the garnishee after the interrogatories and other pleadings were filed on them are not subject to seizure[302].

When immovable property generates income or other fruits while it is being taken, there is a single exemption to the norm that specifies what property and credits are seized and placed in the garnishee's possession. According to Article 466 of the Civil Code, even when these income and other fruits accrue after the interrogatories and other pleadings are served, they are nevertheless considered to be part of the seizure that has already taken place[303]. As real estate is typically not taken by garnishment, this exemption is not very significant[304].

Any profits or interest that may arise from moveable assets that are frequently taken through garnishment procedures, such as corporate securities or deposits in savings accounts, would be subject to the general rule and would not be regarded to fall within the seizure as Article 466 does not apply to mobile property. Practically speaking, the amount of the defendant's assets that are confiscated by a single garnishee is typically inadequate to settle the plaintiff's claim against the defendant. In order to swiftly recover a large portion of the defendant's assets, the plaintiff may, if he knows this before to initiating the garnishment procedures, induce many third parties to be listed as garnishees at the same time[305]. This may become especially wise if there is concern that the defendant would try to keep his assets out of the plaintiff's grasp. This technique carries the risk that the entire amount of assets seized will exceed the amount required to settle plaintiff's claim against defendant, as will be discussed in more detail below. Even though this circumstance is uncommon, the outcome leaves the plaintiff open to culpability for damages due to the defendant's disproportionate seizure. Plaintiff may nevertheless file additional garnishment procedures in an effort to collect more defendant assets if the assets seized in the hands of one garnishee are not adequate to fulfill plaintiff's claim, or if such a shortfall persists even after other people have been named as garnishees.

Even if credits and property that a garnishee receives after the interrogatories and other pleadings are served usually aren't covered by the seizure that was carried out, the plaintiff may, by means of a supplementary petition, have another garnishment procedure initiated against the same garnishee, so effecting a second seizure that will reach any newly acquired assets that are discovered in his hands[306]. Naturally, if the garnishee has already disposed of freshly acquired property and credits prior to the extra seizure, there is no way to access them in a garnishment process. The garnishee is not required to help plaintiff seize the defendant's assets and credits, nor is the garnishee required to stop working with the defendant to get rid of recently obtained assets so that they aren't taken into custody.

The plaintiff may petition the appropriate Court or Courts in accordance with the venue rules if he wants to add more third parties to the list of garnishees in order to make up the shortfall in the amount of assets seized. However, there is a chance that an excessive amount of the defendant's assets may be confiscated whenever a seizure is performed in the hands of two or more garnishees. All of the garnishable assets held by each garnishee listed are seized up to the amount required to settle the claim that the petition indicates the plaintiff has against the defendant, plus a sum for interest and other fees if the garnishment is carried out under a writ of *fieri facias*, unless the plaintiff gives the sheriff particular instructions[307]. This is the required outcome of the constructive seizure procedure used in garnishment, which involves the seizure of assets without the sheriff's selection or identification at the time of the seizure. The possibility of significant damages is increased by the fact that the defendant is not entitled to notice that the garnishees have conducted a seizure, even if the defendant may only suffer minor losses as a result of the disproportionate seizure.

At least two protective measures would be available to plaintiff in order to allow him to make an additional seizure under garnishment process without running the danger of damages for excessive seizure in the event that seizures have already been made under the garnishment process and plaintiff is aware of the amount of defendant's assets that he has seized[308].

The best course of action is to declare that specified assets belonging to the defendant have already been seized in the petition for the citation of the additional party as garnishee. A second safeguard is to let the sheriff know that some assets have already been taken and that he should only take as much of the defendant's assets as the garnishee needs in order to meet the deficit before citing the new party as garnishee[309]. Naturally, it must be acknowledged that the issues around inducing an excessive seizure are mostly theoretical in nature and are unlikely to come up in real-world situations. Although all of the garnishee's assets may be exposed to seizure through the constructive seizure procedure, it is important to keep in mind that there may be a number of procedural and practical obstacles that prohibit the plaintiff from successfully using the seized assets to satisfy his claim. The plaintiff reaps the most benefits from the garnishment procedure when the garnishee provides a genuine and responsive response. Incomplete and dishonest responses given in a way that makes them difficult to find lead to the confiscation of very few or none of the plaintiff's legally granted assets.

5.4.10. *Seizure release*

As mentioned earlier, assets and credits seized through garnishment procedure are not removed from the garnishee at the moment of seizure; rather, they stay in the garnishee's possession until the Court directs them to be turned over to the sheriff. The basic norm is that only the defendant has the right to post bail and get the confiscated assets released since the property and credits that the garnishee has taken belong to the defendant[310]. In such cases, the defendant may not see any benefit in securing the return of the assets as the garnishee is the legitimate custodian of the confiscated property and credits.

Nonetheless, the defendant is free to request the return of the confiscated assets if he believes doing so will be beneficial[311]. The defendant does not have to wait to get the assets released until the plaintiff has been informed of the name of the confiscated property and credits, and the garnishee has responded to his interrogatories[312]. Immediately following the effected seizure and before the garnishee has responded, the defendant may deposit the requisite bail if he wants to release the assets from seizure as soon as feasible. In these situations, the fact that the assets have been taken and later released from seizure does not exempt the garnishee from answering the interrogatories if the defendant leaves the released assets in the garnishee's possession[313]. However, the garnishee is released from answering the interrogatories and the garnishment procedure ends if the defendant is successful in getting the assets released into his own possession[314]. This is predicated on the idea that both parties to the action have removed the property and credits from the garnishee's possession, and as a result, there is no longer any justification for the garnishment procedure to proceed, given that the defendant has posted bond for the release of the assets and the plaintiff has agreed that the surety on the bond is sufficient. It is evident, therefore, that defendant's claim to the assets must grant defendant possession as against the garnishee before he could have released the assets seized into the garnishee's custody. The only times when the requirement that only the defendant post bail and be granted access to assets seized during the process of garnishment is not met are when the garnishment is carried out in accordance with a writ of attachment[315].

Under a writ of attachment, the garnishee may post bond and request the release of the assets that have been seized and are in his possession under consignment or pledge from the defendant[316]. Seized assets held by the garnishee are automatically freed if the plaintiff withdraws the garnishment action. Furthermore, if the traversing delay ends, the defendant's assets that are not confessed in the answer are released from seizure[317].

5.4.11. *The garnishee's procedural and substantive rights*

The garnishee is granted certain rights to protect his interests. These can be categorized as follows: the right to ordinary process; the right to be sued in accordance with the procedures set forth for the garnishment process; the right to raise any defenses he may have against the defendant; and the right to be shielded from double liability. As a stakeholder, the garnishee's obligations are to respond truthfully to interrogatories, provide evidence in support of his answers if necessary, and pay or deliver the assets and credits he is in possession of to whoever the Court may direct[318]. The garnishee must distance himself from other parties' claims to the property and credits in his possession as a stakeholder. He is not permitted to investigate the merits of the dispute between the plaintiff and the defendant[319], nor is he permitted to challenge the garnishment action filed against him by demonstrating the invalidity of the plaintiff's claim against the defendant[320] or the existence of a defense by the defendant that nullifies the claim[321]. Likewise, the garnishee is not permitted to support the rights of the defendant's creditors[322], another garnishee[323], or an intervenor in the garnishment process[324]. The garnishee's only righteous concern is safeguarding his personal interests.

5.4.12. *The response*

He is instructed to respond to the interrogatories by the citation designating the third party as the garnishee[325]. The period of time that the garnishee has to submit his responses shall be discussed below. The garnishee must provide the response, or if the garnishee has given his agent specific permission to respond to interrogatories, the garnishee himself must provide the response[326]. If the Court does not give orders to the contrary, the garnishee is required to respond to the interrogatories by oath in front of a notary[327] and submit them to the Court clerk as soon as possible[328]. Seldom is it necessary to force the garnishee to appear in Court to respond. The garnishee's responses are deemed to be accurate and are eligible for full credit up until they are completed successfully[329].

5.4.13. *Defendant's rights*

Once the garnishee has been served with the interrogatories, the defendant may post bail and gain the release of any assets that have been taken by garnishment under either a writ of *fieri facias* or attachment[330]. It has been established that the defendant may take a ruling on the plaintiff and garnishee contradictorily to show cause why the assets should not be given over to the sheriff to be kept until the litigation if he is unable to post bail to release the property seized in the hands of the garnishee[331]. Although the main concern in garnishment procedures is typically whether the garnishee will ultimately face a judgment, the defendant is not completely barred from intervening to stop the judgment. It is obvious that the defendant might step in to stop a judgment against the garnishee if the plaintiff's claim against the garnishee is invalid[332] or if the defendant has a defense that refutes the claim upon which the garnishment procedure is granted. Additionally, the defense would have the right to bring up the situation during garnishment proceedings if the property held by the garnishee is legally exempt from seizure or if more property has been confiscated than is required to meet the plaintiff's claim[333].

It has been established that the defendant cannot object to an exception of no cause of action at any point throughout the proceedings as the goal of garnishment proceedings is to establish assets in the garnishee's possession that belong to the defendant[334]. Nonetheless, the defendant has been permitted to intervene if his goal is to create a cause of action in the plaintiff's favor. In one instance, the defendant was permitted to step in and challenge the garnishee's claims that it did not hold any assets[335]. It has been decided that the defendant has enough interest as a third party to challenge the garnishment proceedings' ultimate ruling[336]. Furthermore, a decision rendered by the plaintiff in a garnishment process is res judicata solely with regard to the debt or assets that the garnishee was forced to give up during the proceedings[337]. He can then file a lawsuit against the garnishee to prove his culpability for any property or debt that the garnishee was not required to turn over or pay during the garnishment procedure[338].

[1] 15 U.S.C.A. §§ 1671-1677.
[2] *Id.* at § 1671 (a) (1).
[3] *Id.* at § 1671(a) (2).
[4] *Id.* at § 1671(b).
[5] *Id.* at § 1671(a) (3).
[6] *Id.* at § 1671(b).
[7] *Id.* at § 1677.
[8] *Id.* at § 1675.
[9] *Id.* at § 1673(a).
[10] The Department of Labor has produced a methodology for applying the exemptions outlined in Section 1673(a) where the debtor gets paid on a basis other than weekly. The 25% calculation will be used in the same manner as it was for the one work week. In cases where the minimum wage formula is applied in multiples of thirty, the minimum wage is multiplied by the number of weeks included in the pay period. For example, if the worker receives payment every two weeks, the calculation would be 30 X $1.60 X 2. In the event that the employee is paid semi-monthly, the proper value would be 21/6; if the pay period were for a full month, 41/3 would be utilized. See, T. M. FLANAGAN, L. G. SMITH, *Garnishment - State vs. Federal Procedures*, in *Clev. St. L. Rev.*, vol. 20, no. 1, 1971, pp. 134-144.
[11] 15 U.S.C.A. § 1672 (b).
[12] *Ibid.*
[13] See W. BURNHAM, *Introduction to the law and legal system of the United State*, Minnesota, 1995.
[14] Curry v. Woodward, 50 Alabama, 258.
[15] Stevens v. Dillman, 86 Illinois, 233.
[16] In Strong v. Smith, 1 Metcalf, 476, the Supreme Court of Massachusetts said: «The trustee process operates as a species of compulsory statute assignment, by which a creditor may obtain that by operation of law which his debtor might voluntarily assign to him in payment of his debt». See, Campbello. Nesbitt, 7 Nebraska, 300; Sears v. Thompson, 72 Iowa, 61.
[17] Kennedy v. Brent, 6 Cranch, 187; Parker v. Kinsman, 8 Mass. 486; Blaisdell o. Ladd, 14 New Hamp. 129; Burlingame v. Bell, 16 Mass. 318; Swett v. Brown, 178; Tindell v. Wall, Busbee, 8.
[18] Walcott v. Keith, 196; Moore v. Holt, 10 Grattan, 284: Johnson v. Gorham, 6 California, 195; McConnell v. Denham, 72 Iowa, 494. Nevertheless, in South Carolina the Court of Appeals said that: «Our opinion is, that an actual seizure is not essential to create the attachment lien, but that the service of the writ on one in whose custody or control the assets of the absent debtor may be, is sufficient to make the whole assets in his hands secure and liable in law, to answer any judgment that shall be secured and awarded upon that process». Renneker v. Davis, 10 Richardson Eq. 289. In Vermont, garnishment was termed an "inchoate lien". Wilder v. Weatherhead, 82 Vermont, 765.
[19] Parker v. Fart, 2 Browne, 331; Parker v. Parker, 2 Hill Ch'y, 35.

[20] See, American Law Institute, *Restatement of the law, conflict of law as adopted and promulgated by the American law institute*, Minnesota 1971; A. Ehrenzweig, *Treatise on the conflict of law*, Minnesota, 1962.
[21] Hicks v. Gleason, 20 Vermont, 139; Bank of the State of Missouri v. Bred 31 Missouri, 523. See Gause v. Cone, 73 Texas, 289.
[22] Brashear v. West, 7 Peters, 608; Mattingly v. Boyd, 20 Howard Sup. Ct. 128.
[23] Erskine v. Staley, 12 Leigh, 406.
[24] Walcott v. Keith, 2 Foster, 196.
[25] Stiles v. Davis, 1 Black, 101.
[26] Aldrich.v. Woodcock, 10 New Hamp. 99; Parker v, Parker, 2 Hill Ch'y, 35; Loyless v. Hodges, 44 Georgia, 647; Stevens v. Dillmen, 86 Illinois, 233; Adams v. Penzell, 40 Arkansas, 581.
[27] Scholefield v. Bradlee, 83 Martin, 495; Erskine v. Staley, 12 Leigh, 406.
[28] Burlingame v. Bell, 16 Mass. 318; Swett v. Brown, 5 Pick. 178.
[29] Parker v. Kinsman, 8 Mass. 436.
[30] Despatch Line v. Bellamy Man. Co., 12 New Hamp. 205.
[31] Goddard v. Hapgood, 25 Vermont, 851; Clapp v. Rogers, 38 New Hamp. 435; Claflin v. Landecker, 17 Missouri Appeal, 615; Valentine v. Landecker, 20 *Ibid.* 60.
[32] Baughv. Kirkpatrick, 54 Penn. State, 84. The Court said: «It is contended the attachment arrested their power to sell, leaving the goods tied up in their hands. We cannot assent to this. We are bound to take notice of the general usages governing the contracts of factors and commission merchants. By the order to sell, and advances made by the factors, an interest was acquired in the goods with a right to sell, which could not be affected by an after attachment. It would be deleterious to trade, and the rights of those engaged in it, to hold that goods forwarded to a factor to be sold, may be tied up in in his hands until the creditor of the consignor is ready to proceed with his execution to convert them. The attaching creditor stands upon no higher footing than his debtors in relation to the garnishee. What right would the debtor himself have to say to the garnishee, you shall not sell, without tendering him his advances and making him whole? Even an execution cannot be levied of goods in pawn, so as to take them out of the pawnee's possession, without tendering him the money for which he holds them in pledge. So here the garnishees, as factors to sell, having made advancements, had a power coupled with an interest, which was irrevocable except upon a tender of their charges. Added to the injury to them by protracted storage, a fall in price might leave their advances partially unprotected. If the plaintiff was desirous to retain the goods for an advance in price, it was his duty to furnish the money to relieve them of the lien of the garnishees, and to direct the sheriff to take them into custody».
[33] Bank of the State of Missouri v. Bredow, 31 Missouri, 523. See Brown v. Scott, 51 Penn. State, 357; Patterson v. Hankins, 9 Philadelphia, 105.
[34] Parker v. Parker, 2 Hill Ch'y, 35.
[35] Parker v. Farr, 2 Browne, 331.
[36] Consequently, in cases where a devisee's interest in a testator's estate was attempted to be reached through garnishment - even though the testator's estate may never legally vest in her during her lifetime - the Court refused to uphold

the attempt to reach the devisee's interest through that process, even though it held that something with a present and certain existence - even though its possession and enjoyment may be delayed for a while - may be reached through garnishment. Patterson v. Cald well, 124 Penn. State, 455. See Day v. New England L. I. Co., 111 *Ibid.* 507.

[37] Patterson v. Caldwell, 124 Penn. State, 455. See Day v. New England L. I. Co., 111 *Ibid.* 507.

[38] Wolf v. Tappan, 5 Dana, 361. See Godding v. Pierce, 13 Rhode Island, 532.

[39] Wolf v. Tappan, 5 Dana, 861. See Godding v. Pierce, 13 Rhode Island, 532.

[40] Arthur v. Batte, 42 Texas, 159; Noyes v. Brown, 75 Ibid. 458.

[41] Bigelow v. Andress, 31 Illinois, 322. In New Hampshire, in an attachment proceeding in equity, a bill to restrain a garnishee from fraudulently putting his property beyond the reach of legal process in order to prevent the collection of the judgment which he anticipates may be rendered against him as garnishee, was sustained. Moore v. Kidder, 55 New Hamp. 488.

[42] Jones v. Huntington, 9 Missouri, 249.

[43] Illinois C. R. R. Co. v. Weaver, 54 Illinois, 319.

[44] Bailey v. Ross, 20 New Hamp. 802. See Emerson v. Wallace, Ibid. 567; Bergman v, Sells, 39 Arkansas, 97. In Whittier v, Prescott, 48 Maine, 867, it was decided that, provided the case does not reveal that the donor was bankrupt or heavily indebted, a person who received a gratuitous financial present would not be held liable for the debt as a garnishee of the donor, even if the debt was sued for before the gift.

[45] English v. King, 10 Heiskell, 666.

[46] White v. White, 30 Vermont, 888.

[47] Chase v. Currier, 63 New Famp. 90.

[48] Steib v. Whitehead, 111 Illinois, 247.

[49] Beck's Estate, 133 Penn. State, 51.

[50] Keyser v. Mitchell, 67 Penn. State, 473. See White v. Jenkins, 16 Mass. 62; Brigden v. Gill, *Ibid.* 522; Hall v. Williams, 120 *Ibid.* 344; Hinckley v. Williams, 1 Cushing, 490; Mellvaine v. Lancaster, 42 Missouri, 96; Lackland v. Garesche, 58 *Ibid.* 267; Banfield v. Wiggin, 58 New Hamp. 155;

[51] Rogers Locomotive Works v. Kelly, 26 New York Supreme Ct. 399; affirmed in 88 New York, 234.

[52] Girard L. I. & T. Co. v. Chambers, 46 Penn. State, 485; Estate of James McCann, 16 Philadelphia, 224.

[53] Wilder v. Weatherhead, 32 Vermont, 765.

[54] Erskine v. Staley, 12 Leigh, 406; Moore v. Holt, 10 Grattan, 284; Talbot v. Harding, 10 Missouri, 350; Johnson v. Griffith, 2 Cranch, C. C. 199; Arledge v. White, 1 Head, 241.

[55] The Olivia A. Carrigan, 7 Federal Reporter, p. 507.

[56] Woodruff v. French, 6 Louisiana Annual, 62. See also A.N. Yannopoulos, *Louisiana Civil Code*, vol. 1, 2006.

[57] The original meaning of this term is Garner, Garnisher, to warn, to summon, according to Kelham's Norman Dictionary. Notice, Summary, Garneyreint, Garnishment, Garnissement, and Garnishant.

[58] C. D. DRAKE, *cit.*, § 451.
[59] He is also referred to as the factor and the factorizing process in Vermont and Connecticut. *Ibid.*
[60] See, Bliss v. Smith, 78 Illinois, 359; Sievers v. Woodburn, S. W. Co., 43 Michigan, 275. See, also, B. CURRIE, *Attachment and garnishment in the Federal Courts*, in *Mich. L. Rev.*, vol. 59, no. 3, 1961, pp. 337-380.
[61] See, Tate v. Morehead, 65 North Carolina, 681; also, Welch v. Gurley, 2 Haywood, (N. C.), 884; White v. Ledyard, 48 Michigan, 264.
[62] See, Gregg o. Nilson, 1 Legal Gazette R. 128; 8 Philadelphia, 91. In order for the sheriff to carry out the writ, the Court in New York upheld the sheriff's order to open a safe and tin box that belonged to the company in question and contained allegedly defendant property. See, United States v. Graff, 67 Barbour, 304.
[63] See, Bottom v. Clarke, 7 Cushing, 487. However, in Georgia, the defendant placed a box in the garnishee's store without assuming any liability for it, and he allowed the defendant to take it out after the garnishment. Once the contents' value was established, the defendant was held liable as the garnishee. See, Loyless v. Hodges, 44 Georgia, 647.
[64] Schindler v. Smith, 18 Louisiana Annual, 476. The Court said: «The garnishee, in the eyes of the law, is a mere stakeholder, a custodian of the property attached in his hands; he has no pecuniary interest in the matter ; he has no cost to pay, and therefore none to save; his business is to let the law take its course between the litigants; he has no right to accept or waive service of the proceeding, thereby favoring one party at the expense and injury of an-other, and creating actually a privilege with priority in favor of one creditor to the prejudice of another». In the case Roy v. Heard, 38 Mississippi, 544, appears that no question regarding the legality of the proceeding was raised, so it cannot be said that the case militates against the position taken in the text. Despite the fact that the garnishee was not served with process, he appeared, answered, and the Court acted on his response. In Vermont the case Caboon v. Morgan, 38 Vermont, 234, it was determined that serving a trustee (garnishee) and having him accept service gives him the right to keep the money in his possession against a later assignee, where the "trustee process" resembles and has the same effect as a summons. Finally, in the case Freeman v. Miller, 61 Texas, 443, it was decided that when a garnishee has willingly appeared before an officer and there are no rights of an opposing creditor involved, the doctrine mentioned in this section does not apply in the suit of a creditor against the garnishee himself.
[65] See, Hebel v. Amazon Ins. Co., 33 Michigan, 400.
[66] See, Northern Central R. Co. v. Rider, 45 Maryland, 24.
[67] Raymond v. Rockland Co., 40 Conn. 401. See, also, McDonald v. Moore, 65 Iowa, 171.
[68] Harris v. Phonix Ins. Co., 35 Conn. 310; Myer v. Liverpool, L. & G. Ins. Co., 40 Maryland, 595; Tup-per v. Cassell, 45 Mississippi, 352; United States v. Robertson, 5 Peters, 641; Waldron v. Wilcox, 13 Rhode Island, 518; Oregon R. & N. Co. v. Gates, 10 Oregon, 514; Richardson v. Lester, 83 Illinois, 55;

National Bank v. Staley, 9 Missouri Appeal, 146; Fenton v. Block, 10 Ibid. 536; Fitzgerald v. Hollingsworth, 14 Nebraska, 188; Burlington & M. R. R. Co. v. Thompson, 31 Kansas, 180.

[69] Lamb v. Stone, 11 Pick. 527. This was a creditor's suit in relation to a person who the debtor was accused of selling his property fraudulently to. The Court determined that the action could not be continued for two reasons: (i) the property may be subject to attachment both before and after the sale if the transaction was fraudulent; and (ii) if the property could not be located for particular attachment, it might end up in the buyer's possession through garnishment. See United States v. Vaughan, 3 Binney, 394; Henry v. Murphy, 54 Alabama, 246; Lee v. Tabor, 8 Missouri, 322; Lackland v. Garesché, 56 *Ibid.* 267; Strauss v. Ayers, 34 Missouri Appeal, 248. In order to entice A. to join the board, the directors of the company gave him 100 shares of the company's stock. Although he accepted the offer as full payment, he made no payment and was elected to the board. This is a notable example of how a garnishee can be held accountable for money belonging to a defendant that he unlawfully got. But after a few months, he and the other directors couldn't agree, so he sold his shares to one of them for $1200. His stock certificate was then revoked and forfeited, and the firm created a new certificate for the same stock, which it gave to the buyer. After that, A. was called in as the company's garnishee. The Court determined that he may be considered a debtor of the business because of his technical collaboration with the directors, which allowed him to acquire assets that the law considered sacrosanct for the protection of creditors and benefit from their conversion. Eyerman v. Krieckhaus, 7 Missouri Appeal, 455.

[70] Holek o. Phonix Ins. Co., 68 Texas, 66.

[71] Thompson v. Wallace, 3 Alabama 132; Price v. Higgins, 1 Littell, 274 Hammett v. Morris, 55 Georgia, 644.

[72] McEachin v. Reid, 40 Alabama, 410.

[73] Mitchell v. Watson, 9 Florida, 160.

[74] See, Endicott Co. v. Encyclopedia Press, 266 U.S. 285 (288) (1924).

[75] *Ibid.*

[76] Riesenfeld, *Regional Report 72,* Cases 12.

[77] Sniadach v. Family Finance Corp 395 U.S. 337 (1969).

[78] *Ibid.*

[79] *Ibid.*

[80] Fuentes v. Shevin 407 U.S. 67 (1972), reh.den. 409 U.S. 902 (1972).

[81] *Ibid.*

[82] North Georgia Finishing, Inc. v. Di-Chem., Inc., 419 U.S. 601 (1975).

[83] Mitchell v. W. T. Grant Co., 416 U.S. 600 (1974).

[84] D. J. Lawson, *Rights, remedies, and practice, at law, in equity, and under the codes: treatise on american law in civil causes, with digest of illustrative cases*, San Francisco, 1890.

[85] Shaffer v. Heitner 433 U.S. 186 (1977).

[86] International Shoe Co. v. Washington, 326 U.S. 310 (316) (1945).

[87] See, Endicott Co. v. Encyclopedia Press, 266 U.S. 285 (289) (1924).

[88] Bailey v. Layce, 27 Louisiana Annual, 39; Richardson v. Lacey. *Ibid.* 62

[89] See, Code of Virginia, §§ 8.01-511 to 525 (Rep. vol. 1977 & Cum. Supp. 1979). However, the early foreign attachment legislation in Virginia did not foreshadow the current garnishment procedure. Instead, this process was the result of significant legal reforms that happened around a century later.
[90] *In re* Cruff, 280 F Supp. 846, 848 (W.D. Va. 1968); Lynch v. Johnson, 196 Va. 516, 520, 84 S.E.2d 419, 421 (1954).
[91] Ayres v. Harleysville Mut. Cas. Co., 172 Va. 383, 394, 2 S.E.2d 303, 307 (1939); Levine's Loan Office v. Starke, 140 Va. 712, 714, 125 S.E. 683, 684 (1924).
[92] A. C. FREEMAN, *A treatise on the law of executions in civil cases: and of proceedings in aid and restraint thereof,* Dretoit, 2010; S. RIESENFELD, *Collection of money judgments in american law - A historical inventory and a prospectus,* in 4*2 Iowa L. Rev*., 1957, pp. 177-78.
[93] A choice in action is typically understood to be a private right that is recovered through a legal claim rather than being limited to ownership. B. GARNER, *Black's law dictionary*, ed. 5., Arizona, 2016, p. 305. Therefore, the phrase "choses in action" refers to everything of the debtor's personal estate that he does not now hold, including all of his outstanding obligations.
[94] Only the debtor's property and chattels that could be seized at the moment the writ was given to the sheriff were subject to the *fieri facias* lien. C. J. NABIT, *cit*., p. 794.
[95] See, Code of Virginia, § 3601, 1887. There are no significant changes between the 1887 version of the Act and the original 1850 language. See, Code of Virginia, ch. 188, § 3, 1860.
[96] *In re* Acorn Elec. Supply, Inc., 348 F Supp. 277, 280 (E.D. Va. 1972). In contrast, a levy must be made prior to the writ's return date in order for a lien against tangible property to be effective. *The Lien of The Writ of Fieri Factas in Virginia,* 2 VA. L. REG., 704, 705, 706 (1897).
[97] Frayser's Adm'r v. Richmond & A. R.R., 81 Va. 388, 392 (1886); Charron & Co. v. Boswell, 59 Va. (18 Gratt.) 216, 221-22 (1868); Puryear v. Taylor, 53 Va. (12 Gratt.) 401, 408 (1855).
[98] Trevillian's Ex'rs v. Guerrant's Ex'rs, 72 Va. (31 Gratt.) 525, 529-30 (1879); Puryear v. Taylor, 53 Va. (12 Gratt.) 401, 408 (1855). The Court's ruling in Trevillian established that, even if a writ of *fieri facias* is not asserted during the debtor's or creditor's lifetime, it remains unaffected and unimpaired by their passing. The lien can still be enforced through the relevant legislative remedies.
[99] The writ of *capias ad satisfaciendum* was discontinued in 1850, and the Code revisors wanted to create a remedy that was just as effective. To that aim, they created the garnishment procedure. Puryear v. Taylor, 53 Va. (12 Gratt.) 401, 407 (1855). Before 1850, the only method available to a creditor to obtain access to the debtor's non-leviable assets was through the writ of *capias ad satisfactendum*. According to that writ, the debtor's body was executed. The debtor remained in prison until he was released from custody in accordance with the insolvency regulations, at which point the creditor legally acquired title to all of his non-leviable assets. *Id.* See, also, Note, *Body attachment and body execution: forgotten but not gone*, in *Wm. & Mary L. Rev*., 1976, p. 543.

[100] Charron & Co. v. Boswell 59 Va. (18 Gratt.) 216 (1868).
[101] *Id.,* at 223-24.
[102] Even if a judgment regular is assumed to be legitimate on its face, a judgment debtor has the option to contest the legality of the judgment against him by filing a request to stop the garnishment process. Code of Virginia, § 8.01-477 (Repl. vol. 1977).
[103] Lynch v. Johnson, 196 Va. 516, 520, 84 S.E.2d 419, 421 (1954); Ayres v. Harleysville Mut. Cas. Co., 172 Va. 383, 394, 2 S.E.2d 303, 307 (1939); Levine's Loan Office v. Starke, 140 Va. 712, 714, 125 S.E. 683, 684 (1924).
[104] Lynch v. Johnson, 196 Va. 516, 520, 84 S.E.2d 419, 421 (1954).
[105] Bickle v. Chrisman's Adm'x, 76 Va. 678, 691 (1882).
[106] J. ROOD, *Treatise on the law of garnishment,* Minnesota, 1896, § 6. Compared to when a basic principle of law is at issue, the quantity and scope of criteria of construction are significantly more constrained when administering statutory law. A statute is a positive enactment created by a body with the inherent authority to enact laws, and that body is assumed to be fully aware of the meaning of all the terminology it uses. *Ivi*, §§ 8-11.
[107] Bickle v. Chrisman's Adm'x, 76 Va. 678, 691 (1882).
[108] Levine's Loan Office v. Starke, 140 Va. 712, 714, 125 S.E. 683, 684 (1924); Rollo v. Andes Ins. Co., 64 Va. (23 Gratt.) 509, 513 (1873). The only source used in Virginia decisions to support the idea that a garnishment procedure aiding in execution is a civil suit under the terms of that legal definition is C. D. DRAKE, *cit.*, § 452. Drake, on the other hand, mostly depends on two previous Alabama cases: Moore v. Stainton, 22 Ala. 831 (1853); Travis v. Tartt, 8 Ala. 574 (1846). See also J. ROOD, *cit.*, § 3. The idea of the garnishment procedure as a distinct litigation is appropriate given the broad discretion given to the Virginia Courts in establishing the presence and scope of the culpability involved, even if the cases in Virginia that relied on Drake have unquestioningly accepted his authority. Huff v. Huff, 143 Va. 46, 49-50, 129 S.E. 219, 220 (1925); Levine's Loan Office v. Starke, 140 Va. 712, 715-16, 125 S.E. 683, 684 (1924). Many other jurisdictions see garnishment procedures as summary in nature, meaning that a Court cannot decide who is liable in a dispute. See, e.g., Cornelius v. Albertson, 244 N.C. 265, 93 S.E.2d 147 (1956).
[109] Tunstall v. Worthington 24 F Cas. 324 (C.C.D. Ark. 1853) (No. 14,239).
[110] *Ivi*, at 325.
[111] Lynch v. Johnson, 196 Va. 516, 521, 84 S.E.2d 419, 422 (1954) ; Ayres v. Harleysville Mut. Cas. Co., 172 Va. 383, 394, 2 S.E.2d 303, 307 (1939) ; Rollo v. Andes Ins. Co., 64 Va. (23 Gratt.) 509, 512-13 (1873); C. D. DRAKE, *cit.*, § 452; J. ROOD, *cit.*, §§ 8-11.
[112] Fentress v. Rutledge, 140 Va. 685, 687, 125 S.E. 668, 669 (1924).
[113] *Ivi*, at 687-88, 125 S.E. at 669.
[114] Code of Virginia, §§ 8.01-519, -565 (Repl. vol. 1977).
[115] Jetco, Inc. v. Bank of Va., 209 Va. 482, 486-87, 165 S.E.2d 276, 279 (1969).
[116] C. D. DRAKE, *cit.*, § 458; see A. FREEMAN, *cit.*, §§ 159-60. This notion stems from the idea that the garnishment procedure is an action taken against the garnishee by the judgment debtor acting on behalf of the judgment creditor.

[117] C. D. DRAKE, *cit.*, § 460.
[118] Fentress v. Rutledge, 140 Va. 685, 688, 125 S.E. 668, 669 (1924); Frietas v. Griffith & Boyd, 112 Va. 343, 345, 71 S.E. 531, 532 (1911); Boisseau v. Bass Adm'r, 100 Va. 207, 210, 40 S.E. 647, 649 (1902).
[119] C. D. DRAKE, *cit.*, § 551; A. FREEMAN, *cit.*, § 165. See Boisseau v. Bass' Adm'r, 100 Va. 207, 210-11, 40 S.E. 647, 649 (1902); Baltimore & 0. R.R. v. Gallahue's Adm'rs, 53 Va. (12 Gratt.) 655, 665-66 (1855).
[120] See, e.g., Jetco, Inc. v. Bank of Va., 209 Va. 482, 165 S.E.2d 276 (1969); Lynch v. Johnson, 196 Va. 516, 84 S.E.2d 419 (1954); Ayres v. Harleysville Mut. Cas. Co., 172 Va. 383, 2 S.E.2d 303 (1939); Combs v. Hunt, 140 Va. 627, 125 S.E. 661 (1924); Fentress v. Rutledge, 140 Va. 685, 125 S.E. 668 (1924); Boisseau v. Bass' Adm'r, 100 Va. 207, 40 S.E. 647 (1902); Bickle v. Chrisman's Adm'x, 76 Va. 678 (1882); Baltimore & 0. R.R. v. Gallahue's Adm'rs, 53 Va. (12 Gratt.) 655 (1855); Baltimore & 0. R.R. v. McCullough, 53 Va. (12 Gratt.) 595 (1855); Brockenbrough v. Ward's Adm'r, 25 Va. (4 Rand.) 352 (1826).
[121] Boisseau v. Bass Administrator 100 Va. 207, 40 S.E. 647 (1902).
[122] *Ivi*, at 208, 40 S.E. at 648. The insurance stipulated that a certain premium had to be paid for a total of twenty years. Bass passed away well after the writ of garnishment's return date, but before the twenty-year period ended. *Ivi*, at 209-10, 40 S.E. at 648-649.
[123] *Ivi*, at 210, 40 S.E. at 649.
[124] *Ibid*. The Court had previously concluded that there was no existing fixed obligation based on A. FREEMAN, *cit.*, §§ 164-165.
[125] Boisseau v. Bass Administrator 100 Va. at 210, 40 S.E. at 649.
[126] Lynch v. Johnson 196 Va. 516, 84 S.E.2d 419 (1954).
[127] *Ivi,* at 524, 84 S.E.2d at 424. As the Court pointed out, the owner of any other interest in property has no claim to the insurance benefits when someone covers their own interest in it in their own name and at their own expense. *Ivi,* at 523, 84 S.E.2d at 423. See Morotock Ins. Co. v. Cheek, 93 Va. 8, 24 S.E. 464 (1896). In this instance, though, the property was insured for the benefit of everyone with a stake in it. Furthermore, any insurance funds from the property would only be used for its restoration, according to a contemporaneous agreement established with the deed's signing. The Court continued by saying that the evidence did not specify how much money was owed to the judgment debtor, even if he could be personally entitled to a share of the revenues. No specific amount was claimed, hence the creditor was not entitled to seize any of the earnings. *Ivi*, 196 Va. at 524, 84 S.E.2d at 424.
[128] C. D. DRAKE, *cit.*, § 460; see *In re* Acorn Elec. Supply, Inc., 348 F Supp. 277, 281 (E.D. Va. 1972); Shackelford v. Apperson, 47 Va. (6 Gratt.) 451 (1849); Henley's Case, 3 Va. 145 (1805). Code of Virginia, § 8.01-504 (Repl. vol. 1977) stipulates that in the event that a defendant (possibly even a garnishee) gets notice of a lien via a writ of *fieri facias* when there isn't a judgment against them, the plaintiff who initiated the service and the officer who actually served the notice will have to pay the defendant $100 in addition to any further damages that are shown. Regarding the possibility of a wrongful garnishment lawsuit.
[129] Code of Virginia, § 8.01-505 (Repl. vol. 1977).

[130] Code of Virginia, § 8.01-475; see, Richardson v. Wymer, 104 Va. 236, 51 S.E. 219 (1905); Puryear v. Taylor, 53 Va. (12 Gratt.) 401 (1855). It is not permissible to utilize the authority to carry out several executions to needlessly oppress or harm the debtor. Sutton v. Marye, 81 Va. 329 (1886). When a judgment debtor's earnings or salary is being garnished by a judgment creditor, the judgment creditor's ability to issue numerous garnishment summonses is further restricted.

[131] Code of Virginia, § 8.01-425 (Repl. vol. 1977).

[132] Code of Virginia, §§ 8.01-506 to 510 (Repl. vol. 1977 & Cum. Supp. 1979). A recent amendment to the Act states that any party may file an affidavit demanding the production of books of accounts or other documents that are in the debtor's or any third party's possession. *Ivi*, § 8.01-506.1.

[133] *Ivi*, § 8.01-503.

[134] *Ivi*, § 8.01-501.

[135] *Ibid*. See Virginia Mach. & Well Co. v. Hungerford Coal Co., 182 Va. 550, 29 S.E.2d 359 (1944); Charron & Co. v. Boswell, 59 Va. (18 Gratt.) 216 (1868); Evans v. Greenhow, 56 Va. (15 Gratt.) 153 (1859). The phrase referring to assignment that was contained in the 1849 original draft of the Act was first interpreted in the case of Evans v. Greenhow 56 Va. (15 Gratt.) at 159-60. The Evans Court determined that this new and broad lien had a lawful extent that was restricted to prevent harm to other parties' rights.

[136] Shields v. Mahoney, 94 Va. 487, 27 S.E. 23 (1897). In Shields, the Court determined that an insolvent debtor might legitimately transfer a chose in action that he possessed, and that the bona fide assignee would obtain title superior to the claim of *fieri facias* against the debtor for the value of the chose in action. Any intent on the part of the debtor to perpetrate fraud is irrelevant if the assignee is unaware of it. *Ivi*, at 490-91, 27 S.E. at 24.

[137] Bickle v. Chrisman's Adm'x, 76 Va. 678, 691 (1882); see, Lynch v. Johnson, 196 Va. 516, 520, 84 S.E.2d 419, 422 (1954). Additionally, the garnishee has been defined as the Court's agent, with the right to retain the property while his culpability is investigated and with no freedom to act as its owner. Erskine v. Staley, 39 Va. (12 Leigh) 406 (1841); C. D. DRAKE, *cit*., § 453.

[138] *Ut supra*, note 223.

[139] Code of Virginia, §§ 8.01-519, -564 (Repl. vol. 1977). In Bickle v. Chrisman's Adm'x, 76 Va. 678, 691 (1882), the procedure of garnishment was explained as follows: «differing in no essential particular from attachment by levy, except as is said that the plaintiff does not acquire a clear and full lien upon the specific property in the garnishee's possession, but only such a lien as gives him the right to hold the garnishee personally liable for it or its value». *Ivi*. See, also, C. D. DRAKE, *cit*., §§ 450, 456.

[140] Bickle v. Chrisman's Adm'x, 76 Va. 678, 692 (1882).

[141] Code of Virginia, § 8.01-468 (Repl. vol. 1977); see Baltimore & 0. R.R. v. Gallahue's Adm'rs, 55 Va. (14 Gratt.) 563 (1858).

[142] The basic norm is that many people who owe the judgment debtor money jointly have to be added as garnishees. See, e.g., Lyon v. Ballentine, 63 Mich. 97, 29 N.W. 837 (1886). Nonetheless, the Virginia Code offers: «When a judgment is against several persons jointly, executions thereon may be joint against

all of them». Code of Virginia, § 8.01-469 (Repl. vol. 1977). As a result, under Virginia law, only one partner may legitimately receive a summons in an attempt to garnish a debt owed from the partnership to the debtor.

[143] Code of Virginia, § 8.01-15 (Repl. vol. 1977). See, in general, Yonce v. Miner's Mem. Hosp. Ass'n, 161 F Supp. 178 (W.D. Va. 1958).

[144] The overwhelming weight of evidence supports the idea that municipal corporations and their executives who possess property to which other people have a right are not accountable to those people's creditors via a garnishment procedure. E. McQuillin, *Law of municipal corporations*, ed. 3, 1968, § 49.86; K. M. Kanter, *A changing public policy: garnishment of municipal corporations in Ilinois-Henderson v. Foster,* in *DePaul L. Rev*., vol. 25, no. 3, 1976, p. 746. To study how Courts employ public policy concerns to shield municipal corporations from garnishment, go here, City of Roosevelt Park v. Norton Township, 330 Mich. 270, 47 N.W.2d 605 (1951); Welsh Lumber Co. v. Carter Bros. & Bird, 78 W. Va. 11, 88 S.E. 1034 (1916).

[145] Portsmouth Gas Co. v. Sanford 97 Va. 124, 33 S.E. 516 (1899). See, also, Hicks v. Roanoke Brick Co., 94 Va. 741, 27 S.E. 596 (1897).

[146] A municipal corporation's executives, clerks, and workers may have their wages and salaries garnished when a judgment is made against them, according to a law passed in 1898. This privilege was expanded to include all state workers' pay and salary under a different measure. Portsmouth Gas Co. v. Sanford, 97 Va. 124, 127, 33 S.E. 516, 517 (1899). See also Knight v. Peoples Nat'l Bank, 182 Va. 380, 29 S.E.2d 364 (1944).

[147] Slaughter v. Winston, 347 F Supp. 1221, 1222 (E.D. Va. 1972). In Slaughter, an individual who had received a verdict for cruel and unusual punishment against the city sergeant in his official capacity attempted to seize the operational money that City Council had set aside for the city sergeant's office. The city's statutory responsibility to contribute such monies would still exist even if garnishment was allowed, the Court said, since the funds sought to be garnished were used to pay expenditures spent in carrying out a municipal function rather than the city being a "mere shareholder" of such funds. Therefore, the idea of sovereign immunity prevented garnishment of these payments, as it would have been against public policy. *Ivi*, at 1222-23.

[148] Jetco, Inc. v. Bank of Va., 209 Va. 482, 486, 165 S.E.2d 276, 279 (1969).

[149] *Ibid*. In Jetco, the Court recommended that, as an alternative, the garnishment procedure may have been put on hold until a lawsuit was filed to evaluate the third party's claim's legality. *Ivi*, at 487, 165 S.E.2d at 280. Determining the claim throughout the garnishment procedure appears to be the best course of action in order to avoid duplication of effort.

[150] Code of Virginia, § 8.01-5 (Repl. Vol. 1977). See, McDaniel v. North Carolina Pulp Co., 198 Va. 612, 95 S.E.2d 201 (1956); Hogan v. Miller, 156 Va. 166, 157 S.E. 540 (1931).

[151] In Virginia, the writ of *fieri facias* creates a lien on the debtor's intangible personal property that lasts for a year from the execution date and/or until the amount owing by the debtor to a third party is determined, whichever comes first. Code of Virginia, § 8.01-505 (Repl. vol. 1977). The lien expires when the

judgment's right to be enforced goes away (see *Ivi*, § 8.01-251), or it is suspended by the impending giving and forfeiture of a bond, by supersedeas, or by another Court order. *Ivi*, § 8.01-505. See M. BURKS, *Common law and statutory pleading and practice*, ed. 4, Virginia, 1952, § 372.

[152] Whereas a Court of equity was the appropriate forum for redress, Virginia did not allow the garnishment of an executor or administrator to recoup a legacy or distributive share prior to 1932. See, e.g., Bickle v. Chrisman's Adm'x, 76 Va. 678 (1882). In the same year, however, a change was made to the Act that permitted the garnishment procedure to be used against the personal representatives of judgment debtors.

[153] Code of Virginia, § 8.01-511 (Cum. Supp. 1979).

[154] *Ibid.*

[155] *Ibid.*

[156] A. W. PHELPS, *Handbook of Virginia rules of procedure in actions at law*, in *Wm & Mary L. Rev.,* vol. 2, no. 2, 1960, p. 539 ss. See, also, M. BURKS, *cit.*, § 374.

[157] The summons must essentially follow Code of Virginia, § 8.01-512 (Cum. Supp. 1979) in terms of format. This draft summons has the terminology and substantive limitations of the federal wage garnishment legislation on its face. The summons that is issued after July 1, 1980, must to have the exact same format as the statutory model. *Ivi*, § 8.01-512.1.

[158] *Ivi*, § 8.01-511 (Cum. Supp. 1979). See *Ivi*, § 16.1-99 (Cum. Supp. 1979) requiring the *fieri facias* writ to be returned to the general district Court whence it originated within ninety days.

[159] *Ivi*, § 8.01-511 (Cum. Supp. 1979). The relevant portion of the legislation reads: «The summons shall be served on the garnishee, and shall be served on the judgment debtor». The underlying tenet of Virginia's legal system - that every person has the right to notice and an opportunity to be heard - is reflected in this statement. Dorr's Adm'r v. Rohr, 82 Va. 359, 362 (1886). See also Fultz v. Brightwell, 77 Va. 742 (1883); Underwood v. McVeigh, 64 Va. (23 Gratt.) 409 (1873). However, the Virginia Supreme Court has ruled that the garnishee is lawfully before the Court after the summons has been properly served to him, and no more notice of the hearing's time is required. Jetco, Inc. v. Bank of Va., 209 Va. 482, 488-89, 165 S.E.2d 276, 280-81 (1969).

[160] Usually, services are rendered in the way outlined in: Code of Virginia, § 8.01-296(1), (2) (Repl. vol. 1977).

[161] *Ivi*, § 8.01-511 (Cum. Supp. 1979). According to the legislation, the judgment creditor must provide the clerk with an envelope that has first-class postage affixed, along with a certificate stating the debtor's last known address. Furthermore, if the debtor's social security number is available, the creditor must provide it; this information will show up on the summons. *Ibid.*

[162] *Ivi*, § 8.01-513 (Repl. vol. 1977).

[163]*Ibid.* The authorized form of service here differs from the general regulations found at Code of Virginia, §§ 8.01-299,-301 regarding the service of process on companies.

[164] *Ivi*, § 8.01-523.

[165] *Ibid.* Serving the United States Attorney or another representative requires

following the instructions in Federal Rules of Civil Procedure, Rule 4(d)4.
[166] To learn more about the garnishment of government employees' wages to satisfy child support and alimony requirements see J. F. VEHKO, *Enforcement of family support obligations in Virginia,* in *Wm. & Mary L. Rev.*, vol. 21, no. 3, 1980, pp. 881-918.
[167] Code of Virginia, § 8.01-515 (Cum. Supp. 1979). In order to avoid appearing in person or providing a verified statement, the Virginia Act gives the garnishee the option to deliver or pay the amount he is due for to the officer delivering the summons or to the clerk issuing it, before the summons' return date. *Ivi*, § 8.01-520. (Repl. vol. 1977). Additionally, an employer may pay his employee's wages or salary when it is due, regardless of the rules of §§ 8.01-515, -516, as long as the amount is not greater than that which is exempt from federal garnishment limits as specified in *Ivi*, § 34-29 (Cum. Supp. 1979). After that, he has to pay the excess of the wages or salary above the exemption into Court, submit a written declaration to that effect detailing the amount so paid, and be released from any need to reimburse the employee for the earnings or salary withheld. *Ivi*, § 8.01-517 (Repl. Vol. 1977).
[168] *Ivi*, § 8.01-515 (Cum. Supp. 1979).
[169] *Ibid*.
[170] Code of Virginia, § 8.01-518 (Repl. Vol. 1977).
[171] *Ibid*.
[172] Code of Virginia, §§ 8.01-519, -565.
[173] *Ivi*, § 8.01-519 specifies that a jury will not be used in the proceedings when the summons is heard by a general district Court.
[174] Huff v. Huff, 143 Va. 46, 49-50, 129 S.E. 219, 220 (1925); see, also, Levine's Loan Office v. Starke, 140 Va. 712, 715-16, 125 S.E. 683, 684 (1924); Eastern Shore Produce Exch. v. Belote, 138 Va. 707, 123 S.E. 372 (1924).
[175] Code of Virginia, § 8.01-516 (Repl. vol. 1977).
[176] *Ivi*, § 8.01-521.
[177] *Ibid*. There won't be a judgment against the garnishee for costs if he produces or pays what he owes before the summons' return date.
[178] Code of Virginia, §§ 8.01-519, -564.
[179] With the creation of the French East India Company in 1664, the Custom of Paris took precedence over other laws in New France. These included the 1673 "Code Savary" on trade, the 1685 Code noir on slavery, and the 1667 and 1670 "Code Louis" ordinances concerning civil and criminal procedure. Nevertheless, this rule was superseded by Spanish law found in three main documents following the Spanish cession in 1763: the *Siete Partidas, Recopilación de las Indias*, and Nueva *Recopilación de Castilla*. The Bilbao Ordinances controlled commercial law. Leyes de Toro (1505), Fuero de Real, and Fuero Juzgo were among the additional laws. R. A. PASCAL, *Louisiana's mixed legal system*, in *Rev. génér. de droit*, vol. 15, no. 2, 1984, pp. 341-357.
[180] Cfr. T. CURRY, *A new digest of the statute laws of the state of Louisiana: From the change of government to the year 1841*, New Orleans, 1842; and G. DARGO, *Jefferson's Louisiana: Politics and the clash of legal tradition*, Cambridge, 1975.

[181] R. BATIZA, *The verbatim and almost verbatim sources of the Louisiana civil codes of 1808, 1825 and 1870: The Original text,* New Orleans, 1973 and R. A. PASCAL, *Sources of the digest of 1808: A reply to professor Batiza*, in *Tul. L. Rev.*, vol. 46, no. 4, 1972. Of the same author, see R. A. PASCAL, *Of the civil code and Us*, in *Lou. L. Rev.,* vol. 59, 1998.
[182] See S. B. GRONER, *Louisiana law: its development in the first quarter-century of American rule*, in *La. L. Rev.*, vol. 8 no. 3, 1948 and E. F. HAAS, *Louisiana's legal heritage (Studies in Louisiana culture)*, Louisiana, 1983.
[183] M. GRAZIADEI, *Stili dottrinali nell'aerea angloamericana e modelli di civil law*, in *Quadrimestre,* Milano, 1989 and, previously, J. T. HOOD, *The history and development of the Louisiana civil code*, in *Lou. L. Rev.*, vol. 19, no. 1, 1958.
[184] R. H. KILBOURNE, A *history of the Louisiana civil code, The Formative years 1803-1839,* Baton Rouge, 1987.
[185] G. IRELAND, *Louisiana's legal system reappraised*, in *Tul. L. Rev.*, vol. 11, 1973, *passim.*
[186] J. JOHNSON, *Louisiana history: the journal of the Louisiana historical association*, vol. 30, no. 2, 1989.
[187] See the works of A. N. YIANNOPOULOS, *The civil codes of Louisiana,* in *Civ. L. comment. I*, 2008; A. N. YIANNOPOULOS, *Requiem for a Civil Code: a commemorative Essay,* in *Tul. L. Rev.*, vol. 78, 2004, p. 379; and A. N. YIANNOPOULOS, *The early sources of Louisiana law: critical appraisal of a controversy*, in *Studies in Louisiana culture*, 1983.
[188] R. A. PASCAL, *cit.*, p. 346.
[189] The U.S. Constitution states that the U.S. Constitution, laws, and treaties are «the supreme law of the land and that the judges in every state shall be bound thereby, anything in the constitution or laws of any state to the contrary notwithstanding».
[190] R. A. PASCAL, *cit.*, p. 347.
[191] *Ibid.*
[192] M. GRAZIADEI, *cit.*
[193] The Louisiana Code of Practice of 1870, Section 256, mentions "property" as «goods, effects, rights, credits, or right of acts». Both the defendant's physical and incorporeal possessions are covered by this term. The term "property" or credits is sometimes used in this Comment to remind readers that incorporeal rights may also be garnished, despite the term being commonly used to refer solely to corporeal property. Garnishing money owing to another party, such as money in a bank account or profits the defendant's employer owes him, is arguably the most common use of garnishment.
[194] Louisiana Code of practice, Article 241 *et seq.*, Article 269 *et seq.*, (1870).
[195] *Ivi*, Article 641 *et seq.*
[196] An example of this would be if the confiscated property belonged to someone else rather than the defendant. In such a situation, it's likely that the plaintiff would not realize he had not actually taken defendant's property until many later, after the property had been sold. Since the genuine owner is well protected by the law, he need not notify the plaintiff of his error unless he so chooses. The owner may choose to keep silent until the confiscated property is

sold through a formal Court proceeding, at which point he can file a simple lawsuit for damages against the sheriff and the creditor who took it. Duperon v. Van Wickle, 4 Rob. 39, 39 Am. Dec. 509 (La. 1843). But this is not the only recourse available to the true owner. He could decide to hold off on launching a third opposition until right before the property is sold. Louisiana Code of Practice, Article 396 *et seq.*, (1870). Regarding this, see also, *ivi*, Articles 298(7), 299, 399, and 400. The owner has a third option available to them. The owner may execute a "third party affidavit" at any point prior to the property being sold, which would require the sheriff to get an indemnity bond from the seizing creditor in order to shield the sheriff from liability for an unlawful seizure and sale. R.S. Louisiana 13:3869 (1950). This results in a return of property in a significant proportion of situations. As a result, it appears that the plaintiff may be wholly misled about the value of the defendant's property that he has been able to seize, and he is unable to determine if the defendant is sufficiently defending his rights or supplying a sufficient amount of money to satisfy his judgment.

[197] Shexnayder v. Carter Packet Co., 132 La. 293, 61 So. 379 (1918); Batte v. Reed, Manning's Unreported Cases 833 (La. 1877-1880); Duperon v. Van Wickle, 4 Bob. 39, 38 Am. Dec. 509 (La. 1843).

[198] D. J. McDonald, B. J. Carter, *cit.,* p. 448.

[199] *Ibid.*

[200] *Ibid.*

[201] *Ibid.*

[202] In certain situations, the plaintiff already has the right to get the defendant's property that is in their possession from third parties as a result of the action brought against the defendant, thus there is no need to employ the garnishment procedure. Let's take a scenario where co-defendant A owes co-defendant B enough money to cover the judgment rendered against them. It has been decided that the judgment creditor cannot garnish A to satisfy the obligation owing by A to B in an attempt to collect the whole judgment from B. The reason given is that, since both 4 and B are accountable for the full amount of the judgment, garnishment of A is prohibited. Such actions could not increase 4's culpability with respect to the verdict. Previous instances concerning the garnishment of a co-defendant under a judgment *in solido* came to the same conclusion, concluding that the co-defendant could not be classified as a "third person" under Louisiana Code of Practice, Article 246(1) (3) (1870), and so the garnishment procedure was not possible. Terry & Co., 27 La. Ann. 89 (1875), J. T. Bailey & Co. The Court specifically rejected this analysis in A. M. & J. C. Dupoce, Inc. 1. Boudreaux, 182 Bo. 184 (La. App. 1038). Produced when an immovable is being taken, its fruits are deemed to be a part of the seized property and benefit the person executing the seizure. Louisiana Code of Practice Article 656 (1870); Civil code Louisiana Article 466 (1870). Therefore, since plaintiff is legally entitled to receive rent, there is no need to garnish the lessee's income when plaintiff seizes defendant's rental property. In Summers & Brannins v. Clark, 30 La. Ann. 436 (1878), the plaintiff garnished the tenant in addition to seizing the defendant's rental property through a *fieri facias*. The

judge stated in its ruling that given the «the process of garnishment was unnecessary, and constituted simply another seizure of what was already under seizure». *Ivi*, at 439.

[203] Blitz v. Guenin, 187 So. 690 (Ta. App. 1939); Bank of Monroe v. Ouachita Valley Bank, 124 La. 798, 50 So. 718 (1909); Levy, Loeb, Scheuer & Co. v. Acklen, 37 La. Ann. 545 (1885); McDonald v. Mechanics' & Traders' Ins. Co., 32 La. Ann. 594 (1880); Lannes v. Courege, 31 La. Ann. 74 (1879); Safford v. Max-well, 23 La. Ann. 345 (1871); A. & J. Trounstein v. Rosenham, 22 Ba. Ann. 925 (1870); A. F. Flournoy & Co. v. Milling, 15 La. & Co. v. Simpson, 9 La. Ann. Ann. 473 (1860); S: O. Nelson 311 (1854): Rightor v. Slidell, 9 La. Ann: 602 (1854); but ef. Carl v. Young, 9 La. Ann. 272 (1854).

[204] See, Louisiana Code of Practice, Article 246, (1870) and dicta in Ozan Lumber Co. v. Goldonna Lumber Co., 124 La. 1025, 50 So. 839 (1909).

[205] Louisiana State Law Institute, *Code of practice revision: exposé des motifs*, vol. 1, 1953, p. 8.

[206] *Ibid.*

[207] This Comment does not address the grounds for obtaining a writ of attachment. Louisiana Code of Practice, Article 240, (1870).

[208] O. K. Realty Co. v. John A. Juliana, Inc., 1 La. App. 19 (1924); A. Roos & Co. v. Merchants' Mutual Insurance Co., 28 La. Ann. 319 (1878); Matta Thomas, 21 La. Ann. 37 (1869); Pollock v. Williams, v. 9 La. Ann. 460 (1854); Erwin v. Commercial and Railroad Bank of Vicksburg, 3 La. Ann. 188 (1848): Raboteau v. Valeton, 11 Rob. 218 (La. 1845).

[209] Frellson, Stevenson & Co. v. Stewart, 14 La. Ann. 832 (1859).

[210] The sheriff serves the plaintiff's petition in the defendant's action, the petition for the issue of garnishment proceedings, the interrogatories, the citation, and the notice of seizure to the third party when designating them as garnishees, as will be explained in more detail below.

[211] Chalmette Petroleum Corp. v. Myrtle Grove Syrup Co., 175 La. 969, 144 So. 730 (1932); Ugana v. Bringier, 24 La. Ann. 164 (1872); Matte F. Thomas, 21 La. Ann. 37 (1869). In certain instances, dicta suggest that it is adequate if a valid writ has been requested at the moment the sheriff serves the garnishee with the petition and interrogations. Pollock y. Williams, 9 La. Ann. 460 (1854) ; Raboteau v. Valeton, 11 Rob. 218 (La. 1845). If the sheriff returns the writ without keeping a copy after having it in his possession during the petition and interrogation service, the garnishment's legality is unaffected. Egana y. Bringier, 24 La. Ann. 164 (1872). See also Dockham v. New Orleans, 26 La. Ann. 302 (1874).

[212] Frellson, Stevenson & Co. v. Anderson, 14 La. Ann. 65 (1859); Copley v. Fretwell, 2 La. Ann. 310 (1847).

[213] Simpson v. Allain, 7 Rob. 500 (La. 1844).

[214] Lehman, Stein & Co. v. E. Martin & Co., 132 La. 231, 61 So. 212 (1918); Rothschild v. Dennis & Davey, Gunby'a Dec. 75 (1885). See also Collins v. Jones, 152 So. 802 (La. App. 1934).

[215] The Section on attachments contains the fundamental guidelines for garnishment under the Code of Practice of 1870. It is specified in Article 246 that

garnishment under *fieri facias* must be carried out: «in the same manner and with the same regulations as are provided in relation to garnishees in cases of attachment». The situation is reversed under the proposed code's provisions, which are covered in the Section on the execution of decisions. Exposé des motifs No. 18, bk. vii, Special Provisions, tit. I, Provisional Remedies, Article 3 states as follows: «Except as otherwise provided, the provisions applicable to garnishment under *fieri facias* apply also to garnishment under attachment or sequestration».

[216] D. J. McDONALD, B. J. CARTER, *cit.,* p. 452.

[217] *Ibid.*

[218] *Ivi*, pp. 464-506.

[219] Garnishment procedures may be initiated by justice of the peace Courts. Goodwin v. Southern Kraft Co., 6 So.2d 783 (La. App. 1942).

[220] Marqueze & Co. v. LeBlanc, 29 La. Ann. 194 (1877). The ruling in this case resolved disagreements between the authorities on the location of garnishment under write-of-attachment and *fieri facias*. The Code of Practice from 1870 has no provisions about venues. The proposed Code of Practice codifies the venue rules in the Marqueze case. See, Louisiana State Law Institute, *Code of practice revision: exposé des motifs*, *cit*., Article 44, p. 31. The location of the writ of attachment and the writ of sequestration is the same under this clause. For an explanation of the garnishee's bearing on the case's merits as they pertain to the plaintiff and defendant collectively as well as to each of them personally.

[221] The rejection of mandamus requested to compel payment of a judgment directly against defendant cannot be argued as res judicata to a garnishment process launched to execute the judgment because the litigation against defendant and the garnishment case under *fieri facias* are regarded separate and distinct. Bullis v. Town of Jackson, 203 La. 289, 14 So.2d 1 (1943).

[222] Marqueze & Co. v. LeBlanc, 29 La. Ann. 194 (1877). The proposed Code of Practice codifies this venue provision. See, also, Alter y. Pickett, 24 La. Ann. 513 (1872); Featherstone'h v. Compton, 3 La. Ann. 380 (1848); Manuel Motor Co. v. Graham, 69 So.2d 64 (La. App. 1953). The defendant in a garnishment procedure under *fieri facias* is not a party and is not notified of the proceedings.

[223] Louisiana Code of Practice, Article 89, (1870). This regulation frequently creates difficulties for defendants who work for big companies, such railroads, whose headquarters are located far from the defendant's home. This regulation effectively prevents the plaintiff from using the garnishment process in many of these situations. See Manuel Motor Co. v. Graham, 69 So.2d 64 (La. App. 1953).

[224] Louisiana Code of Practice, Article 240(2), (1870); Louisiana Laws Revised Statutes, 13:3952 (1950).

[225] In this case, the Court handling the proceedings may name many non-residents from the parish as garnishees. If any of these garnishees finds themselves in possession of the non-resident's property, jurisdiction will be established.

[226] Germania Savings Bank v. Peuser, 40 La. Ann. 796, 5 So.
75 (1888): Rose & McCarthy v. Whalet & Edwards, 14 La. Ann. 374 (1859); Oliver v. Gwin, 17 La. 28 (1841). It would seem that the plaintiff might still attempt to obtain jurisdiction in the same Court later on by using garnishment

procedures based on nonresident attachment, even if the plaintiff's complaint was dismissed under these circumstances. In these processes, the plaintiff may want to include more third parties as garnishees, or even request that the same third parties be listed as garnishees again in the hopes that, in the interim, they may get defendant property. While technically no nonresident property has been attached, it should be remembered that even though the garnishee has no nonresident property, the Court's jurisdiction will still be upheld if the garnishee refuses to respond and a judgment *pro confesso* is rendered against him. Spring v. Barr, 120 So. 256 (La. App. 1929).

[227] Until the Court's jurisdiction is established, the primary demand against the defendant cannot be heard on its merits. With the possible exception of lack of jurisdiction over the defendant's person, any effort at a merits trial would be subject to the time constraints.

[228] Louisiana Laws Revised Statutes, 13:3952 (1950).

[229] Spring v. Barr, 120 So. 256 (Ia. App. 1929).

[230] Kahn & Bigart v. Sippili, 35 La. Ann. 1039 (1883).

[231] Louisiana State Law Institute, *Code of practice revision: exposé des motifs*, *cit.*, p. 26.

[232] Louisiana Code of Practice, Article 248 (1) (3), (1870).

[233] About the naming of a co-defendant as a garnishee in cases where many defendants have been found guilty in *solido*. *Ut supra*, note 300.

[234] Converse v. Dicke, 179 La. 889, 154 So. 17 (1934).

[235] Swift & Co. v. Centerville Co., 161 La. 183, 108 So. 408 (1926). In this case, the Court noted that a different outcome is obtained in other states. The choices are typically supported by municipal laws that allow for this kind of activity. This activity is not permitted by any Louisiana legislation.

[236] Brode v. Firemen's Insurance Co., 8 Rob. 244 (1844).

[237] Kelly & Frazier v. Robertson, 10 La. Ann. 303 (1855). The case's declared bases of conclusion were that the debtor's rights were to supersede those of any creditor, and that the husband could not file a lawsuit against the wife to retrieve the common debt. The Court in Summers & Brannins v. Clark, 30 La. Ann. 436, 466 (1878), a garnishment case, notes that this reasoning is flawed.

[238] Louisiana Code of Practice, Article 246(3) would appear to mandate that before a judgment creditor may utilize garnishment under *fieri facias*, the creditor must have "reason to believe" that a third party has defendant property or is obligated to him. *Ivi*, Article 246(1) a person could only be declared a garnishee if the plaintiff "knows or thinks" that the potential garnishee has defendant property in his possession, according to the provision allowing for garnishment under writ of attachment. Practically speaking, the threshold of mere suspicion - which disregards the basis of that suspicion - amounts to allowing the plaintiff to garnish anybody they choose. There were no cases that the Court looked into to determine if the plaintiff had "knowledge or suspicion" or "reason to suspect" that the garnishee was in possession of any assets or credits that belonged to the defendant. Certain rulings have allowed garnishment in situations that seem to suggest these rules are not followed. The relevant provision in the proposed Code of Practice states that «by petition the

[plaintiff] may compel a third party to be listed as a garnishee», omitting the requisite of "knowing or suspicion" or "reason to believe". Louisiana State Law Institute, *Code of practice revision: exposé des motifs*, *cit.*, p. 26. It should be mentioned that even while the authors of the new code that is being proposed have not set further restrictions on who can be declared garnishee, they have provided some respite from the dangers and burdens that come with being made garnishee. As will be mentioned later, in order for parties to respond to the garnishment interrogatories, the code's compilers have added additional protections to protect the garnishee from the possibility of being held entirely accountable for the plaintiff's claim under a decision *pro confesso*: J. D. MCDONALD, J. B. CARTER, *cit.*, p. 479.

[239] Isaac v. Commission Reguladora del Mercado de Henequen, 204 La. 1, 14 So.2d 865 (1943).

[240] *Ibid.* Under a single *fieri facias* writ, this was carried out.

[241] Regardless of whether the attachment creditor's control is based on legal authority, it would seem that de facto control by a third party over the defendant's property is sufficient possession to prohibit the use of the attachment procedure. Buddig v. Simpson, 83 La. Ann. 875 (1881). Article 262 of the Code of Practice of 1870 deals with the garnishment of defendant property that the garnishee may hold, regardless of its legal title, as well as any amounts he may be owed by the defendant, whether or not they are yet due. According to the ruling in Ivens v. E. M. Ivens & Co., 30 La. Ann. 249, 250 (1878), "title" in this article refers to the right that the garnishee enjoys under the defendant as a lessee, bailee, or in any other capacity. Ivens v. B. M. Ivena & Co., *supra*. Even if the property actually belongs to the defendant, the garnishment procedure cannot access it when the garnishee responds and claims title. The revocation action or the declaration of simulation action cannot be replaced by the garnishment procedure.

[242] See Louisiana Code of Practice, Articles 842, 24, (1870).

[243] *Ivi*, Article 844.

[244] *Ivi*, Article 644.

[245] In situations where the cause of action originated outside of this state, the defendant's wages are free from garnishment by Louisiana Laws Revised Statutes, 13:3912 (1950), provided that the wages were both earned and paid outside of this state. It states that, in certain situations, the garnishee must use this exception unless the defendant is actually served with legal notice. Note that if the earnings were paid in Louisiana or were earned there, this exemption would not be applicable.

[246] Whether an employee works for a private company, the state government, or one of its political subdivisions, or both, and whether pay is given in the form of wages, salaries, or commissions, this exemption covers all employments. Louisiana Code of Practice, Article 644(2), (1870). The previous case law, such as Wild v. Ferguson, 23 La. Ann. 752 (1871), which held that state officials' wages were immune from seizure, was reversed by the 1942 change to Article 644(2). Similarly, the subtle difference that developed over the meaning of the word "laborer" was eliminated by the amendment's wide

provisions. Groves & Rosenblath v. Atkins, 160 La. 489, 107 So. 316 (1926), is one example.

[247] Louisiana Code of Practice, Article 644(2), (1870). «If [the employee] earned as much as $60, [he] should get not less than $60, but that, if he got more than $60, 20 percent of total should be subject to seizure, provided that the deduction from the total of 20 percent should not lower the balance available to the employee to less than $60», was the correct way stated in Civic Agency v. Quealy, 172 So. 555, 556 (La. App. 1937) about the computation of this exemption. See, also, Jones v. Commagere, 189 So. 603 (La. App. 1939) the overall pay sum was the subject of a judicial probe.

[248] Squairs v. Hall, Gunby's Dec. 24 (La. 1885); Thomas v. Young, 71 So.2d 368 (La. App. 1954). However, under the "Small Loan Act", only 10% of the employee's income may be assigned to the lender, and the employer must provide written authorization before any earnings may be assigned for a loan. Louisiana Revised Statutes, 6:587, 588, as (1952). It is unclear if this restriction on the proportion of assignable compensation forbids an employee from assigning ten percent of his pay to a second lender after he has already given ten percent of his earnings to a first lender.

[249] Thomas y. Young, 71 So.2d 368 (La. App. 1954). Even if the defendant is a resident of Louisiana, does work in this state, and is always paid in Louisiana, the Full Faith and Credit Clause of the US Constitution may be used to avoid the garnishment procedure even when a foreign judgment is obtained against the garnishee. Refer to the case of Williams v. St. Louis & S.W. Ry. Co. (1902), 109 La. 90, 33 So. 94.

[250] Silverman v. Grinnell, 165 La. 587, 115 So. 789 (1928): Humphrey Midkift, 122 La. 939, 48 So. 331 (1909): Maduel v. Mousseaux, 29 La, Ann. 228(1877); Blanchard v. Cole, 8 T.a. 160 (1835); Simon v. Hulse, 124 So. 845 (La. App. 1929). Since seizure takes place after the interrogatories and other pleadings are sent to the garnishee, the usual rule is that it only affects those property and credits that are susceptible to garnishment and that are in the garnishee's control at the time of seizure. Article 4607 of the Civil Code of 1870 has an explicit exemption to this provision, stating that the fruits of immovable property gathered or generated during a seizure are deemed to be part of the seizure itself. Louisiana Revised Statutes, 13:3921-3927 (1950) has a second exemption to this law, which deals with pay or salary garnishment.

[251] Louisiana Code of Practice, Article 246 (1870). Property and credits are seized in accordance with Article 246(3) as soon as the interrogatories are served. Regardless, even when the property is seized, the garnishee is not required to turn it over to the sheriff until the appropriate period for payment or delivery has passed. The Court will not make this decision in garnishment proceedings involving writ of attachment until after the defendant has been found guilty. See, also, Silverman v. Grinnell, 165 La. 587, 115 So. 789 (1928); Maduel v. Moussenux, 29 La. Ann. 228 (1877). It should be emphasized that even in cases where the garnishee argues that the defendant owes them nothing owing to some cause (such as breach of contract), the garnishment procedure can be utilized to take amounts owed by the defendant under an executory or

finished contract. In these situations, the plaintiff may cross-examine the garnishee's responses and try to compel a resolution of the disagreement resulting from the defendant and garnishee's contract during the traverse trial, which is a rather brief procedure. If the issue is tried in the garnishment action instead of in a lawsuit between the garnishee and the defendant, it might substantially disfavor the garnishee. Because of this, the law allows the garnishee to object to having these matters tried during the garnishment process. Nonetheless, the garnishee forfeits his right to have the matter decided through standard procedure if he doesn't oppose. These circumstances are covered in further detail. J. D. McDonald, J. B. Carter, *cit.*, p. 481.

[252] See, Ober, Nanson & Co. v. Matthews, 24 La. Ann. 90 (1872); Blanchard v. Cole, 8 La. 160 (1835); Brode v. Firemen's Ins. Co., 8 Rob. 244 (La. 1844); Frazier v. Willcox, 4 Rob. 517 (1843): Helme v. C. W. Pollard & Co., 14 La. Ann. (1859); White v. Bird, 20 La. Ann. 188 (1868); Cargill v. Otwell, 3 La. App. 197 (1925).

[253] Silverman v. Grinnell, 165 La. 587, 115 So. 789 (1928); Maduel v. Mousseaux, 29 La. Ann. 228 (1877); Coleman, Britton & Withers v. Finnimore, La. Ann. 253 (1861) (if a defendant fails to finish a building contract on time, the payment they owe will be forfeited and cannot be garnished). Naturally, the payment may be garnished if it is unquestionably due at the time the interrogatories are served. See Morehouse Lumber & Bldg. Material Co. v. Jacob & Walker, 139 So. 713 (La. App. 1932), 144 So. 190 (La. App. 1932), aff'd, 177 La. 76, 147 So. 504 (1933). See Annot., 82 A.T.R. 1115 (1933).

[254] First National Bank & Trust Co. v. Drexler, 171 So. 151 (La. App. 1936). This choice is also supported by the argument that allowing garnishment would complicate the estate's management. Regarding the heir's share of an unliquidated succession in which no executor or administrator has been named.

[255] National Park Bank v. Concordia Land & Timber Co., 159 La. 86, 105 So.234 (1925); Peet, Yale & Bowling v. J. J. McDaniel & Co., 27 La. Ann. 455 (1875).

[256] See Appalachian Corp. of La. v. Compania General de Petroleo, 162 La.774, 111 So. 160 (1927); Marchand v. Bell, 21 La. Ann. 33 (1869).

[257] A third exception emerges for reasons and policy reasons unrelated to the type of claims the defendant has against his property that is in the garnishee's possession. Assets pledged by the defendant to the garnishee may be seized by the plaintiff; however, the sale of such assets is contingent upon the claim of the garnishee-pledgee. Oldham v. Kirkpatrick & Co., 38 La. Ann. 553 (1886). This ruling is based on the legal principle that a debtor's property is the common pledge of all of his creditors, and that the pledgee's only privilege over the plaintiff is the right of precedence on the profits of the property's sale.

[258] In order to understand the rulings in the cases of Buddig v. Simpson, 88 La. Ann. 375 (1881), and J. E. Ouachita Excelsior Saw and Planing Mills, Fay & Egan Co. v. 50 La. Ann. 205, 23 So. 312 (1898), connected case, 51 Ta. Ann. 1708, 28 So. 388 (1899), it appears that this rule was originally articulated in the case of Humphrey v. Midkift, 122 La. 939, 48 So. 831 (1909). In the instances of United States v. Feazel, 49 F. Supp. 679 (W.D. La. 1943), and Simon v. Hulse, 124 So. 845 (La. App. 1929), this rule was most recently acknowledged.

[259] In the related case, 51 La. Ann. 1708, 28 So. (1889), J. E. Fay & Egan Co. v. Ouachita Excelsior Saw and Planing Mills, 50 La. Ann. 205, 23 So. 312 (1898). The case of Coleman, Britton & Withers v. Fennimore, 386 16 La. (1861) Ann. 258 established that a defendant's installment under a building contract cannot be garnished if the contract is not completed on time, forfeiting the installment.
[260] Black's Law Dictionary, defines *in esse* as: "in being" or "actually existing". According to the Fay Dictionary (4th ed., 1951), «it may be stated that defendant possessed some contract right at the time the interrogatories and the pleadings were served upon him in the 6 Egan case (referred to as 13110 above) ». However, Buddig v. Simpson, 33 La. Ann. 375 (1881), allowed the seizure of funds within garnishee's control following the service of interrogatories, although on the same day. According to the ruling in Humphrey v. Midkift, 122 La. 939, 48 So. 831 (1909), the deposit was *in esse* on the day it was made and may be seized. This case would seem to imply that the writ question's seizing authority, which forms the basis of the garnishment procedure, has a longer lifespan. These examples don't seem to have anything in common that may lead to the development of a rule that would indicate how the Court would handle a particular case. Additionally, refer to the 1929 Louisiana App. case Simon v. Hulse, 124 So. 845.
[261] Louisiana Revised Statutes, 18:3921-3927 (1950). There is a common term for this statute: "Continuing Garnishment Statute".
[262] Before this legislation was passed, the defendant's accumulated earnings may only be garnished under Article 246 of the Code of Practice of 1870. See, Humphrey v. Midkiff, 12 La. 939, 48 So 331 (1909).
[263] Exposition Ry. & Improvement Co. v. Canal St. Expositions Ry., 42 La. Ann. 370, 7 So. 627 (1890); Summers & Brannins v. Clark, 30 La. Ann. 436, 439 (1878). «The idea that the of his debtor must be taken *cum grano salis*, and is not absolutely true», as stated in the *Summers* case. See, also, 17 La. Ann. 258 (1865) Relf & Co. v. Boro. Many instances indicate the opposite position in broad strokes, ignoring the intricacies involved. The rights of a creditor who is taking money through a garnishment procedure are measured precisely by those in Kelly & Frazier v. Robertson, 10 La. Ann. 303 (1855).
[264] Louisiana Civil Code, Articles 2642, 2643 (1870). Summers & Brannins v. Clark, 80 La. Ann. 436 (1878).
[265] Louisiana Civil Code, Articles 1922, 1923 (1870). Summers & Branning v. Clark, 80 La. Ann. 436 (1878). See, also, Relf & Co. v. Boro, 17 La. Ann. 258 (1865).
[266] Louisiana Acts, 1932, no. 18.
[267] Louisiana Revised Statutes, 13:8921-3927 (1950). These clauses will stay in the Revised Statutes and not be included in the proposed Code of Practice.
[268] Louisiana Code of Practice, Article 250 (1870). Koningh v. Knecht, 48 So.2d 409 (La. App. 1950). Under LA. R.S. 13:3601 (1950), the petition has to be validated.
[269] Louisiana Code of Practice, Article 250 (1870). The proposed Code of Practice does not include express consent to issue supplementary petitions for the garnish-

ment procedure. The Louisiana State Law Institute, *Code of Practice Revision: Exposé Des Motifs*, no. 7, tit. 1, *Pleading*, c. 7. *Amended and Supplemental Pleadings*, 1954, provides general authority for additional petitions.

[270] Bird v. Cain, 8 Ta. Ann. 248 (1851). In order to inform the garnishee of the value of the assets taken and the obligation that would be incurred should the defendant refuse to answer the interrogatories, a statement of the claim against the defendant is required. It is possible to insert the petition in the interrogatories even though it is the more suitable approach. Garnishment procedures are deadly if the particular amount claimed against the defendant is not included in the petition or the interrogatories. National Park Bank v. Concordia Land & Timber Co., 159 Ta. 86, 105 So. 284 (1925); Copley v. Snow, 4 La. Ann. 521 (1849). See also Bird v. Cain, 6 La. Ann. 248 (1851).

[271] When earnings, salaries, or commissions are garnished, it is necessary to allege employment.

[272] Rice Stix Dry Goods Co. v. Saunders, 130 La. 627, 58 So. 413 (1912); Bean v. Mississippi Union Bank, 5 Rob. 833 (La. 1843).

[273] State v. Rightor, 49 La. Ann. 696, 22 So. 245 (1897). The garnishee often responds to the interrogatories in front of a notary public while testifying under oath.

[274] Plaintiff is required to approach the Court to set a date for the garnishee's appearance whenever it deems appropriate to ask the garnishee questions that must be answered in public. If the plaintiff doesn't follow through on this, the garnishee is released from the requirement to appear in public. Additionally, if the plaintiff goes to trial without securing a day's appointment, the plaintiff forfeits his right to have the garnishee respond to questions. Petway v. Goodin, 12 Rob. 445 (La. 1846). See also Cockfield v. Tourres, 24 La. Ann. 168 (1872); Dwight v. Webster & Co., 7 La. Ann. 538 (1852); Spears v. Nugent, 2 La. Ann. 11 (1847); Parmely v. Bradbury, 13 La. 351 (1839).

[275] The plaintiff would now just assert the amount of the judgment he has secured, as opposed to the full amount of money he had initially sought from the defendant. It goes without saying that the writ of *fieri facias*, not a writ of attachment, is what has to be prayed for.

[276] The petition has the same title and docket number as the lawsuit in which the judgment was given if the garnishment procedure is issued by the same Court that decided the main demand. In Bank of Monroe v. Ouachita Valley Bank, 124 La. 798, 50 So. 718 (1909), the Court determined that the plaintiff's garnishment proceedings were null and void when the plaintiff filed a petition with a different name and docket number than the matter in which the *fieri facias* was issued and the judgment in the major demand was made. Whether this case would still be upheld in the modern era is up for debate. Kunnes v. Kogos. 168 La. 682, 128 So. 122 (1929)

[277] In this petition, the plaintiff will often request a writ of *fieri facias*. Nonetheless, the plaintiff has the option to seek his *fieri facias* from the Court where he received his judgment against the defendant and instruct the clerk to forward the writ to the parish sheriff in the third person's residence. Featherstone'h v. Compton, 3 La. Ann. 380 (1848).

[278] In Isac v. Comision Reguladoro del Mercado de Henequen, 204 La. 1, 14 So.2d 865 (1943), in one petition, 49 distinct garnishees are listed.
[279] First National Bank v. Moss, 52 La. Ann. 170, 26 So. 828 (1899); Smith v. McCall, 122 So. 149 (La. App. 1929).
[280] Mitchell v. Murphy, 131 La. 977, 60 So. 636 (1913); Parmely v. Bradbury, 13 La. 351 (1839). It should be emphasized that the Mitchell case refers to an order issuing the garnishment procedure, while the Parmely case refers to an order requiring the garnishee to respond. The question posed by both is whether the garnishee has a legal duty to acknowledge the legitimacy of the actions that have been initiated against him. Typically, a Court will issue an order for the garnishment procedure to begin when it issues an order for the garnishee to respond. Typically, an order for the garnishment procedure to be issued closely mirrors the petition's plea. However, an order is required if the garnishee is to be forced to respond in public. Dwight v. Webster & Co., 7 La, Ann. 588 (1852).
[281] It appears from the phrasing in the early case of Elder v. Rogers, 11 La. Ann. 606 (1856) that the order is not required when the interrogatories are just appended to the petition. But this argument is dubious in light of the strong wording employed in the Mitchell case.
[282] There is no clause in the Code of Practice of 1870 mandating that the garnishee get notification of the seizure. However, Ornelas v. Silvan Newburger Co., 139 La. 832, 72 So. 372 (1916), supports this. The case of Billenudeaux v. Manuel (1925) established that an heir's interest in an unliquidated inheritance could not be garnished due to the absence of a designated legal agent who could receive notice of seizure. See Koningh v. Knecht, 48 So.2d 409 (La. App. 1950) for a case showing that serving of a notice of seizure is necessary. Article 40 (Execution of Judgments) of the Proposed Code of Practice specifically provides for the delivery of notice of seizure on garnishee.
[283] Louisiana Code of Practice, Article 252, (1870). See also Koningh r. Knecht, 48 So.2d 409 (La. App. 1950). When a supplemental petition is used to obtain a garnishment under attachment, the garnishee may only be properly served by receiving both the original and the subsequent petition. Cartwright v. Lovell, 17 La. 547 (1841). It is most likely sufficient to serve the additional petition in a garnishment under *fieri facias*. The garnishment procedure is void if the third party is not provided with notice of the citation as garnishee. Ouachita Excelsior S. & P. Mill v. J. A. Fay & Egan Co., 51 La. Ann. 1708, 26 So. 386 (1899). The order in which the sheriff serves these pleas is not required to adhere to any certain pattern. Louisiana Code of Practice, Article 256, (1870). Matthews v. Crescent City Mutual Insurance Co., 26 La. Ann. 386, (1874). Concerning a partnership's citation as a garnishee, see Dupierris v. Hallisuy, 27 La. Ann. 132 (1875); Bell v. R. H. Short & Co., 25 La. Ann. 312 (1873); Ferguson & O'Dowd v. Murphy & Co., 10 La. Ann. 53 (1855); Felt & Tarrant Mfgr. v. Sinclair Agency 4 La. App. 121 (1926).
[284] Louisiana Code of Practice, Article 246, (1870). Service cannot be accepted even by a properly authorized representative. Morgan v. Dickson & Co., 6 La. Ann. 562 (1851). It is assumed that the sheriff's return, which shows garnishee

service, is accurate. In Mercantile Adjustment Agency v. Fabacher (La. App. 1931), 133 So. 175 was decided.

[285] John Phelps & Co. v. Broughton, 27 Ta. Ann. 592 (1875); Schindler v. Smith, Bullins & Co., 18 La. Ann. 476 (1866).

[286] Louisiana Revised Statutes, 13:8471 (10) (1950).

[287] It has been established that service of a notice of seizure on the defendant judgment debtor is not a prerequisite for garnishment under *fieri facias*. Myrtle Grove Syrup Co. v. Chalmette Petroleum Corp., 175 La. 969, 144 So. 780 (1932). There is no case law or statute that mandates that the defendant get notice of seizure when the garnishment is carried out pursuant to a writ of attachment. By comparison, since notification to the debtor is not required for nonresident attachment, garnishment would also not be required under attachment.

[288] In Lehman, Stern & Co. v. B. Martin & Co., 132 La. 231, 61 So. 212 (1913) and Matta v. Thomas, 21 La. Ann. 37 (1869), the seizure that was thus carried out was referred to as a "constructive" seizure.

[289] Louisiana Code of Practice, Article 246, (1870). As was previously said, a legal seizure cannot be carried out without first serving the petition and citation, even if Article 246 of the Code of Practice 1870 exclusively addresses the serving of interrogatories. Although technically a seizure can occur without serving the garnishee with a notice of seizure, as mentioned *infra*, serving the garnishee with a notice of seizure is a necessary condition for a genuine seizure to take place. In jurisprudence, it is sometimes stated that a seizure cannot be lawfully effected unless the sheriff has the writ of attachment, or *fieri facias*, in his possession when the interrogatories and other pleadings are served to the garnishee. This is the basis for the garnishment procedure. According to the ruling in Pollock v. Williams, 9 La. Ann. 460 1854, the garnishee may need documentation proving the issue of a current, valid writ before he may be served legally.

[290] The amount owing to the defendant was in doubt at the time the seizure was carried out, and the garnishee even said during questioning that there was no debt. However, the claim was later settled by a settlement between the garnishee and the defendant. According to the ruling, the compromise amounted to an admission of prior debt that was covered by the seizure and that was related to the date of the seizure. Appalachian Corp. of La. v. Companis General de Petroleo, 162 La. 774, 111 So. 160 (1927); Marchand v. Bell, 21 La. Ann. 33 (1869).

[291] Practically speaking, the authors of Statute 53 of 1889, which established the previous garnishment act, and the Code of Practice of 1870 could not have meant for this supplemental process to wind up being more severe than seizure pursuant to a writ of attachment, or *fieri facias.* Furthermore, it would be utterly implausible to maintain that the intention was for someone who used the garnishment procedure to be at danger of paying damages for an excessive seizure, for example, under Article 642 of the Code of Practice of 1870, just because the garnishee happened to possess assets that belonged to the defendant that exceeded the plaintiff's claim against the defendant. Conversely, as previously said, it is likely that the garnishment method was added to

Louisiana law in order to facilitate a safer and more efficient seizure than could be achieved by the use of a straightforward writ of attachment or *fieri facias*.

[292] «The sheriff shall...collect and hold such much of whatever property the debtor may possess within the parish over which his powers extend amount requested in the action», states Article 256 of the Code of Practice of 1870. The article refers to notifying the garnishee «if there be such made party to the action», therefore it is reasonable to assume that the amount of property that the sheriff would seize in an attachment case would be the same even if it is intended to be equivalent in value to the provisions applicable to seizure under a writ of attachment without the use of the garnishment procedure, *i.e.*, "seize and detain" defendant's property. Writs of *fieri facias* permit garnishment «in the same and with the same rules as are given in respect to garnishees in situations of attachment, and according to specific statutes», that stated in Article 642. It should be noted that Article 651, which deals with *fieri facias*, states that «the sheriff shall seize the debtor's property to a sufficient amount to satisfy the judgment, as well as interests and costs; he may even confiscate anything over this amount, to pay the interest which may become due, and the expected expenses of the seizure and sale». In contrast, Article 250, which deals with attachment, permits seizure in an amount equal in value to the sum claimed in the action. Because of this, the maximum amount of assets that may be taken through a garnishment process varies depending on the specific writ that is the basis for the garnishment procedure.

[293] *Ut supra*, note 390.

[294] Lehman Stern & Co. v. E. Martin & Co., 132 La. 231, 61 So. 212 (1913); A. & J. Dennistoun & Co. v N. Y. Croton & Steam F. Co., 6 La. Ann. 782 (1851); Caldwell v. Townsend, 5 Mart (N.S.) 307 (1827); Scholefield v. Bradlee, 8 Mart. (O.S.) 495 (1820). It is not possible to require the garnishee to give the sheriff the property or credits until after the plaintiff has won the primary demand judgment against the defendant.

[295] King v. Cram, Gunby's Dec. 26 (1885); A. & J. Dennistoun & Co. v. N. Y. Croton e Steam F. Co., 6 La. Ann. 782 (1851). Following the seizure, the garnishee assumes liability to the plaintiff for any money given to the defendant or another party. Payne & Gilman v. Citizens Bank, 21 La. Ann. 380 (1869): Mississippi Union Bank v. Bean, 5 Rob. 333 (La. 1843).

[296] See Dockham v. New Orleans, 26 La. Ann. 302 (1874).

[297] Louisiana Code of Practice, Article 722, (1870). Dockham v. New Orleans, 26 La. Ann. 302 (1874): Marchand v. Bell, 21 La. Ann. 33 (1869) (*fieri facias*). If plaintiff later obtains a judgment against defendant, the attachment of defendant's property grants plaintiff a privilege on the assets and credits seized from the time of seizure. The case of I.S.U. Board of Supervisors v. Hart (1946) 210 La. 78, 26 So.2d 861. Regarding garnishment under a writ of attachment, no cases were located that applied this rule. That being said, the fact that the attachment was made through garnishment procedures will not impact how this regulation operates. The Louisiana State Law Institute, Louisiana State Law Institute, *Code of practice revision: exposé des motifs*, Article 7, *cit.*, codifies this case with regard to both attachments and sequestration. The fact that the

seizure is carried out through a garnishment procedure as opposed to a straightforward seizure under writ of attachment or *fieri facias* without more does not alter the precedence among privileges conferred on the same property or credits. Refer to Dockman v. New Orleans, supra; Louisiana Oil Refining Corp. v. Hammett, 145 So. 38 (La. App. 1932); Gomilla v. Milliken, 41 La. Ann. 116, 5 So. 548 (1889). Additionally, seizures may be used to halt medication. Refer to Concordia Land & Timber Co. v. National Park, 159 La 86, 105 So. 234 (1925).

[298] Article 466 of the Civil Code of 1870 states that when immovable property is taken, the proceeds and other fruits generated by the property during the seizure are considered to be part of the seizure. According to Louisiana Revised Statutes 18:8921-3927 (1950), both earned and unearned earnings are considered to be subject to seizure when wages or salaries are garnished.

[299] Silverman v. Grinnell, 165 La. 587, Midkift, 122 La. 939, 48 So. 381 115 So. 789 (1928); Humphrey v. (1909) (garnishment of future wages was later permitted by La. Acts 1932, No. 181); Murphy v. Thielen, 8 Rob. 288 (La. 1843); Simon v. Hulse, 124 So. 845 (La. App. 1929). See, also, United States v. Heazel, 49 F. Supp. 679 (W.D. La. 1948), and Gomilla v. Milliken, 41 La. Ann. 116, 5 So. 548 (1889).

[300] «The property and effects in the custody of a third person, belonging to defendant, or debts owed by him to such defendant, will be regarded to be levied as by the sheriff, from the date of service of the interrogatories on such individuals», states a portion of Article 246 of the Code of Practice of 1870. «Seizure of such property or debts under garnishment must take effect upon serving of the petition, citation, and interrogatories», reads Article 39 of the Louisiana State Law Institute, *Code of Practice, Exposé des motifs, cit.* Neither of these clauses would rationally support the assumption that more property and credits that come into the garnishee's possession should also be subject to seizure for a longer period of time than is thought.

[301] Writs of attachment are *stricti juris*, meaning that failure to carefully adhere to the required procedures and criteria may result in the nullity of the document. 45 La. Ann. 846, 12 So. 504 (1893) Lehman v. Brous Bard. This is a well-established premise. The Section on attachments contains the fundamental guidelines for garnishment under the Code of Practice of 1870. Garnishment under *fieri facias* is to be carried out «in the same way and with the same restrictions as are specified in connection to garnishees in cases of attachment», according to Article 246.

[302] Humphrey v. Midkiff, 122 La. 989, 48 So. 831 (1909) (garnishment of future wages was later permitted by La. Acta 1982, No. 181); Simon v. Bulse, 124 So. 845 (La. App. 1929). See also United States v. Feazel, 49 F. supp. 018 (W.D. La. 1948).

[303] Louisiana Civil Code, Article 466, (1870). Seizures made pursuant to a writ of *fieri facias* or writ of attachment are covered by this clause. New Orleans Compress Co. v. Katz, 185 La. 174 170 So. 244 (1936) 723, (*fieri facias*); Posey v. Fargo, 187 La. 122, So. 175 (1937) (attachment). No garnishment procedure was used to achieve the seizure in any of these situations. There were no incidents of garnishment utilizing Article 466 that could be located.

However, since the garnishment procedure is just an ancillary matter, it seems likely that this rule also applies to seizures made in connection with the garnishment process.

[304] This item may be used in the event that the garnishee failed to object to the use of the garnishment procedure to test the ownership of the property after the defendant had made a simulated sale of immovable property to them.

[305] Even when the plaintiff requests in one petition that two or more people be listed as garnishees, a separate garnishment procedure is started against each garnishee.

The garnishee is not involved in any other legal proceedings except from his own. First Natchez Bank v. Moss, 52 La. Ann. 170, 26 So. 828 (1899).

[306] It is likely that the plaintiff should state in his petition that since the last garnishment procedures were carried out, it is thought that the garnishee has acquired additional property and credits. If the initial writ of *fieri facias* or attachment was still in existence and legal, then no other writ would need to be obtained in order to carry out the second seizure. It would be required to obtain the issue of a new writ in order to carry out the seizure if the first one had expired or had been returned in some other way by the sheriff. See, *supra*.

[307] There is no other conclusion that can be drawn from Article 256 of the 1870 Code of Practice. The amount that the plaintiff is requesting from the defendant needs to be included in either the interrogation or the petition. See, *infra*.

[308] If just one individual has been designated as the garnishee and the plaintiff wants to file further garnishment actions against the same garnishee in order to collect assets that have come into the latter's control after the first seizure, there doesn't seem to be any risk of an excessive seizure. No matter how many times the garnishee was mentioned, it would seem irrational to presume that more was sought of them than the amount claimed in the complaint. However, if assets had been taken into possession by someone else prior to the garnishee's second garnishment, that would present a distinct issue.

[309] The amount of assets that the garnishee will have seized might be specified by the sheriff in the notice of seizure that is given to them. See, note 390.

[310] Louisiana Code of Practice, Article 259, (1870). It has been established in Brown & Co. v. Richardson, 1 Mart. (N.S.) 210 (La. 1823); Lecesne v. Cottin, 10 Mart. (O.S.) 174 (1821) that the defendant has the right to post bail in order to release asset attached under the garnishment procedure. Release of goods confiscated pursuant to *fieri facias*: Louisiana Revised Statutes, 13:3411 (1950).

[311] See, note 409. It has been held that the defendant may take a rule on the plaintiff and garnishee contradictorily to show cause why the assets should not be turned over to the sheriff and be held by the sheriff pending the litigation in the event that the defendant is unable to post bond to release the property seized in the hands of the garnishee. Rochereau & Co. v. Guidry, 24 La. Ann. 294 (1872).

[312] Brown & Co. v. Richardson, 1 Mart. (N.S.) 210 (La. 1823).

[313] *Ibid.*

[314] *Ibid.*

[315] It should be mentioned that the Draft Code includes clauses that permit

garnishment in response to a sequestration writ. A second set of exclusions will be established if the legislature approves these measures. See, *infra*.

[316] Louisiana Revised Statutes, 18:3941 (1950). The writ of sequestration is likewise covered by these rules.

[317] *Ibid*. Johnson v. Bolt, 146 So. 875 (La. App. 1938).

[318] Johnson v. Murphy, 124 La. 143, 49 So. 1007 (1909); Schindler v. Smith Bulling & Co., 18 La. Ann. 476 (1866): Hazard v. Agricultural Bank, 11 Rob. 326 (La. 1845); Bean v. Mississippi Union Bank, 5 Rob. 333 (Ta. 1843); Frazier v. Wilcox, 4 Rob. 517 (La. 1843); Kimball v. Plant, 14 La. 511 (1840); Manuel Motor Co. v. Graham, 69 So.2d 64 (La. App. 1953); Goodwin v. Southern Kraft Corp., 6 So.2d 783 (La. App. 1942).

[319] Johnson v. Murphy, 124 La. 143, 49 So. 1007 (1909); Brode v. Fire Ins. Co. of New Orleans, 8 Rob. 2A4 (La. 1844); Frazier v. Willeox, 4 Rob. 517 (La. 1843); Lee & Hardy v. Palmer, 18 La. 405 (1841).

[320] Brode v. Firemen's Ins. Co. of New Orleans, 8 Rob. 244 (La. 1844).

[321] Whitney Central Trust & S. Bank v. Norton, 157 La. 199, 102 So. 806 (1924) (property exempt from seizure); Frasier & Adams v. Banks, 11 La. Ann. 31 (1856) (debt discharged by bankruptcy); Goodwin v. Southern Kraft Corp., 6 So.2d 783 (La. App. 1942) (wages exempt from seizure). *Contra*, Smith v. Paderas, 1 Orl. App. 239 (La. App. 1904).

[322] Louisiana Oil Refining Corp. v. Hammett, 145 So. 38 (Ta. App. 1932).

[323] First Natchez Bank v. Moss, 52 La. Ann. 170, 26 So. 828 (1999).

[324] Lee & Hardy v. Palmer, 18 La. 405 (1841).

[325] Louisiana Code of Practice, Article 252, (1870). However, the Court order ordering the garnishee to transfer the property releases the garnishee from answering the interrogatories if the defendant posts bonds to release the property confiscated into the garnishee's possession before the response can be submitted. Brown & Co. v. Richardson, 1 Mart. (N.S.) 210 (La. 1823). It may be legal for the garnishee to decline to respond to any one or all of the interrogatories. Attorney-client privilege was asserted by the garnishee attorney in Shanghnessy v. Fogg, 15 La. Ann. 330 (1860). When a garnishee responds to interrogatories, it becomes evidence against the person who asked the questions. H. B. Merril & Co. v. Cator, 16 La. Ann. 187 (1861).

[326] Citing Lewis v. Franks, 18 La. Ann. 564 (1866), the case of Zenero v. Pressey, 1 La. App. 347 (1924) suggests that the garnishee may be bound by the replies of an agent lawfully authorized to answer the interrogatories. This decision in Dickson & Co. v. Morgan, 7 La. Ann. 562, (1851), in turn, served as the foundation for the Lewis case. It should be mentioned that this final case was later appealed, and the Court decided as follows in Dickson & Co. v. Morgan, 7 La. Ann. 490, 491 (1852): «The power of answering interrogatories on oath, we do not think can be conferred by one person on another». Given the intervening jurisprudence, it is probable that the Courts will continue to find that an agent can be given the power to respond to interrogations. The judgment on appeal in this case appears to have eluded the Courts' notice in the subsequent rulings on the matter.

[327] State v. Rightor, 49 La. Ann. 698, 22 So. 245 (1897).

[328] Parol evidence can be used to show the responses' nature in cases when the Court clerk misplaces the answers that the garnishee filed with him. McGee v. Taylor & Knapp, 19 La. Ann. 374 (1867). When the answers were really entered into the case record in the clerk's office, a judgment *pro confesso* will not be rendered if the clerk neglected to mark the answers as "filed" or to put the filing on the docket, and if the garnishee neglected to pay the filing fee. Livingston Finance Corp v. Baudin, 120 So. 401 (La. App. 1929).

[329] Henry v. Bew, 43 La. Ann. 476, 9 So. 101 (1891).

[330] Release of goods seized under attachment: Louisiana Code of Practice, Article 258, (1870). Release of goods seized under *fieri facias*: Louisiana Revised Statutes, 13:3411 (1950).

[331] Rochereau & Co. v. Guidry, 24 La. Ann. 294 (1872).

[332] See, Brode v. Firemen's Insurance Co., 8 Rob. 244 (La. 1844).

[333] Frasier & Adams v. Banks, 11 La. Ann. 31 (1856).

[334] Carroll v. Powell, 136 So. 210 (La. App. 1931).

[335] Rochereau & Co. v. Bringier, 22 La. Ann. 129 (1870).

[336] First National Bank v. Lagrone, 164 La. 907, 114 So. 832 (1927).

[337] Robeson v. Carpenter, 7 Mart. (N.S.) 30 (La. 1828).

[338] *Ibid.*

6. Garnishment in India

6.1. *Introduction*

Today's Indian law can be seen as the interweaving of a properly *Indian* law[1], *i.e.,* applicable indiscriminately to every inhabitant of India, and various personal laws, *i.e.,* applicable according to the religion professed by the individual. Thus, among the latter we find a Hindu law, a Muslim law, a Canon law and a Parso law[2], all enclosed within the wide meshes of a secular Indian law of British origin.

A Sanskrit-speaking population settled in India[3] around the beginning of the 2nd millennium B.C., as part of the great Indo-European migratory flow that characterized those years[44], and they were the bearers of a very peculiar conception of the celestial world and of man[5]. According to the sacred scriptures of the Jewish, Christian, and Muslim religions, all men are equal before God and are created in his image and likeness, according to the Hindu conception man is a mere abstraction[6].

The only thing that characterizes him is the social category to which he belongs by virtue of birth. This gives rise to castes[7], linked to a traditional trade or occupation[8], and to which are associated completely unequal tasks, rewards[9], and duties. Moving from one caste to another is not allowed[10].

Another peculiarity of the Hindu tradition are the rules of conduct[11] that men bust abide by and that depend on the goals pursued by the individual[12]. The *dharma* is a set of religious, ethical, preventive and dispute resolution precepts[13]. They constitute a projection of the cosmic order that a few enlightened sages have been able to discern and have tried to translate into words, enclosed in collections, the *dharmasatra*[14]. The *dharma* presents itself as the supreme source of cosmically derived and therefore unparalleled rules. However, it does not exclude the presence of other sources that regulate the behavior of individuals. Custom is accepted: the sages themselves recommend avoiding those behaviors that are disliked by society even if they are not condemned by the *satras* of reference[15]. The law is accepted, an instrument that the ruler uses to maintain order, without forgetting that the rules of *dharma* are superior. Finally, the principles of justice and equity are recognized, which are drawn upon in the absence of other binding rules[16].

As far as jurisprudence is concerned, it must be said that within Hindu society the judge is highly respected, his decisions may deviate from the dharma in order to avoid unjust solutions in the individual case, although there is no possibility of changing the *dharma* itself. Precedent is not a source[17].

The Islamic presence in India began to manifest itself from the 8th century A.D. and became full-fledged rule from 1200 onwards[18]. The conquerors replaced royal jurisdictions[19] and established the application of Muslim law in state Courts. However, they left the popular methods of dispute resolution intact: in particular the *panchayat*, adjudicative assemblies that settled intra-caste matters, continued to operate undisturbed[20].

English interest in India grew more and more during the 1700s until it turned, a century later and officially from 1805, into total control to the detriment of the Islamic rulers[21]. The new conquerors did not try to impose English law of the population of India but, especially with regard to private law endeavored to apply rules already familiar to the natives. Hindu law and Muslim law[22] were thus placed on an equal footing and applied in all disputes that required a decision on the basis of these rules. Despite the colonizers' good intentions[23], the British judges called upon to apply Hindu law, wrongly identified with the *dharma*, were faced with a series of extremely complex texts written in a language unknown to them. While waiting for codification that could solve these problems, the British magistrates availed themselves of the help of pundits, experts who, on the basis of the *dharmasatra* (and *nibandhas*[24].

In addition, local customs were gradually collected and applied in a general way, some rules of Hindu tradition were judged to be unjust and therefore eliminated, where Hindu law was deficient, rules of English law were inserted. At the same time, decisions followed one another and also began to be collected: by virtue of the rule of *stare decisis* imported from the English tradition, they became binding precedents[26].

On another front and starting from the realization that not all the population was Hindu or Muslim, a general Indian law was created that could be applied to those who did not profess these religions. In addition, significant regulatory works were completed in those areas where Hindu law had not been applied in the first place. Thus, we see the enactment of a Code of Civil Procedure in 1859, a Penal Code in 1860, and a Code of Criminal Procedure in 1861[27]. The *modus operandi* had not been correct and Hindu law had been distorted and modified to a large extent[28].

The law of India prior to independence from British rule, which did not take place until 1947, is an English-derived law, but one that does not perfectly follow the British system or even fully incorporate its principles. The various attempts to draft a Civil Code and the absence of distinction between equity and common law as sources of law are only the most conspicuous examples of this phenomenon[29].

India ceased to be a British colony and became independent in 1947. From then on, a series of important changes took place[30].

With independence, India saw the breakaway of Pakistan and Bengal, where a large part of the Islamic population resided[31]. In 1950, the Constitution of India came into force[32], transforming the country into a federal republic or, more precisely, a union of states consisting of twenty-eight main states and seven territories, all with autonomous parliaments and governments[33].

Executive and legislative powers are shared between the Union and the individual states. Although each state makes its own language choices[34], at the federal level the unifying language remains English. Its replacement by Hindi, the most prestigious of the various languages spoken in India and perhaps a descendant of Sanskrit itself, still seems a long way off. The Constitution also expressly cancelled the caste system, prohibiting it in Article 15[35].

With regard to marriage, an important reform took place with the Hindu Marriage Act 1955, which decreed the elimination of many anachronistic elements of the institution[36]. In 1956, new regulations were drawn up concerning minor age, guardianship, adoptions, and succession[37]. All these changes did not, however, eliminate the existing system whereby each individual sees his or her private life relations regulated by a personal statute, which differs according to the religion professed. This situation should have been overcome with the drafting of an Indian Civil Code, as Article 44[38] of the Constitution itself would require. So far, however, a different path has been followed, hinged on targeted and occasional legislative interventions, not systematic and "codifying" enough to finally provide for a unified discipline of Indian law.

On the judicial system side, the post-independence legislation of the Indian Republic provides for a pyramid structure, with the Supreme Court of India at the top. It is the only Court that operates at the federal level and acts as the Court of last resort[39] for the High Courts, the highest Courts in each state of the Union. Below these are various subordinate Courts[40].

It should also be pointed out that, without prejudice to the superiority of the law as the source of law, the *ratio decidendi* contained in the decisions of the Supreme Court and the High Courts is recognized as having the value of binding precedent for the interpretation of normative texts[41].

6.2. *An overview of the Indian legal system*

In the Indian legal system[42], the amendment adopted in 1976 marked a noteworthy historical and legislative moment because it introduced the concept of garnishee order into the Civil Procedure Code (CPC) Order 21 Rule 46 A to Rule 46 I of the 1908. The competent Court issues a garnishee order, which instructs the garnishee to refrain from paying a certain sum directly to the judgment debtor because the latter is the one who is obligated to the decree-holder. This order's aim is to safeguard the decree-holder's interests and ensure that some of his debts are paid on time[43]. This power is codified in Order 21, Rule 46 A of the Code. The Court may or may not decide to issue this type of order, depending on the situation, and sometimes it may cause undue harm to the garnishee. However, the Court's discretion is not unlimited and must be applied judiciously.

Before to the 1967 amendment, some Courts believed that they did not have the authority to order a garnishee to pay a debt in Court. In fact, if the garnishee denied the debt at the time of appearance, the Court's responsibility was to find out whether the debt was owed and, if so, it was not lawful to order him to pay the amount in Court, except under specific circumstances[44]. However, following the Code's amendment, a new clause was added to safeguard the rights of those in whose favor the decree had been issued. Following the recent amendment, a new direct provision was added to the code, giving the Court the authority to make an order that effectively protects the decree-holder's interests. Although the Court may choose to pass an order that effectively complies with the current circumstances, it is not required to grant the order[45].

The purpose of the recently added Rule 46 A (1) is to allow the decree holder to execute the debt owed by the judgment debtor, rather than forcing him to appear in Court. The principal aim of a garnishee order is to enable the decree holder to execute the judgment debtor's outstanding debt without forcing them to appear in Court[46]. In the event of a debt (excluding debt secured by a mortgage or charge) that has been attached under Rule 46, the Court may, upon the application of the attaching creditor, issue a notice to the garnishee liable to pay said debt, requesting that he either appear and show cause why he should not do so, or pay into Court the debt owed from him to the judgment debtor, or as much of it as may be sufficient to satisfy the decree and costs of execution. The Court has the discretion to refuse to make the order proposed by Rule 46 A if it is not equitable[47]. That discretion though must be exercised judiciously. Under this rule, the Court should not intervene if it determines that there is a legitimate dispute against the claim and that the dispute is not baseless or unfounded[48]. However, some assets are not subject to garnishment. Statutory exemptions are designed to prevent a debtor from being left without any means of support. For instance, the amount of income from work that can be garnished is limited[49].

In terms of the judgment debtor, the garnishee's payment made to the Court in accordance with the notice will be regarded as a legitimate discharge. The Court has the authority to order that the decree holder receive this sum in order to satisfy the decree and cover execution costs[50]. In the event that the garnishee fails to provide the required payment to the Court or fails to show cause in responding to the notice, the Court has the authority to enforce the order as if it were a decree against the garnishee[51]. The Court has the authority to determine the amount of the costs of the garnishment proceedings[52]. In addition, orders issued during foreclosure proceedings are equally appealable as decrees[53].

6.3. *Garnishee proceedings*

As already noted, garnishment is a judicial proceeding in which a creditor asks the Court to order a third-party debtor to deliver to the creditor any of the debtor's property held by that third party. Being an inquisitorial process, it offers a severe and exceptional remedy. It is an oddity, a statutory invention sui generis, unrelated to any common law action. Although it is a seizure technique, it is not a levy in the sense that the word is commonly used. It is a legal process that allows a creditor to legally get priority over other creditors. It is similar to a creditor's bill in that it involves sequestering a debtor's assets into the debtor's possession[54]. In this case, the plaintiff is trying to obtain the defendant's rights and assets by bringing into Court a third party who either owns those assets or owes them money. Although a garnishment proceeding serves the same functions as an attachment or execution, it is a legal process intended to obtain a new judgment rather than being a levy on property. Proceedings for garnishees are conducted both in *personam* and in *rem*. They work both on the debt and the garnishee's person. Consequently, they are categorized as a *quasi in rem* proceeding[55].

In Kuchimanchi Nagamani v. Mantri Prasada Agnihotrudu and others, the petitioner filed suit for recovery. The order of garnishee of amount lying with Government Department was passed during the pendency of the suit; however, no government authorities objected at that time, so the order became final. Subsequently, the government authorities objected to the petitioner's request to withdraw the amount. In rejecting the objections, the Court ruled that the objections could not be sustained because the authorities did not raise them at the appropriate time[56].

In another case, the enforcement petition in Fargo Freight Ltd v. Commodities Exchange Corporation sought to enforce the English award. According to the Honorable Court, it fell under Sections 46 to 49 of the 1996 Arbitration and Conciliation Act. The enforcement in these proceedings must inevitably occur between the award's parties. In this proceeding it was not possible to rule on the contributory liability of third parties as the dispute concerned the discrepancy or otherwise of the documents presented. The division Court ought to have instructed the appellants to have that dispute resolved by the appropriate Court in a proper proceeding, according to the ruling of the Honorable Supreme Court.

Furthermore, based on the provisions contained in Part II of the 1996 Act, Courts are prohibited from resolving disputes with third parties in arbitration and conciliation proceedings. In this case, the division Court is right in this regard. A disagreement like this could not have been resolved during the proceedings. However, the Supreme Court held that the division Court erred in referring the case to the next stage under Order 21, Rule 46 CPC, because the latter deals with garnishee proceedings[57]. These rules are applicable when third parties hold the judgment debtor's funds. The liability of the issuing bank in a case involving a letter of credit is totally separate from any other liability. It cannot be said that the payment of the sums owed by the bank are debtor sums. Therefore, any dispute, if any, can only be resolved through separate and distinct legal proceedings which the appellants should have initiated[58].

6.4. *Prohibition against garnishee*

The case Greater Cochin development Authority, Kadavanthara v. Harrisons Malayam Ltd. & Anr concerned issuing a notice inviting the defendant to show cause against the plaintiff's prayer in his application. However, however, the notice had not been issued in a compliant manner, *i.e.,* within Form no. 5.

The Kerala High Court ruled that the order cannot be invalidated on the grounds that the Form 5's purpose was substantially met. Form no. 5 was compared to the prohibitionary order that was actually served to the garnishee. It revealed some discrepancies, such as the fact that Form no. 5 envisages directing the Amin to request that the defendant provide security, while the prescribed form directed the garnishee to «the above named garnishee and to affix at the Court house».

The impugned order did not mention directing the defendant to provide security, and instead directed the garnishee to refrain from paying the specified debt or any portion of it to anyone other than the Court. Nonetheless, the Court resorted to issuing a separate notice calling upon the defendant to show cause against the prayer in the application, which also mentions security, as there was no illegality. This was because there was no specific form required by law by which the amin, to whom the warrant in Form no. 5 is addressed, should call upon the defendant to furnish security. The Court accomplished the goal of the previous Section of Form no. 5 by issuing a separate notice[59].

6.5. *Monetary decree execution*

The executing Court has the authority to reclaim any money that the judgment debtor has that is held by another party. However, the Court lacks the authority to give any person an order or direction, even if it is the judgment debtor's regular financier who pays the debt or the judgment debtor's decretal amount, or if it is assumed that the guarantee will be able to recover the amount from the judgment debtor or that the judgment debtor will pay the garnishee. The executing Court in the case State of Bikaner and Jaipur v. Additional Dist. & Sessions Judge, has not ruled that any of the judgment debtor's funds, which they do not possess, are lying with the petitioner bank. The executing Court held that the petitioner could not be ordered to impose liability on himself to pay the decree holder under any legal provisions, even if the petitioner had the possibility of recovering the money from the state or the judgment debtor.

Therefore, the order of the executing Court is in violation of Rule 46 B of order 21 of CPC and may be set aside. It is essentially a directive to impose a liability on the bank instead of paying any debt amount or deposit amount of the judgment debtor to the decree holder[60].

6.6. *Purpose and nature of the provisions of the Code of Civil Procedure*

6.6.1. *Notice to garnishee: Order 21 Rule 46 A*

According to the provisions of Rule 46-A, a garnishee must receive notice prior to the issuance of a garnishee order against him. The order would be void if no notice of this kind was given and no hearing was granted prior to it being passed[61]. According to the law, such an order does not exist, and any action taken in compliance with or to enforce such an order would likewise be illegal[62]. This rule's goal is to give the decree holder access to the judgment debtor's unpaid debt in execution rather than forcing him to file a lawsuit. It is applicable to debts attached under Rule 46-A, excluding debts secured by charges or mortgages. This new rule (Rule 46-A), unlike the Calcutta rule, also applies to a debt arising from a negotiable instrument. The word "may" in the rule denotes discretion; namely, the Court may refuse to act in accordance with it.

Garnishee proceedings cannot be initiated in relation to a debt that is not attachable under Rule 46 or that has not been attached in accordance with this rule. As a result, the firm in execution decree prohibits the garnishee proceedings from being brought against the partners in their individual capacities for any debt[63]. Furthermore, only in cases where the judgment debtor has an immediate right to recoup the debt from his judgment debtor (the garnishee) may a decree holder take legal action against the garnishee. Should funds be disbursed to the judgment debtor exclusively under specific circumstances, both the decree holder and the judgment debtor would be equally disabled and would have to wait for the occurrence of that situation[64]. This is the case because, should he so choose, the judgment debtor may compel payment of the attachable debt. There is a difference, though, between an existing debt whose payment is postponed and one whose debt and payment are due in the future. The debt is attachable in the first scenario, but not in the second[65]. Even if the exact amount of the debt that is owed or accruing is not ascertained, a garnishee order *nisi* may still be issued[66].

In Syndicate Bank v. Vijay Kumar, the customer provided the bank with a bank guarantee in support of the high Court and gave the bank two properly discharged fixed deposit receipts, granting the bank custody of the receipts and renewals of the same. According to the Honorable Supreme Court, it turns into a general lien. The party's liability may be offset by the bank against the receipts. The garnishee must appear in Court if the fixed deposits are linked to the bank. The remaining amount, following the bank's claim adjustments, will be sufficient to fulfill the decree[67].

In another case the garnishee responded to the letter by showing up in Court and submitting a counter-affidavit in which they raised a few points of contention. It was decided that even in the absence of a formal notice under Order 21 Rule 46 C[68] to order that the disputed matter be adjudicated as an issue and to decide the matter, his arguments, having been raised in his counter-documentation, could be considered objections covered by the above rule. The lower Court did not consider the merits of the appellant's dispute in issuing the impugned orders[69].

6.6.2. *Mode of notification*

The garnishee will be asked to provide justification in the submitted notice. A money decree was obtained in a specific case through compromise. In fact, as Executive Engineer, KSE Board v. JH Sharma stated at the request of the decree holder, a prohibitory order was used to attach, prior to judgment, a certain amount of money purportedly belonging to the judgment debtor and held by the appellant garnishee. However, the garnishee was never served any notice under Order 21 Rule 46 by the execution Court. The Court only ordered a letter to be written asking the garnishee to remit the amount specified in the summons or notice[70]. Thus, the case does not fall under Order 58 Rule 5[71].

It is useful to note that in the case that two people jointly own a bank account, their shares are deemed equal unless there is proof to the contrary[72]. A banker may set off one account against another that belongs to the same individual[73]. The Order 21 Rule 46 prohibits attaching a check. It is attached in accordance with Order 21 Rule 51 concerning negotiable instruments[74].

You cannot attach a contingent debt. For instance, if the building contractor is only to be paid upon the architect's certificate in accordance with the terms of the building contract, funds in the owner's possession cannot be used to satisfy a debt owed to the contactor until the certificate is issued[75].

6.6.3. *Order against garnishee: Order 21 Rule 46 B*

Rule 46 B of Order 21 gives the Court the authority to order the garnishee to comply with the terms of the notice and to issue an enforcement order if the garnishee fails to show cause or fails to appear in response to the notice under Rule 46 A. This kind of order is considered a judgment in favor of the judgment creditor and against the garnishee. The subsequent actions are directed at the garnishee and are intended to carry out that decree[76]. The authority to issue the order is discretionary and may be withheld for good reason, such as when the judgment debtor is acting in a trustee capacity and has no personal stake in the debt[77].

6.6.4. *Trial of disputed questions: Order 21 Rule 46 C*

For the purpose of appeal or not, the legislator intended to treat some of the orders issued by the executing Court as decrees. In order to make a final decision on such matters, it was also intended to treat certain orders as if they fell within the original jurisdiction of the Court. Accordingly, jurisdiction had been expressly conferred pursuant to Order 21 Rule 46 C[78] and Rule 101[79] of the CPC. However, the orders issued under Rule 46 C and Rule 101 have a different legal basis. Therefore, should the garnishee contest their debt to the judgment debtor or assert that the debt is not enforceable, the Court must mandate that the matter be brought up and resolved. A trial is required even in cases where there is a reasonable doubt[80].

6.6.5. *Resolution of the conflict*

In this regard it is useful to observe the case of the Global trust bank Ltd. v. Fargo Freight ltd. & ors which concerns a letter of credit opened by the bank and the Court issues an *interim* order in response, but the bank disputes its obligations under the terms of the letter, it is improper to issue a decree based on an arbitration award without first determining the bank's liability. The reasoning of the Delhi High Court was as follows: «For all intends and purposes the appellant is a third party to the decree. The first question for our consideration is that whether decree could be enforced in the same execution proceedings against a third party, not being party to the decree. Before that question is taken up for consideration, we have to see the nature of letter of credit. Letter of credit as commonly understood confers authority upon the person to whom it is addressed to advance money or furnish goods on the credit of the writer. It is in the nature of negotiable instrument and is a letter whereby a person requests another to advance money or give credit to a third person and promises to repay person making advancement. A letter of credit has been defined as an offer by a bank or other financial institutions to be hound to person to whom it is directed, when accepted and acted on by him according to its stipulations and is in substance an authority to him to draw on the bank in accordance with the terms stated and a promise by the bank to accept and pay bills or drafts so drawn»[81].

6.6.6. *Trial of the contested issue*

In the case where the ban contested its obligations under the letter of credit, it was noted that a letter of credit, as it is generally understood, gives the recipient authority to advance funds or provide goods on the writer's credit. This letter, which is a negotiable instrument, asks someone else to advance money or grant credit to a third party with the understanding that the person making the advance will reimburse the recipient. Furthermore, Rule 46 A of Order 21 covers debts under negotiable instruments in addition to debits that are not secured by mortgages or charges that have been attached in accordance with Rule 46 of Order 21 of the CPC. The process in cases where the garnishee contests the judgment debtor's debt or claims the debt is not attachable is outlined in Rule 46. An issue must be brought up and tried by the Court's order. The case ought to go to trial even in cases where there is a legitimate doubt. Before an issue regarding liability can be raised and an order made, the garnishee must establish a prima facie case. According to the words, he would reveal information from which one could reasonably conclude that there is a legitimate disagreement regarding his claimed culpability. Similar to Rule 46 C of Order 21, once the bank has contested its obligation to pay, the Court must make a decision[82].

6.6.7. *Garnishment before judgment*

In the case under consideration, given the temporary nature of the Court order in this case and the fact that the garnishee still had the opportunity to provide security, there was no urgent need to physically seize the money. In fact, a prohibition order had already been issued under these circumstances. The garnishee or the defendant is not prejudiced in any way by the order's specific form of service because it contains no directive that is not permitted by law. The specific order that is actually served to the garnishee clarifies any ambiguity regarding the availability of the prescribed form and makes it clear that the Court has placed restrictions on payment. It should be noted that since this is a debt attachment, Order 21 Rule 46 applies with regard to how the attachment order is carried out, and Order 21 Rule 46(2)[83] allows for the prohibitory order to be served on the garnishee in addition to being affixed to the Court's notice board. Here, each of these prerequisites has been met. Order 21 Rule 46(2) does not require that the defendants also receive a copy of the prohibitory order[84].

Since the money subject to the attachment allegedly belonged to the judgment debtor and was in the possession of the appellant, the garnishment before the judgment was executed in accordance with Order 38 Rule 5 CPC and would be affected by a prohibition order. Order 38 Rule 11A CPC states that: «the provisions of the code are applicable to an attachment made in execution of the decree shall, so far as may be, apply to an attachment made before judgment which continues after the judgment by virtue of provisions of R 11»[85]. According to Rule 11 «[w]here property is under attachment by virtue of the provisions of this order decree is subsequently passed in favour of the plaintiff, it shall not be necessary upon an application for execution of such decree to apply for a re-attachment of the property»[86].

6.6.8. *Bank's liability*

Continuing the analysis of the case Global trust bank Ltd. v. Fargo Freight ltd. & ors, when the bank contested its obligation under the credit letter, the Court issued a decree in the form of an arbitration award that established the bank's liability rather than making a decision about the bank's liability. Nevertheless, the orders were enforceable because the bank was not a party to the arbitration. An issue must be brought up and tried by the Court's order. The case ought to go to trial even in cases where there is a legitimate doubt. Before his liability can be ordered to be raised, the garnishee must establish a *prima facie* case. Stated differently, he would reveal information that would allow one to reasonably conclude that there is a legitimate disagreement regarding his purported culpability. «On the same analogy, as contained in R 46 C, there must be adjudication by the Court, once the bank had disputed its liability to pay [...]»[87].

6.6.9. *Acceptance of appeal*

Orders issued under Rule 46 C and Rule 101 have a different legal standing than orders issued under Order 21's provisions, despite the latter's intention to treat all of these orders as decrees. Orders passed under Rule 46 C and Rule 101 are orders passed in exercise of the original jurisdiction of subordinate Court, and those orders shall come within the purview of Clause (ii) of S 5 of Kerala HC Act. Since the executing Court has not been granted original jurisdiction in deciding claims under Rule 58 CPC, an appeal from such orders shall not lie to the division bench[88].

6.6.10. *Undertaking to pay compensation*

In cases where the garnishee obtained possession from the tenant with a commitment to pay an agreed compensation, in the lawsuit filed by the creditor the garnishee was ordered to deposit the amount due in Court. In the case being considered, the Tamil Nadu Industrial Development Corporation Limited known as TIDCO acquired land belonging to the Government of India's salt department with a commitment to compensate the department and its tenants. In accordance with the government of India's order dated 6-1-99, the salt department has also transferred the entire tract of land to TIDCO. The terms of the transfer that were favorable to TIDCO by the Indian government were as follows: TIDCO will compensate tenants who were forced to give up their lease rights prematurely. It was further stipulated that TIDCO would be responsible for satisfying all claims and that the salt commissioner would not be involved in any legal proceedings related to the amount due to the lessees[89].

6.6.11. *Procedure where debt belongs to third person: Order 21 Rule 46 D*

The expression in Rule 46 D CPC «where it is suggested or appears to be probable that the debt belongs to some third person» would mean that the pledgee indicates this or that the Court believes it from the acts[90]. Similar to this rule, it has been held in England that the garnishee must notify the Court of any claim to or lien upon the debt, and if, in spite of this knowledge, he pays the garnisher anyway, he will be responsible for paying the claimant[91]. According to this regulation, the Court must issue an order obliging the third person to appear and state his or her right to the debt and provide the relevant documentation.

6.6.12. *Order as regards third person: Order 21 Rule 46 E*

The rule in question states that: «After hearing such third person and any person or persons who may subsequently be ordered to appear, or where such third or other person or persons do not appear when so ordered, the Court may make such order as is hereinbefore provided, or such other order or orders upon such terms, if any, with respect to the lien, charge or interest, as the case may be, of such third or other person or persons as it may deem fit and proper»[92]. For the analysis of this rule, it is useful to look at the case R Viswanatha Pandaram & Co v. Surajmal Ganeshmal Bansali where «the appellants in tithed the suit for recovery of Rs. 13,300, against one Sarajmal Ganeshmal Bhansali. On the same day, an application was filed for attachment before judgment of a sum of Rs. 10,000 in the hands of the Canara Bank Ltd, at Salem, as belonging to the debtor. The garnishee, *i.e.*, the Canara Rank Ltd., tiled a counter-statement, stating that the money did not belong to the debtor, but to the Lakshmi Bank Ltd., which was carrying end business in the Bombay State. Notice was thereupon issued to Lakshmi Bank Ltd., under the provisions of Order 21, rule 46-D»[93]. The Madras High Court held that «the decision of the question as to the title to the money in deposit with (the Canara Bank Ltd.,) was kept pending, and the present application for execution must be considered merely as a reminder to the Court of the necessity to decide that question first and grant reliefs thereafter. It was the duty of the lower Court, to have decided that question. Its order referring the parties to a suit cannot therefore be sustained»[94].

6.6.13. *Payment by garnishee to be valid discharge: Order 21 Rule 46 F*

The Rule 46 F of the Code provides that payments made by the garnishee are considered to be a valid discharge of debt against him. In fact, the expression «under Rule 46 A or under any such order» means that the pledgee is discharged from his liability only if payment is made under Rule 46 A or an order issued under Rules 46 B, 46 C, 46 E[95]. Therefore, the pledgee would not obtain a valid release under this rule if he or she made the payment by private agreement instead of through the garnishment proceeding[96]. Despite the decree in execution of which the Rule 46 A application is made, or the order rendered in the proceedings under such an application, being set aside or reversed, the garnishee receives a valid discharge. This also applies in cases where the judgment debtor has been found insolvent and the judgment creditor may be required to return the funds to the receiver in bankruptcy.

In Food Corporation of India v. Sukh Deo Prasad, the Hon'ble Supreme Court held that «the garnishee proceedings are governed by Rules 46 and 46A to 46F of Order 21 of the Code. Sub-para (1) of Rule 46 A provides that in the case of a debt (other than a debt secured by a mortgage or a charge) which has been attached under Rule 46, upon the application of the attaching creditor, the Court may issue notice to the garnishee liable to pay such debt, calling upon him either to pay into Court the debt due from debtor or to appear and show cause why he should not do so. Rule 46B provides that where the garnishee does not forthwith pay into Court the amount due from him to the debtor and does not appear and show cause in answer to the notice, the Court may order the garnishee to comply with the terms of such notice, and on such order, execution may issue as though such order were a decree against him. Rule 46C provides that where the garnishee disputes liability, the Court may order that any issue or question necessary for the determination of liability shall be tried as if it were an issue in a suit, and upon the determination of such issue shall make such order or orders as it deems fit. It would thus be seen that the amount due by a garnishee, if disputed has to be determined as if it was an issue in the suit and the Court can appropriate order determine the extent of liability of the garnishee. In this case, there was no adjudication of the amount payable by FCI. Whatever amount that was due in pursuance of the order dated 27.5.1996 in regard to one go down taken on lease in June 1994, was deposited by FCI and the plaintiff bank at whose instance the order was made has no complaint or grievance»[97].

6.6.14. *Preventing a garnishee order*

A person or the primary debtor may stop a Court from granting a garnishee order. He may submit an application for the same thing to a Court of law. Nonetheless, the application may be rejected by the Court based on a number of variables and conditions. The principal debtor has several significant options at his disposal to stop the Court from imposing a garnishee order on him:

1) Pay off the entire amount owed: if the principal debtor pays the creditor's entire debt within the stipulated time frame, the Court will not issue a garnishee order against him. Rather than issuing a garnishee order, the Court may decide to extend the deadline for paying the debt to the creditor. But the Court has full authority to issue a garnishee order against the principal debtor in the event that he fails to make the payment by the deadline.

2) Repayment options: In order to repay the debt in a way that works for both parties, the principal debtor may arrange specific

terms with the creditor. In this case, the creditor has the option to lower the principal amount and lengthen the debt's repayment period. The best method to avert or prevent a garnishee order is thought to be the agreement between the principal debtor and the creditor regarding the outstanding debt. That being said, the creditor is not required to accept the debtor's offer. The creditor has the option to accept or reject the debtor's offer of an arrangement or settlement. The principal debtor should not receive any personal benefit from the solution; instead, it must be advantageous to the creditor.

3) Make installment payments: The principal debtor has the option of appearing before the Court and committing to pay off the outstanding debt through installments imposed by the Court. One way for the principal debtor to pay the debt in installments is to submit his or her financial report to the Court. The garnishee order will end and the debtor will pay the amount owed in installments if the Court grants the application. Nonetheless, the Court may deny the application for one of two reasons. First, if it will take too long to pay the debt amount to the creditor; second, if the analysis of the debtor's financial situation indicates that the debtor is unable to pay the amount due as determined by the Court.

4) The 2016 Bankruptcy and Insolvency Code: The garnishee order against the principal debtor will be terminated if he filed a defense under the Insolvency and Bankruptcy Code, 2016[98].

It is argued that if someone is found insolvent under the act's provisions, the Court lacks the authority to order them to pay the outstanding balance. When a Court declares a debtor insolvent and bankrupt, it is assumed that they are completely free of all debts. Any garnishee order issued against him will therefore be null and void and halted.

6.7. *Brief concluding remarks*

In light of everything considered the law analyzed must be handled carefully. It is the Court's responsibility to determine whether the case is prima facie before making such an order. The Court also has an obligation to ensure that the discretionary power is not abused and that no innocent person is harassed.

Thus, one of the crucial components of the Code for approving an order for the execution of a decree is the garnishee order. The Court must take into account a number of small details when deciding whether to issue a garnishee order. It is the Court's responsibility to issue an order that will be helpful to the judgment creditor.

Notes

[1] See R. SACCO, A. GAMBARO, *Sistemi giuridici comparati*, Turin, 2008, p. 363. See also D. RENÉ, J. SPINOSI, *I grandi sistemi giuridici contemporanei*, Padua, 2004, R. SACCO (Italian edition edited by), p. 421 and p. 435.
[2] Corresponding to the most widespread religions of India.
[3] On the history of India see, generally, M. TORRI, *Storia dell'India*, Rome-Bari, 2000; and M. TORRI, *Storia dell'India*, Milan, 2004.
[4] See R. SACCO, A. GAMBARO, *cit.*, p. 364.
[5] *Ibid.* For a general overview of the Hindu tradition from its origins to the 1960s, see, R. LINGAT, *La tradizione giuridica dell'India. Dharma, diritto e interpretazione*, Francavilla (Italian translation by), Milan, 2003. Also, in general, see, A. PIZZORUSSO, *Sistemi giuridici comparati,* Milan, 1998, pp. 86-87, with particular attention to the bibliographical references in the footnotes.
[6] D. RENÉ, J. SPINOSI, *cit.*, p. 422.
[7] In the Hindu population we can find thousands of castes and sub-castes, traditionally divided into Brahmins, the priests, Kshatriyas, the warriors, Vaishyas, the traders, and Sudras, servants and common labourers.
[8] See P. GALLO, *Grandi sistemi giuridici,* Turin, 1997, p. 447.
[9] It would not be quite correct to speak of rights in the Western sense, a concept foreign to the Hindu tradition, which is based on the concept of duties. They vary by caste but also by age. See D. RENÉ, J. SPINOSI, *cit.*, p. 423.
[10] See K. ZWEIGERT, H. KÖTZ, *An introduction to comparative law,* T. WEIR (translated edition by), Oxford, 1998, p. 340. It should also be pointed out that caste discrimination was long accompanied by discrimination against women, who were deemed unworthy of embracing the divine and were therefore denied immortality. See R. SACCO, A. GAMBARO, *cit.*, p. 365.
[11] These rules of conduct are contained in work known as *Sâtra*, which will also be discussed later in this paragraph. See D. RENÉ, J. SPINOSI, *cit.*, p. 422.
[12] See D. RENÉ, J. SPINOSI, *cit.*, p. 423, R. SACCO, A. GAMBARO, *cit.*, p. 365, K. ZWEIGERT, H. KÖTZ, *cit.*, p. 340. P. GALLO, *cit.* p. 447.
[13] See D. RENÉ, J. SPINOSI, *cit.*, p. 424. R. SACCO, A. GAMBARO, *cit.*, pp. 366-367. K. ZWEIGERT, H. KÖTZ, *cit.*, p. 340. P. GALLO, *cit.* p. 447.
[14] The most famous are those of Manu, Yajnavalkya and Narada, probably written between the 1st century BC and the 14th century AD. See R. SACCO, A. GAMBARO, *cit.*, p. 366. For references to pseudo-legal literature predating the *dharmasatra*, in particular the *dharmasutra* and *smritis*, see K. ZWEIGERT, H. KÖTZ, *cit.*, p. 341.

[15] See R. Sacco, A. Gambaro, *cit.*, pp. 367-368. D. René, J. Spinosi, *cit.*, p. 424. R. Lingat, *cit.* pp. 198 ss.
[16] See R. Sacco, A. Gambaro, *cit.*, p. 368, D. René, J. Spinosi, *cit.*, p. 424. See also D. Amirante, *India*, Bologna, 2007, pp. 31 ss.
[17] See D. Amirante, *cit.*, pp. 28 ss.; and R. Sacco, A. Gambaro, *cit.*, p. 368.
[18] See P. Gallo, *cit.* p. 449, R. Sacco, A. Gambaro, *cit.*, pp. 370 ss., D. René, J. Spinosi, *cit.*, pp. 427 ss. and C. Antons, *Legal culture and history of law in Asia*, in C. Heath (ed. by), *Intellectual Property Law in Asia*, London, 2003.
[19] India was divided into principalities. Each principality had within it three degrees of jurisdiction in order to ensure the most correct application of the rule. On this subject, see R. Sacco, A. Gambaro, *cit.*, p. 369.
[20] R. Sacco, A. Gambaro, *cit.*, p. 370 ss.; D. René, J. Spinosi, *cit.*, p. 427 ss.
[21]For a reconstruction of the transition from Muslim to English rule, see, R. Sacco, A. Gambaro, *cit.*, p. 370 ss.; and M. Mukherjee, *Colonial order, British law: The empire and India: justice, war, and the imperium: India and Britain in Edmund Burke's prosecutorial speeches in the impeachment trial of warren hastings*, in *L. & Hist. Rev.,* vol. 23, 2005, pp. 589-630.
[22] We will now speak mainly of Hindu law and not Muslim law because Hindu law applied, as a personal right, to most of the population of India. Muslim law also continued to apply, in certain matters, if the dispute concerned individuals of the Islamic religion. Similar to what would happen with Hindu law, judges would seek help from Muslim law experts to try to reach a just settlement of disputes. See on this point R. Sacco, A. Gambaro, *cit.*, p. 374.
[23] For some comments on British colonization and beyond see K.M. Parker, *The Historiography of difference*, in *L.& Hist. Rev.,* vol. 23, 2005, p. 685 ss.; and E. KOLSKY, *A note on the study of Indian legal history*, in *L. & Hist. Rev.,* vol. 23, 2005, p. 703 ss.
[24] In this regard, please refer to footnote no. 181.
[25] See D. René, J. Spinosi, *cit.*, pp. 428 ss. and P. Gallo, *cit.* p. 449.
[26] See D. René, J. Spinosi, *cit.*, pp. 430 ss. and R. Sacco, A. Gambaro, *cit.*, pp. 372 ss.
[27] See P. Gallo, *cit.* p. 450; and R. Sacco, A. Gambaro, *cit.*, p. 376 ss.
[28] See K. Zweigert, H. Kötz, *cit.*, p. 342 ss.
[29] In this regard, see D. René, J. Spinosi, *cit.*, p. 432 ss.; and R. Sacco, A. Gambaro, *cit.*, p. 376 ss.
[30] For a more in-depth look at the post-colonial era see also M. Mukherjee, *A History of the present*, in *L. & Hist. Rev.*, vol. 23, 2005, p. 697 ss.
[31] R. Sacco, A. Gambaro, *cit.*, p. 377. This has resulted in the growth in importance of Hindu law, which now belongs to a much higher percentage of subjects.
[32] For an interesting insight into the relationship between international law and the Indian Constitution. See, S.C. Kashyap, *Constitution of India and International Law*, in B.N. PATEL (edited by), Leiden, 2005.
[33] For further details, please refer to G. Franceschini, F. Misuraca, *India: diritto commerciale, doganale e fiscale*, Milan, 2006, pp. 1 ss.
[34] There are about 15 major languages in India and an even larger number of

languages spoken by minorities. In this regard, see G. FRANCESCHINI, F. MISURACA, *cit.*, p. 1 ss.; and R. SACCO, A. GAMBARO, *cit.*, p. 378.

[35] Article 15 «(1) The State shall not discriminate against any citizen on grounds only of religion, race, caste, sex, place of birth or any of them. (2) No citizen shall, on grounds only of religion, race, caste, sex, place of birth or any of them, be subject to any disability, liability, restriction or condition with regard to: (a) access to shops, public restaurants, hotels and places of public entertainment; or (b) the use of wells, tanks, bathing ghats, roads and places of public resort maintained wholly or partly out of State funds or dedicated to the use of the general public. (3) Nothing in this article shall prevent the State from making any special provision for women and children». See D. RENÉ, J. SPINOSI, *cit.*, p. 433. The English version of the Indian Constitution, updated with amendments in 2007, is available at: . (Last accessed 11 June 2010).

[36] Before this law, the woman had no freedom to choose her spouse but was offered as a gift by her parents to her future husband. Polygamy was also tolerated and the indissolubility of the bond was imposed. Now monogamy is the rule and divorce are provided for. The possibility of the payment of a maintenance pension for the divorced code was also introduced. See D. RENÉ, J. SPINOSI, *cit.*, p. 433.

[37] In particular, the Hindu Minority and Guardianship Act 1956, the Hindu Adoptions and Maintenance Act 1956 and the Hindu Succession Act 1956 were enacted. These acts, and particularly the latter, are part of the attempt to equalize the right of men and women that has resulted in various post-independence regulatory acts. According to traditional Hindu law, a deceased person's property only belonged to those who could provide him or her with spiritual benefits, and women were not able to do so. See D. RENÉ, J. SPINOSI, *cit.*, pp. 433-434; and P. GALLO, *cit.*, p. 450.

[38] See the text of Article 44: *The State shall endeavor to secure for the citizens a uniform civil code throughout the territory of India.* Available at . (Last accessed 11 June 2010).

[39] As well explained in G. FRANCESCHINI, F. MISURACA, *cit.*, p. 6 ss., the tasks of the Supreme Court go far beyond those of a Court of appeal from decisions of the High Courts. It performs, among others, the function of a review Court for decisions of the lower Courts, settles disputes arising between the central state and individual states or those of the states among themselves.

[40] See G. FRANCESCHINI, F. MISURACA, *cit.*, pp. 29 ss.

[41] See G. FRANCESCHINI, F. MISURACA, *cit.*, p. 29 ss. There, it is also pointed out that the Supreme Court is the only Court that is not bound by its own precedents, although, it is then pointed out, the rule applies that decisions taken with a higher number of members prevail over those taken with a lower composition.

[42] On the Indian legal system, see R. LINGAT, *La tradizione giuridica dell'India*, D. FRANCAVILLA (translated by), Milan, 2003; D. FRANCAVILLA, *Il diritto nell'India contemporanea. Sistemi tradizionali, modelli occidentali e globalizzazione,* Turin, 2011; S. YILDRIM, *Expanding secularism's scope: an indian case study,* in *The Am. J. Comp. L.*, 2004; D. AMIRANTE, *India*, Bologna, 2007; H.P. GLENN, *Comparative legal families and comparative legal traditions*, in

R. ZIMMERMANN, M. REIMANN, *The Oxford handbook of comparative law*, Oxford, 2006, *passim.*; R. SACCO, *Legal formants: a dynamic approach to comparative Law (Installment II of II)*, in *Am. J. comp. L.*, vol. 39, no. 2, 1991.

[43] The creditor always benefits from a garnishee order because it shields him from losses brought on by the judgment debtor's inability to provide funds. It serves as an alternative mechanism for collecting the balance from the debtor in the event that the debtor is unable to do so within the time stipulated in the parties' agreement. P. RAMANATHA AIYAR, *Advanced law lexicon. the encyclopaedic law dictionary with legal maxims, latin terms, words & phrases*, ed. 6, vol. 4, Nagpur, 2019.

[44] Global Trust Bank Ltd. V. Fargo Freight Ltd., Bank of Rajasthan Ltd. and others, AIR 2002 Delhi 13.

[45] *Ex multis*, C. K. THAKKER, *Code of civil procedure*, Lucknow, 2009.

[46] See, V. RAJORA, *Power of Indian Courts to issue garnishee 0rder*, 2010. Available at SSRN: https://ssrn.com/abstract=1539347.

[47] Code of Civil Procedure 1908, Order 21 Rule 46 A (2) stated that: «An application under sub-rule (1) shall be made on affidavit verifying the facts alleged and stating that in the belief of the deponent, the garnishee is indebted to the judgment-debtor». And Rule 46 A (3) stated that: «Where the garnishee pays in the Court the amount due from him to the judgment-debtor or so much thereof as is sufficient to satisfy the decree and the costs of the execution, the Court may direct that the amount may be paid to the decree-holder towards satisfaction of the decree and costs of the execution».

[48] In the case Mackenzie & co. v. Anil Kumar AIR 1975 Cal 150, the Calcutta High Court said «The appellant has denied the judgment-debtor's claim based on the bill submitted by the judgment-debtor. It has disputed the validity of the claim and the judgment-debtor's right to recover the same. It has further said that owing to the default and negligence of the judgment-debtor in discharging his duties as the Stevedore it has suffered loss and damages in a very large sum of money. It has claimed to set-off a sum of Rs. 31,500/- which according to it is due to the judgment-debtor against such claim and it has said that after such set-off nothing will be due and payable to the judgment-debtor by the garnishee. The dispute raised by the garnishee with regard to the claim made by the judgment-debtor cannot in our view be said to be frivolous and without substance. Some of the particulars of negligence and default on the part of the judgment-debtor have been set out in the letters addressed by the appellant to the second respondent. It is true that a charge of negligence and default is a matter of proof. But the garnishee ought not to be deprived of the opportunity to substantiate its claim by producing evidence in support of its claim». Where the garnishee disputes his liability, the Court must raise an issue, and determine the liability of the garnishee.

[49] As per 15 U.S. Code § 1673, entitled Restriction on garnishment, is stated that «[…] the maximum part of the aggregate disposable earnings of an individual for any workweek which is subjected to garnishment may not exceed (1) 25 per centum of his disposable earnings for that week, or (2) the amount by which his disposable earnings for that week exceed thirty times the Federal

minimum hourly wage prescribed by section 206(a)(1) of title 29 in effect at the time the earnings are payable, whichever is less». Garnishment is subject to due process requirements since it entails the taking of property. The Wisconsin statute that permitted pretrial wage garnishment without a right to a hearing or to present a defense was overturned by the U.S. Supreme Court in Sniadatch v. Family Finance Corp. of Bay View, 395 U.S. 337, 89 S. Ct. 1820, 23 L. Ed. 2d 349 (1969). The Court claimed that garnishment infringed upon basic due process rights since it occurred without prior notice or hearing.

[50] Code of Civil Procedure 1908, Order 21 Rule 46 E, 46 F, 46 G.

[51] Code of Civil Procedure 1908, Order 21 Rule 46 B, Rule 46 H.

[52] Code of Civil Procedure 1908, Order 21 Rule 46 G.

[53] Code of Civil Procedure 1908, Order 21 Rule 46 H.

[54] P. RAMANATHA AIYAR, *cit.*

[55] L. RAJ SUBASH, *Power of Indian Courts to issue garnishee order,* in *Int. J. R. A. Rev.,* vol. 4, no. 4, 2017, pp. 326-328.

[56] Kuchimanchi Nagamani Vs. Mantri Prasada Agnihotrudu and others, 2001 (1) ALT 385. From an extract of the judgment, the Court states the following: «Neither any such objection was raised nor these applications were contested even though the authority was represented through the Assistant Government Pleader. [...] Thus, the proceedings have come to an end and the orders of garnishee attachment have become final since they remained unchallenged. [...]».

[57] See, C. K. TAKWANI, *Civil procedure*, Lucknow, 2003.

[58] Fargo Freight Ltd v. Commodities Exchange Corporation, AIR 2004 SC 4109. The Court's reasoning was as follows: «In the alternative, he submitted that even if this Court holds that the time had been validly extended and that the presentation was within the validity period of the Letter of Credit, the documents presented were not in accordance with the Letter of Credit and were discrepant. He submitted that the Court could not have been, in these proceedings, decided whether there were discrepancies and could not have been called upon the 3rd Respondent to pay the amount. We have heard the parties. In our view, Mr. Sanghi is right that a Letter of Credit is an independent transaction. The issuing bank is not at all concerned with the contract and/or dispute between the opener and the beneficiary. Also, to be noted that the 3rd Respondents were not parties to the Arbitration proceedings and there is no Award directing payment by the 3rd Respondent. In our view, Mr. Sanghi is also right that the Court should not have been passed an interim order, which affected the rights of an issuing banker. In the absence of fraud or some other act on the part of the issuing bank, they cannot be called upon to extend the validity period. At the highest the Court could have directed the 1st Respondent to keep alive the Letter of Credit. By directing an issuing bank to keep a Letter of Credit alive, the Court is likely to cause prejudice to the issuing bank inasmuch as the value of the security may deteriorate. We cannot accept the submission of Mr. Sanghi that the 3rd Respondent was not bound by the interim order. However, wrong the order may be the 3rd Respondent was bound by the order. By not immediately challenging the order and keeping the Letter of

Credit alive, the 3rd Respondent took the risk of having to pay, if documents in conformity with the Letter of Credit, were presented to it. They were bound to extend from time to time the validity period of the Letter of Credit. The 3rd Respondents were negligent in not pursuing their application and in not having the orders directing them to keep the Letter of Credit alive, set aside or challenged in a high of form. However, obeying an order of the Court does not amount to acquiescence and does not stop 3rd Respondent from contending that they cannot be made liable as documents presented are discrepant».

[59] Greater Cochin development Authority, Kadavanthara v, Harrisons Malayam Ltd. & Anr., AIR 2002 Ker. 119.

[60] The conclusion of the Rajasthan High Court is as follows: «So far as factual aspect is concerned, the executing Court has not held that any of the amount of the judgment-debtor is lying with the petitioner bank. The executing Court also did not hold that the petitioner under any of the provision of law can be directed to create liability upon itself to pay the amount to the decree holder even under assumption that petitioner may recover the amount either from the judgment-debtor or from State. The executing Court only proceeded on the assumption that since there is an account of the respondent judgment-debtor with the petitioner bank and transactions are carried in the account and the bank, number of times issued over draft to the judgment-debtor and the petitioner bank even stayed the withdrawal of the amount from the account No. 71, therefore, the petitioner bank can be directed to pay the decretal amount for the judgment- debtor. The executing Court appears to have not looked into the relevant provision of law to find out for what type of order can be issued against the garnishee». The order of the executing Court is, therefore, in violation of the Rule 46B of Order 21 CPC, which authorizes the executing Court to direct the garnishee to pay the «amount due from him (garnishee) to the judgment-debtor». In view of the above, the order of the Trial Court is absolutely contrary to law and is virtually a direction to create liability for the bank, rather than to pay any debt amount or deposit amount of the judgment-debtor to the decree holder. [...]». See the case State of Bikaner and Jaipur v. Additional Dist. & Sessions Judge, Jodhpur, AIR 2005 Raj 246.

[61] Code of Civil Procedure 1908, Order 21 Rule 46 A(1): «The Court may in the case of a debt (other than a debt secured by a mortgage or a charge) which has been attached under rule 46 upon the application of the attaching creditor, issue notice to the garnishee liable to pay such debt, calling upon him either to pay into Court the debt due from him to the judgment-debtor or so much thereof as may be sufficient to satisfy the decree and costs of execution, or to appear and show cause why he should not do so».

[62] See the case Surinder Nath v Union of India, AIR 1988 SC 1777, where the Supreme Court of India said that: «It is manifestly clear from the observations of the Enquiry Officer extracted above that he could not come to a finding that a sum of Rs. 8,56,377.55 in respect of which the garnishee order was, passed was actually due by M/s. Krishna Kapoor & Co. to M/s. Indo-Kashmir Carpets & Handicrafts. It is true that the Enquiry Officer has observed that both the firms did not co-operate in the matter, but it is equally true that the Revenue

had failed to substantiate that the said sum was due by Krishna Kapoor & Co. to the other firm. The most glaring fact that has been found by the Enquiry Officer is that although the IAC (Astt.), Range-II, Amritsar, issued a show cause notice to Krishna Kapoor & Co. under Section 226(3) in respect of Rs.3,86,450, yet he issued a garnishee order for Rs. 13,5d,377.55. It has been observed by the Enquiry Officer that it was due to the carelessness of the officer concerned that he did not issue the show cause notice for the sum of Rs.8,56,377.55 for which a garnishee order was issued. but such carelessness, in our opinion, is unpardonable. Moreover, as stated already, there is no satisfactory evidence before the IAC (Asstt.), Range-Il, Amritsar, that a sum of Rs.8,56,377.55 was due by the firm, Krishna Kapoor & Co., to M/s. Indo-Kashmir Carpets & Handicrafts, inasmuch as the Enquiry Officer himself has been unable to come to a finding in respect of that amount. Thus, without giving the firm, Krishna Kapoor & Co., an opportunity of showing cause in respect of the sum of Rs.8,56,377.55 under section 226(3) of the: Act, a garnishee order in respect of that amount was passed under section 226(3)(x) and a very valuable property of the firm was put up to auction and sold to the petitioner».

[63] In the case Kurseong Hydro-Electric Supply CO Ltd. v. Lakshmi Narayan Sukhani, AIR 1941 Cal 364, the Calcutta High Court states that: «We cannot therefore accede to the argument of the appellant's advocate, which he at first advanced, that we must take the debt to be a debt due to the firm because it is on that footing that the learned subordinate Judge proceeded. In continuation of his argument, he also drew our attention to some items of evidence which would suggest that the debt was due to the firm, Sundar and Rai, e. g., Exs. F to F (2) and the deposition of N. B. Rai. The resolutions of the share-holders which have been exhibited are equivocal in terms. We therefore accept the suggestion of the respondents' advocates, to which the learned advocate of the appellant agreed in the end, that for the ends of justice the point as to whether the engineering remuneration was payable to the firm, Sundar and Rai, or to P. M. Sundar and N. B. Rai individually should be further investigated in the lower Court on the evidence on the record and on such additional evidence as the parties may be advised to lead. We accordingly set aside the order appealed against, save and except for the sum of Rs. 1160, and remand the case to the lower Court for investigation of the point indicated above, the parties being at liberty to adduce additional evidence. If the Court finds that at the dates when the prohibitory orders issued under Order 21, Rule 46 were served on the company the debt was due to the firm, Sundar and Rai it would dismiss the garnishee proceedings except with regard to the above-mentioned sum of Rs. 1160. If, however, the finding be otherwise the questions which have been discussed in the judgment under appeal would be material questions. In order that the said questions may not be further mooted in the lower Court we give our decision thereon in the paragraph following».

[64] See, Kazim Jawaz Jung vs Mir Mohamad Ali Jaferi and Anr, AIR 1972 AP 70.

[65] In the case O'Driscoll v. Manchester Insurance Committee, 1915 3 KB 499, CA, «the Court of Appeal considered the meaning of the word "debt" in the

context of fees payable by the National Insurance Committee to a panel doctor. There, the Insurance committee had entered into agreements with the panel doctors of their district by which the whole amounts received by the committee from the national Insurance Commissioners were to be distributed among the panel doctors in accordance with a scale of fees. The contention was that there could not be a debt until the amount had been ascertained and that contention was sought to be supported by citing cases relating to unliquidated damages». Swinfen Eady L J who distinguished the cases so cited, observed: «Here there is a debt, uncertain in amount, which will become certain when the accounts are finally dealt with by the insurance committee. Therefore, there was a "debt" at the material date, though it was not presently payable and the amount was not ascertained».

[66] «On an application for a garnishee order the affidavit in support stated, on information and belief, that a particular debt was due from the garnishee to the judgment debtor. The garnishee, by affidavit, denied the existence of that specific debt. Held, that on such an application an affidavit of information and belief is sufficient. Held, also, that in such a case the inquiry is not limited to the existence of the particular debt alleged, and consequently that the garnishee might be called upon to depose that he did not owe any debt to the judgment debtor, and that, on his refusal to do so, an order absolute could rightly be made». See, De Pass v. Capital & Industries Corp, 1891 1 QB 216.

[67] Supreme Court of India in the case Syndicate Bank v. Vijay Kumar, AIR 1992 SC 1066 came to this conclusion: «We have already held that the appellant Bank has a general lien over those two FDRs. The High Court having held that the two FDRs can be attached gave a further direction dismissing the objection of the Bank that the Bank should deposit an amount of Rs. 35,000/-. As rightly contended by the learned Counsel for the appellant Bank, the Bank in the instant case has the liberty to adjust from the proceeds of the two FDRs towards the dues to the Bank and if there is any balance left that will only be the amount which would belong to the depositor namely the Judgment-debtor in this case and only such amount, if any, can be attached in discharge of a decree. It is also submitted that the liability of the Judgment-debtor to the appellant Bank was far in excess of the amounts covered by the two FDRs and therefore nothing is due from the Bank to the Judgment-debtor. This is a matter for verification. However, in the view taken by us above namely that the Bank has a general lien over the two FDRs we set aside the order of the High Court directing the appellant Bank to deposit an amount of Rs. 35,000/-. The High Court shall, however, consider the objections raised by the Bank, namely that no amounts are due to the Judgment-debtor, in the light of the above principles laid down by us and then decide whether there is any amount left for being attached by the Decree-holder in execution of his decree. With the above directions the appeal is accordingly allowed. In the circumstances of the case, there will be no order as to costs».

[68] Code of Civil Procedure 1908, Order 21 Rule 46 C stated that: «Where the garnishee disputes liability, the Court may order that any issue of question necessary for the determination of liability shall be tried as if it where an issue

in a suit, and upon the determination of such issue shall make such order or orders as it deems fit: Provided that if the debt in respect of which the application under rule 46A is made is in respect of a sum of money beyond the pecuniary jurisdiction of the Court, the Court shall send the execution case to the Court of the District Judge to which the said Court is subordinate, and thereupon the Court of the District Judge or any other competent Court to which it may be transferred by the District Judge shall deal with it in the same manner as if the case had been originally instituted in that Court».

[69] See Executive Engineer, KSE Board v. JH Sharma, AIR 1988 Ker 288.

[70] In the above case the High Court's reasoning are: « [...] We are therefore of the opinion that prior to the passing of the impugned order garnishee was not served with a notice under Rule 46A. Notice was not ordered to the garnishee either in the E.P. or in the E.A. referred to earlier. The appellant appeared in Court only in response to the letter and filed counter affidavit raising certain contentions. Since he raised his contentions in the counter-affidavit, the same can be treated as objections contemplated under Rule 46C, even in the absence of a formal notice under Rule 46 A. That being so, the Court below had a duty under Rule 46C to order that the disputed question be tried as it were an issue in a suit and to decide the issue. In the impugned order the Court below did not consider the merits of the dispute raised by the appellant. The view taken by the Court below that the contention raised that no amount is available with him is not open to him is unsustainable. The observation of the Court below that garnishee had no case that he is not the garnishee does not convey any meaning. He is a garnishee in the sense that he received a prohibitory order. But it is open to him to contend that he does not have any money belonging to the judgment-debtor or due to the judgment-debtor. If such a contention is raised at the appropriate stage in response to notice under Rule 46 A the Court has a duty to consider the same».

[71] Code of Civil Procedure 1908, Order 58 Rule 5 stated that: «Where a claim or an objection is preferred and the Court, under the proviso to sub-rule (I), refuses to entertain it, the party against whom such order is made may institute a suit to establish the right which he claims to the property in dispute; but, subject to the result of such-suit, if any, an order so refusing to entertain the claim or objection shall be conclusive».

[72] In the case Balaraman v. Varadammal, AIR 1987 Mad 99, the petitioner is one of the sons of the judgment-debtor and 3rd respondent in that execution. According to the ruling: «The immediate question is whether the petitioner has made out a case to claim the entire balance with the bank on the demise of the judgment-debtor. The petitioner's specific case is that the whole money belonged to him and that out of respect to his father, the judgment-debtor, he opened the said account in the joint names of judgment-debtor and himself on terms either or survivor'. Except an argument and an averment in the counter filed by him, the petitioner has not proved his said case. The other alternative is that both the judgment-debtor and the petitioner have equal share. In the circumstances of the case, the only inference is that both have equal share. If so the respondent is entitled to attach a moiety of the amount in bank deposit».

Because in this case «[…] the petitioner has not let in any evidence. Indeed, the burden is on him to prove that though the account was in the joint name of himself and the judgment-debtor, the money was exclusively his. The burden is not discharged».

[73] Instead, in the case United Bank of India v. Venugopalan, AIR 1990 Ker 223 the Court's Reasoning state that: «We should in this connection remember that money lodged with banks as fixed deposits stricto jure is a loan to the bank. The banker in connection with the "fixed deposit", therefore is a debtor. The depositor accordingly would cease to be the owner of the money in fixed deposit. The said money becomes the money of the bank, enabling the bank to do as the bank likes, that however, with the obligation to repay the debt on maturity. The direction given by the executing Court to deposit Rs. 8,812/- made mention of in the petition E.A.878/87 treating the bank as a garnishee, in the light of the discussion above, is beyond challenge».

[74] Code of Civil Procedure 1908, Order 21 Rule 51, establishes that: «Where the property is a negotiable instrument not deposited in a Court, not in the custody of a public officer, the attachment shall be made by actual seizure, and the instrument shall be brought into Court and held subject to further orders of the Court».

[75] See, Dunlop & Ranken Ltd v. Handall Steel Ltd (1957) 1 ALL ER 347.

[76] See Code of Civil Procedure 1908, Order 21 Rule 46 B.

[77] Roberts v. Death, (1882) 8 QBD 819.

[78] Code of Civil Procedure 1908, Order 21 Rule 46 C determines that: «Where the garnishee disputes liability, the Court may order that any issue of question necessary for the determination of liability shall be tried as if it where an issue in a suit, and upon the determination of such issue shall make such order or orders as it deems fit: Provided that if the debt in respect of which the application under rule 46A is made is in respect of a sum of money beyond the pecuniary jurisdiction of the Court, the Court shall send the execution case to the Court of the District Judge to which the said Court is subordinate, and thereupon the Court of the District Judge or any other competent Court to which it may be transferred by the District Judge shall deal with it in the same manner as if the case had been originally instituted in that Court».

[79] Code of Civil Procedure 1908, Order 21 Rule 101, establishes that: «All questions (including questions relating to right, title or interest in the property) arising between the parties to a proceeding on an application under rule 97 or rule 99 or their representatives, and relevant to the adjudication of the application, shall be determined by the Court dealing with the application and not by a separate suit and for this purpose, the Court shall, notwithstanding anything to the contrary contained in any other law for the time being in force, be deemed to have jurisdiction to decide such questions».

[80] In Executive Engineer, KSE Board v. J H Sharma AIR 1988 Ker 288, the garnishee responded to the letter by showing up in Court and submitting a counter-affidavit in which they raised a few points of contention. The ruling stated that even in the absence of formal notice under Order 21 Rule 46 C to order that the disputed question be tried as an issue and to decide the issue, his

contentions could be regarded as objections contemplated under Order 21 Rule 46 C because he had raised them in his counter-affidavit. The lower Court disregarded the merits of the appellant's dispute in the impugned orders. In another case, Surinder Nath Kapoor v. Union of India & Ors 1988 AIR 1777, the Supreme Court ruled that a garnishee order is a powerful tool of the Court that should be used fairly and in accordance with the circumstances at hand.

[81] Global trust bank Ltd. v. Fargo Freight ltd. & ors., AIR 2002 Del. 13.

[82] *Ibid.*

[83] Code of Civil Procedure 1908, Order 21 Rule 46(2).

[84] Greater Cochin development Authority, Kadavanthara v. Harrisons Malayam Ltd. & Anr., AIR 2002 Ker. 119.

[85] Code of Civil Procedure 1908, Order 38 Rule 11 A.

[86] Code of Civil Procedure 1908, Order 38 Rule 11.

[87] As ruled by the Delhi Hight Court in the case Global trust bank Ltd. v. Fargo Freight ltd. & ors., AIR 2002 Del. 13.

[88] See C.G. Manoj v. infant Jesus Church & Ors, AIR 2000 NOC 43 (Ker) where: « […]by the learned counsel appearing for the 1st respondent that an appeal before a Division Bench is not maintainable against an order of the execution Court, and as per S. 5 of the Kerala High Court Act, an appeal before a Division Bench would lie only against a decree passed in exercise of the original jurisdiction of subordinate Court». S. 5 of the Kerala High Court Act, 1958 reads: «Appeal from judgment or order of Single Judge. An appeal shall lie to a Bench of two Judges from (i) a judgment or order of a single Judge in the exercise of original jurisdiction; or ii) a judgment of a single Judge in the exercise of appellate jurisdiction in respect of a decree or order made in the exercise of original jurisdiction by a subordinate Court». Clause ii) makes it clear that an appeal before a Division Bench would lie only against an order or decree passed in exercise of the original jurisdiction by a subordinate Court. In this case the appeal is dismissed.

[89] See the case K Jayaraman & etc. v. TS Ravi & Ors., AIR 2001 Mad 422

[90] Code of Civil Procedure 1908, Order 21 Rule 46 D states that: «where it is suggested or appears to be probable that the debt belongs to some third person, or that any third person has a lien or charge on, or other interest in such debt, the Court may order such third person to appear and state the nature and particulars of his claim, if any, to such debt and prove the same».

[91] See the case The Leader (1868) L R 9 A & E 314.

[92] Code of Civil Procedure 1908, Order 21 Rule 46 E.

[93] See R. Viswanatha Pandaram & Co v. Surajmal Ganeshmal Bansali, AIR 1964 Mad 49; Syndicate Bank v. Vijay Kumar, (1992) 2 SCC 330.

[94] *Ibid.*

[95] Code of Civil Procedure 1908, Order 21 Rule 46 F states that: «Payment made by the garnishee on notice under rule 46A or under any such order as aforesaid shall be a valid discharge to him as against the judgement-debtor and any other person ordered to appear as aforesaid for the amount paid or levied, although the decree in execution of which the application under rule 46A was made, or the order passed in the proceedings on such application

may be set aside or reversed».

[96] See Turner v. Jones (1858) 26 LT Exclusive 62.

[97] See, Food Corporation of India vs Sukh Prasad, AIR 2009 Supreme Court 2330. The Court noted that a garnishee may set off his claim against the money the debtor owes him. Therefore, the Court may notify the garnishee creditor who is responsible for the debt and ask him to pay the debt to the debtor in Court or to appear and give reasons why he should not do so.

[98] The Gazette of India *Extraordinary Insolvency and Bankruptcy Code*, 2016, no. 31. Available at: The Gazette of India Extraordinary Insolvency and Bankruptcy Code, 2016, no. 31. Available at: https://www.mca.gov.in/Ministry/pdf/TheInsolvencyandBankruptcyofIndia.pdf.

7. Garnishment in Africa: the cases of Nigeria and Cameroon

7.1. *Introduction*

Nigeria is a presidential federal republic, organized into 36 states and 1 territory. Each state has its own legislative body (House of Assembly) and legal system. The Nigerian legal system is a mixed legal system, based on English common law and traditional customary law. Other sources of law are the constitution and jurisprudential precedents. The main sources of law, apart from the Constitution (in force since 1999), are federal and state laws. Since 1999-2001, Islamic law (*Sharia*) on family law has been in force in 12 northern states for people of the Muslim religion. The law is applied within a democratic system in which 12 northern federal states, with a Muslim majority, have adopted *Sharia* law to regulate certain aspects of the personal law of citizens of the Islamic religion[1].

In the Nigerian legal system[2], garnishment procedures are a frequently used method of enforcing monetary a judgment. The primary objective of the garnishment procedure is to guarantee the recovery of the judgment amount and the accomplishment of the goals of justice by preventing the debtor from denying the creditor the benefits of his judgment[3]. Garnishment proceeding is a post-judgment procedure that a creditor may initiate to collect a sum of money from a debtor. This legal procedure involves the seizure or attachment of a debtor's outstanding debts that are part of his or her assets and that can be used to enforce a judgment, with the goal of enforcing a monetary judgment. A garnishment proceeding is a type of enforcement of a debt that is not subject to standard enforcement procedures. The judgment creditor applies to the Court for a garnishment proceeding (*i.e.,* the initial application in a garnishment proceeding is filed *ex parte*) without adding the judgment debtor as a party[4]. In other words, upon receiving a judgment from a competent jurisdictional Court ordering the payment of a certain amount of money to an individual, that individual may request that the Court order a third-party holding funds on behalf of the accused individual to transfer those funds directly to the individual who is entitled to the Court-ordered payment[5].

It is crucial to note at this point that the Sheriffs and Civil Process Act (SCPA), Part V, Sections 83-91, boldly titled «Attachment of debts by garnishee order», contains the substantive law governing garnishee proceedings in Nigeria. The adjectival law is contained within the Act as a subsidiary law and is referred to as Order VIII of the Judgments (Enforcement) Rules (JER)[6]. All things considered, Section 287 of the 1999 Constitution of the Federal Republic of Nigeria (CFRN) states that all authorities, persons and Courts of subordinate jurisdiction shall enforce the judgments of the Supreme Court, Court of Appeal, Federal High Court, State High Courts and all other Courts established by the Constitution in any part of the federation[7]. Garnishment proceedings before the Federal High Court are also governed by the Federal High Court (Civil Procedure) Order 37 of 2019[8]. This is not unusual because it is in accordance with Section 254 of the 1999 Constitution, which gives the Chief Justice the authority to make rules governing the practices and procedures of the Court, subject to the provisions of any law of the National Assembly[9].

There are essentially several parties involved in garnishment proceedings, and for a better understanding of the terminology used, we will begin with a lexical and legal review: (i) Garnishee represents a third party who has custody of the judgment debtor's money or is indebted to him; at the request of the judgment creditor, this party is called upon to settle the judgment debt from the judgment debtor's credit in his third-party account or from his debt to the judgment debtor[10]; (ii) Garnishor or Judgment Creditor, according to the law, is anyone who has the temporary right to enforce a money judgment. Similarly, he is defined as someone who has obtained or has the right to enforce a judgment or order[11]; (iii) Judgment Debtor is one to whom a money judgment has been issued but who has not yet satisfied it. The garnishee proceedings are the result of his failure to comply with the judgment[12].

7.2. *Nature of garnishee proceedings*

Salami J.C.A. (as it then was), in P. P. M. C. Ltd v. Delphi Pet. Inc. sums up the garnishment process as follows: «A garnishee proceedings although incidental to the judgment pronouncing the debt owing, the appellants being judgment debtor are not necessary party to the said proceedings. The procedure whereby the judgment creditor obtains the order of the Court to attach from any person within the jurisdiction of the Court assets of judgment debtor to satisfy the judgment debt is described as attachment of debt and is one of several methods of executing judgment. The proceedings for this separate and distinct action is between the respondent, herein the Guaranty Trust Bank plc., the garnishee which has not appealed the said decision»[13]. In this regard, in addition to the definition of garnishment proceedings provided in the description above, it can also be inferred that these proceedings are distinct from the original action, the significance of which lies in the fact that they are only ancillary to the action that produced the judgment. This was deemed by His Lordship, Kekere-Ekun J.C.A. (as he then was), in Denton-West v. Muoma, when his declared that: «There is no doubt that garnishee proceedings are separate proceedings between the judgment creditor and the person or body who has custody of the assets of the judgment debtor, even though it flows from the judgment that pronounced the debt owing»[14].

Once more, it would seem that garnishee procedures are significantly different from execution. In the Purification Tech. (Nig.) Ltd. v. Attorney General of Lagos State case, as reported by Galadima, J.C.A. (as he was then), garnishee proceedings were explained as follows: «Again, given the distinction that exists between execution and garnishee proceedings for the enforcement of a judgment, I do not think the existence of an application seeking for an order staying execution of a judgment does preclude a judgment creditor from seeking to use some other legal method to enforce judgment. There is clear distinction between execution of judgments and other methods of enforcing judgments, such as garnishee proceedings. The distinction is brought out by the definition of 'writ of execution' in Section 19 of the Sheriffs and Civil Process Act, Cap. 407, Laws of the Federation, 1990. Writ of execution includes writ of attachment and sale, writ of delivery, writ of possession and writ of sequestration. It excludes a garnishee proceeding»[15]. His Lordship's stance above implies that execution will still be necessary in the end even if garnishee proceedings, in any form, fail. It makes sense, then, that some of Their Lordships have felt it appropriate to refer to the garnishee process as an auxiliary or ancillary means of enforcing judgment in certain situations. For instance, Omoleye, J.C.A. discussed garnishee proceedings in the Nitel Plc. v. I.C.I.C. (Directory Publishers) Ltd. case: «A garnishee proceeding or attachment of debts is a method auxiliary to that of execution for the enforcement of a judgment or order for the payment of money into Court enabling the judgment creditor to attach money due to the judgment debtor from a third person called the garnishee, who must be within the jurisdiction of Court»[16]. As a result, while garnishee procedures are solely related to financial judgments, writ of execution procedures are not. Second, unlike writ of execution, which is typically directed against the judgment debtor's assets, ultimate execution under garnishee proceedings typically occurs on the garnishee's assets. Not to mention, compared to writ of execution, garnishee proceedings are typically a quicker way to enforce a Court order.

The fact that garnishee proceedings resemble an equitable charge placed on the judgment debtor's assets by a third party sets them apart from other methods of judgment enforcement. In the case of C.B.N. v. Auto Import Export, Saulawa J.C.A. succinctly sums it up as follows: «However, it must be emphatically made clear, that the mere service of the garnishee order nisi on the garnishee does not necessarily operate as a transfer of the ownership of the debt to the judgment creditor. Conversely, it merely creates an equitable charge on the debt in his favour and the garnishee cannot pay the debt to anyone but the judgment creditor without the risk of having to pay it over again»[17].

A further feature of garnishment proceedings is that not all debts are attachable. A debt must be owed or accrued by the judgment debtor for it to be attachable in garnishment proceedings[18]. The debtor must be the rightful owner of the debt, or the debt must be real and existing. In Seabrook Estate Co., Ltd. v. Ford Hallett, J. elaborated on this point. His Honor observed the following: «In order that a sum can be attached there must be an actual debt existing at the time the order is sought, though the debt need not be then payable. There has been a good deal of discussion and authority about the words 'debts owing or accruing' [in R.S.C., Ord. 45, r. 1], but I think that the position is reasonably clear having regard to the judgment of the Court of Appeal in Webb v. Stenton. It is now well settled that a sum of money may properly be the subject of a garnishee order although the time for payment of it is in the future - *solvendum* in future - provided that it constitutes *debitum in praesenti*, *viz*., a sum of money the obligation to pay which is in existence at the date when the garnishee order is sought»[19]. Therefore, it is safe to say that if the debt to be attached has not yet become due to the judgment debtor, garnishee proceedings cannot be started by a judgment creditor[20].

The preceding makes clear the following regarding the character of garnishee proceedings: (i) garnishee proceedings are among the various ways judgments can be enforced; (ii) the person in possession of the judgment debtor's financial assets, known as the garnishee, and the judgment creditor usually engage in separate and distinct actions during garnishee proceedings; (iii) the first application (*ex parte*) that resulted in the garnishee order nisi does not require the judgment debtor as a party.

7.3. *Parties to garnishee proceedings*

As anticipated in the introduction, the parties involved in the garnishment process are Judgment creditor or applicant and the garnishee or respondent[21]. The party who has custody of the debtor's funds, called the garnishee, is the one called by the creditor to make payments from the debtor's account to the creditor, because the judgment creditor is the one in whose favor the Court rendered a judgment and is entitled to the judgment sum[22]. The judgment debtor, instead, are not necessary party to the said proceedings. As the Court of Appeal has repeatedly stated although foreclosure proceedings are ancillary to the judgment pronouncing the debt owed, the judgment debtors are not necessarily parties to said proceedings. This is because garnishment proceedings are separate and distinct actions between the creditor and the garnishee. This seems to have been the tendency adopted, in almost all cases already decided, by the Court of Appeal, such as the case: Denton-West Muoma[23], P.P.M.C. Ltd. v. Delphi Pet. Inc[24], U. B. A. v. Ekanem[25]. However, this position is believed to be the result of the inability or negligence of the Courts, particularly in the cases highlighted above, to grasp the difference between a garnishee order nisi proceedings and garnishee absolute proceedings with respect to the questions submitted to the judge. In particular, an in-depth analysis of some of these cases will highlight that the sentences adopted did not refer to the issues submitted to the decision, thus relegating the decisions to the level of *obiter dicta*[26].

In details, the question of parties in garnishee proceedings did not come up in U.B.A. v. Ekanem because the ruling made in that regard were *mere obiter*. What was in issue was a case of staying further execution filed by the garnishee[27]. While Denton-West v. Muoma is a case that deals with garnishee order nisi, the statement made in that case is vague enough to cover garnishee order nisi and garnishee order absolute proceedings[28]. In P.P.M.C. Ltd. v. Delphi Pet. Inc., instead, he led judgment by Garba, J.C.A. did not make any pronouncement on the issue of garnishee proceedings at all. But when it came to garnishee orders, Salami, J.C.A. (as he was then) addressed the matter and decided that the judgment debtor, who was the appellant, could not appeal the order because they were not involved in the proceedings. This stance merely conveys the idea that the ruling in that case applies to both garnishee order absolute and nisi proceedings[29]. As a result, it is essential to distinguish between the nisi and absolute procedures when determining who the right parties are in garnishee proceedings. It is safe to say that only the judgment creditor and the garnishee are parties to the garnishee order nisi proceedings because of the nature of the application filed. It should be mentioned that the judgment debtor is not included in the action because it is brought *ex parte*[30]. Therefore, it can be said that any decision stating that the judgment debtor is not a party at this point represents the proper legal position. However, three parties are considered if the case reaches the point where an absolute seizure order is issued. These three parties are: (i) the garnishee; (ii) the judgment debtor; and (iii) the judgment creditor.

In light of what has been considered, in the context of garnishee order absolute proceedings, the active participation of the debtor is shared because first, as stated in the Sheriffs and Civil Process Act's Section 83(1), an oral examination of the judgment debtor is anticipated, either prior to or following the issuance of the order nisi. In order to prevent the judgment debtor from losing the asset, it is justified to do so after the order nisi is granted but before the order is made absolute, even though it may not be practical to do so prior to the order nisi[31]. This implies that at this point in the process leading up to the creation of the order absolute, the judgment debtor is entitled to a hearing. As additional evidence that this is the case the fact that Section 83(2) requires the order nisi to be served to the judgment debtor at least fourteen days prior to the hearing where the order nisi will be made absolute serves. This is definitely to allow him to show up in Court on the postponed date. By serving the judgment debtor, this merely constitutes an invitation to be heard, thereby incorporating him into the proceedings.

The judgment debtor must be served with the order nisi in accordance with Section 83(2), which implies that the judgment debtor is not only a party to the garnishee proceedings but also a necessary party. The Act would not have required the order nisi to be served on the judgment debtor if this had not been the intention. According to Nwodo, J.C.A., in the case of Wema Bank Plc. v. Brastem-Sterr (Nig.) Ltd., the purpose of serving an order nisi on a judgment debtor is recognized[32].

7.4. *Procedure in garnishee proceedings*

7.4.1. *Order nisi*

Considering that the foreclosure procedure is a *sui generis* procedure, it mainly consists of two phases which can be started on the basis of the following orders: order nisi and order nisi absolute[33]. The order nisi is a provisional order of Court that, barring specific conditions, will become final or effective at a later time. The origin of the term nisi (also known as decree nisi or rule nisi) comes from Latin and means 'unless'. In practice, an order nisi requires the garnishee to appear in Court, on a specified date, to show cause why an order should not be made requiring him to pay the debtor's outstanding debt to the creditor[34]. In particular, Article 83(1) SCPA provides that the first stage, the creditor initiates legal proceedings by filing an *ex parte* application[35]. This application must be accompanied by a sworn statement that the judgment has been obtained and has not yet been satisfied. The latter can be presented by the judgment creditor or by his lawyer. It is also anticipated that the affidavit will specify the amount of the unsatisfied debt as well as the fact that the judgment debtor owes a third party within jurisdiction[36]. The affidavit supporting the *ex parte* application must have a certified true copy of the judgment attached if the garnishee proceedings are taking place before a different Court than the one that issued the judgment[37]. Thereafter, and if these conditions have been met, the Court issues an attachment order nisi when it considers that the creditor has the right to attach the debt. The garnishment order nisi, issued in accordance with Form 25-26, requires the garnishee to appear in Court on a designated date to give cause why an order will not be made against him that would require him to pay the debtor's outstanding debt in the against the judgment creditor. Furthermore, a copy of the order nisi must be served on the judgment debtor and garnishee at least 14 days before the date of the hearing at which the garnishee's appearance and justification is scheduled[38].

Order nisi service on the garnishee binds the debt in the garnishee's possession[39]; any payment of the debt to the judgment debtor or its alienation without the Court's permission is void[40]. After serving the order nisi on him, the garnishee has eight days to pay the amount the judgment debtor claims is his due from him[41]. If that amount is more than enough to cover the judgment debt and costs, he may also pay the debt and costs. The actions against the garnishee will be halted upon payment of the specified sum into Court[42]. Therefore, according to Section 84 of the SCPA, before the Court can issue an order nisi, the relevant officer's consent must be obtained if the money to be attached is in the custody of a public officer acting in his official capacity or in the custody of the Court[43].

Where a garnishee disputes his liability to pay the debt, he does not have to make any payment into Court, but to appear in Court on the return date and dispute his liability and the Court may order that any issue or question necessary for determining his liability be tried or determined in any manner in which any issue or question in any proceedings may be tried or determined or may refer the matter to a referee[44]. Furthermore, a garnishee may argue that a lien or charge has been placed on the debt in question by a third party, or that the debt itself belongs to a third party. If the third party does not show up, the Court may proceed to make an order as if the third party has appeared based on proof of service of the order nisi. In this scenario, the Court may order the third party to appear and state the nature and specifics of his claim upon such debt[45].

In case the third party comes forward, the Court may order execution to collect the amount due from the pledgee, or it may decide to try and determine any issue or problem. It may also decide to freeze the third party's claim or issue any other order it deems appropriate, subject to such conditions as the Court deems appropriate in connection with any lien or charge[46].

Finally, if the garnishee fails to appear as directed, does not contest the debt, and fails to pay the amount owed to the Court within the allotted time frame, the Court may declare the garnishee order nisi absolute upon proof of service[47].

7.4.2. *Order nisi absolute*

An order absolute is an order nisi which – because the party against whom it was issued has not provided reasons why the order should not be made absolute – has now become complete and unconditional[48]. In fact, the Court may establish a garnishee order nisi absolute if, on the return date, the garnishee fails to appear in Court or does not contest the amount that is allegedly owed from him to the judgment debtor. Through this act the judgment creditor orders the garnishee to pay the judgment debtor the full amount owed by him, or the portion of the judgment debt that is sufficient to cover the judgment debt and the costs of the garnishee proceedings[49].

In order to follow up the order absolute, just like any other money payment order, it is possible to use: a writ of *fifa*, a charging order, a writ of sequestration, an order of committal on a judgment debtor's summons, including garnishee proceedings against the garnishee's debtor[50]. If a garnishee fails to pay the garnisheed amount, he becomes an automatic judgment debtor and is subject to garnishee proceedings to recover the judgment debt. This applies to any garnishee against whom an order absolute is made[51]. It bears mentioning that the granting of an absolute garnishment order is at the discretion of the Court. If there is uncertainty about the ownership of the attached claim, an attachment order nisi would not be made absolute[52].

Similarly, an order absolute made in error by the pledgee and judgment creditor may also be set aside upon application[53]. In addition, the absolute garnishment order is a definitive decision of the Court, it is not interlocutory. The Court would become *functus officio*[54] once the absolute order is issued, and the garnishee's only chance to challenge the order would be to file an appeal[55]. Consequently, if, in spite of having the means to do so, a judgment debtor disregards a garnishee order absolute without good reason, Forms 48[56] and 49[57] may be used to serve him. The judgment debtor thus runs the risk of receiving a jail sentence if found guilty and could receive a contempt citation.

7.5. *Garnishee proceedings and other forms of judgment execution*

An enforceable judgment can be enforced not only through garnishment proceedings but also through other means, such as: a writ of *fieri facias*, a charging order, a writ of sequestration or an order of committal on a judgment debtor's summons[58].

In this regard, it is useful to give a definition, albeit brief, of these orders: (i) While a garnishee proceeding is directed at money in the possession of a third party that is owed to or accruing to the judgment debtor, the writ of *fieri facias*, also known as the writ of *fifa* or the writ of execution, is directed at the judgment debtor's goods, chattel, or immovable property that may be seized and sold to realize money to satisfy the judgment debt. (ii) Regarding the charging order, the Black's Law Dictionary defines a charge as «an encumbrance, lien or claim over property»[59]. A charge implies the discharge of a specific debt from a specific fund or item of property. A charge order imposes the obligation to pay a debt owed under a judgment. Unlike garnishee proceedings, which focus solely on money in the hands of a third party and thereby limit the option of the judgment creditor, it broadens the creditor's options for satisfying the judgment debt by adding property or funds that may be charged for payment of the debt to the list of options. (iii) Sequestration is legal procedure consisting of the temporary deprivation of a person of his property[60]. A writ of sequestration may be issued to enforce judgments or orders in accordance with SCPA Section 82 and Order XI Rules 8 and 9 of the JER. Unlike garnishee proceedings, which are directed against the garnishee and the money that belongs to the judgment debtor that is in his custody and control, the writ is directed against both movable and immovable property, including chose in action. (iv) The judgment summons is a process used to procure the committal of a judgment debtor[61]. Based on the writ of summons, issued at the request of the creditor, the debtor is required to appear and be questioned under oath with respect to his or her means[62]. Sections 55, 58, 60, and 65 of Part IV of the SCPA specifically address the use of summonses to enforce judgments. Failure to appear in Court to contest liability may be construed as an admission of liability and result in the issuance of a summons. In contrast, in foreclosure proceedings, failure to appear in Court after service of the order nisi causes the order to become absolute.

7.6. *Garnishee proceedings and stay of execution*[63]

A party who dissatisfied with a Court decision has the legal right to appeal it, especially if the decision was not made by the Supreme Court, which is the highest Court in the nation[64]. In this regard, after filing an appeal to challenge the decision, a petition for a stay of execution of the appealed decision is usually filed concurrently in order to safeguard the appellant's interests. This is because the appeal does not always automatically operate to stay the execution of the judgment[65]. A stay of execution is just a Court's decision to delay, halt, or suspend its judgment. A stay of execution's main purpose is to protect the suit's subject matter, prevent a *fait accompli* from being imposed on the appellate Court, and prevent a scenario in which a party that prevails on appeal creates a pyrrhic victory after the appeal's subject matter has been exhausted[66].

In SPDC Nigeria Limited v. Amadi & Ors[67], the Supreme Court, capturing this point succinctly enthused as follows: «A stay of execution stops temporarily the beneficiary of the judgment from enjoying the fruits of the judgment while the appeal is being heard. It is usually granted before the hearing of the appeal and stays in force right through the hearing of the appeal. The aim being to protect the res from destruction, thereby avoiding a situation where the Court hearing the appeal is presented with a fait accompli»[68].

The question is whether garnishee proceedings are distinct from other proceedings and, as such, a judgment creditor may still attempt to use garnishee proceedings to enforce the judgment even in the event that an application for a stay of execution is filed. This stance is supported by the argument that a garnishee proceeding is a different process from the customary modes of judgment execution listed in SCPA, Part III, Section 19[69]. In this regard, the majority opinion on this matter is the Court of Appeal's ruling in Purification Techniques Nig Ltd v. A.G. Lagos State, where His Lordship Galadima, JCA, wich held as follows on: «There is clear distinction between execution of judgments and other methods of enforcing judgments, such as garnishee proceedings. The distinction is brought out by the definition of "writ of execution" in Section 19 of the Sheriffs and Civil Process Act, Cap 407, Laws of the Federation 1990. Writ of execution includes writ of attachment and sale, writ of delivery, writ of possession and writ of sequestration. It excludes a garnishee proceedings»[70]. This distinction allowed His Lordship Galadima, JCA, to go further in holding that a judgment debtor can enforce the judgment even while an application to stay the execution of the underlying judgment is pending. To quote him: «Given the distinction that exists between execution and garnishee proceedings for the enforcement of a judgment, I do not think the existence of an application seeking for an order staying execution of a judgment does preclude a judgment creditor from seeking to use some other legal method to enforce judgment»[71]. It should be noted, however, that the same Court of Appeals questioned this position in WAEC & Ors v. Mrs Nkoyo Edet Nkang, in which Her Ladyship, Akaahs, JCA held that: «However I am still at a loss as to the reasonableness of a Court to deal with a pending application for stay of execution of the judgment and proceed to grant the *ex parte* garnishee application»[72].

In the most recent ruling of Nigerian Breweries v. Dumuje, where the Court deviated from earlier rulings, the rationale for the decision was one of the significant issues that came up for decision before the Court of Appeal. The Court disagreed with the fine distinction made between the different ways judgments are executed and garnishee proceedings, believing that garnishee proceedings are just another way judgments are executed[73].

The Court rejected the fine distinction that was being made between the different ways that judgments were executed and garnishee proceedings, concluding that the latter are merely additional ways in which judgments are executed. especially in terms of the targeted effects and consequences.

In light of this, it is entirely incorrect to attempt to allow a judgment creditor to continue enforcing a judgment against which a stay of execution has been requested through garnishee proceedings. Because, as the Supreme Court stated in Vaswani Trading Company v. Savalakh & Company, (*ut supra*) the law is against imposing an accomplished state of facts on the appellate Court. Instead, the Supreme Court has continued to uphold this attitude in all cases that have been decided to date. The following supports the belief that the position of the Court of Appeals is not perfectly adherent to the law. The definition of writ of execution found in Section 19 of the Sheriffs and Civil Process Act was incorrectly relied upon by the Court of Appeal in each of these cases when drawing a distinction between the execution of judgments and other means of enforcing judgments, such as garnishee proceedings. Unfortunately, it doesn't appear that this distinction is the goal of the provision.

The Court of Appeals' attempt to draw a distinction is fallacious on purpose, because the goal of all the different ways of enforcing judgments is the same. It all boils down to a procedure or method that the debtor uses to obtain the benefits of his judgment. When the process of enforcing a judgment is executed while an appeal and a motion for stay of execution are still pending, the appellate Court will undoubtedly be rendered completely powerless, depriving the debtor of his constitutional right to appeal.

Furthermore, it appears from the Court of Appeal's decisions that the terms "execution of judgment" and "enforcement of judgment" have somewhat different meanings. The word "enforcement" was given a wider meaning from the different rulings of the learned Justices, whereas the word execution was given a restricted meaning based on those modes contained in the definition of writ of execution in Section 19. The word "includes" in the definition of "writ of execution" in Section 19, above, indicates that the modes of enforcement that are mentioned are not all exhaustive.

The definition of "includes" according to Black's Law Dictionary, is "To contain as a part of something"[74]. In the case C.H.S. Co. Ltd. v. Migfo (Nig.) Ltd., Galadima J.S.C. provided the following definition of the word "includes": «The word 'includes' when used in a statute or written enactment can enlarge the scope of the subject matter it qualifies or tend to qualify, only to an extent permitted by law»[75]. Among other things, the interpretation of the word "includes" implies that garnishee proceedings may be included in a "writ of execution". The Judgments (Enforcement) Rules' Order VIII, Rule 7(1), which defines "writ of execution" as follows, supports this: «Execution against the garnishee under Section 86 of the Act shall be by a writ of execution in Form 27». It is safe to assume that garnishee proceedings will be included in the definition of "writ of execution" as per Order VIII, Rule 7(1) of the judgments Enforcement) Rules.

Furthermore, it appears from the Court of Appeal's decisions that the terms "execution of judgment" and "enforcement of judgment" have somewhat different meanings. The word "enforcement" was given a wider meaning from the different rulings of the learned Justices, whereas the word "execution" was given a restricted meaning based on those modes contained in the definition of "writ of execution" in Section 19. The decisions also suggest that, although a stay of execution application in progress will prevent a judgment creditor from "executing" his judgment while employing any of the methods of execution specified in Section 19's definition of "writ of execution", a stay of execution application will not prevent a judgment creditor from enforcing his judgment through the use of other methods of execution not specified in the aforementioned Section 19's definition of "writ of execution". As an example, it essentially means that garnishee proceedings – which are not covered by the aforementioned definition – cannot be stopped by requesting a stay of execution because they are not a means of carrying out a judgment[76].

As they are used interchangeably, the terms "execution" and "enforcement" actually have the same meaning when taken into appropriate consideration. Fidelis Nwadial defines execution of judgment as follows because of this: "By execution of a judgment is meant the enforcement of that judgment, that is, giving effect to it. It is the process whereby a judgment or order of a Court is enforced or given effect to according to law"[77].

It is important to observe that the laws, customs, and procedures controlling garnishee proceedings in Nigeria seem to be aligned with those in England. Chukwuma-Eneh, J.C.A. held as much in the Sokoto State Govt. v. Kamdex (Nig.) Ltd. case stating that: «Although, the law as well as practice and procedure governing garnishee proceeding locally appears codified as per the Sheriffs and Civil Process Act and the judgment (enforcement) Rules they are (*mutatis mutandis*) in tandem with the law and practice and procedure in England. It is for this that reference are constantly being made to England cases as regards the guiding principles in such matters; for instance, the case of Richardson v. Richardson (1927) AER (Reprint) 92»[78].

Based on the above decision, the English case of Re: Overseas Aviation Engineering (G. B.), Ltd., Lord Denning, M.R., on the meaning of "execution" stated thus: «In the light of what I said earlier in this judgment, I propose to approach that Section as it now stands without recourse to previous state of the law. So, approaching it, I am clearly of opinion that when a judgment creditor obtains a judgment charge on a specific land of a company, he thereby issues 'execution' against the land of the company»[79]. The Act doesn't define the term execution, but it is possible, in this regard, to draw on the definition contained in that precious ancient book of J. Rastell, Termes de la Ley: Certain difficult and Obscure Words And Terms Of The Common And Statute Laws Of This Realm, Now In Use, Expounded And Explained, New Jersey, 2012, where it says: «Execution is, where judgment is given in any action, that the plaintiff shall recover the land, debt, or damages, as the case is; and when any writ is awarded to put him in possession, or to do any other thing whereby the plaintiff should the better be satisfied his debts or damages, that is called a writ of execution; and when he hath the possession of the land, or is paid the debt or damages, or hath the body of the defendant awarded to prison, then he hath execution»[80].

It is crucial to remember at this point that filing an appeal is a requirement for being able to request a stay of execution. Therefore, the locus to file an appeal is essential in determining the competence to request a stay of execution. To ensure that the distinction between enforcement and execution with regard to the appropriate parties in garnishee proceedings is deemed legitimate, it is imperative to carefully consider the type of proceedings to be adopted[81]. Therefore, in garnishee order nisi proceedings, only the judgment creditor and garnishee, and not the judgment debtor, have the right to appeal and, consequently, to apply for a stay of execution. However, the judgment debtor also has the right to appeal and, consequently, the right to request a stay of execution in the event of garnishee order absolute proceedings, as previously mentioned. Section 109(1)[82], which affirms the judgment debtor's ability to request a stay of proceedings with regard to garnishee actions, serves as additional support for this. As a result, any decisions that contradict this stance ought to be regarded as having been made per incuriam. For example, in the previous case of Nitel Plc. v. I. C. I. C. (Directory Publishers) Ltd., the following was stated by His Lordship in the dictum of Omoleye J.C.A.: «having found as earlier on stated in this ruling that, the judgment debtor is a total stranger to a garnishee proceeding, especially after a garnishee order absolute has been made, it becomes manifestly clear that he, that is, the judgment debtor, cannot be heard on it except in a proper appeal»[83].

7.7. *Brief final considerations*

In light of what has been considered so far, it is possible to argue that the practice and procedure of foreclosure proceedings are a little-studied area of law, in fact much of the material on foreclosure proceedings is found in case law. Nonetheless, garnishment proceedings are becoming increasingly popular as a way to enforce money judgments, particularly against the government and its agencies. On the other hand, however, it is also useful to underline that the Nigerian legal system actually requires some interventions, especially with respect to some of the positions previously highlighted, such as the question of the oral examination of the debtor and the right to be heard during the garnishment proceedings. In this regard, a revision of the legal provisions may be necessary to expressly exclude both the oral examination and the right of hearing granted to the judgment debtor, as occurs for example in Section 109 of the Sheriffs and Civil Process Act. At the current state of jurisprudence, however, it appears that the provisions of the statute in question are more per *incuriam*.

7.8. *Cameroon*

7.8.1. *Brief overview of the discipline of Anglophone Cameroon*

Cameroon's legal system has been progressively influenced by local, religious and traditional law systems as well as colonial law.

Before the arrival of Europeans, Cameroonian laws were closely linked to culture and religion. Over time, a real work of Islamisation increasingly extended the power of this religion over community life until the imposition of Islamic law, which adapted well to past customary laws[84].

The arrival of colonizers in the 19th century changed the Cameroonian social framework: Europeans sought to change the collectivist culture in favour of a more individualist one and to impose a state-religion relationship more similar to that of the West. In order to achieve these goals, the colonizers slowly introduced land privatization and favored the development of Christianity. In order, they were followed by the Portuguese, the Germans and then the British and the French[85].

The Germans helped to profoundly change the local culture by changing the legal system. They succeeded in profoundly changing local values, especially through education, and soon introduced a double law: one for European settlers, which was based on German law, and one for the natives, which consisted mainly of imposing free labour on the settlers and banning all local rituals[86].

The British arrived in Cameroon in the early 1900s and were confronted with a strictly Islamic legal-political system, called *lamidate*, in which power was divided into territories and held by chiefs who exercised both political and religious power. After the First World War, they began to implant Common Law, which was initially directed only at the Westerners present there and coexisted with Islamic law, which was directed instead at the local natives[87].

As for the French, however, when they arrived in 1916, they found themselves in a territory deeply marked by the German presence. From 1945 Cameroon came under the protection of the United Nations and began to enjoy great autonomy, with a very small percentage of Europeans in charge of politics. During these years, the ferment for the country's independence began on the French side, which in 1958 was granted by the United Nations with French approval, leading to the birth of the Republic of Cameroon, to which the southern part, run by the British, was added from 1961 after a local referendum. On 21

February 1960, the first constitution of the new republic was approved and the first president was elected. The colonial works and the various forms of traditional and religious law that existed in the country before independence strongly influenced Cameroonian jurisdiction, creating a system that is a meeting, or perhaps a mixture, of all the various systems that have emerged over time[88].

Even today, the legislative system is based on Common Law, Civil Law and Customary Law with various influences from the various religious beliefs and group and, finally, from the various international agreements to which Cameroon is a party. Common Law is applied in the English-speaking areas and Civil Law is preponderant in the eight French-speaking regions, while customary law has a great influence only in the northern part, where it is the primary law, while in the rest of the country it is generally applied only to specific cases.

7.8.2. *Cameroon and OHADA*

Cameroon is part of the Organization for the Harmonization of business law in Africa (OHADA, in French *Organisation pour l'Harmonisation en Afrique du Droit des Affaires*) since December 1996. An intergovernmental body promoting legal integration is called the body for the Harmonization of Business Law in Africa, or OHADA for short. It was created by the Treaty of October 17, 1993, which was amended in Quebec, Canada, on October 17, 2008, and signed in Port Louis, Mauritius[89].

The Organization for the Harmonization of Business Law in Africa currently has seventeen member states: Benin, Burkina Faso, Cameroon, Central African Republic, Côte d'Ivoire, Congo, Comoros, Gabon, Guinea, Guinea Bissau, Equatorial Guinea, Mali, Niger, the Democratic Republic of the Congo (DRC), Senegal, Chad, and Togo[90]. The Organization is still open to any state that is not a member of the African Union or any state that is invited to join by consensus of the OHADA member states. The primary goal of the Treaty is to alleviate the judicial and legal instability that exists within member states[91].

Amidst a severe economic crisis and a sharp decline in investment in Africa, OHADA was established. One of the main reasons investors are distrustful has been recognized as legal and judicial uncertainty. Legal instability resulted from the rules controlling economic activities being outdated, inconsistent, and inaccessible, which made it impossible to decide which rule applied in a particular situation. The scenario was made worse by the deplorable conditions of the Courts, the insufficient judicial staff, the absence of corporate law training for stakeholders, the judicial backlog, and ethical dilemmas. In order to address the problem, OHADA was assigned the duty of simplifying business laws to ensure the judicial and legal stability of economic operations, with the goal of attracting investment and establishing a new progress horizon in Africa. To achieve this, OHADA: produces a simple, up-to-date, harmonized and suitable business laws for its Member States, in order to facilitate business activities. The law is contained in Uniform Acts which, once adopted, apply equally in all Member States. Ten Uniform Acts have been adopted so far; ensures that the harmonized law is applied with due diligence, under conditions that guarantee the legal security of economic activities. This objective is achieved by securing the legal settlement of business litigations and by promoting alternative methods of dispute resolution.

OHADA intervenes upstream by developing a set of rules contained in "Uniform Acts". Simplicity and modernity, the basic characteristics of these rules, help to simplify business. The effectiveness of these rules is ensured by their direct effect in all member states. these, once adopted by the Council of Ministers, can be invoked by any party in legal proceedings before the Courts of a member state, irrespective of the existence of a text in national law. The principle of direct effect thus guarantees the effectiveness and enforceability of the rules contained in the Uniform Acts[92]. OHADA also intervenes downstream through the establishment of a supranational Court, the Joint Court of Justice and Arbitration (CCJA), whose role is to ensure the common interpretation and application of the Treaty, Regulations and Uniform Acts. The CCJA thus performs three functions: advisory (it issues opinions on the interpretation of the OHADA Act), judicial (as a last resort, it hears appeals from the judgments of the Supreme Courts of the Member States concerning the application of the OHADA Act) and arbitration (it has an institutional arbitration centre originally regulated by the Arbitration Rules of 11 March 1999)[93]. On 23 and 24 November 2017, the Council of Ministers renewed its right to arbitration by adopting a new uniform law that comes to modernize the 1999 law. Under the Council's final communiqué, the adoption of this text revolutionizes the OHADA system for alternative dispute resolution and is likely to enhance the transparency, speed and efficiency of arbitration procedures in the OHADA space. The objective of this new text is to strengthen the confidence of local and foreign investors, and significantly improve the business climate in the OHADA area.

7.8.3. *OHADA's new procedure on debt recovery*

The injunction to pay and the injunction to deliver or return property are two straightforward legal processes that a creditor may use to force its debtor to fulfill its obligation. They are organized by the Uniform Act establishing simplified recovery procedures and measures of execution (UASRPME)[94].

Regarding measures of execution, the UA arranges the regulations regarding coercive execution and governs the different types of restraints: temporary seizures (of real estate, obligations, rights of shareholders, and movable property) and enforceable seizures (seizure and sale, garnishee, attachment of earnings, and attachment of immovable property)[95]. The Permanent Secretary was given permission by the OHADA Council of Ministers to evaluate the UASRPME's implementation in order to strengthen the laws governing debt collection and strong enforcement[96]. The easy, quick, and efficient recovery of debt by creditors throughout the 17 OHADA member states is one of the key tenets of the legal framework established by the Organization for the Harmonization of Business Law in Africa. To help achieve this goal, the OHADA Council of Ministers approved the updated Uniform Act Organizing Simplified Recovery Procedures and Enforcement Measures (the "Revised AUPRSVE") on October 17, 2023. The Uniform Act, which was published in the OHADA Official Gazette on November 15, 2023, repealed and replaced the earlier Uniform Act Organizing

Simplified Recovery Procedures and Enforcement Measures (1998), and went into effect on February 16, 2024.

Not retroactively, is the Revised AUPRSVE. This indicates that for enforcement actions and streamlined recovery processes started before to February 16, 2024, the provisions of the 1998 Uniform Act will still be valid. However, as of this date forward, recovery processes and executions must be carried out in accordance with the revised rules of the Revised AUPRSVE. According to article 5, the President of the competent Court has three days after being referred to issue an order. The same provision now mandates that the order for payment, which is not subject to the creditor's appeal, be justified in the case that the request is denied in whole or in part[97].

The amended article 10's objection period to a payment order has been shortened from 15 to 10 days after the order is served. The opposing party is now obliged to serve the order on the bailiff or the body in charge of the sale, in addition to the parties and the registry of the Court that issued the order (updated article 11). The amended article 12 states that within 15 days of the judge's appointment, the Court will name a judge who will oversee conciliation in chambers. Even if the order for payment contains the enforceable formula, it is replaced by the subsequent report in the event that conciliation produces a favorable result. The judge will only make a note of it and forward the matter to the next hearing if this attempt fails. The new article 12 gives the Court two months from the date of the initial hearing to rule on the opposition in this particular instance[98]. Articles 15 and 16 of the appellate Court regulations were simplified, lowering the appeal term from 30 to 15 days following the delivery of a conflicting judgment or the notice of the decision made by default.

The Revised AUPRSVE makes a distinction between nullities for substantive faults (new articles 28-3 and 28-4) and those for formal deficiencies (new articles 1-16) in essentially different Sections. Bailiffs and/or authorities authorized to serve either on paper or electronically may address (new article 1-5) or serve (new article 1-8) documents for the preservation or recovery of debts. Articles 1-8 through 1-10 provide specifics on the formalities for service. The beneficiaries of immunity from execution are made clearer by the Revised AUPRSVE, which limits them to juristic people subject to public law (article 30, paragraph 1).

It is expected that the OHADA member states' legal framework for debt recovery and enforcement would significantly improve as a result of the amended Uniform Act[99].

Enforcement of a Court decision may occasionally require tracing the judgment debtor's funds to a third party, despite the fact that usually the judgment creditor is obligated to trace and enforce the judgment and Court orders against the judgment debtor named in the action. In this scenario, the third party would not be involved in the decision-making process. A judgment cannot be executed or enforced against a party that was not a defendant in the case in which it was rendered, with the exception of this. It is unconstitutional to carry out a decision against an individual who was not a party to the action, as stated in the preamble of the Constitution of 1996 read in conjunction with Article 65. This is because it violates the individual's right to a fair hearing. Such a legal anomaly cannot exist in any civilized system. If the debtor refuses to comply with the judgment and turn over the money to the judgment creditor, the garnishee proceedings allow the judgment creditor to seize the recalcitrant judgment debtor's funds from a third party, such as a bank. The garnishee procedure is currently governed by articles 153-172 of Part IV Book II of the OHADA[100] Uniform Act, which organize the simplified recovery proceedings and measures of execution, despite the fact that common law Courts have long utilized this procedure. Though there are important distinctions between the two procedures, the garnishee is conceptually the same under both the common law and the OHADA dispensation. In particular, garnishment under OHADA as it has changed much of the common practice to the point of reduction will be examined here.

7.8.4. *Requirements for initiating garnishment proceedings*

Typically, a Court with the necessary authority must make a final decision before the garnishee procedure can be used. This principle is essential because, according to Article 3 of the Uniform Act, a judgment is an enforceable right that can be enforced through the OHADA dispensation. Article 153 of Part IV of Book II must be read in conjunction with this clause, which states that: «Any creditor in possession of a writ of execution in proof of a debt certain and due immediate payment may in order to secure payment, attach any sum of money owed the debtor by a third party subject to the special provisions relating to the attachment of earnings»[101].

In *Affair Société Afrocom-Ci of Citibank*, the highest Court of the OHADA legal system interpreted this expansive dispensation. Here, the CCJA made it very evident that in order for the proceedings to proceed, the judgment debtor's funds had to be in the possession of a third party and there had to be a judgment against him. To provide more clarity, the Court defined a third party as «a person who has in his keeping and independently, sums of money belonging to the debtor»[102]. According to the interpretation provided in the *Affair Société Afrocom case*, the rules of the Uniform Acts concerning the garnishee proceedings place individuals, banks, and other financial institutions carrying out bank functions in consideration of the third party (the garnishee) against whom the proceedings may be brought. Through the garnishee procedure, organizations such as post offices, saving banks, and corporative societies that hold judgment debtors' funds may be ordered to turn over the funds they are holding to the judgment creditor[103]. However, the process cannot be used to seize funds from a judgment debtor's employee. Article 153 of the Uniform Act makes it clear that garnishee proceedings may only be used for liquidated debts that are certain and past due. As a result, the Court of Appeal in Buea held in Camtel v. Pastel[104] that the garnishee procedure could only be used to enforce an award that was liquidated.

7.8.5. *The garnishment process*

According to common law, the judgment creditor must file a motion to detain the money if, following a thorough investigation, it is discovered that a bank or other third party is holding funds that belong to the judgment debtor. The motion must be supported by an affidavit. The motion adds the third party as a party. The OHADA statute and an odd executive practice directive from the minister of justice combine to form the present Anglophone Court procedure.

Despite these executive party directives, the minister of justice and keeper of the seals issued Circular No. 17 of 4/6/2002 and another of 12/7/2002, which established the requirement of serving a preliminary summons to the judgment debtor for payment before a debt can be attached. Despite these executive circulars, Part III of the Uniform Acts' article 92 mandates that the preliminary summons be served with payment, and this requirement must be strictly adhered to[105].

According to the same provision, the garnishee paperwork that is to be served to the debtor must include an account of the amounts claimed «in principle, cost, and accrued interest» along with a statement of the interest rate. Under the current OHADA dispensation, the process is far more technical than it was under the common law. In fact, as stated in Article 92, failure to comply with the prescribed requirements nullifies the proceedings, in contrast to common law, which prohibits technicalities from undermining the goals of substantial justice[106]. Article 157 of Part IV requires a bailiff, not a Court, to prepare and serve a writ of attachment on the third party[107].

The writ of attachment is deemed null and void by the *Cour Commune de Justice et d'Arbitrage* (CCJA) decision in Arrêt no. 007/2002[108] if it does not contain the items specified in Article 157. In actuality, the CCJA had overturned the Duala Court of Appeals' ruling permitting a writ of seizure that omitted to mention the accrued interest, which is presently set at 6% per Article 2 of Law no. 2004/015 of 21/4/2004. In contrast to common law procedures, the OHADA garnishee procedure only attaches the actual amount and incidental costs[109].

Citing both Ordinance no. 1364 of September 5, 2002, and Article 164 of the Uniform Act[110], Mba Acha has pointed out that if the amount is attached to a third party, it must be disclosed to the judgment debtor within eight days, failing which the garnishee process will be null and void. She accurately points out that a deed containing four elements must be used for disclosure. A copy of the writ racient and a bolded statement stating that (i) an opposition may be raised, (ii) such an opposition is admissible only if made within a month of the deed's notification or service, (iii) the date the period will expire, and (iv) the Court in which disputes may be resolved, must be attached to the deed[111].

The CCJA's extremely stringent interpretation of the aforementioned requirement in Société Banque Commerciale Du Niger v. Hamadi Ben Damma[112] is consistent with Mba Acha's perspective. In this case, the OHADA supreme Court ruled that a disclosure deed was invalid because it failed to include the expiration date and the Court's determination, as stated in items 3 and 4.

The Uniform Act's Article 156, which mandates that the third party disclose the amount it is holding for the judgment debtor, is also very important. If this requirement is not met, the third party will be accountable to the judgment creditor for the full amount owed, including damages[113].

7.8.6. *Temporary execution*

Temporary executions refer to the conditional application of a Court's ruling. This is a typically French legal concept that was created by civil law to lessen the severity of the autocratic practice of preventing the enforcement of pronouncements. Due to a purposeful strategy by an omnipotent executive to undermine the judiciary and subjugate the Courts, both have been introduced into Cameroon and extended to the Courts in the Anglophone regions. Discretionary provisional execution and provisional execution of right are the two categories of provisional execution. On the other hand, the mandatory provisional execution is one that is mandated by law in a statute as of right. Since a statute mandate that a particular judgment or ruling must be automatically enforced through a provisional order of execution, the judge in this case has no discretion[114].

Section 67 of the Civil Status Registration Ordinance 1981, which mandates the mandatory enforcement of alimony for a deceased wife and children in a judgment through a provisional order of execution, serves as a prime example for Anglophone Courts[115].

When a judge exercises his discretion to make an order in a case where the law expressly provides for it, this is known as discretionary provisional execution. An excellent example of this can be found in Law No. 92/008/14/8/92's article 3, which states as follows: «Notwithstanding the provisions of Section 2(1) above a Court seized of a matter may in case of a judgment delivered after full hearing or considered to have been delivered after full hearing order the provisional execution of the judgement regardless of an appeal»[116].

The following situations are listed in Article 3 as ones in which this discretion could be ordered: (i) «Matters relating to maintenance claims, contractual outstanding debt, eviction based on the land certificate which confers unchallenged rights or a written lease». (ii) «Compensation for damage resulting from acts causing bodily harm for covering justified expenses and costs incurred to meet emergency medical treatment in particular costs of transportation or transfer of person concerned, costs of drugs hospitalization and medical expenses». (iii) «In cases relating to undisputed salaries»[117].

In Yonta Maurice Ngosso v. Ouambo[118], Asuagbor CJ held that in cases where the justice of the case requires that the *status quo* be maintained in order to prevent the appeal from being rendered nugatory, an order of provisional execution will be reversed. In this case, the applicants, through counsel, requested a stay of execution or a modification of the terms set forth in the judgment no. LM/116/05-06. The application was made via motion on notice. In accordance with Section 3 (1) of Law No. 92/008 of August 14, 1992, as amended by Law No. 97/018 of July 8, 1997, the lower Court had ordered the defendants to give the plaintiff immediate possession, without regard to any appeal. This ruling addressed the matter from three angles: the application's admissibility, the Court's authority to modify the lower Court's ruling, and the viability of the stay request.

The learned Cj held that regarding the first issue «under our procedure where files are first brought to the Chief Justice for assignment and constitution of the panel» a stay applicant cannot know the date of the hearing in advance in order to notify the opposing party in accordance with the law's five-day deadline. Consequently, she came to the conclusion that «failure to notify the date of within 5 days cannot be attributed to eh applicant who should not be made to suffer as result of administrative bottlenecks». To put it plainly, this established a strong precedent that a party would not face consequences for the registry's mistakes in either the trial or appeals Courts. Regarding the second matter, the knowledgeable Cj denied the request to alter the terms stated in the ruling No. LM/ 116/05-06, citing that because «this Court is sitting a Court of original jurisdiction in matters of applications for stay of provisional execution, it cannot in this capacity arrogate to itself the powers of an appellate Court sitting on the substantive appeal» prior to determining that «we lack the competence to vary the contents of the orders of the lower Court». In essence, the Court of appeals agreed that the statute governing the execution of Court orders only gives the Court the authority to grant or deny a lower Court's request for a stay of a provisional execution order. Regarding the final matter, the Court noted that there was a query as to whether the order for provisional execution was in compliance with the law before coming to the following conclusion: «The question here is not concluding the respondent has land certificate but wis het the hand certificate confers unchallenged rights on its owner. At the lower Court, in their notice and grounds of appeal and before this Court applicants have always raised the crucial issue of vacant possession in other words challenged the rights of the owner to enter into possession. In order not to render the appeal nugatory, we shall refrain from examining this issue but having regards to its fundamental nature in the determination of the rights of parties; it is in the interest of justice that the parties maintain the status quo ante».

A labor Court may, in accordance with Section 146 of the Labor Code, direct the prompt execution of all or part of the awards made in a labor judgment, regardless of any petition for a stay of execution or appeal. This ruling, which might be issued on an as-needed basis, is commonly known as a "provisional execution" order[119]. While Section 146 lists the types of awards that are considered wages and unquestionably due, as previously said, legislation No. 92/008 of August 14, 1992, lays out the specifics of the rules governing the implementation of Court orders, including, naturally, labor actions.

According to Section 3 of this legislation, a Court that is handling a dispute involving the payment of salaries, wages, and leave allowances that are due may, in the event that a decision is delivered following a complete hearing or is deemed to have been delivered following a full hearing, order the judgment's provisional execution regardless of the outcome of an appeal. The conditions of Section 3 above must be strictly followed by the order of provisional execution in order for it to be deemed competent[120].

First of all, it is evident from a straightforward reading of this clause that an order of provisional execution cannot be granted till the case is decided on the merits. An award in a default judgment cannot be enforced by an order of provisional execution. Secondly, before an order for interim execution can be obtained, it must be proven that the award pertains to «salaries, wages and leave allowances due». The unassailable stance is that salaries, wages, and leave allowances that are not yet due cannot be ordered to be placed under provisional execution. A labor Court is undoubtedly not permitted to grant claims for future salary and earnings since, according to Section 3, such an award cannot be the subject of a temporary execution order[121].

The Supreme Court's ruling in University of Buea v. Mbua Teke Daniel[122] upheld this statutory position, ruling that the trial Court in Buea had found in favor of the plaintiff worker and awarded him 5.214.420 francs, among other amounts. This particular award was for the worker's wages for the four years of service for which the worker would have worked, had he been permitted to reach the retirement age of sixty years. The trial Court ordered provisional execution of this amount, regardless of any appeal, and the South West Court of Appeal confirmed the order of provisional execution. However, the Supreme Court ruled that the order of provisional execution «did not fall within the ambit of Section 3 of law No. 92/008/of 14 August 1992» given the circumstances of the case[123].

The Supreme Court cited the fact that these earnings were «in future, covering as they did the four years period between the date of his forceful retirement at age 56 and the statutory retirement age of 60 years» as justification for overturning both

Courts' rulings. This ruling makes it abundantly clear that an order for provisional execution can only be granted in cases where the award relates to wages, salaries, or allowances that are unquestionably due.

In addition to the requirement that wages become payable prior to the order's issuance, the guidelines outlined in Harp Distribution Services v. Nfonba B Joseph[124] also apply to provisional execution. These extra tenets were identified as follows by M. A. Mbeng JCA: (i) where the award is less than 600.00 FRS without a surety as a result of the 15/12/1993 Prime Ministerial Decree No. 93/754/PM; (ii) if the judgment debtor receives an award exceeding 600,000 FRS, they are required to provide a surety; (iii) if the award exceeds 600,000 FRS, the Court may still grant provisional execution as long as it is related to salaries and requirements and is not subject to dispute. However, the Court held firmly to the opinion that none of these things – medical costs, severance compensation, notice to pay, or allowance in lieu of income – were «part of a salary or a requirement or an accessory to a wage or salary»[125]. The Court postponed the temporary execution of the awards granted to cover these products on the grounds that they did not represent fresh salaries or an accessory[126].

However, the effect of the Uniform OHADA guidelines on the application for a stay was not mentioned. According to B. Martor et al., the enforcement measures established by the Uniform Act can be divided into two main categories: (a) measure execution, which allows a creditor to enforce a judgment against his debtor's assets, and (b) provisional measures, which allow a creditor to secure a judgment while waiting for a final ruling on the merits[127]. It is evident that the first scenario does not apply to labor decisions; however, the same cannot be said of the second scenario. Given that a labor judgment is «a Court decision which has been deemed enforceable» as described by Article 33 of the Uniform Acts, it is unquestionably an enforceable right[128].

Since this is the case, it must abide by the Uniform Acts, including the OHADA regulations regarding the stay of execution. The seizure of the judgment debtor's goods under Article

49 or the attachment of his finances in accordance with Article 163 and 104 of the Uniform Act may serve as the first step in the execution of a labor judgment[129].

According to a system established by Article 104, the judgment debtor has 15 days to object to the seizure of his assets or cash by filing an application, most likely with the Court that issued the enforcement order. In this process, the Court «may either order payment to be made to the creditor or refund of the funds to the debtor…». The penultimate language of Article 104 makes it clear that the Court has the authority to order the restoration of the confiscated assets to the judgment debtor in order to halt the execution of the judgment.

The OHADA Uniform Acts, not the customary appeals laws[130], are what cause the delay. Alternatively, the Court may order the debtor's cash to be kept by a third party while it stays a judgment under Article 104 until the enforcement actions are resolved.

There are no hard and fast rules controlling stay of enforcement under the new OHADA method since the subject is primarily left to the assessment of the judge who must nonetheless act carefully in the interest of[131]. Nonetheless, a wise use of this discretion must emphasize the need to ensure that no judgment creditor is arbitrarily denied the opportunity to profit from the decision, as would be required by the requirements of a just system of the administration of justice. On the other end of the spectrum, it is equally crucial to remember that an obviously erroneous ruling shouldn't be quickly put into effect[132].

It is apparent that OHADA regulations have made it harder for judgment creditors to enforce rulings that have been rendered in their favor. It needs to be condemned to this degree. for undermining the idea of justice even further for the entire society. This is especially true as the country's judicial system's whole appeal process applies to objections to enforcement as separate processes[133].

7.8.7. *Stay of execution*

Systems of democratic law People all throughout the world are aware that allowing Court rulings to become official is best for both the litigants and society as a whole. This idea was first stated in English in the Annot Lyle case of 1886, when Bowen L. J. decided that «a victorious plaintiff or party has a claim to the fruits of his judgment», but added that «the Courts would not make practice at the request of a failed litigant of depriving a successful one of the fruits of the decision in his favor»[134].

Put in another way, the aforementioned concept states that a judgment remains enforceable until it is revoked by a regular appellate Court ruling. It is uncommon and weird to prevent the ruling from having this impact before an appeal is heard and decided, as it deprives plaintiffs of any sense in the judicial system. Section 2(1) of Law No. 008/14/8/1992, however, stipulates that the filing of an appeal in civil proceedings stays the judgment appealed against in Cameroon, as has previously been mentioned.

Even after the bailiff has started carrying out the judgment, it is still possible to halt its implementation. It is established that, as of the enactment of Law No. 2007/001 on April 19, 2007[135], the president of the Court that rendered the decision or a judge nominated by him is the competent Court to decide any matter pertaining to challenges in carrying out a judgment, even though the circumstances under which this may be done may differ based on the particular facts. According to article 3 of this statute, a request to stay the ruling of the Court of first instance Kumba was denied as the appeals Court pronounced itself ill-equipped to consider the issue.

Notes

[1] Regarding African legal systems, see, A.N. ALLOT, *The Future of law in Africa*, London, 1960; P. BROWN, *Patterns of authority in west Africa,* in *Africa,* vol. XXI, no. 4, 1951; A. GAMBARO, R. SACCO, *Sistemi giuridici comparati,* Turin, 2018, p. 391 ss; P.F. GODINEC, *Le Droit African - evolution et sources*, Paris, 1968; Y. M. MOHAMED, A. KOPPEL, *Mixed legal systems, east and west*, New York, 2015; J. N. MOINE, *The place of customary law in modern Africa*, in *Annales de la Fac. de Droit du Cameroun*, no. 3, 1972; R. SACCO, *Il diritto africano*, (coll.) M. GUADAGNI, R. ALUFFI BECK-PECCOZ, L. CASTELLANI, Turin, 1995; R. J.W. SALACUSE, *An introduction to the law in French-speaking Africa, volume 1 - South of the Sahara*, Charlottesville, 1969. With a focus on the Nigerian legal system, see O. ACHIKE, *Nigerian law of contract*, Enugu, 1972; T.O. ELIAS, *The Nigerian legal system*, London, 1963;

C. Mwalimu, *The nigerian legal system: public law*, vol. 1, New York, 2005; *Id.*, *The Nigerian legal system: private law,* vol. 2, New York, 2005; A.M. Olong, *The Nigerian legal system: an introduction*, Lagos, 2007; A.E.W. Park, *Sources of Nigerian law*, London, 1963.

[2] See, O. Obaloluwa, *The Nigerian legal system I*, 2023. Available at: https://www.academia.edu/91390000/JIL_201_The_Nigerian_Legal_System_I?email_work_card=view-paper. See, also, for a comparative law overview, H.P. Glenn, *Comparative legal families and comparative legal traditions*, in R. Zimmermann, M. Reimann, *The Oxford handbook of comparative law*, Oxford, 2006, *passim*; R. Sacco, M. Guadagni, R. Aluffi Beck-Peccoz, L. Castellani, *Diritto africano*, in *Rev. int. dr. comp.*, vol. 49, no. 3, 1997.

[3] See *infra*, Sequestration, Judgment summons, and Writ of *fifa* are additional means of enforcing a judgment.

[4] F. Nwadialo, *Civil procedure in Nigeria*, ed. 2, Lagos, 2000, p. 1011. In a similar vein, the following is how Halsbury's Laws of England define garnishee in terms of orders: «Third party debt orders, formerly known as "garnishee orders", are one of the methods of enforcing a money judgment. Upon the application of the judgment creditor, the Court may make an order (a "final third-party debt order") requiring a third party to pay to the judgment creditor (1) the amount of any debt due or accruing due to the judgment debtor from the third party; or (2) as much of it as may be sufficient to satisfy the judgment debt and the judgment creditor's costs of the application. The Court will not make a final third-party debt order without first making an interim third-party debt order». Halsbury's Laws of England, ed. 4, vol. 17, no 1, United Kingdom, 2002, p. 128. In addition, the Black's Law Dictionary, defines garnishee proceeding as: «a statutory proceeding whereby a person's property, or credit in possession or under control of, or owing by, another are applied to payment of former debt to third person by proper statutory process against debtor and garnishee». B. Garner, *Black's law dictionary*, *cit.*, p. 612.

[5] In the case C.B.N. v. Auto Import Export, [2013] 2 NWLR (Pt. 1337) 80 p. 126 paras. E-F, the Honourable Justice Saulawa provided succinctly to definition of garnishment procedure: «Garnishee proceedings are special specie of process by which a judgment creditor may attach (or garnishee) debts due in satisfaction of the judgment debt. The debt owed by the third party to the judgment debtor, on being attached, shall ultimately be paid by him to the judgment creditor on the order of Court. Thus garnishee proceedings involve the attachment of debt due from a third party to the judgment debtor, and the use of the amount of that debt in liquidating the judgment debt. In garnishee proceedings, the third party indebted to the judgment debtor is called the garnishee. The judgment creditor, on the other hand, is referred to as the garnishor».

[6] Sheriff and Civil Process Act & Judgments (enforcement) Rules: Cap S6, *Laws of the federation of Nigeria*, 2004. Since its passage on June 1, 1945, the original Act has essentially not changed. The SCPA also contains a number of forms, specifically: (i) form 25 describes the contents of the affidavit in support of the attachment order; (ii) form 26 specifies the form of the attachment order;

and (iii) form 27 specifies the form of the writ of execution against the garnishee under Section 86 of the SCPA.

[7] E. Ojukwu, C. N. Ojukwu, *Introduction to civil procedure*, Nigeria, 2002, p. 261.

[8] See Federal Republic of Nigeria, *Official Gazette*, vol. 106, no. 72, Lagos, 2019. Available at: https://olumidebabalolalp.com/wp-content/uploads/2021/01/FHC-Rules-2019-Federal-High-Court-Civil-Procedure-Rules-2019-1.pdf.

[9] It is important to note that the provisions of Order 37 regulations are virtually identical to those of the SCPA.

[10] Briefly, a garnishee is a third party indebted to the judgment debtor. See STB Ltd. v. Contract Resources (Nig.) Ltd., [2001] 6 NWLR (Pt. 708) 115 at 123, paras. G-H.

[11] B. Garner, *cit.*, p. 721. See also Halsbury's laws of England, *cit.*, p. 18.

[12] See also the definition of the term's judgment creditor, judgment debtor, given in the case U. B. A. v. S. G. B. Ltd. [1996] 10 NWLR (Pt. 478) 381 at 389, paras. G-H.

[13] P. P. M. C. Ltd v. Delphi Pet. Inc. [2005] 8 NWLR (Pt. 928) 458 at 484, paras. D-F.

[14] Denton-West v. Muoma (2008) 6 NWLR (Pt. 1083) 418 at 442 D-E, Kekere-Ekun. It is important to remember, though, that the judgment debtor is typically not involved in the early stages of garnishee proceedings, which are limited to the judgment creditor and the garnishee.

[15] Purification Tech. (Nig.) Ltd. v. Attorney General of Lagos State, [2004] 9 NWLR (Pt. 879) 665 at 678 paras. E-G.

[16] Nitel Plc. v. I. C. I. C. (Directory Publishers) Ltd., [2009] 16 NWLR (Pt. 1167) 356 at 387, paras. F-G.

[17] C.B.N. v. Auto Import Export [2013] 2 NWLR (Pt. 1337) 80 at 128, paras. E-F.

[18] Section 85 of the Sheriffs and Civil Process Act, 1945, Ch. S6, LFN 2011, states: «Service of an order that a debt due or accruing to the judgment debtor shall be attached, or notice thereof to the garnishee, in such manner as the Court may direct, shall bind such debt in his hands». See, moreover, Sections 83, 86 and 90 of the Sheriffs and Civil Process Act where the words "debt due" or "amount due" has been used.

[19] Seabrook Estate Co., Ltd v. Ford, (1949) 2 All ER 94 at 95, para. E- G. See also the cases of C.B.N. v. Auto Import Export [2013] 2 NWLR (Pt. 1337) 80 at 126, paras. G-H and Webb v. Stenton (1883) 11 Q.B.D. 518; L.J.Q.B. 584.

[20] Consider the following case: can a judgment debtor's bank account loan amount be attached as debt owed to him to pay off a judgment debt? In this regard, see FIB Plc. v. Effiong [2010] 16 NWLR (Pt. 1218) 199, where the Court of Appeal determined that a judgment debtor's bank account balance, which is a loan from his bankers, cannot be considered a credit debt that qualifies for garnishment proceedings.

[21] The Nigerian Supreme Court provided a very useful definition of necessary parties in its locus classicus decision in Green v. Green [1987] 3 NWLR (Pt.

61) 480, p. 492-493. As stated by the Court: «Necessary parties are those who are not only interested in the subject matter of the proceedings but also who in their absence, the proceedings could not be fairly dealt with».

[22] Standard Trust Bank Ltd v Contract Resources Nig. Ltd (2001) 6 NWLR (Pt. 703) 115 at 123.

[23] In Denton-West v Muoma, (2008) 6 NWLR (Pt. 1083) 418 at 442, paras D-E., the Court of Appeal, per Kekere-Ekun, J.C.A. (as it then was), argued that: «There is no doubt that garnishee proceedings are separate proceedings between the judgment creditor and the person or body who has custody of the assets of the judgment debtor, even though it flows from the judgment that pronounced the debt owing». Regarding the possibility that the debtor can be heard in a garnishment proceeding, see also the position D. O. available at SSRN: https://ssrn.com/abstract=3186411.

[24] Similarly, also, the Court of Appeal in P.P.M.C. Ltd. v. Delphi Pet. Inc., [2005] 8 NWLR (Pt. 928) 458 at 484, paras C-G. per Salami, J.C.A., argued the following: «The reason for inability of the appellants to appeal against a garnishee order is for the simple fact that it is a product of proceedings between the judgment creditor and the person in possession of the assets of the judgment debtor. In the instant case, Guaranty Trust Bank is the garnishee or a person holding the assets of the judgment debtor, the appellants herein, while the respondent is the judgment creditor. A garnishee proceeding although incidental to the judgment pronouncing the debt owing, the appellants being judgment debtor are not necessary party to the said proceedings. The procedure whereby the judgment creditor obtains the order of the Court to attach from any person within the jurisdiction of the Court assets of judgment debtor to satisfy the judgment debt is described as attachment of debt and is one of the several methods of executing judgment. The proceedings for this separate and distinct action is between the respondent, herein and the Guaranty Trust Bank Plc., the garnishee which has not appealed the said decision. There is no substance respectfully in the submission of the learned counsel for appellants that the decision of Aderemi, J.C.A. In Re Diamond Bank Limited (2002) 17 NWLR (Pt. 795) 120 is *obiter dictum*. The issue in that decision was an existence or otherwise of an appeal and, the person competent to bring an appeal in a garnishee proceedings».

[25] Accordingly, the case of U. B. A. v. Ekanem [2010] 6 NWLR (Pt. 1190) 207 at 222, para. B-D., Orji-Abadua J.C.A. held thus: «A close scrutiny of the aforestated provisions reveals that a judgment debtor is merely a nominal party whose money in the custody of the garnishee is being recovered by the judgment creditor. He is not the one requested to appear before the Court to show cause why the order nisi should not be made absolute. It is only the garnishee, and, only the garnishee is expected to inform the Court if there is third party's interest in the said judgment debtor's money in its custody. So, in all ramifications, it is only the garnishee that is expected to react if the law was not properly followed or observed».

[26] Moreover, though, the majority of the rulings have been recognized as precedent in later rulings. For e.g., in the case Purification Tech. (Nig.) Ltd. v.

Attorney General of Lagos State [2004] 9 NWLR (Pt. 879) 665., the crux of the matter concerns the cancellation of the order nisi. Rather than being limited to this, the judgment passed, which has since been followed in all other cases, is as if to cover both the garnishment order nisi and the garnishment order absolute proceedings.

[27] U. B. A. v. Ekanem [2010] 6 NWLR (Pt. 1190) 207.

[28] Denton-West v. Muoma, [2008] 6 NWLR (Pt. 1083) 418. See. also, the reconstruction carried out by L. OPEYEMI, *Enforcing judgments through garnishee proceedings in Nigeria - Crossing the hurdle of inconsistent decisions,* Oxford, 2017, pp. 1-16. Available at: https://papers.ssrn.com/sol3/papers.cfm?abstract_id=3138097.

[29] P.P.M.C. Ltd. v. Delphi Pet. Inc., [2005] 8 NWLR (Pt. 928) 458.

[30] «The word 'jurisprudence of new wine in an old bottle' aptly refers to the inconsistent and conflicting decisions that have emanated from the Court of appeal on the position of the judgement debtor in garnishee proceedings [...]». It is important to note that different judges have made different rulings regarding the required parties in garnishee proceedings. A garnishee proceeding is purely between the garnishor and the garnishee, according to certain Court decisions, and the judgment debtor is not a party in the strict sense of the word. However, other Court decisions hold that the judgment debtor is an essential party in the garnishee proceeding. See M.O.I., NWABUOKU, K.O. MRABURE, *Garnishee proceeding and enforcement in Nigeria. The jurisprudence of a new wine in an old bottle,* in *U. J. P. P. L.,* vol. 5, no. 2, 2020, p. 390-402.

[31] See U. M. MGBEAHURU, *Interlocutory applications. Trial and appellate practice,* ed. 3, Lagos, 2019, pp. 463-481.

[32] Nwodo, J.C.A., held thus: «Under S. 83(2) Sheriffs and Civil Process Act, order nisi must be served with the originating process or any other order affecting the interest of the judgment debtor on him. Service of mandatory process is fundamental to the jurisdiction of the Court when there is a specific provision that a party is to be served in a specific manner and it is not observed the jurisdiction of Court against that party has not been invoked. Mohammed v. Mustapha (1993) 5 NWLR (Pt. 292) p. 22. The learned trial Judge erred when she held that the complaint of non-service is unmeritorious. The statutory provision on service is mandatory. Service of the order nisi on judgment debtor is a condition precedent to the jurisdiction of the Court to make an order absolute. Consequently Issue 1 is resolved in favour of the appellant». Wema Bank Plc. v. BrastemSterr (Nig.) Ltd. [2011] 6 NWLR (Pt. 1242) 58 at 80, paras A-D.

[33] See J. OTU ENYIA, *The law of banking in Nigeria: Principles, statutes and guidelines*, Lagos, 2018, p. 173; I. OLAWUNMI, *A judgment debtor in garnishee proceedings in Nigeria: to be seen or to be heard?*, 2021, pp. 1-21. Available at: https://ssrn.com/abstract=4012038; also, the case Nigeria Agip Oil Company Limited v Peter Ogini (2017) LPELR-42859.

[34] The jurisdiction of the Court (jurisdiction) in a garnishment proceeding is a matter of crucial importance. Indeed, if a Court were found not to have juris-

diction over a matter, even if conducted accordingly, the proceeding would be declared null and void. See A. WODI, *Jurisdiction in garnishee proceedings: The Nigerian position*, 2022, pp. 1-17. Available at: https://ssrn.com/abstract=4397466. In the case of Madukolu & Ors v. Nkemdilim, (1962) All NLR (Pt. 2) p. 581, the Supreme Court ruled that the following elements had to be met in order for a Court to have jurisdiction: «(a)the proper parties are before the Court; (b)the subject matter falls within the jurisdiction of the Court; (c)the composition of the Court as to members and qualifications; and (d)the suit is commenced by due process of law and upon fulfillment of any conditions precedent to assumption of jurisdiction». The legislation pertaining to garnishee proceedings attempts to address the question of jurisdiction by stating that even though the debt exceeds the Court's jurisdiction, garnishee proceedings may be brought before a magistrate's Court. See, Judgments (Enforcement) Rules, Order VIII, rule 1. The garnishee proceedings may be conducted in any Court where the judgment debtor could have sued the garnishee to recover the debt, or even in the same Court that delivered the judgment sought to be enforced. See, Judgments (Enforcement) Rules, Order VIII, rule 2 (a) and (b). The second leg of Order VIII rule 2 of the JER proposes a "debt recovery test". Since no specific Court is mentioned in the rules, there isn't a quick fix available. Thus, it might be challenging to apply the test, especially if the garnishee is the Federal Government or one of its Agencies, or a garnishee banker.

[35] The creditor must meet the following requirements to seize the debtor's funds held in the hands of another person: (i) provide the Name, address and occupation of the Judgement creditor, Judgement debtor and the Garnishee(s); (ii) present an existing Court judgment in its favour; (iii) show that the judgement sum remains unsatisfied/unpaid; (iv) clearly specify the amounts payable; (v) show that the judgment debtor carries on business, is employed or resides within the Court's jurisdiction. See, A. OLUWATOSIN, *The efficacy of garnishee proceedings in the enforcement of judgement debt*, pp. 1-8. Available at https://www.oakwoodlegalng.com/assets/files/Ganishee-Proceedings.pdf. (Consulted March 2024).

[36] Accordingly, by Section 83(l) of the act, a garnishee proceeding against a garnishee who is not a resident of the State from which the order nisi was issued is incompetent and subject to being dismissed. In other words, a bank or any other corporate entity existing in Lagos State, Nigeria, cannot be compelled to appear in Akwa Ibom State on the basis of an order nisi issued by a Court of that State if it has no establishment and proving the reason for the order in question should not be made final. C. N. OGBONNA, O. C. NWABACHILI, *A critical analysis of garnishee proceedings in Nigeria,* in *J. Comm. Prop. L.*, 2023, pp. 69-82.

[37] Judgments (Enforcement) Rules, Order VIII, rule 3(1)(b).

[38] I. J. GOLDFACE-IROKALIBE, *Law of banking Nigeria,* Lagos, 2007, p. 110; J. OTU ENYIA, *cit.,* p. 99. It should also be noted that the oral examination of the debtor should take place before or after the order nisi is issued. In practice, however, this aspect is often overlooked. The notification of the nisi order

established in Section 83(2) is a prerequisite of essential relevance for a Court to assume jurisdiction. In the Drexel Energy & 2 Ors case against Trans International Bank Ltd & 2 Ors, that failure to notify the original trial as required by the Rules of Court and the Sheriffs and Civil Process Act is a failure to comply that raises questions of fair trial, which is essential for the exercise of the Court's jurisdiction. Drexel Energy & 2 Ors v. Trans International Bank Ltd & 2 Ors (2008) 12 SC (Pt II) 240.

[39] Sheriffs and Civil Process Act, Section 85.

[40] Sheriffs and Civil Process Act, Section 92. See, for example, the FMBN Ltd. v. Desire Gallery Ltd. case, where the garnishee paid out money following the order nisi's service, the Court held that any money paid by the garnishee without the Court's permission following the order nisi's service is void under Section 92 SCPA. FMBN Ltd. v. Desire Gallery Ltd. (2004) 13 NWLR (Pt 891) 522, 541-542 [B-D]; [A-C]. Any payments made to the judgment debtor after the order nisi is served to the garnishee will be deemed void and the alleged debt will be attached. However, the attachment is null and void if the garnishee legitimately settles the debt with the judgment debtor prior to service, since there is no longer any debt to be attached. See A. OBI-OKOYE, *Essays on civil proceedings*, Anambra, 1997, p. 68.

[41] Judgments (Enforcement) Rules, Order VIII, rule 5(1). Notification represents a formality of absolute importance for the start and hearing of a trial. In fact, failure to notify the order nisi is not considered a mere irregularity but a fundamental defect which renders the proceedings null and void. In particular, the creditor must ensure that both the garnishee and the debtor are served with the order nisi as provided in Section 83(2) of the SCPA and Or. 8r. 4 of the JER otherwise risks rendering the proceedings null and void, since an absolute order obtained in absentia can be annulled for precisely these reasons. See A. WODI, *Garnishment law and practice in Nigeria, UK and U.S.,* Nigeria, 2023, p. 48 ss.

[42] Judgments (Enforcement) Rules, Order VIII, rule 5(2).

[43] Depending on whether the public officer is employed by the Federation or a State as a public servant, the term "appropriate officer" described the Attorney General of that state or the Attorney General of the Federation. See, Sheriffs and Civil Process Act, Section 84(3). When funds are under *custodia legis*, or in the custody of the Court, Court authorization is required. Section 84 is interpreted narrowly with respect to the definition of "public officer" just mentioned. In fact, under Article 84 of the SCPA, the Lagos Executive Development Board (LEDB), a corporation, was not considered a public officer, according to Barclays Bank, D.C.O. v. Baderinwa: Re L.E.D.B. (1962) 2 All NLR 731. See also CBN v. Hydro Air Pty Ltd (2014) 16 NWLR (Pt. 1434) 482, p. 521-522; and Ibrahim v. J.S.C. (1998) 14 NWLR (Pt 584) 1 (Iguh, JSC), cases in which the meaning of "public official" has been equated with that of "public department", encompassing any official or department entrusted with the performance of public functions. In opposition to CBN v. Njamenze (2015) 4 NWLR (Pt 1449) 276, in which the Court held that the CBN is not a public official for the purposes of foreclosure proceedings. Also,

the Court of Appeal provided a narrow definition of the term "public officer" in C.B.N. v. Interstella Comms. Ltd. (2015) 8 NWLR (Pt 1462) 456, ruling that the term "public officer" relates to the holders of the office as reflected only in Section 318(1) of the Federal Republic of Nigeria, 1999 (as amended). Section 84 of the Sheriffs and Civil Process Act defines a public officer as an individual who holds a public office. Although Central Bank of Nigeria officers are considered public officers, it is not appropriate to categorize them as such since the bank serves as a banker to the Federal Government of Nigeria regarding credit balances in the Federal Government of Nigeria's accounts. The issue of the requirement for consent by the Central Bank of Nigeria was explored taking into account the basic constitutional principles, such as: separation of powers, independence of the judiciary, access to the Court, due process, equality and the state by right. in this regard, please refer to the analysis of E. F. AGHEDO, *Attorney general's consent in garnishee proceedings versus costituzionalism: appraising the status of the central bank of Nigeria*, in *O.A.U.L.J.*, vol. 1-2, 2018, pp. 1-22. See, also, O. KEHINDE, *The attorney-general's consent in garnishee proceedings: Are view of the law,* in *Int. J. Comp. L. & Leg. Phil.*, vol. 1, no. 2, 2019, pp. 49-56; C. ONUZULIKE, *An analysis of the consent requirement of section 84 of the sheriff and civil process act 2004 and the judgment enforcement powers of Courts*, 2020. Available at: https://ssrn.com/abstract=3662960.

[44] Sheriffs and Civil Process Act., Section 87.

[45] Sheriffs and Civil Process Act, Section 88.

[46] E. UDIM, *Principles of garnishee proceedings in Nigeria*, Princeton, 2015, *passim.*

[47] See the case Diamond Bank Ltd. [2002] 17 NWLR (Pt. 795) 120 at 134, para. G.

[48] See G. NWAEZE, *Garnishee proceedings in Nigeria: the effects of order absolute,* 2022, pp. 1-7. Available at: http://dx.doi.org/10.2139/ssrn.4175690.

[49] A. BABALOLA, *Enforcement of judgments*, ed. 1, Nigeria, 2003, p. 106; T.A. NWAMARA, *The law of execution of judgments*, ed. 1, Nigeria, 2007, p. 258.

[50] A. OBI-OKOYE, *cit.,* p. 71.

[51] See, for instance, the case of Ifeanyichukwu Okonkwo v. Zenith Bank Plc.& CBN (Unreported Suit No. FHC/EN/CS/39/07) in which Zenith Bank failed to pay a judgment debt in an earlier case (Ifeanyichukwu Okonkwo v. Govt. Anambra State & Zenith Bank Plc, unreported Suit No. FHC/EN/CS/173/06) and became the Judgment Debtor with CBN as the garnishee in the instant case.

[52] See, *ex multis*, the case where the Court had to order an investigation to determine the ownership of the debt owed by Baderinwa to the LEDB in Barclays Bank DCO v. Baderinwa: re LEDB (1962) 2 All NLR 731 because it was alleged that the funds in the hands of the LEDB belonged to him jointly with three other members of his family.

[53] In this regard, in Moore v. Peachey (1892) 8 TLR 406 a bank had a customer named Frederick Peachey, while the garnishment order issued against the bank bore the name Henry Frederick Peachey. It was decided that the judgment cred-

itor, who mistakenly thought the order applied to the bank's customer, could not keep the money that the bank had paid him.

[54] See UBN Plc. v. Boney Marcus Ind. Ltd (2005) 13 NWLR (Pt 943) 654, 665 [A]; 667 [B-D].

[55] *In re*, Diamond Bank Ltd (2002) 17 NWLR (Pt 795) 120, 134-135 [G-A].

[56] Sheriffs and Civil Process Act, Form 48, *Notice of consequences of disobedience to order of Court.*

[57] Sheriffs and Civil Process Act, Form 49, *Notice to show cause why order of attachment should not be made.*

[58] Govt. of Gongola State v. Tukur (1989) 4 NWLR (Pt 117) 592.

[59] B. GARNER, *op. cit.*, p. 248.

[60] J. BURKE, *Osborn's concise law dictionary*, ed. 6, London, 1976, p. 303.

[61] *Ivi*, p. 187.

[62] J.B. SAUNDERS, *Words and phrases legally defined*, ed. 3, vol. 2, London, 1989, p. 496.

[63] Although a litigant has obtained a judgment in his favor in a garnishment proceeding, he may, however, encounter a number of difficulties relating to the enforcement of the judgment itself. Indeed, according to Afe Babalola: «Enforcement is the last stage of judicial process after the legal right, claim, or interest has been converted into a judgment or order which remains to be enforced. Therefore, a party who has successfully obtained a final order or signed judgment against another has only won the first round in the fight». A. BABALOLA, *cit*, p. 1. In this regard, see also the analysis carried out by D. NNAMDI, O. OLAOYE, A. ADEROGBA, O. OJOGBO, J. ONELE, *Efficacy of garnishee proceedings against closed banks/Nigeria deposit insurance corporation (NDIC)*, 2015, pp. 1-19. Available at: http://dx.doi.org/10.2139/ssrn.2651075.

[64] See Section 235 of the 1999 Constitution of the Federal Republic of Nigeria (as amended) which states that there is no right of appeal against a decision made by the Supreme Court to any other body or person.

[65] See, Section 18 of the Court of Appeal Act, Section 24 of the Supreme Court Act, Emir of Kano v. Agundi [2006] 2 NWLR (Pt. 965) 572; Josiah Comelius Ltd. & Ors. v. Chief Cornelius Okeke Ezenwa [1996] 4 NWLR (Pt. 443) 391.

[66] See Integration (Nig.) Ltd v. Zumaform (Nig.) Ltd [2014] 4 NWLR (Pt. 1398) 479, p. 494, para. D.; see also the case of Vaswani Trading Company v. Savalakh & Company (1972) 12 S.C 50 at 57, Lines 24-32. where Coker, J.S.C. held thus: «Whilst by virtue of the provisions of the Section, an appeal or the filing thereof could not *eo ipso* operate as stay of execution, clearly in practice, the position should be different where apart from filing an appeal, the prospective appellant also files an application in this Court, by which a stay of execution of the same judgment is sought. In such circumstances, a general appraisal of the whole situation is absolutely necessary and it is most desirable that the Court should ensure that, at that stage of the proceedings, it is not possible for any party to present it with a fait accompli». Similarly, Thomas, J.C.A. concurred with the lead judgment in Julius Berger (Nig.) Plc. v. T. R. Comm. Bank [2007] 1 NWLR (Pt. 1016) 540 at 549, paras. B-C., but held as

follows: «Once a notice of appeal is filed and served on the other party and the lower Court, especially in the instant appeal where the applicant is challenging the judgment sum and has urged at the lower Court for stay of execution, it is a clear position that the appellate Court is now in total control of the matter, and the other parties and the lower Court are prohibited from tampering with the respondent».

[67] SPDC Nigeria Limited v. Amadi & Ors [2011] LPELR-3204(SC), p. 34, paras. A-F.

[68] See also the reasoning in Lingo (Nig.) Ltd. v. Nwodo [2004] 7 NWLR (Pt. 874) 30 to the effect that «The whole essence of granting a stay of execution is the preservation of the res. If the Court will allow a judgment debtor to be in possession of the res and retain its enjoyment, then the whole essence of stay of execution is defeated».

[69] Sheriffs and Civil Process Act., Part III, Section 19, entitled *Enforcement of judgments and orders executions and committals,* in the definition of writ execution «includes writ of attachment and sale, writ of delivery, writ of possession and writ of sequestration».

[70] Purification Techniques (Nig.) Ltd v. A.G. Lagos State [2004] 9 NWLR (Pt.879) 665, p. 678. In addition, in the case N.A.O.C. v. Ogini 147, [2011] 2 NWLR (Pt. 1230) 131 at 152-153 para-D-G., Owoade, J.C.A. approved the exact quotation above in and holds that a garnishment proceeding is *sui generis* proceeding, belonging to a separate class, and must be distinguished from other proceedings for the enforcement of judgments, such as those conducted by writ of execution. In the same way, in in U.B.A. Plc. v. Ekanem, *supra*, at 224, paras. C-E, Orji-Abadua, J.C.A. adopted the stance mentioned above and held the following: «Be that as it may, it cannot be overemphasized that there is a distinction between the enforcement of a judgment by a writ of execution, and by garnishee proceedings. In Purification Techniques (Nig) Ltd. v. Attorney General of Lagos State (2004) 9 NWLR (Pt. 879) p. 665 it was held that, the existence of an application seeking for an order of stay of execution of a judgment does not preclude a judgment creditor from seeking to use garnishee proceedings to enforce the judgment. It was further held that the contention of the respondent that the appellant was not entitled to enforce the judgment in its favour by garnishee proceeding because the respondent had filed an application for stay of execution is untenable». See also the case of Nitel Plc. v. I. C. I. C. (Directory Publishers) Ltd [2009] 16 NWLR (Pt. 1167) 356 at 388, para-D.

[71] See a similar decision of the Court of Appeal in Denton-West v. Muoma [2008] 6 NWLR (Pt. 1083) 418 where the Court held that «Garnishee proceedings are legitimate exercise of his right to employ auxiliary methods to enforce the judgment obtained in his favour and they are competent notwithstanding the pendency of a motion for stay of execution».

[72] WAEC & Ors v. Mrs Nkoyo Edet Nkang [2011] LPELR-5098 (CA).

[73] Nigerian Breweries Plc v. Dumuje [2016] 8 NWLR (Pt. 1515) 536.

[74] B. Garner, *op. cit*, p. 77.

[75] C.H.S. Co. Ltd. v. Migfo (Nig.) Ltd. [2012] 18 NWLR (Pt. 1333) 555 at 593,

paras. G-H. Also, in Uhunmwangho v. Okojie, [1989] 5 NWLR (Pt. 122) 471 at 490, para-D., Nnaemeka-Agu, J.S.C. defined the word 'include' as follows: «The word includes is of course used in order to enlarge the meaning of the words and phrases occurring in the body of the statute. It means that the types of orders contemplated must be construed as comprehending not only the three types of orders enumerated in the definition but also other similar orders». See also Mandara v. A-G., Federation [1984] N.S.C.C. Vol. 15, 221 at 233, lines 47-52.

[76] This distinction was further highlighted by the learned Justices of the Court of Appeal in Denton-West v. Muoma [2008] 6 NWLR (Pt. 1083) 418 at 443, para C-D., wherein Their Lordships denied the application to set «aside the Garnishee Order Nisi and further hearing of the garnishee proceedings by the lower Court while granting a stay of execution of the original judgment and all or any enforcement processes pending the determination of the appellant/applicant's appeal against the said judgment».

[77] F. NWADIALO, *cit.*, p. 965.

[78] See, Sokoto State Govt. v. Kamdex (Nig.) Ltd [2004] 9 NWLR (Pt. 878) 345 at 380, paras. F-G.

[79] Re: Overseas Aviation Engineering (G. B.), Ltd., [1962] 3 All E.R. 12 at 16, paras. D-I.

[80] J. RASTELL, *Termes de la ley: certain difficult and obscure words and terms of the common and statute laws of this realm, now in use, expounded and explained*, New Jersey, 2012.

[81] M. BANIRE, *Emerging issues in garnishee proceedings in Nigeria*, 2018. Available at: https://mabandassociates.com/emerging-issues-in-garnishee-proceedings-in-nigeria/#_ftnref92. (Consulted March 2024).

[82] Sheriffs and civil process act, Section 109(1).

[83] Nitel Plc. v. I. C. I. C. (Directory Publishers) Ltd [2009] 16 NWLR (Pt. 1167) 356 at 389-390, paras H-A.

[84] See, C.F. FISIY, *Colonial and religious influences on customary law: the Cameroonian experiences*, in *Africa: Riv. trim. studi doc. dell'Istituto Italiano per l'Africa e l'Oriente,* no. 2, 1988, pp. 262-275.

[85] See E.M.K. DISSAKE, *Language and legal proceedings. Analysing Courtroom discourse in Cameroon,* 2021, p. 10 ss.

[86] See, M.C. FOMBAD, *Managing legal diversity: Cameroonian bijuralism at a critical crossroad*, in V.P. VERNON, Y. M. MOHAMED, A. KOPPEL, *Mixed legal systems, east and west*, New York, 2015, pp. 101-119; N.N. RUBIN, *Cameroun: an african federation*, London, 1971; H.R. RUDIN, *The Germans in the Cameroons 1884-1913: a case study in modern imperialism*, New Haven, 1938, pp. 9-75.

[87] See M.C. FOMBAD, *Managing legal diversity, cit.*; C. ANYANGWE, *The Cameroonian judicial system,* Yaoundé, 1987.

[88] See D. E. GRADINIER, *Cameroon-United Nations challenge to French policy,* Oxford, 1963.

[89] Shortly after the declaration of war on 1 September 1939, the French government adopted, on 9 September 1939, a series of decrees and other acts by

which it prohibited (or at least subjected to public order restrictions) the export of capital, foreign exchange transactions and gold trading. The application of the provisions of these decrees was also extended to Overseas France (DOM) and the African and Asian colonies. Thus was created what would later become the "Franc Zone", *i.e.,* the set of former colonies that chose to adopt a common exchange rate system, regulated by common institutions within a single economic-monetary system. At the end of World War II, on 26 December 1945, the same day it ratified the Bretton Woods agreements, France created two new currencies, at that time stronger than the French franc itself, which was suffering from devaluation: the CFA franc (*franc des Colonies Françaises d'Afrique*) and the CFP franc (*franc des Colonies Françaises du Pacifique*). With particular reference to the African colonies, between 1954 and 1962 many of them gained independence from France. This renewed geopolitical context of the African continent did not lead to the disappearance of the "*franc zone*", but radically redefined its nature and structure. The new African states remained in the "*franc zone*" and the West African and Central African states retained their monetary union with each other, the West African Monetary Union (*Union monétaire ouest-africaine*) - UMOA - and the Central African Monetary Union (*Union monétaire de l'Afrique centrale*) - UMAC - respectively. The CFA franc consequently changed its name to franc de la *Communauté Financière Africaine* for the member states of the UMOA, and to franc de la *Coopération Financière en Afrique Centrale* for the member states of the UMAC. In addition, the two monetary unions each provided themselves with an issuing institution: the *Banque centrale des Etats de l'Afrique de l'Ouest* (BCEAO) and the *Banque des Etats de l'Afrique centrale* (BEAC). In the early 1970s, new monetary cooperation agreements were signed. The French presence on the boards of the BCEAO and the BEAC was reduced and the headquarters of the two institutions were moved to Africa: in 1977 the BCEAO moved to Dakar, Senegal, and the following year the BEAC to Yaoundé, Cameroon. In 1984, the UMAC extended its geographical perimeter with the accession of Equatorial Guinea (future signatory state of the OHADA Treaty) to the Union. It is in this common economic-monetary as well as political and cultural substratum that the foundations of the legal integration between the OHADA member states are laid. The project of progressive harmonisation of the droit des affaires en Afrique agreed upon by the Ministers of Finance of the "Franc Zone" at the Ouagadougou summit tended towards the creation of a legal zone favorable to business initiatives; In April 1991, it was decided to achieve this objective by, on the one hand, bringing closer together legal systems that are separate from each other but share a common language and currency and a similar colonial past (which directly influenced the legal tradition of the individual legal systems), and, on the other hand, improving the judicial system. In its almost twenty-five years of history, OHADA has adopted a number of Uniform Acts on collective proceedings for the assessment of liabilities, general commercial law, warranties, law of inland transportation of goods, law of commercial companies and economic interest groups, law of cooperative societies, simplified procedures for debt recovery and enforcement procedures, organization and harmonization of entity accounting, accounting and financial reporting (known by the acronym AUDCIF); plus the Uniform Act on Mediation and the Uniform Act on Arbitration adopted on 23 November 2017.

[90] See, https://www.ohada.com/l-ohada/presentation-de-l-ohada.html. (Last accessed 02 June 2024).

[91] For a detailed overview of OHADA's history, objectives and structure see S. Mancuso, *Diritto commerciale africano*, Naples, 2009. See, also, P. Meyer, *La sécurité juridique et judiciaire dans l'espace OHADA*, in *Penant*, vol. 116, no. 855, 2006.

[92] For an in-depth commentary on OHADA Uniform Acts, see S. Mancuso, *Diritto commerciale africano*, *cit.*, p. 65 ss.

[93] *Id.*, p. 38 ss.

[94] Date and place of adoption: April 10, 1998 in Libreville (Gabon), Date of publication in the OHADA Official Gazette: June 1st, 1998, Entry into force: August 31, 1998. The English translation of the Uniform Act on simplified debt collection procedures and enforcement proceedings is available at: https://www.droit-afrique.com/uploads/OHADA-Uniform-Act-1998-simplified-recovery-procedures.pdf. (Last accessed on 02 June 2024). Part II (Simplified procedure for delivery or restitution of specific personal property) of Book I of the UA is dedicated to the mentioned legal processes. On this topic, see also S. Mancuso, *Diritto commerciale africano*, *cit.*, p. 303 ss.

[95] Enforcement proceedings are regulated in Book II of the UA. See, also, S. Mancuso, *Diritto commerciale africano*, *cit.*, p. 311 ss.

[96] M.T.T. Tatsi, *The Uniform act on arbitration as a simplified debt recovery procedure within the OHADA Zone: A critical appraisal*, in *journal of corporate governance and international business Law*, vol. 4. no. 1, 2021. The article focuses on the cases of the streamlined debt recovery process for cash, products, and services that apply in Cameroon in light of national laws passed after the country's independence as well as local laws of regional and subregional political and economic communities. Emphasizing the novelties and benefits of the uniform acts under consideration, it aims to show how the uniform act on arbitration may be utilized as a streamlined mechanism for the recovery of contractual debts.

[97] The old article 5 simply stated that «Where, upon examination of the documents submitted, the petition appears to be wholly or partially well-founded, the President of the competent Court shall issue a mandatory injunction to pay the amount determined by him» and that «Where the President of the competent Court dismisses the petition in whole or in part his decision shall not be subject to appeal by the creditor. The creditor's only remedy shall be an ordinary civil claim».

[98] Prior to the amendment, article 12 stated that «The Court in which the opposition is filed, shall attempt conciliation. Where the conciliation succeeds, the President shall draw up a conciliation report which shall be signed by the parties. One copy thereof shall contain the executory formula. Where the conciliation fails, the Court shall immediately rule on the claim for recovery,

even in the absence of the debtor who filed the opposition and the Court's decision shall have the effect of a judgment delivered after adversary proceedings».

[99] T. ENAW, *Transnational harmonised Court practices: a critical assessment of the injunctive processes under the OHADA uniform act on simplified recovery procedures and measures of execution,* in TDM 5, 2018. Available at: WWW.TRANSNATIONAL-DISPUTE-MANAGEMENT.COM. (Last accessed 02 June 2024).

[100] M. S. TUMNDE, *Harmonization of business law in Cameroon: issues, challenges and prospects,* in *Tul. Eur. & Civ. L. F.*, vol. 25, 2010, pp. 119-137.

[101] Ohada Uniform Act, part IV, book II, Article 153.

[102] M. A. YANOU, *Practice and procedure in civil matters in the Courts of records in anglophone Cameroon,* Cameroon, 2015, p. 176.

[103] *Id.,* pp. 176-177.

[104] Camtel v. Pastel Suit No CASWP/48/2002.

[105] Ohada Uniform Act, part III, Ch. 1, Article 92 establish that: «The attachment shall be preceded by a preliminary summons to pay served on the debtor at least eight (8) days before the attachment and shall under pain of nullity contain; 1) a reference of the writ of execution by virtue of which the attachment exercise was carried out, with a separate detailed account of all the sums payable by way of the principal, costs and accrued interest, as well as an indication of the interest rate. 2) a summons to pay the debt within eight (8) days, failing which it shall be recovered by the forced sale of his movable property».

[106] *Ibid.*

[107] Ohada Uniform Act, part IV, Ch. I, Article 157: «The garnishor shall commence attachment through a writ served on the garnishee by the bailiff or process server. […]».

[108] Courte Commune de Justice et D'Arbitrage, Arrèt no. 007/2002 of the 21 March 2002. For a more detailed discussion about the aforementioned Court see E. ASSEPO ASSI, *La Cour commune de justice et d'arbitrage de l'OHADA: un troisième degré de jurisdiction?,* in *Rev. Int. Dr. Comp.*, 2005, pp. 943-955.

[109] M. A. YANOU, *cit.*, p. 178.

[110] Ohada Uniform Act, part IV, Ch. II, Article 164, provides that: «The garnishee shall make payment to the garnishor on presentation of a certificate from the registry to prove that no opposition was filed within one month following disclosure of the attachment, or on presentation of the enforceable decision of the Court dismissing the opposition. Payment may equally be made before the expiry of the time limit for opposition, where the debtor declares in writing that he is not opposed to the attachment».

[111] M. A. YANOU, *cit.*, p. 178.

[112] Société Banque Commerciale Du Niger v. Hamadi Ben Damma Arrêt n. 008/2004 of 26/2/2004.

[113] Ohada Uniform Act, part IV, Article 156 states that: «The garnishee shall be required to declare the extent of his obligations to the debtor to the garnishor. He shall also disclose any terms likely to affect his obligations, and where necessary any previous transfer of claims, assignment of debts or any prior attachments. He shall hand over any documents in proof thereof. The above

declaration and the handing over of the documents shall be done on the spot to the bailiff or process server or within five days of service of the act of attachment where same was not served personally on the party. The act of attachment shall make mention of any declaration made and any documents handed over on the spot. Any inexact, incomplete or late declaration shall engage the liability of the third-party debtor to pay the claim, without prejudice of an order to pay damages».

[114] M. A. YANOU, *cit.*, p. 179.

[115] The Civil Status Registration, Ordinance No. 81-02 of 29 June 1981, Article 67 states that: « (1) The President of the Republic may, for serious reasons, authorize the marriage of the two persons, one of whom is deceased, after the formalities stipulated in Article 53 et seq of the present Ordinance have been fulfilled. (2) The deceased spouse shall be represented at the registration of the marriage by his father, mother, brother, sister, relative in the ascending or descending line or by the customary head. Mention of the authorization by the President of the republic shall be made in the margin of the marriage certificate».

[116] Law no. 92/008 of 14 august 1992 relating to the enforcement of Court judgements.

[117] M. A. YANOU, *cit.*, p. 180.

[118] Yonta Maurice Ngosso v. Ouambo CASWP/21m/C/2007 Unreported.

[119] Labor Code, Article 146, states that: «The judgment may provisionally order immediate execution, notwithstanding any motion for a stay of execution of any appeal, with exemption from surety up to a sum to be fixed by a statutory instrument. In respect of amounts in excess, provisional execution may be ordered on condition that surety is furnished; but it may be ordered without such condition, and in any amount, notwithstanding a motion for stay or an appeal, in the case of wages and perquisites recognized as due and not in dispute». Available at: https://www.emploiservice.cm/en/candidat/detail_droits.php?p=23&at=1.

[120] Law no. 92/008 of 14 august 1992 relating to the enforcement of Court judgements.

[121] *Ibid.*

[122] University of Buea v. Mbua Teke Daniel Appeal No. 16/s/02-03.

[123] These were the opinions that served as the foundation for this choice. Refer to Justice Epuli's supplemental report, folio 6. However, the uppermost was deemed inadmissible as it was submitted outside the 15-day window for filing labor appeals.

[124] Harp Distribution Services v. Nfonba B Joseph Suit No BCA/1LM/2008 Unreported.

[125] The Court determined that house allowance, seniority bonus, and transportation allowance are perks, characterizing severance compensation and payment in place of notice as damages given to a rightful party in a lawsuit involving termination of employment. *Ibid.*

[126] *Ibid.*

[127] B. MARTOR, N. PILKINGTON, D. S. SELLERS, S. THOUVENOT, *Business law in*

Africa: Ohada and the harmonization process, London, 2002, p. 231.
[128] *Ivi*, p. 232.
[129] Ohada Uniform Act, artt. 49, 104, 163.
[130] About customary Courts see, G. SERTORIO, *L'applicazione del diritto consuetudinario nella regione delle Nigeria Occidentale con particolare riguardo alle Customary Courts*, in *Riv. trim. stud. doc. dell'Istituto italiano per l'Africa e l'Oriente,* no. 4, 1966, pp. 339-374.
[131] M. A. YANOU, *cit.*, pp. 185-186.
[132] *Ivi*, p.186.
[133] *Ibid.*
[134] Annot Lyle (1886) 11 P D 144.
[135] Law No. 2007/001 on April 19, 2007. Available at: http://197.159.3.34/index.php/en/instruments-and-laws/laws/233-law-n-2007-001-of-19-april-2007-to-institute-a-judge-in-charge-of-litigation-related-to-the-execution-of-judgements-and-lay-down-conditions-for-the-enforcement-in-cameroon-of-foreign-Court-decisions-public-acts-and-arbitral-awards.

8. Garnishment in Iran

8.1. *Introduction*

The institutional history of today's Iran appears very complex, being the result of a millennial evolution, often little known and misinterpreted by the Western observer. The basic issue is that the Islamic State is investigated and described using parameters, and sometimes stereotypes, that are purely Western, whereas this country represents a peculiar experience even with respect to the Arab world itself, being characterized by a multi-level and multi-polar social, political, institutional and religious system. It is therefore essential to outline at least a frame of reference within which to evaluate the affirmation of the modern State of Persia, which started from the will of the Safavid dynasty (1501-1722) to unite the Turkoman tribes of the region, reinforcing the sense of community identification above all through the adoption, as official religion, of Dodo-Deciman Shiism, thus clearly differentiating the new State from the Ottoman Empire, the largest Islamic empire of the time[1].

Iran's strategic geographic position was the object of the expansionist aims of Russia, for whom it constituted an essential alternative route to the Persian Gulf and the Indian Ocean bypassing the Ottoman Empire, and for England, for whom it represented an essential protective position for the "Indies Route". Thus, Moscow and London managed over time to carve out real enclaves in the north and south of the country respectively[2]. The Constitutional Revolution of the early 20th century brought ideas and strands of thought of Western origin into the Persian political community, including rationalist approaches close to contractualism, the offspring of the French Enlightenment and English liberalism, socialist thought, nationalism and parliamentarism, while from Russia came the socialist-radical component[3].

It was up to a special Constituent Assembly to approve the 1906 Constitution, a fundamental charter destined to become a model for many countries in the Arab world. Article 27 of the annex to the 1906 Constitution clearly stated on the separation of executive, legislative and legal forces that in the second paragraph of this article it was stated that: «Judicial and sentential force is established to identify rights and this force is specific in religious Courts in Shariah cases and justice cases in others». Iran's modern era effectively began with the end of the Qajar dynasty and the accession to the throne of Reza Shah Pahlevi. The evolution of the legal system in the era of Reza Shah's reign began with the appointment of a minister of justice by the name of Ali Akbar Davar who had completed his legal studies in Switzerland and had a career as a judge behind him and was much more open to European legal systems such as Switzerland, France and Germany and therefore proposed a law to parliament on 17/02/1927 in which the Court system was changed and the religious Courts were eliminated and merged into the normal Courts of justice[4].

Davar's appointment initiated a codification of laws in a form adopted by European countries such as France and Belgium[5].

The era of the reign of the Pahlevi ended with the Islamic revolution of 1979 with the leadership of Ayatollah Khomeini who founded the only country in the world with a constitution based on Shiite Islam. The reform policy inevitably clashed with the religious hierarchy, which saw its sphere of competence progressively shrinking due to new legislation on commercial, criminal and civil matters[6].

Of particular interest is the Civil Code, which was issued between 1928 and 1935 and amended several times. This Code is one of the few civil codes of an Islamic country that, while being closely anchored to the sources of Islamic law and observing the principles of *Shiite Imamite* law, inserts these religious sources within the modern logic of codification of a European matrix, combining them with the most advanced aspects found in the French code and other countries on the continent. From a substantive point of view, in fact, there are many convergences and parallels between the solutions of Roman law, especially Justinian law, the provisions of many European codes and the solutions provided by the Iranian Islamic code, especially in the area of obligations and contracts.

The current wording of the Iranian Civil Code derives from the amendments introduced following the 1979 Revolution, innovations made with the aim of adapting civil law to the cardinal principles of the Islamic Republic, whose Constitution in Article 4 provides that: «all laws of the State shall be in accordance with the precepts of Islam». In the 20th century, however, Iran was under British and Soviet occupation during the Second World War, a period of great instability[7].

Although the cultural influence of the mandating power was inevitable, no real awareness of common law was ever established, as was the case in the Indian subcontinent and Sudan. The law of the Mandate power, then, exerted its influence in a mediated, and therefore less rigorous, manner through Anglo Indian law, which, by trying to graft itself into a context already influenced by the Ottoman season and inclined to civil law, did not take root. Consequently, during the British Mandate, a version derived from Anglo-Indian law took the place of the former legislation[8].

8.2. *The legal system in Iran*

After the constitutional revolution in Iran, the first modern Iranian constitution in its history came into force. It provided for a parliament, a senate, the prime minister and the king, who was only supposed to rule and not govern and had more of a symbolic function. He began the codification and passing of various laws in parliament, the most important of which are the Civil, Criminal and Trade Codes. Due to the fact that most of the jurists of that time who sat on the legislative committees of the parliament or were university professors had studied at European universities, especially French, Swiss and Belgian universities, they had introduced the "Roman-Germanic" legal system and as such a direct effect one encounters actual translations made from the legislative codes of France, Belgium and Switzerland and this effect can also be found in the Constitution of that time. Although the Iranian legal system can be traced back to the Roman-Germanic family, the content of the laws is based on the rules of Shiite Islam, which itself has detailed laws on private law. After the Islamic revolution in 1979, a new constitution came into force that, while still taking into account the legal roots of the Roman-Germanic system, absolutely insists that all Iranian laws and codes approved for parliament must be laws with Shia Islamic content, and thus we have a kind of authoritative Islamic government that calls itself the Islamic Republic and has at the head of power the spiritual leader who possesses the highest legislative power in the country, even more than parliament itself[9].

Article 4 of the Constitution of the Islamic Republic of Iran provides: «All civil, criminal, financial, administrative, cultural, military, political etc. laws and legislations must be according to the norms of Islam. This principle includes all articles of the constitution and all other laws in force that such application will be evaluated through the religious members of the negahban (Senate) council». The legal organization in Iran after the Islamic revolution was established following Article 61 of the constitution, which states: «The function of judicial power is applied by the Courts, which should be established according to Islamic rules and should judge in cases and protect public rights and expand and apply justice and establish the limits set by God'. The Judges of the Courts are obliged to abstain from the application of state approvals and regulations that are against Islamic laws and regulations or are outside the authority of the executive force and any person may request the annulment of such in the Court of Administrative Justice».

And on the other hand, Article 3 of Civil Procedure states: «The judges of the Courts are obliged to abide by the laws in cases assigned to them and must render appropriate rulings and cease hostilities between the parties. If the rules are incomplete or contradictory, or there is no law regarding the matter, the judge must refer to authentic Islamic sources or Fatwa and valid legal principles that do not contradict the religious rules, and issue judgement, and may not with the excuse of silence of the law or imperfection, or contradiction of the laws, abstain from the case and issuing a verdict that will be criminally punished in this case. Clause - If the judge is a Mojtehed and finds the law illegal, the case will come to another Court of the same jurisdiction». Thus, in every case the judge must issue a verdict and the source of Law in Iran in the absence of law is Fatwa and social customs and habits.

The foundation of the Iranian legal system is Islamic jurisprudence, which is a civil law system. The three volumes and 1,335 articles that make up the Iranian Civil Code were adopted between 1928 and 1935, and its contents have only undergone minor revisions since then. The primary source of law used by Iranian Courts to ascertain the legal and economic rights of natural and legal people is the Civil Code. The rulings rendered by Iranian Courts are not enforceable as precedent by other Courts handling cases with comparable facts. Nonetheless, in extraordinary circumstances, the Supreme Court's General Board rulings in related cases set precedent that other Courts must abide by[10].

The Civil Procedure Code outlines the guidelines for proceedings that all Courts, including the Supreme Court, Revolutionary, Public, and Appeal Courts, must follow.

The judge has ultimate authority. In accordance with Islamic law, judges are all certified, and most, but not all, are members of the governing clergy. Iran's Courts include the Supreme Court, Appellate Courts, Courts of First Instance (public Courts with jurisdiction over most criminal and civil issues).

The Iranian legal system is notable for its excellent integration of Western and Islamic legal systems, drawing from both Islamic and Roman-German legal traditions[11]. Nonetheless, considering that Islamic law is far less evolved in process than in substance, the Court system is similar to and heavily influenced by the French system[12]. Because of this, the Iranian judicial system's framework is similar to that of European legal systems, making it recognizable to European audiences. Iran has a number of Courts and tribunals with the authority to hear various kinds and classifications of cases and allegations. The "Act on the Establishment of General and Revolution Courts" of 1994 is the legislative act that governs Court organization. The main judicial institutions under this Act will be normal Courts and a special Court known as the Revolution Court. However, additional laws have led to the establishment of several more Courts with the authority to hear particular kinds of cases.

Apart from the judicial Courts, there are other administrative Courts and tribunals that operate mainly as semi-judicial authorities, with the majority possessing exclusive authority.

8.3. *General Courts*

As its name implies, general Courts have the broadest authority to consider a variety of issues. In light of this, all civil, criminal, and business issues need to be heard in general Courts unless specific claims are required by law to be decided by special tribunals. The fact that general Courts are separated into criminal and civil branches, each with exclusive jurisdiction, is a crucial caveat. As a result, each kind is covered separately here[13].

8.3.1. *Civil Courts*

The offices of civil Courts are located in the majority of the cities in the Islamic Republic of Iran, and they serve the whole nation. Civil Courts are concentrated in a number of judicial buildings spread across the city's many districts in big cities like Tehran, the capital[14].

The majority of civil cases, including those involving real estate, contracts, and torts, can be heard by civil Courts. These Courts are notable for having the authority to decide business issues involving corporations, negotiable instruments, and bankruptcy. While a wide range of subjects are under the jurisdiction of civil Courts, conflicts involving more specialized matters are assigned to specialist branches in major cities[15].

Currently, disputes involving intellectual property, banking, and insurance matters and those related to judicial review of arbitral awards are adjudicated by specialized branches of civil Courts. It is to be noted that these branches maintain their general jurisdiction and are competent to hear other cases, if necessary. Currently, specialist divisions of civil Courts handle cases pertaining to intellectual property, banking, insurance, and judicial review of arbitral rulings. It should be mentioned that these branches continue to have universal jurisdiction and can, if needed, hear additional cases. It is important to remember that conflicts must be valued at least 200,000,000 IRR in order to be eligible for arbitration in civil Courts. Small claims magistrate Courts known as Dispute Resolution Committees (DRCs) must hear disputes below. Moreover, some real estate partition issues that are within the purview of the Property Registration General Office (PRGO) and lease disputes that are under the DRC's purview are not included from the jurisdiction of civil Courts[16].

8.3.2. *Appellate bodies*

Criminal and civil Courts' rulings, awards, and decrees are appealable. The Appellate Court and the Supreme Court are the two forums that are in responsibility of examining these Court rulings. The Iranian political system is monist in nature, in contrast to federal plans. Nonetheless, the nation is split up into 31 provinces, each of which has a restricted amount of administrative power. Each of these provinces has formed an appellate Court with authority over all of the province's family, criminal, civil, and Revolution Courts. The appellate Court has three seasoned judges in each of its branches. The appellate Court's rulings are final and enforceable against the parties. They are rendered by a simple majority[17].

8.3.3. *The Supreme Court*

The Iranian justice system's highest Court is the Supreme Court. The Supreme Court performs a number of duties. As the highest appellate authority, it makes sure that lower Courts follow relevant procedural standards when they issue judgments or make other judicial decisions. Additionally, it is the top authority overseeing the offices of prosecutors. Moreover, it is the legal jurisdiction for the prosecution of powerful government figures, such as the President. Appeals Court judgments and rulings are subject to a procedural review by the Supreme Court[18].

The matter is referred to a Court at the same hierarchical level each time the Supreme Court reverses a decision. Another duty assigned to the Supreme Court is to render judicial evaluations on retry requests. Furthermore, in cases when subordinate Courts' jurisdictions dispute, the determining body normally makes the final decision. An essential role of the Supreme Court is to integrate diverse rulings among the lower Courts. When contradictory rulings are made in cases that are similar to one another, a General Assembly of the Supreme Court's justices convenes and issues an opinion that lower Courts must follow in matters that fall under its purview. The efficiency and transparency of the Iranian legal system seem to have been generally strong, particularly at the top echelons of the Court hierarchy. Iranian Courts are somewhat more dependable at the appeal level, yet they may nevertheless save nasty surprises for the first instance. Furthermore, corruption cases can be reported and looked into, as Courts are often overseen by higher authorities. In Iran, the process of adjudication commences with the submission of a petition to an appropriate Court. The claimant may submit a petition with the Court office when the claim has been specified and the appropriate Court has been identified. The claimant may then pursue its claims until a final decision is issued and upheld[19].

8.4. *The definition of garnishment in Islamic jurisprudence*

The definition of garnishment has never been discussed in Islamic jurisprudence. According to jurisprudence, the claimant should be given what he claims if it cannot be refuted. This opinion may have been formed by scholars of this school of thought depending on their particular circumstances and in certain cases (such as when the defendant remains silent in response to the plaintiff's claim)[20].

Although some scholars believe that garnishment is against Islamic law, the mechanism in question is consistent with Islamic jurisprudential principles and does not conflict with any established legal principles. Three jurisprudential principles can generally be linked to the establishment of the concept of garnishment: (i) dominion principle; (ii) the judge is legal guardian for refuse; (iii) principle of no harm.

The dominion principle states that no illegal agent may prevent the owner from exercising dominion or control over their property or any related properties, and that the owner has the sole legal authority to occupy their properties.

Because possession and ownership are only recognized when they are consistent with Sharia law, the generalities of the dominion principle are occasionally broken by Islamic lawmakers and have been limited and conditioned. This is because Islam's Sharia law has not established the principles of dominion and possession based on the free will of humans, but rather on God's will. A clause that was added to the dominion principle limits possessory ownership in order to protect the rights of others. For example, it is against the law for someone to be bankrupt and for the mortgagor to take possession of the mortgagee's belongings when the mortgagee is denied their rights. It is also against the law for mentally ill or insane people to own property. As another restriction on possessory ownership to uphold creditors' rights, garnishment may be used. In order to protect the plaintiff's rights and implement "the principle of no harm", the judge may, therefore, disrupt the defendant's possessory ownership under legal circumstances and seize the owner's property. This is based on the idea that "the judge is the legal guardian for refuse"[21].

On the other hand, instead, the no-harm principle specifically prohibits causing harm to individuals.

The no-harm principle must be applied in garnishments, just as the judge must intervene in possessory ownership. This means that there will inevitably be a conflict between the no-harm and monarchy principles, with the no-harm principle taking precedence. The lawmakers have created the monarchy, so any harm caused should be balanced against the no-harm principle, and it should be made clear that the lawmaker is not endorsing the monarchy in this case because doing so would impose harm and increase the damage[22].

Inevitably, it should be noted that although garnishment was not foreseen in Islamic jurisprudence explicitly, it complies with the rules of jurisprudence and is implicitly confirmed by Islamic *Sharia*. It is impossible to foresee every law that will need to be created in order to modify the legal relationships amongst members of society at any given time. However, the extensive body of Islamic jurisprudence has established a foundation for the establishment of appropriate legal rules at each stage of social change by understanding the fundamental principles that are in line with human nature.

8.5. *The definition and nature of a garnishment order*

All of the above considered, the Iranian legislature has provided a mechanism by which to protect the rights of the creditor by ensuring that he or she obtains what is deduced in his or her claims, whether it is a sum of money or a specific measure, from the very beginning of the proceedings, without the need to wait for the enforcement phase.

In this way, the creditor is protected about the possibility of the debtor transferring his assets, making the Court action unsuccessful. This institution serves as a guarantee and is precisely known as garnishment. This provision intervenes to deal with those dilatory and depleting practices of the debtor's assets, preventing the defendant who decides to conceal his assets in order to evade the payment of debts, or in the event that he learns of the commencement of the proceedings by a proceeding creditor, he obstructs the natural outcome of the proceedings, implementing "colorable transactions"[23].

In this sense, a garnishment order is limited to the seizure or confiscation of the defendant's property, which while a highly effective measure, its obtaining is based on simplified formalities compared to normal cognitive procedures.

Before delving into the core of the issue, it is important to discuss the definition, linguistic ramifications, and substantive implications of a garnishment order. We will begin with a lexical and legal analysis in order to achieve this.

8.6. *Definition of the constituent elements of garnishment*

8.6.1. *The concept of securing through an order*

From an etymological point of view, the word *Qarar* (*i.e.*, Order) implies «stability, strengthening, determining and emphasizing»[24].

In another vocabulary, it stands for "unbreakable verdict". In other words, it concerns the Court's decision in adversarial trials that does not end the debate[25].

The term *Ta'amin* (*i.e.,* Securing) is derived from the root *Aman* which means «he who has sought shelter and is now safe»[26] and lexically speaking, it means to make safe, to preserve, to maintain trust, and to act truthfully.

Garnishment (*Ta'mine Qarar*)[27] is defined by the legislature as follows: «garnishment consists of confiscation of movable and immovable property» (Article 121 of the Law on Civil Procedure (hereinafter LCP).

According to common usage, garnishment implies «seizure (impound) of assets including movable or immovable property belonging to the debtor and sums due from third parties». Two types of attachment are mentioned in legal and jurisprudential texts to safeguard the rights of creditors in claiming their debts; these include "personal and objective titles"[28].

In personal guarantees, such as in sponsorship and personal surety cases, a third party is also responsible for the principal debtor's performance. The creditor has preemption rights over unsecured creditors in cases of objective guarantees, where the creditor has a real and objective right (*jus in re*) to a particular asset belonging to the creditor. From the perspective of the Iranian system, at first, personal guarantee was the norm; however, over time, it became common practice to entrust or deposit assets (movable or immovable) as collateral and pledge with creditors. In this way, objective guarantees took the place of personal guarantees: by resorting to this mechanism, creditors decreased the risks associated with a possible bankruptcy of the principal debtor but also of the sponsor or a guarantor, since they had the availability of the assets deposited with them[29].

In view of this description, it can be inferred that garnishment falls under the category of objective securities in the Iranian system.

8.6.2. *Relief (Sought)*

From a lexical point of view, the word relief in Persian is a past participle and means "that which is sought after or intended"[30] or "that which is desired"[31].

In the legal language, this term denotes the remedy sought, that is, it is made to coincide with the *petitum*[32] of the dispute. The expression *relief* is sometimes used in the same way as the term remedy, recalling the structure of English law, according to which every right also has a procedural action for its protection: a non-actionable right is a non-right[33].

The definition of garnishment is unanimously understood among jurists, who translate it into operational terms as a precautionary measure through which the plaintiff confiscates the object of the claim or its economic equivalent from among the assets owned by the defendant until the end of the trial. This act precludes the transfer of assets for the purpose of satisfying a credit claim[34].

According to the current law, (Article 108-129 LCP), a garnishment consists of a request filed by a beneficiary with the competent authority for the garnishment of property belonging to a defendant or property or sums owed to him by a third party or equivalent.

This request, in observance of the conditions on which the parties had agreed, is filed prior to the final judgment, in order to safeguard the object of the claim, inhibit its transfer, and facilitate its satisfaction when the time comes to enforce the judgment[35].

8.6.3. *Nature of garnishment order*

A trial Court's decision on a garnishment has the same executive force as a judgment while lacking two basic elements, namely (i) being relevant to the merits of the dispute and (ii) also having an intermediate character (Articles 299 LCP).

As such, and in view of the contraposition deducible from this article, and because a decision made on a garnishment application does not meet the aforementioned prerequisites, the doctrine qualifies the garnishment order as an order.

However, the legislature has repeatedly reaffirmed this interpretation and stressed that an attachment is regarded as an order (see, for example, LCP Articles 112, 115, 116, 117, 119, and 120).

That being the case, the doctrine questions the type of order to which a garnishment is attributable; in other words, should it be considered as a final, semi-final, or interlocutory order.

(i) Definitive orders are defined as those orders for which, once issued, the case file will not be on the agenda of the Court before which it is pending.

(ii) A semi-definitive order in turn means those decisions which, when granted, place the file in question in a state of dormancy but without being set aside or removed from the workload of that judicial body (Iranian doctrine refers to the case of an order concerning the lack of capacity of one of the parties to the case). Cases in which the file is transferred to another internal adjudicative board, rather than to another Court, also fall into this category. Typical cases in the latter category are orders deciding a plea of jurisdiction or jurisdiction.

(iii) Interlocutory orders are defined as those orders granted for the purpose of preparing the discussion of a case for the delivery of a final judgment. Orders of inspection, investigation, and oath could be listed among these mentioned interlocutory (preparatory) orders.

Given the initial description of the garnishment order, the latter does not fit neatly into any of the three categories just described. On the other hand, it is a collateral injunction issued on an *interim* basis. More specifically, the *raison d'être* of these orders is to safeguard the future rights of one of the litigants. In other words, because garnishment injunctions are granted to secure the plaintiff's rights, they should be classified as a security injunction of a provisional nature.

8.7. *Conditions for requesting a garnishment order*

The garnishment request is subject to observance of certain conditions of a general nature, which are equally applicable to any Court application. In addition, there are requirements of a specific nature that apply necessarily and exclusively to the measure under discussion here.

8.7.1. *Claimant's application*

The issuance of a garnishment order is subject to the plaintiff's request, and in the absence of the latter, this results in wrongdoing[36].

In the same way, it is considered wrongful for the Court to ignore such a request once it has been made[37].

According to Article 108 LCP, «Before submission of the application for the principal claim or concurrent therewith and until such time as a final judgment is yet to be rendered, the claimant has the discretion to request for security from the Court and the Court has to oblige […] ».

Technically, three moments can be distinguished for filing a garnishment order, namely:

- Application before institution of the proceedings;
- Application concurrent with the institution of the proceeding;
- Application after to institution of the proceedings.

In fact, the claimant will be able to apply to the Court for a garnishment order before submitting his main application to the Court, following when provided by Article 112 of the LCP. If the applicant for such an order does not file his or her main application within 10 days from the date of issuance of the order, the Court, upon request of the defendant, will cancel the order[38].

In addition, such an application could be filed at the same time as the main claim, and if so, the creditor could express his claim in the same application form in which he states his main and substantive claims[39].

Likewise, a certain amount of time elapses between the registration of an application until the hearing and the time when the judgment is rendered, potentially allowing the claimant the opportunity to seek an order, and that is until the final Court order is made[40].

Hence, an application for garnishment is admissible: (i) after the filing of the main application; (ii) while the proceedings are ongoing; (iii) and during the period when the final verdict is being prepared.

Moreover, this application could be filed either during hearings before a Court of first instance or at the appeal phase. One noteworthy point is that, such an act advanced in one of the three steps above does not require the filing of a formal petition. Obviously, as a general rule, to obtain an order valid for the purposes of the law, an application must be made to a judicial body; but the Iranian legislature provides a simplified procedure that exempts the proceeding party from following excessive formalities[41].

Article 108 LCP, on the one hand, refers to a garnishment application and, on the other hand, to the registration of a tracking number in the online database of judicial bodies, which does not always indicate the submission of an application. Consequently, before the system went digital, it was not necessary to file a garnishment application on designated forms in order for it to be registered with the Court clerk's office, and, in fact, there have been several instances where applications have been processed without having been written on the aforementioned forms. Currently, through specific desks operating online, which appear to be connected to the Court system, it is possible to file a garnishment claim; and although the practice of these offices is to provide for the drafting of a separate application to obtain a garnishment order, before the main application is granted, this formal requirement appears to be without merit.

8.7.2. *Legal standing and plaintiff's interest*

In accordance with Article 2 LCP: «no Court can entertain a dispute unless an individual(s) with interest therein asks for a hearing of that dispute according to law».

Also included in the legal provision just mentioned is the application for garnishment, whereby individuals can go to a Court and seek protection of their rights against another legal entity. The implementation of this right is carried out through a specific legal act that is known as "bringing a case"[42].

According to Article 2 LCP, a dispute could be considered only when the claimant(s)' interest in the matter is identified; and garnishment is no exception to this rule. Therefore, anyone wishing to apply for the issuance of such an order must demonstrate to the Court that he or she has an interest in the matter. Moreover, as for the concept of interest, lexically it means profit or gain, and indicates an active element of the relationship that is the opposite of loss and damage[43].

In legal terminology, however, interest means that if a claim made by the claimant is proven, the claimant would benefit. As such, standing for a writ of garnishment should, in principle, satisfy the characteristics of interest, namely (i) legitimacy, (ii) constancy, and (iii) immediacy. To this end, a plaintiff through a counterclaim or even a third-party intervener may make such a claim, if, however, other conditions will also be met: there is nothing, in fact, to prevent us from thinking that they, too, might have an interest such as the one described above. Nevertheless, it is clear from the wording of Article 114 that the legislature has recognized the possibility of making a claim even in cases where the claimant's interest has not yet accrued, by virtue of the exceptional legal nature of the institution of garnishment. The requirement for this condition to exist is such that: «the Court has to satisfy itself of the interest of a claimant before granting of a garnishment and consequently, if the documentation and evidence affixed to the application are in such a manner that a suspicion concerning lack of interest is possible, the Court must reject the application due to this reason and such a request must be repudiated»[44].

It is in light of this provision that the defendant has the right to oppose a request for garnishment, claiming the lack of interest of the claimant (*ex* Article 116 LCP).

In addition, in cases where a person other than the proponent (e.g., an attorney, guardian, or benefactor) brings such a claim before the Court, the Court must ascertain that the requirement of standing is satisfied. As a result, there should be no doubt as to who is representing the proponent in a dispute; in fact, the proper evidence must be attached to the pleadings that have been filed in order to establish the proponent's relationship with the petitioner (as an attorney, guardian, authorized signatory, *etc.*). For this reason (and because of the nature of *norma specialis*), in cases where there is uncertainty as to standing, the Court will dismiss the attachment order (Article 84(10) LCP), and similarly, if a Court grants an garnishment order without due consideration of the plaintiff's legal standing, the defendant will have the right to object to such an order within the time limit set forth in Article 116 of the LCP, and the Court, on review, may revoke the order issued (Article 118 LCP).

8.7.3. *The remedy's unconditional nature*

The remedy sought must be definite and enforceable, that is, its realization must not be contingent on the occurrence or non-occurrence of a future event. For in this case, immediate enforcement would not be possible.

A similar fate occurs in the case of a conditional right, that is, a right that will be effectively enforceable once an external (and yet to be realized) condition is fulfilled[45].

In other words, if the remedy sought is not unconditional, it will not be possible to apply for and obtain a garnishment order, even if the application filed by the plaintiff is supported by evidence of law, official or jurisdictional acts, or if the document underlying the application is likely to become ineffective due to the passage of time. Furthermore, even in these two prior cases – which tautologically require the claim to be unconditional and nondependent – it cannot be deduced from Article 114 LCP that they are exceptions to the requirement of unconditionality. The only exception is when Article 114 LCP's other requirements are satisfied, in which case the time limit is relaxed.

8.7.4. *Term for obtaining Relief Sought*

Another condition for remedy sought is that it be due and effective. The creditor cannot demand payment until the date of performance of an obligation or payment has passed.

In other words, where the time limit to qualify for relief sought has not elapsed, the element of interest is missing, which must exist from the time of the commencement of the dispute and remain throughout the dispute.

8.8. *Determination of the remedy*

A remedy must be definite and identifiable. A definite or specified asset is that which can be identified, separately from other assets, and such that it can be divided or held in undivided shares. Article 113 of the LCP establishes that: «a request for a garnishment order is granted only when the relief sought is clear or when it is a specific object». Determinability is, literally, the opposite of indeterminacy: the property must be measurable, otherwise it could not be seized or confiscated.

In the case where an asset appears as a whole it will be equally sizeable as long as it is distinguishable after indicating its number, weight, and quantity (e.g., 1,000 kilograms of wheat or 50 sheep)[46]. In cases where seizure was not possible, Article 123 prepares a solution by stipulating that: «if the relief sought is not a specific object or it is such but not sizable, the Court shall confiscate the monetary equivalent of that property from among the other assets owned by the defendant».

According to the provisions of Article 113 LCP, regarding the requirements of the determination of the remedy sought and the specificity of the object, some jurists believe that even the shares of an SPA could be considered as assets, since they are determined in their amount, can be disposed of and, therefore, could be subject to seizure.

The aforementioned issue has also been raised in doctrinal symposia, but the jurisprudential formant[47] in its majority argues that in this case, the claim filed by the plaintiff is neither determined nor provided by a specific object, rather representing a kind of faculty to dispose of the asset.

In conclusion, both views are not entirely convincing; for the authors, it is more reasonable to hold that, as a common rule, joint stock companies have assets separate from those of the shareholders and that, therefore, the latter cannot be subject to attachment for the debts of an individual shareholder[48].

8.9. *Effects of garnishment order*

Obtaining an attachment order implies a positive outcome, both for the applicant and for the Court system; at the same time, this generates critical issues for the defendant. Moreover, in legal terms, the adoption of such a measure result in a number of effects on the attached property, which will be examined below.

8.9.1. *Non-transferability of seized property*

The inability to transfer the property covered by the order is among the garnishment's most significant effects. The Iranian legislature has sanctioned the cancellation of transactions for any transfer made after the seizure; these transactions will not be legally enforceable[49].

In this context, Article 56 of the Law on the Execution of Civil Decrees specifies that: «any transfer, including definitive, provisional and through pledge which involves the seized property is null and void and without any force or effect». In addition, Article 57 of the same law states: «unless otherwise agreed to by the beneficiary, any and all contracts and/or promises regarding the seized asset are not binding after the seizure enters into effect».

It follows from the combination of the two provisions just cited that: (i) Article 56 considers null and void all transactions that transfer the title of the seized property, because such transactions are to the detriment of the seizure beneficiary and, moreover, are contrary to the *raison d'être* of the garnishment itself; (ii) Article 57, on the other hand, dwells on contracts and obligations that do not transfer the title, but only create rights for third parties, which if unfavorable to the seizure beneficiary, will not be binding (some examples of such transactions are: the right of easement, the right of exploitation or the use loan).

Regarding the non-transferability of the seized property, the view of the doctrinal formant is not uniform.

According to some authors, in fact: «Concerning the implementation, the provisions of Articles 663 to 665 of prior legislation prohibited the transfer of the seized property once such confiscation had been communicated to the debtor. In implementing official documents too, Article 71 of the Bylaw for Execution of Official Document entails the same content. In both cases, the debtor or the losing party's conduct is contravention to the afore-mentioned laws as they pass the property through various means to a third party. This transaction is non-binding and unauthorized and it could be rendered binding upon approval of the beneficiary»[50].

Other part of the doctrine, however, holds that: «after seizure, the title rights remain suspended and they continue to be so for the duration of the seizure, until a definite verdict is handed in. If the judgment is granted in favor of the defendant, seizure is repealed. Otherwise, this seizure for security transforms into an executive seizure and the title of assets is removed from the debtor. This final ruling does not create a right merely and just brings it to light. As such it is retroactive and the confiscated property will be hypothecated to the beneficiary from the seizure date»[51].

The latter position could, however, be subject to criticism because it views the transfer of ownership to the garnishment applicant as a mandatory act following the final judgment.

However, the issuance of an executive decree does not automatically transfer the ownership rights of the assets; an offer in line with the provisions of Articles 113-ff of the LCP will be required to transfer the property to the beneficiary.

In addition, if the object of the measure is an immovable property, duly registered, the transfer of ownership of the property will take place only with compliance with the relevant formalities (Article 22 of the Law on Registration). In particular, if the defendant transfers the property to a third party during the trial and a judgment is subsequently issued against him or the seizure is annulled for any reason, the doctrine questions whether or not such a transfer can be considered null and void.

In this regard, the previous legislation (Article 264) imposed a prohibition on the transfer of such assets but, at the same time, it could have been argued that if the seizure had been annulled, such transfer could have been considered enforceable and binding. Currently, however, taking into account (i) Article 126 of the LCP which states that the seizure of movable or immovable property must be carried out under the conditions set out in the Law on Implementation of Civil Decrees, and (ii) Article 39 of this act, any transaction on such property must be considered as binding. Any possible derogation could only be reviewed in the light of Article 663 of the Islamic Penal Code, which is directed at the offender.

A different interpretation has also been put forward, according to which in cases where a transaction relating to a seized property takes place and, for whatever reason, the order is subsequently revoked, the effects of that transaction must be considered valid[52].

That being said, «taken from the standpoint of Civil Procedure Law, a void transaction (in the civil law sense) is without any effect when its annulment is requested by a beneficiary from a competent authority and a final verdict is issued in this regard. The beneficiary under this scenario is primarily an individual to whose benefit an asset is seized, transferee is also could be counted as a beneficiary until such time as the property is confiscated. But whenever seizure is terminated for any cause, it must be concurred that none of the above individuals are beneficiaries in a dispute concerning the void transaction»[53].

In the situation just described, even if the transaction could be considered null and void, on the basis of civil law principles, there seems to be an impasse that makes it technically impossible to declare the contract null and void, since there is no beneficiary in such a case. In other words, the maxims of civil procedure would prevent the issuance of a deed of annulment for such a transaction, making it valid and hindering its revocation at this stage.

In support of the above, it could be argued that a clear manifestation of Article 56 of the Law on Implementation of Civil Decrees occurs only when an asset is transferred during an enforceable seizure (*i.e.,* when the seizure occurs following the issuance of a final judgment). Thus, if, as a result of garnishment, an asset is confiscated by virtue of an enforcement order, whereas it enjoys the protection afforded by Article 56, there is no doubt that that protection persists only for the duration of the garnishment.

As such, if the seizure is annulled, for whatever reason, the previous transaction on this property may still be null and void, because the rationale of Article 56, *i.e.,* the protection of the rights of the beneficiary of the garnishment, no longer exists. This hermeneutical reconstruction is also supported on the basis of substantive principles and maxims.

In particular, the seizure of property, whether as security or as an enforcement measure, does not nullify the ownership relationship between the owner of the asset and the latter; It only tends to limit the owner's imperium over that particular asset, acting as a barrier that precludes its transfer. Thus, even if an asset is placed under enforceable attachment after a final judgment has been issued and a transaction subsequently takes place on that property, and subsequently the attachment is annulled, that operation will not fall within the scope of Article 56 and will be binding, even if it was concluded at the time of confiscation.

8.9.2. *Establishment of a right of priority*

The ultimate goal of the garnishment application is to protect the rights of the applicant. The establishment of a right of priority in the garnishment guarantees the creditor, who first initiated the procedure to seize the debtor's property, a right of first refusal on the sums accrued from the sale of the seized property. This right can be examined in two distinct stages: (i) firstly, during the trial and until the final judgment is given; (ii) secondly, when the verdict has been rendered and it will be executed through a call for tenders and the proceeds of the confiscated property will be distributed.

First, the garnishment gives the claimant an objective right that has certain consequences for the debtor and other creditors. The applicant is protected from a transfer which is null or non-binding, pursuant to Articles 56 and 57 of the Law on the Implementation of Civil Decrees and Article 126 of the LCP[54]. That being so, as long as the defendant is still the owner of the property, he cannot transfer it without respecting the priority of the claimant of the garnishment deed; therefore, if another creditor wishes to seize the same confiscated property, will have to submit to the title of the first applicant. The attached debtor may deposit the sums equivalent to the value of the seized property in order to obtain its release, if these also include the costs of litigation and damages, directly to the bench of the competent Court: in this way, the assets subject to the lien will be immediately released (Article 55 of the LCP).

In the second case, when the judgment pronounced becomes final and enforced, the advantage of the person who has a garnishment right is considerable, especially in the event that the debtor's assets are not such as to be able to satisfy all the claims of the creditors: in this case, Article 148 (1) LCP provides that the creditor who has obtained a garnishment order in his favor, has a right of priority over the other applicants. However, it is possible that the content of Article 128 LCP is subject to derogations in special cases and priority is waived[55].

Article 128 provides: «in cases of bankruptcy, if the seized asset is a specific property and object of a claim by an applicant, that applicant shall enjoy precedence compared to the rest of creditors». The wording of this article in conjunction with Article 148 of the Law on Implementation of Civil Decrees, as it states that only in insolvency disputes, and only when the seized asset is a definite or specific object, does the priority mechanism apply. In other disputes, with the exception of bankruptcy (which does not fall within the scope of Article 128), it is not possible to establish a right of priority for the applicant. In fact, this is particularly evident because, in many cases, fictitious actions are brought and, in agreement with the defendant, the latter's assets are confiscated by means of a garnishment, using Article 148 and thus preventing the real creditors from obtaining the sums due to them.

All things considered, and with the new laws taken into consideration, it seems that the person who filed for the garnishment still has the upper hand over other creditors. Stated differently, it is not possible to interpret Article 128 as restricting the applicability of Article 148. Consequently, exclusivity with respect to precedence cannot be established solely in situations where the property in question is a particular asset and the dispute relates to bankruptcy. Indeed, Article 128 represents a limit to the extension of two judgments rendered by the Supreme Court which establish a uniform and, as such, non-restrictive practice of Article 148. One of these judgments' states that: «since in accordance to Article 58 of the Law Concerning Liquidation, there is a specific hierarchy for utilization of the seized assets for creditors, and this hierarchy needs to be respected. There is no limit or contingency for creditors who have sought garnishment from the property of the debtor. As a consequence, all creditors, except for the ones explicitly mentioned by Law, can use the confiscated assets and the text of Article 269 of the LCP (as ratified in 1939) does not entail any provision on differentiation and [...]»[56].

Similarly, in the event of the insolvency of an entrepreneur (disqualified from any commercial activity), if a judgment has been issued and enforced, concerning the debts of the entrepreneur, in favor of some of his creditors, all other enforcement actions and transfers that result in damage and prejudice to the other claimants, fall within the scope of Article 423 of the Commercial Code and are considered null and void.

It is evident that neither the beneficiaries of a bankruptcy judgment (judgment no. 561, dated 18/06/1991) nor the applicant for a garnishment (judgment of 09/01/1961) are regarded as having priority over other creditors by the Supreme Court when it issues rulings creating a uniform practice[57].

On the basis of the above, it appears that the wording of Article 128 of the LCP, which provides that in an insolvency dispute if the asset is a specific object, the garnishment claimant has a right of priority over the other creditors, was drafted to limit the operation of the Supreme Court's case-law. Therefore, the same provision does not have a repealing effect of Article 148. In addition, the omission of the provisions of the previous Article 269 in the new legislation is due to the fact that its content has in fact been reaffirmed in Article 148 of the Law on Implementation of Civil Decrees.

In view of the reference to the new legislation (Article 126) regarding the hierarchy of titles in the event of seizure in Article 148, the legislator only wanted to avoid redundancy and, therefore, this omission should not be interpreted as a deprivation of the right of priority for the applicant for a garnishment order.

The wording of Article 128 of the new law is specifically drafted in this way, as has been repeatedly stated, to grant a creditor who has seized a particular item from the debtor's assets a right of first refusal and to separate the issue from the two Supreme Court rulings previously discussed. Essentially, one of the most significant aspects of a garnishment order is that it preserves the applicant's right of priority over other creditors through the garnishment deed.

8.9.3. *Payment of sums due to the creditor of the seized property*

The ultimate intent of a writ of attachment is that the applicant can obtain what is due to him through a deed of disposal of the seized property. Of course, this is only achieved by issuing a final judgment in its favor; in this way, the garnishment order becomes an enforceable title.

Following the final decision and the fulfilment of the requirements listed in Articles 1, 3 and 49 of the Law on Implementation of Civil Decrees, the aforementioned change in the nature of the order occurs.

Depending on the type of property seized, the way in which the plaintiff can enforce his or her claim varies. Thus, if the plaintiff has provided a third-party attachment on a sum of money, the third party must deposit that sum with the Court against a receipt. The latter serves as proof of payment or satisfaction of a debt (Articles 88 and 89 of the Law on Implementation of Civil Decrees).

When the subject of the seizure is the salaries and benefits of the employees of a government, government-affiliated or private institution, the procedure for asserting one's rights is quite simple: the organization is notified of the request to freeze funds, and the head of the organization must deduct the designated amount and send it to the relevant authorities (Article 98 of the Law on the Implementation of Civil Decrees).

If the seized property is movable property, pursuant to Article 113 of the Law on Implementation of Civil Decrees, after an inventory has been drawn up and after agreement on the place and time of the sale between the parties to the lawsuit, it shall be sold through a bidding process observing the provisions of Articles 122-125 of the Law on Implementation of Civil Decrees, and from the proceeds generated the creditor shall obtain what is due to the creditor. In the event that the asset remains unsold, the winning party has the option of indicating an alternative asset and requesting its seizure, or it could accept the asset itself in satisfaction of its debt at the estimated price without recourse.

Another option is to request that the bidding process be held again, in which case the asset will then be sold at whatever price the buyer proposes (Article 131 of the Law on Implementation of Civil Decrees).

According to the foregoing, there are two ways to have one's claim satisfied when the seized property is movable: (i) sale of the property by tender and payment of the debt with the cash thus generated (Article 128 of the Law on Implementation of Civil Decrees); (ii) transfer of the property to the creditor, according to the appraised price, in lieu of payment of the debt owed (Article 131 of the Law on Implementation of Civil Decrees).

Finally, if the attached property is immovable in nature, the creditor's claim action follows the same path; the property will be sold and the amount will be paid to the plaintiff. If the real estate remains unsold, the claimant is entitled to receive title to the property, while taking into account the exception provided in Article 144 of the Law on Implementation of Civil Decrees[58].

8.10. *A comparison of garnishment and related institutions*

It should be noted that there are certain distinctions between garnishment order, on the one hand, and a notarial executive writ, an interim order and an executive seizure, on the other.

These differences concern: enforcement criteria, procedures, and legal implications.

8.10.1. *Garnishment and executive seizure*

Seizure is commonly understood as the prohibition of an act or measure otherwise considered permissible. In operational terms, through seizure a person's property is taken from his or her disposal[59].

In Persian, seizure means arrest, detention; in legal language, the purpose of seizure is to create an obstacle to the transfer of the object of an obligation or subject, promise or duty[60].

It will be vital to first examine the idea of property seizure in a garnishment order and the same act in a garnishment in order to identify and, consequently, compare these two institutions.

As previously stated, a garnishment is a preventative action that is carried out at the plaintiff's request via a Court-issued injunction.

Taking into account the above definition and others provided by the doctrine, it could be argued that the attachment of assets is precautionary in nature and is intended to temporarily preclude the transfer of assets by the defendant. In this way, the plaintiff's interest is safeguarded through the defendant's assets and any activity by the debtor on those assets is temporarily inhibited until the Court reaches a final decision.

In the event that the Court rejects the plaintiff's claim, the asset freeze will be lifted and the assets will be returned to the defendant, who will also have the option to claim damages under Article 120 of the LCP.

Executive seizure is the garnishment of a debtor's or losing party's assets through the relevant judicial bodies[61].

With the garnishment, the assets of the losing party are seized, forfeited, and put up for sale. The winning party in the lawsuit is then able to satisfy itself with the proceeds. Consequently, the issuance of an enforceable title, the passing of time, and a final judgment are prerequisites for an executive seizure.

In this regard, Article 49 of the Law on Implementation of Civil Decrees reads: «if the losing party to a dispute, does not abide by the content of the judgment within the timeline provided therein or does not enter into arrangements with the winning party, or does not furnish assets and no property belonging to him has been attached, then the winning side could make a request to the effect that property equal to the amount of judgment is seized from the assets owned by the other side». Therefore, the losing party has ten days to execute the judgment, which means they must either reach a mutual agreement with the other party or identify the assets that the creditor can use to satisfy its claims.

In addition, the other side may file a petition to seize the losing party's assets for a sum equal to the judgment's specified amount if none of these actions are taken.

If the defendant does not possess any assets, the plaintiff has the option, by law, to request an arrest order against the losing party.

Upon receipt of such a request, the Court, in compliance with Article 2 of the Law Concerning Financial Convictions, will issue an arrest record against the losing party, which will be held until payment is made or until his insolvency is proven.

If the plaintiff filed a petition for garnishment at the start of the case or during the trial, and if an order was issued resulting in the seizure of property, the successful party will receive the seized property if it is in currency, the proceedings are over and a decree of execution has been issued. If not, an expert's assessment of the seized property's value is obtained after the deadlines have passed, and the judicial auction process is started.

In accordance with the above considerations, the following points are noteworthy regarding a garnishment order and an executive seizure:

(i) The plaintiff has the right to apply for a writ of garnishment before the main one. However, seizure may be requested only after the trial and when the writ of execution has been served and the statutory time limits have elapsed.

(ii) To apply for a garnishment, it is sometimes necessary to deposit some sums of money with the procedure fund at the Court; but, to apply for an executive seizure, since the judgment is pending and the Court has already decided on the legitimacy of the plaintiff's claims, the deposit of sums as security is not necessary.

(iii) For enforcement of a garnishment order, in cases where no property is found or when the property named by the plaintiff belongs to a third party, detention of the defendant is not possible; detention is an option only when executive seizure proves futile.

(iv) The goal of garnishment is to prohibit the transfer of assets belonging to the defendant but, in the meantime, seizure is carried out in order to implement the final judgment.

In summary, there exist similarities between the garnishment order and the executive seizure resulting from the issuance of a final judgment condemning the defendant to deliver assets or pay sums due. In both cases, the assets covered by the two procedures are removed from the debtor's disposal. From this moment, the asset can be transferred to the winning party or it will be sold so that the plaintiff can receive the proceeds up to the amount established in the judgment.

8.10.2. *Garnishment and notarial executive writ*

In order to compare these two concepts, it is first necessary to make a definitional clarification of them.

Garnishment has been covered exhaustively before, so we will avoid repeating its constituent elements. As far as the notarial executive writ is concerned, first of all the meaning of executive writ must be clarified, then the concept of executive notarial writ will be outlined and finally, some points relating to the Law on Registration will be illustrated.

Dr. Jafari Langrudi defines writ as: «an official piece of document prepared in observation of detailed administrative formalities at a judicial organ. It entails an order, or content of an enforceable document or a specific decree, such as an enforcement writ for a binding official document and a tax executive order with municipal fees and the like. A notarial executive writ, is an enforcement issued by bureaus for registration of deeds and notary offices in observation of applicable rules and is a distinct concept from a Court-issued executive writ».

Article 92 of the Law on Registration of Deeds and Property states that: «the content of all official documents concerning sums due and other movable property are enforceable without any need of referral to Courts. The earlier provision excludes instances wherein the issue is a surrender of a movable object at the hand of a third party who claims title thereto".

Continuing the reading of Article 93 of the same law: «All official documentation concerning transactions of already registered estates are enforceable independently and without any need for judicial recourse». Official acts have the potential to be enforced with regard to monies owed and movable property. While is specifically excluded: «surrender of a movable object at the hand of a third party who claims title thereto». This exception concerns the ownership of an object and not that of the availability of a property for reasons such as rental, deposit and loan.

According to a decision by the Main Chamber of the Supreme Court establishing a uniform practice: «in light of the fact that the Judiciary is the general venue for legal recourse for disputes, thus except for those instances specified by law, all other disputes including conflicts related to official documents and enforceable instalment receipts could be heard before tribunals. The provision of Article 92 of the Law on Registration of Deeds and Properties indicating no need for a judicial recourse for implementation of the content of official documents relevant to sums due and other movable assets, is not in conflict with the right and discretion for bringing a case before Courts. Enforceability of those documents is a prerogative granted to these documents so that their proprietors act by any suitable means to vindicate their rights [...] »[62].

Having regard to Articles 92 and 93 and Article 15 of Regulation for registration of matrimony and divorce and paragraphs 3 e 4 of the Bylaw of Unification of Matrimony and Divorce and Article 1 and 245 of the Implementing Bylaw for Provisions of Official Documents, and the procedure for entertaining claims concerning execution process and Article 2 of the Law on Checks and Article 15 (as amended) of the Law on Interest-Free Banking an executive writ could be issued for the following documents: (i) official documents relating to sums due and movable property; (ii) official documents relating to registered immovable property; (iii) official documents relating to a lien and a rental object, whether or not registered; (iv) registered payment receipts; (v) official act of marriage; (vi) obligations assumed upon registration of marriage, divorce and revocation; (vii) cheques issued to banks; (viii) bank contracts concluded pursuant to the Law on Interest-Free Banking and un-official documents of persons receiving loans from Keshavarzi Bank; (ix) other cases listed in specific legislation, such as an affidavit notified under Article 10 bis of the Law on Ownership of Apartments (as amended in 1358)[63].

According to the definition of a notarial executive writ and the explanations given above, this kind of act is granted for official documents and similar acts, but the authorities issuing the official documents and the documents considered as such are different. The bodies authorized to grant such acts include: (i) notarial offices; (ii) marriage and divorce registration offices; (iii) bureau for Registration of Deeds. However, this does not mean that the beneficiary can turn to one of these bodies for a ruling.

The jurisdiction of each of those authorities is given by the classification designated for official acts; each institution may issue an act for a document it has registered[64]. Naturally, the content of a document registered with a notary office must be clear and immediately enforceable, without the need to initiate additional procedures, in order for the title of the document to be enforceable. Therefore, the issuance of a document to be reviewed before the Court is not possible: deputy to grant a notarial executive writ is a notary office or a registration unit[65].

For the married side and the commitment at the time of the transcription of the marriage and the divorce, the grantor is the office that has drawn up the deed, except of course if they are present in the deed of immovable property. Therefore, this type of writing cannot be issued as a result of an arbitral award or a Court award and the document must meet the requirements established by law.

Given the foregoing, the following distinctions between a notarial executive writ and a garnishment can be made: a) Garnishment is an institution through which the plaintiff may request a guarantee before presenting the principal application (at the same time or at any time) and before the final judgment. The attachment establishes the prohibition of a possible transfer of the defendant's assets.

On the other hand, a notarial executive writ has as its object the content of all official documents or those considered as such and these acts could be performed without the need for Court intervention; b) the judiciary shall be the competent authority to issue a garnishment whereas the competent body for the granting of a notarial executive writ shall be the registration office or a notary office, depending on the circumstances; c) there are cases in which an order for attachment is adopted following the deposit of sums with the Judiciary Fund but this hypothesis does not concern the notarial executive writs, because their object is an official or similar document already enforceable. Therefore, the synthetic differences indicated here show a certain autonomy between the two measures. Another noteworthy aspect is that, when it comes to official executive documents, it is enough to turn to the notary offices and the executive bureau of the Registration Organization and, consequently, recourse to the Courts appears to be a superfluous activity since these acts are already executable in themselves. However, if the beneficiary were to apply to the Court, his application would still have to be examined for acceptance by the designated Court, given the qualification of the judicial system as the general body of the dispute settlement State (as clarified by the aforementioned opinion of the Supreme Court). There is no unanimity in doctrine on the point, such as that of Dr. Katooziyan, who considers that, since there is no additional advantage obtainable by a passage through the Courts, the applicant's application should be rejected[66].

8.10.3. *Garnishment orders and Interim orders*

Garnishment Orders and *Interim* Orders have the following similarities:

(i) Both shall be of a timely nature and the Court must grant them even before the main application is made, if the conditions are met, as will be explained below.

(ii) They shall be temporary, that is, their object may not be the transfer of title to the plaintiff but may only be to seize the equivalent of the claim. However, both continue until the final judgment is issued.

(iii) The deposit of funds with the Judiciary is the condition for the granting of both. The amount of such deposit will be determined at the discretion of the tribunal if the subject matter of the main claim is not specified. Practice requires 15 to 20 percent of the relief sought in the main application.

(iv) The issue of a judgment in a Court of first instance shall not render ineffective any of these injunctions, which may remain in force before the higher Courts; both shall remain valid until the final verdict has been delivered.

(v) In order to obtain the issue of both orders, a summary examination shall be carried out on the substance of the main application, without an examination of the merits of the law underlying the request.

(vi) Another formality concerns the form and time limit for lodging the application: a) if the application is filed before the main application, it shall be made out on appropriate forms; b) if it is filed together with the main action, it shall be accompanied by the main action; c) in the event that it is requested to the Court after the trial has begun, it could be presented in writing or orally.

(vii) The grounds for exclusion are common to both orders and include: the removal of the cause of issue, the deposit by the defendant, the failure to submit the principal application within the prescribed time limits (10 and 20 days). Dismissal of the order on the basis of the defendant's objections, unsuccessful failure in the main proceedings, withdrawal of the application and withdrawal of the proceedings[67].

Nevertheless, in relation to the distinctive characteristics of the garnishment orders and the *interim* measures are as follows:

(i) The garnishment shall be issued in an unheard-of manner in part to the defendant, but the interim orders shall be adopted in his presence.

(ii)When issuing the attachment order, the Court may not seek security for any future damage if the matter falls under Article 108 (a, b, c) of the LCP. In contrast, the guarantee is mandatory following an interim order according to the provisions of Article 319 of the same law.

(iii) The protection provided for in the garnishment order shall be of a monetary nature, as provided for in Article 108(D) of the LCP; whereas other forms of financial sureties for an interim order shall also be considered permissible, based on the fact that the law does not pronounce on it.

(iv) In accordance with Article 112, if the foreclosure claimant fails to file an application for his principal claim within 10 days of the date on which the attachment was granted, the Court may revoke that order on application by the defendant. This period is extended to 20 days for the cancellation of an *interim* order.

(v) The respondent shall have the right to seek compensation for the damage resulting from the execution of an order for attachment which has given rise to it within 20 days of the judgment becoming final (Article 120 LCP); to do this, there is no need to open formal proceedings. However, in order to obtain such compensation, it is necessary to prove the amount thereof in the course of the proceedings in the case of a different protective measure (Article 324 LCP); in that case, however, the limitation period is one month from the date of delivery of the judgment.

(vi) According to the provisions of Article 113 of the LCP, garnishment concerns only the seizure of property; whereas interim orders may include an injunction to act or to refrain from carrying out an act, in addition to the confiscation of property (Article 316 of the LCP).

(vii) Article 108 of the LCP prohibits the granting of an attachment order, but under Article 315 of the same act, there is no obligation on the part of the Court to issue an interim order.

(viii) Article 116 of the LCP leaves open the possibility of opposition to the garnishment within ten days, while an interim order is not open to appeal.

(ix) Although the Court seized of the main claim is also the body competent to deal with interim orders, in cases where the subject matter of the interim order falls within the jurisdiction of another Court, the appellant shall apply to that Court for the order in question (Article 312 LCP). However, for foreclosure, jurisdiction always lies with the Court of the place where the object of the judicial action is located[68].

8.11. *Concluding observations*

Sometimes, the time between the filing of an application initiating the procedure and the delivery of a final judgment is considerably longer.

Therefore, the defendant could transfer its funds and assets, thereby precluding the execution of the judgment in favor of the winning party.

In addition, this interval of time can also open the way to the occurrence of vices, devaluations and deterioration of the goods discussed in the classroom; but to avoid these complications, the legislator has found a solution through a garnishment order.

Islamic jurisprudence (*Imamai*) does not explicitly provide for a similar institution, but in the light of the principles that justify it legally, as the principle of not harming and the principle that a competent public official could act against those who obstruct the exercise of a right, Muslims have been able to avail themselves of garrisons similar to relief sought.

Article 108 of the Law on Civil Procedure grants the claimant the right to request an act of attachment; this right can be exercised before the beginning of the procedure, at the same time or after the beginning of the process and until it is resumed.

In the event that the plaintiff decides to avail himself of the garnishment before submitting the main application, the latter, then, must be filed no later than ten days from the date on which the order will be issued in his favor.

As described above, it appears that the rationale behind this ten-day time limit laid down in Article 112 of the Act is that the legislator assumes that the claimant will pursue the substance of the dispute.

In addition, the abovementioned rule provides that the Court must grant or reject the application for attachment on the same day as the application is made; if this is not the case, the date of the decision will be considered as a benchmark for the 10-day period.

There are also requirements that must be met in order for a garnishment order to be issued. They are: (i) general requirements, such as the applicant's capacity, interest and the like; (ii) the specific requirements, which stipulate that the object of the attachment is clear and defined.

The Court will then issue an order, taking into account the preliminary provisions of Article 108 of the Law on Civil Procedure. If one or more of these circumstances are not met, the Court will dismiss the application.

In the countries where the islamic tradition is prevalent, civil and commercial topics have been translated at the codified level. Even now, the Islamic tradition plays a co-protagonist role in the legal system given the rising non-confessionalism of some areas of law, both from a diachronic standpoint and because it may offer an authoritative cover for the codicistic solutions that are implemented. In actuality, modern codes are the result of two processes that have solidified transpositions: first, Islamic law, which was embraced by all adherents of that faith during the Middle Ages due to its authority and effectiveness; second, Franchised Roman law's methods and answers. As the pioneer of this progression, the *Majalla* as a pivot for subsequent advancements. In fact, the Ottoman codification collects the core of Islamic tradition within a formal framework inspired by French design. Subsequently, this exoskeleton will be gradually reinforced by norms, this time of material provenance (mostly French), which came in various parts of the globe[69].

The Egyptian (1949) and Iraqi (1951) Civil Codes concretized the advocated idea of stimulating legal development by incorporating more advanced law, essentially European in its French declension, but without neglecting the indigenous "Islamic legal tradition". The circulation of these two examples was rampant, with the Iraqi text able to take root even in legal systems that had been subject to British jurisdiction, where the present codification was characterized by being governed by an example drawn from the Anglo-Indian experience, to which the regulation of extensive segments of law was delegated to the Muslim tradition, due to an operative implementation of jurisprudence that was not only *Sharia*[70].

In this phase of the codification process, «theory seems to give way to practice due to the inclusion in the codes and legislation of certain norms *praeter or contra ius islamicum* ... that intervene to regulate sectors [...] now widely established in almost all Islamic legal systems. Rules that make it possible, however, to mitigate, at least in part, the excessive distancing of commercial law from the rules of common law, which was witnessed during the first period»[71].

Islamic *fiqh* serves as the basis for the development of modern Islamic law, just like Roman law did for European law. Islamic *fiqh* does not lend itself to the modern day due to a flaw in the law itself, but rather to its inability to change throughout time. Stated differently, the jurists stopped modifying it to fit novel situations[72]. The need to adapt to trade trends are well known. The Islamic system was not releasable, especially in light of several of its clauses that deal with technical and economic issues without first being modified to meet the demands of contemporary society[73].

Notes

[1] After the ancient era came the Islamic era, which began with the invasion of Persia by the Arabs some 1400 years ago during the Nahavand War that ended the Sassanid dynasty that had ruled for 416 years, and this invasion and domination completely changed the Iranian legal system and the course of law. Islamic laws came into force with the utmost severity to such an extent that with the destruction of Iranian libraries and culture, the Persian language of that era was also lost and replaced with a Persian that is still used in Iran, which is a mixture of Arabic and Old Persian, and they imposed the Arabic script in place of the Sanskrit and Pahlavi and violated the equal rights between men and women that had existed before. See P. Holt, A. Lambton, B. Lewis, *The Cambridge history of Islam*, vol. 1A, *The central islamic lands from pre-islamic times to the first world war*, Cambridge, 1977.

[2] To give at least a minimal definition of Shia Islam, it is necessary to go back to 632, the date of the Prophet Muhammad's death. Starting from this moment, in fact, Islam was traversed by internal fragmentations and divisions, a reflection of the different currents of thought regarding the determination of the possible criterion for the succession to the leadership of the Islamic community: in the absence of a clear indication from the Prophet regarding the appointment of his successor, already denied at the time by the Shiites, recourse was made to the customary election expressed through the council of sages, *shūrā*, which was supposed to be a meeting place for the various interests between the parties. To the political diatribe over the succession of the Prophet Muhammad must be added that concerning the legitimacy of a religious authority claimed by the descendants of *'Alī*, considered by *Shi'ism* as the only ones to whom the title of *Imām* could be recognized. See, generally, F. Castro, *Il modello islamico*, ed. 2, G.M. Piccinelli (edited by), Turin, 2007.

[3] On the foreign influences, see I. M. Lapidus, *Storia delle società islamiche. I popoli musulmani*, vol. 3, Turin, 2000; T. J. Röder, *The separation of powers in Muslim countries. Historical and comparative perspectives*, in R. Groter, T. J. Röder, *Constitutionalism in Islamic countries. Between upheaval and continuity*, Oxford - New York, 2012, p. 326; L. De Grazia, *Costituzionalismo ed esperienze costituzionali in Iran*, in *Riv. AIC*, no. 2, 2015.

[4] F. Rescigno, *Le "Mille e una notte" del costituzionalismo iraniano. Metodo comparato, teocrazia islamica e diritti delle donne quali diritti universali*, in *Federalismi.it*, 2023, p. 4.

[5] *Id.*, p. 5.

[6] The secularization of the judicial system reached its climax in 1936, when the employment of clerical judges was abolished by a law that required a law

degree from the Faculty of Law in Tehran or a foreign university in order to exercise judicial power. L. De Grazia, *Il diritto islamico nel sistema delle fonti dell'ordinamento iraniano*, in *DPCE Online*, 2011, p. 309.

[7] See, generally, P. Petrilllo, *Iran*, Bologna, 2008. The book discusses the characteristics of the Iranian legal system, especially when compared to other legal systems, by drawing on the country's constitutional history. The relationship between the state and its citizens is shaped by the system of government, which was established after the revolution of 1979. This structure highlights certain unique aspects of the system, such as the President of the Republic's marginal role (which is emphasized by Western media) in comparison to the Supreme Leader and the Guardian Council. The nuclear problem, international relations, and the possibilities for Iranian society's growth - which depends on the quantity and diversity of intellectual ideas as well as the youth population - are given special consideration. See more in detail, M. Papa, *Introduzione al codice civile iraniano*, in *Iranian code civil*, R. MAURIELLO, (Italian translation edited by), Rome, 2015.

[8] F. Castro, *cit.*, pp. 141-142.

[9] F. Sabahi, *Storia dell'Iran*, Milan, 2006.

[10] A. Borroni, M. Firouzan., P. F. Giuggioli, M. Mapa, F. Periale, *Diritto commerciale iraniano*, Padua, 2023, p. 423.

[11] S. Abdollhossein, *Introduction to the science of law*, ed. 1, 2020, p. 187.

[12] N. Katouzian, *Introduction to the science of law*, Tehran, 2018, p 46.

[13] The Act Establishing General and Revolutionary Courts (6 July 1994) available at https://rc.majlis.ir/fa/law/show/90416. See also, the Act on Enforcement of Civil Court Decisions, (23 October 1977), available at: https://rc.majlis.ir/fa/law/show/97591.

[14] A. Shams, *Civil procedure; elementary course*, ed. 26, vol. 1, 2015, p. 138.

[15] A. Borroni, M. Firouzan., P. F. Giuggioli, M. Mapa, F. Periale, *cit.*, p. 435.

[16] E. Jahromi, E. Mostafa, *Civil Procedure*, ed. 1, vol. 2, 2018, p. 89.

[17] A. Borroni, M. Firouzan., P. F. Giuggioli, M. Mapa, F. Periale, *cit.*, p. 440.

[18] A. M. Amin, A. N. Hossein, *Assessing the position and competencies of the supreme Court and the Court of administrative justice*, in *New Research Admin. L. J.*, no. 1, 2016, p. 137.

[19] A. Borroni, M. Firouzan., P. F. Giuggioli, M. Mapa, F. Periale, *cit.*, p. 445.

[20] M. J. Jafari Langeroudi, *Law schools in Islam*, ed. 2, Tehran, 2001, p. 442.

[21] A. K. Haqani Dehkordi, *A jurisprudential review on garnishment*, Tehran, 2016, p. 115.

[22] S. M. Mousavi Bojnourdi, *Jurisprudential rules*, 1993, p. 69.

[23] A "colorable transaction" is defined as a «transaction which presents an appearance which does not correspond with the reality and is intended to conceal or to deceive». See, Osborn v Osborn, 102 Kan 890, 172, p. 23.

[24] A. A. Dehkhoda, *Dehkhoda dictionary*, no. 1, Tehran, 1993, p. 514.

[25] M. J. Jafari Langeroudi, *Extended law terminology*, 2007, p. 531.

[26] L. A. M. Ma'luf, *Translated by: Ahmad bandar Beigi*, Tehran, 2002, p. 35.

[27] As a preventive measure, garnishment is employed to take possession of the

defendant's assets (equivalent to what the plaintiff is claiming) until the trial is over and to render such assets non-transferable, allowing the plaintiff to collect his obligation. This legal act is not peculiar to Islamic jurisprudence; it has existed since ancient Persia and even earlier. According to legend, «in ancient Persian and a thousand years before that, the plaintiff could ask the Court for an immediate order to seize money or another kind of property with the same value (from the debtor) and keep it as a collateral until the trial is over». A. SHAMS, *Civil procedure rules*, ed. 6, vol. 3, 2006, p. 427.

[28] N. KATOOZIAN, *Definite contract*, Tehran, 2011, p. 396.

[29] S. S. SALEH, *Garnishment order*, in *Legal coll. J.,* no. 113, 1994, p. 265.

[30] M. MOEEN, *Persian dictionary*, Tehran, 1982, p. 265.

[31] A. A. DEHKHODA, *Glossary*, Tehran, 1994, p. 435.

[32] In the Italian civil procedural law, the *petitum* is the subject matter of the judicial claim; it constitutes (with the parties and the *causa petendi*) one of the identifying elements of the proposed action. It is customary to distinguish between (i) the immediate *petitum*, which is the measure that is sought from the Court (e.g., the judgment of conviction, attachment of property etc.); (ii) and the mediate *petitum*, which is the thing that is the subject of the claim, *i.e.,* the "good of life" that is sought from the debtor (payment of a sum of money, delivery of movable property etc.). In this regard, part of the doctrine, distinguishes between procedural *petitum* and substantive *petitum*. For further details see, Article 163 and 414 c.p.c.

[33] J. LANGRUDI, M. JAFAR, *Legal terminology*, Tehran, 1997, p. 502.

[34] M. SADRZADEH AFSHAR, *Code de procédure civile et commerciale*, Téhéran, 2006, p. 337.

[35] S. A. MUSAVI, *Prompt trial; garnishment orders*, ed. 2, vol. 1-2, 2021, p. 141.

[36] For a comparative analysis, it should be remembered that the Code of Criminal Procedure also provides for the possibility for criminal Courts to issue garnishment orders. In particular, Article 107 states that: «the plaintiff could ask for a guarantee that damages to his/her will be compensated. If there is acceptable evidence, the magistrate will issue a garnishment». Therefore, «if a garnishment issue seizes the defendant's properties, the magistrate will have to consider this issue in issuing a criminal garnishment». Article 108 of this law specifies the following regarding the provision of the property: «if what the plaintiff wants is not specific, or is specific but cannot be seized, the magistrate seizes its equivalent from other properties belonging to the accused». The garnishment order can only be executed after notification to the defendant, without prejudice to the 10-day period provided for the exercise of the right of objection. Pursuant to Article 109 of the Code of Criminal Procedure «garnishment order is executed according to the civil procedure rules on executing criminal convictions in the related Court».

Furthermore, as the authorities in charge of carrying out criminal convictions, the magistrate or the judge are the ones who must resolve issues related to execution.

[37] M. R. HOSSEINI, *The law on civil procedure in judicial precedent*, Tehran, 2002, p. 102.

[38] The 10-day window for pursuing the primary lawsuit in article 112 appears to arise from the legislator's assumption that the plaintiff will pursue the lawsuit, respond to the plaintiff's request the same day, and approve or disapprove a garnishment.
If not, he ought to have adhered to the core principle and begun the deadline on the day the garnishment was made. See the reconstruction provided by Z. N. Sani Abadi, M. Jafari Harandi, D. Dadashnejad, *A review on garnishments from legal and juridical perspectives,* in I.J.M.M.U., vol. 6, no. 1, 2019, pp. 956-967.

[39] M. Shrifi, A. Masud, *Conditions and instances of garnishment orders*, Tehran, 2018, p. 21.

[40] Otherwise, however, the issuance of a criminal garnishment depends on the presentation of logical reasons to the Court. In addition, the request for criminal garnishment cannot be filed before the lawsuit is filed. If, as previously noted, moreover, in civil garnishment the main suit must be filed with the Court within 10 days of the issuance of the garnishment, in criminal garnishment, on the other hand, according to Article 15 of the Rules of Criminal Procedure, the deadline for following a suit on damages resulting from the crime is before the end of the trial. It is, also, possible to capture further differences between the two types of proceedings, namely, before bringing a lawsuit in a civil case, a garnishment request ought to be properly documented. There must be a written request submitted with the lawsuit and during the trial. But in criminal cases, the garnishment request is adequate on its own; a verbal request is also acceptable. Whereas in civil cases the commission of a crime is not required, in criminal garnishments the damages must be the consequence of one. Article 108 of the Civil Procedure Rules states that in civil cases, where the lawsuit is based on an official document, property is being wasted, or commercial papers are being investigated, the issuance of a garnishment does not require the possibility of damage being inflicted, but in criminal cases, there is no requirement to cause damage at all. It's obvious why. In the event that the plaintiff files a case, the defendant has already wronged him or her, and in order to obtain damages, the plaintiff is requesting garnishment. In addition to the garnishment remaining in force, requiring him to deposit potential damages would constitute a further abuse consistent with the accused's offenses, and the plaintiff could decline to pursue the case further defendant and is requesting garnishment in order to accomplish their goal of receiving damages compensation. For further discussion see the differences and similarities highlighted by Z. N. Sani Abadi, M. Jafari Harandi, D. Dadashnejad, *A review on garnishments from legal and juridical perspectives, cit.*, p. 962 ss.

[41] A. Russo, S. A. Mousavi, *Funzioni e obiettivi del pignoramento nel diritto iraniani: un'analisi comparativa*, in A. Borroni, M. Firouzan, P. F. Giuggioli, M. Papa, F. Periale, *Il modello di common law*, Padua, 2023, p. 287.

[42] N. Katooziyan, *Definite contract*, Tehran, 2008, 73.

[43] M. Moeen, *cit.*, p. 256.

[44] A. SHAMS, *Security in a garnishment order*, in *J. L. R*, no. 16-17, 1996, p. 2.

[45] M. SADRZADEH AFSHAR, *Code de procédure civile et commerciale*, Tehran, 2006, p. 337.

[46] In this regard, it should be noted that, Article 126 of the civil procedure rules establishes that: «seizure of property, whether moveable or immoveable, creating an inventory and evaluating and preserving the seized properties and seizure of salaries and moveable properties that are given to a third party follow a sequence that has been predicted in the civil procedure rules». It is also presumed that the plaintiff may seek seizure of all property except that mentioned in Article 65 of the Rules of Civil Procedure, if he does not expressly claim it. Therefore, the assets specified by the above article are: (i) clothes and objects that are necessary for the losing party and his/her family; (ii) food and groceries necessary for one month; (iii) simple tools and equipment of farmers and workers; (iv) properties and objects are unseizable by specific laws (such as tools exclusive for farmers). In addition, according to article 61 of the rules governing the execution of legally binding official documents, the following assets and property are excluded from debt and will not be seized: (i) an appropriate house for the needs of the losing party and his/her spouse and children; (ii) clothes and objects that are extremely necessary for the losing party and his/her family; (iii) food and groceries for 3 months; (iv) work tools and equipment for workers and farmers that are required for making a living; (v) a vehicle appropriate for the needs of the committed party and his/her family; (vi) specific laws cannot seize other properties and objects. Along these lines, see Z. N. SANI ABADI, M. JAFARI HARANDI, D. DADASHNEJAD, *A Review on garnishments from legal and juridical perspectives, cit.*, p. 962.

[47] Formant theory, although unknown to Iranian law, is the basis of comparative study and methodology. First elaborated by Prof. Rodolfo Sacco, and appearing in the first edition of *Introduction to comparative Law*, it has since been revived countless times in other venues. Among them: A. GAMBARO, R. SACCO, *Sistemi giuridici comparati*, Turin, 2008; G. AJANI, D. FRANCAVILLA, B. PASA, *Diritto comparato. Lezioni e materiali*, Turin, 2018; R. SACCO, *Legal formants: a dynamic approach to comparative law (Installment I of II)*, in *The American journal of comparative law*, vol. 39, no. 1, 1991, pp. 1-34; R. SACCO, *Diversity and uniformity in the law*, in *The Am. J. Comp. L.*, vol. 49, no. 2, 2001, pp. 171-189; R. SACCO, *One hundred years of comparative law*, in *T. L. Rev.*, vol. 75, no. 4, 2001, pp. 1159-1176; R. SACCO, P. G. MONATERI, *Legal formants*, in *2 The new Palgrave dictionary of Economics and the Law*, 1998, p. 531.

[48] Juridical Symposia, *Issues relevant to civil procedure*, Tehran, 2009, p. 85.

[49] Some attorneys have said: «issuing a garnishment, as long as it is not implemented, does not do any damage to the defendant and in fact, an order which means the existence of financial commitments does not do any material or moral damage to both parties» According to Article 4 of the law governing the execution of financial convictions, if a person transfers their property in order to avoid paying their debts, financial commitments, or financial convictions,

and the remaining portion of their property is insufficient to cover the outstanding balance, this act will be deemed unlawful. In this instance, the transferred property will be retrieved from the transferee; if not, the person will be ordered to forfeit the equivalent amount in cash. See, A. SHAMS, *Civil procedure rules*, *cit.*, p. 469.

[50] See J. LANGRUDI, M. JAFAR, *cit.*, p. 25.

[51] M. SADRZADEH, *cit.* p. 337.

[52] S. BONAKI, *Civil responsibility regarding the damages of a temporary order and garnishment*, Tehran, 2012, p. 99.

[53] A. SHAMS, *Civil procedure law*, Tehran, 2019, p. 85.

[54] A. RUSSO, S. A. MOUSAVI, *cit.*, pp. 282-284.

[55] *Ibid.*

[56] *Ibid.*

[57] *Id.,* at 285.

[58] *Id.,* pp. 286-288.

[59] J. LANGRUDI, M. JAFAR, *Legal terminology*, Tehran, 2018, p. 181. But the seizure order can also consist of the deprivation of liberty of a person. In this regard, consider the criminal garnishment in primary investigations. In particular, the defendant - in accordance with the principle of presumption of innocence - has the right to remain at liberty during the primary investigation process. Consequently, the authority will issue an order based on the importance of the crimes committed, the grounds for the charge, the likelihood of flight or destruction of evidence, the defendant's background, and his physical and personal condition after informing him of the charges (other than an order not to leave the country). See H. SATTARI, *A comparative study on criminal garnishments in the new bill of criminal procedure rules and in the old rules*, Qom, 2013, p. 95. Criminal seizures are thus considered interlocutory orders that are granted to gain access to the defendant, collect evidence, conclude the primary investigation, and prepare the criminal case. Articles 132 and 133 of the Rules of Criminal Procedure, approved in 1999 and subsequently ratified in 2002, cover criminal seizures. They contain the following information: (i) obligation to attend by a promise; (ii) obligation to attend by determination of penalty clause; (iii) seizing bail; (iv) seizure collateral (cash or bank guarantee for immovable, movable); (v) order to detain the defendant within the nation or temporary detention. The number of criminal garnishments has increased to ten in chapter 7 of the newly approved criminal procedure rules in 2013. Article 217 of the new law has added the following items to the list of the five previously mentioned items: (i) «obliged not to exit the legal jurisdiction by a promise»; (ii) «obliged not to exit the legal jurisdiction by a penalty clause»; (iii) «obliged to introduce himself/herself weekly or monthly to the Court by a penalty clause»; (iv) «making official servants or members of armed forces be present at Court by a penalty clause»; and (v)«obliged not to leave the house or the determined residence by a penalty clause, using electronic surveillance». Additionally, in accordance with note 1 of Article 217 regarding the issuance of bail, the performance bond does not accept four of the ten orders listed by the

accused. Article 237 of the new law on temporary detention states that the general rule is not to make a temporary arrest. The article also states that the order of temporary detention (which was previously required) has been removed, with the exception of the rules pertaining to the armed forces. H. AMIRI, *Criminal garnishments and legal supervision in criminal procedure rules*, Tehran, 2013, p. 85. *De facto*, garnishment in criminal Courts is a procedure that legislators have thought of as a way to increase the likelihood of recovering the victim's losses. The accused's property will be seized, and if he is found not guilty, his property will be released. However, the judge will grant this request for logical reasons, taking into account that the accused is still merely an accused person and may prove innocent before or during the trial. For instance, if the plaintiff can demonstrate in some way that the defendant is trying to sell or transfer his or her assets, as demonstrated by the testimony of the individual who has purchased the defendant's assets. Another important element is that the request and the plaintiff's claims must be made explicit and present in order for the request to be granted. Garnishment can be requested once it is able to be monitored and assessed. Following the issuance of the garnishment, the accused is notified before the order is carried out, with the exception of situations in which the accused cannot be promptly notified and the property is being wasted. Therefore, the accused may contest this order within ten days of the parquet's issuance, but a Court-issued garnishment is final. A third party may object during implementation if their property is seized, in which case the Court will follow the rules of civil procedure. The following actions can render the garnishment ineffective: (i) the plaintiff can request it; (ii) the lawsuit can be terminated; (iii) the plaintiff can lose the claim resulting from a crime; (iv) the plaintiff can cancel the request; or (v) the plaintiff can fail to present the damage lawsuit to the Court. For a discussion of the similarities and procedural differences between criminal and civil garnishment, see Z. N. SANI ABADI, M. JAFARI HARANDI, D. DADASHNEJAD, *A review on garnishments from legal and juridical perspectives, cit.*, pp. 962-963.

[60] V. REZAIE RAJANI, *Execution of civil judgments*, Tehran, 2007, p. 26.

[61] J. LANGRUNDI, M. JAFAR, *cit.*, p. 181.

[62] Legal glossary of deeds and estate registration, Tehran, 2006, p. 120.

[63] G. R. SHAHRI, *Law of registration of deeds and estates*, Tehran, 2005, p. 199.

[64] J. A. MADANI, *Execution of civil judgments*, Tehran, 2000, p. 27.

[65] A. MIRZAVI, *Practical registration law*, Tehran, 2005, p. 230.

[66] J. A. MADANI, *Civil procedure law*, Tehran, 1997, p. 31.

[67] S. A. MUSAVI, *cit.*, p. 171; M. S. ABBAS, *A practical perspective on garnishment orders*, ed. 3, 2012, p. 51.

[68] S. A. MUSAVI, *cit.*, p. 172.

[69] F. CASTRO, *Il modello islamico*, 2nd edition, G. M. PICCINELLI, (edited by), Turin, 2007.

[70] G. M. PICCINELLI, *Le codificazioni nell'era moderna*, in M. OLIVIERO, M. PAPA, forthcoming G.M. PICCINELLI, *Introduzione al diritto comparato dei paesi islamici*, 2021.

[71] *Id.*, *Il diritto agli interessi nei paesi arabi,* in *Diritto del commercio internazionale*, 1996, p. 35.

[72] S. M. Roesler, *Modern legal reform in Egypt: shifting claims to legal authority*, in *Cardozo J. Int'l & Comp. L.*, vol. 14, 2006, p. 393.

[73] T. S. Twibell, *Implementation of the United Nations Convention on contracts for the international sale of goods (CISG) under shari'a (Islamic law): will article 78 of the CISG be enforced when the forum is in an Islamic state?,* in *Int. legal persp.*, 1997, p. 25.

9. Conclusion

The praxis of chasing a debtor's property that is in the possession of a third party, according to the historian of law, started in in England's trading centers, in particular the "Custom of London".

The first epiphany originated in the attachment of assets of a nonresident debtor, that were in the hands of a third party. At the doors of the 1900, this process almost disappeared in England, on the intent to expand the jurisdiction of this institution.

Under English law, the third chapter of the Law on Civil Procedure, which was approved in 1996, contains the regulations pertaining to requests for writs of attachment against the property of debtors or respondents in the English legal system. Occasionally, this institution takes the shape of a garnishment procedure. This denotes a procedure by which money owed to the losing party, which make up a portion of his assets, is seized and frozen in order to carry out financial judgments.

As such, it is a type of execution pertaining to amounts owed in which standard procedures – such as the sale of a collateral – do not apply. In order to recover the money owing, garnishment orders are issued in two stages: first, an executive writ is issued, and then an absolute order is issued. In this case, the claimant will get payment from a third party for the amounts that are in his possession. He may also choose to take the decision made by the master or registrar and file an objection with the Court.

The other institution is called a "Mareva Injunction", which is comparable to the French system's *Saise Contservatoire*. This enables the plaintiff to seize the respondent's property up until the issuance or execution of a judgment. The claimant may seek a writ prohibiting the transfer, concealment, or removal of the respondent's property from the jurisdiction of the Court where the case is pending if he is successful in establishing the admissibility of his claim, can support it, and can demonstrate that the respondent's property is in imminent danger of being hidden away.

The judge may, in carrying out this order, compel the defendant to present evidence, proof, and a comprehensive list of his creditors and the bank or banks where he has an account, as well as prohibit him from taking any assets out of the country.

Upon the fulfillment of these four requirements, this writ is issued: 1. A disagreement history with the Common law or Civil law countries; 2. A case that is admissible and well justified; 3. The respondent's property is present in the district that the Court has jurisdiction over; 4. The presence of a legitimate danger that makes asset concealment tenable.

The claimant must create a request on prescribed forms and present it to the Court in the location of the defendant's assets. This form includes a thorough claimant description along with the title of the remedy being sought. In urgent situations, the stand-by judge can issue the writ over the phone without even requiring an appointment or hearing. The claimant should provide suitable security to safeguard the respondent's rights. The Court makes the decision on the sum. Certain regulations on this subject are included in Article 5 of the Law on the High Court of England.

The fact that this remedy is not among the more traditional common law ones leads to the point that it would have been impossible to resort to it without a proper statute. But, nowadays, the garnishee proceedings regained importance, if not predominance due to the predominant monetary nature of modern transactions, and the garnishment is used against people whose only source of income is from their employment.

In this field, numerous persistent issues have existed spanning national boundaries. They cover issues such as whether there is only one garnishee process or several, if earnings or other civil debts are attached, if the third debtor's money claims or tangible property are targeted, and, lastly, the main formal requirement of garnishment: whether it can be started by an enforceable document, as in all other enforcement methods, a Court order, or even the garnishor acting on their own initiative. Other recurring difficulties are the status of the garnishee, the implications of garnishment, and the interactions between many creditors seeking to garnish the same claim of their shared debtor.

Answers to these and similar topics sometimes vary even within legal families. It would therefore seem wise to use a functional strategy in this instance, concentrating on the issues, instead of the legal families per se.

It has to be stressed that, operationally, the garnishment procedure is not a pleading; rather, it is a means to bring the garnishee before the Court.

Given the discussion so far, one may claim that the practice and method of foreclosure procedures is an understudied area of the law; in reality, a large portion of the information on foreclosure proceedings can be found in case law. However, garnishment procedures are becoming more and more common as a means of upholding financial judgments, especially those directed against the government and its departments.

There are situations where there is a significant delay between the filing of the application that starts the process and the delivery of the final verdict. As a result, the defendant could move its assets and money, stopping the winning party's decision from being executed. Furthermore, this period of time may also lead to vices, devaluations, and depreciation of the products covered in class; nevertheless, the legislator has devised a garnishment order as a measure to prevent these issues.

From a comparative perspective[1], we assist to a legal transplant of a legal institution that moving from the United Kingdom moved to all the dominions and, if in the original place it vanished progressively, it remains in force in the landing area, along with the peculiarities of the case.

Similar to other common law nations, US law requires the submission of a request that includes the claimant's and respondent's identities, address, request specifics, and any justification provided by the applicant. Property may be seized, and a garnishment order may be issued after this requirement is met.

Apart from the British-style garnishing order, there exists an alternative procedure for taking possession of property, referred to as a "seizure of income," "earning order," or "attachment".

These are employed when the plaintiff asks the Court for a writ that would allow him to seize money immediately from the defendant's paycheck in the event that the defendant refuses to pay the claimant's outstanding debts. From the perspective of the extent of property that can be seized, this procedure is comparable to the French legal system's *Sasie-Conservatoire*. This process is used by Courts in several States until a decision is made.

Similar to the British system, the granting of an order is subject to the fulfillment of several conditions in order to prevent plaintiff misuse. Current laws have intended garnishment as a means of assisting against a respondent who is malicious and has good intentions. Individuals who typically plan to alter or remove their belongings in order to impede the right course of events. On the other hand, this can give rise to abuse by the opposing party and result in damages for the defendant. Accordingly, in the event that the claimant loses the case, the other party is entitled to reimbursement for any future losses, as per the idea of reasonable and proportionate orders.

In Iran, although Islamic jurisprudence does not specifically call for a similar institution, Muslims have been able to take advantage of garrisons that are comparable to the relief they have requested in light of the legal justifications for it, such as the idea that no one should injure another person and the idea that a capable public official may take action against those who obstruct the exercise of a right. Given the protracted legal proceedings necessary in many civil matters, the Iranian legislation has recognized the concept of "garnishment".

This is acknowledged in part because of the potential for abuse on the part of the defendant, which would nullify the arbitration process, as well as to make it easier to execute the ruling, take into account pertinent exigencies, and achieve favorable results for this institution. The same strategy has been used by several well-known legal systems. The most important piece of legislation is found in Articles 108-ff of the Law of Civil Procedures, which was ratified in 2000. It allows the Courts to support the claimant by preserving the subject matter of his claim, giving him hope to continue the proceedings, and improving the effectiveness of the trial.

This institution's foundation is found in Islamic law, or *fiqh*, where it is understood to mean "securing the remedy sought", which is a notion that is entirely foreign. As a result, this institution may be found in Iranian legal texts. The following components determine the number of general and particular criteria needed to apply this concept: Subject of the main claim, supporting materials, proof, and effects provided by the claimant.

Given these prerequisites, the responsible authority managing the case simultaneously protects the proceedings' legitimacy and takes the defendant's rights and interests into consideration. The issuing of injunctive relief and its associated consequences often follow formal procedures that are relevant in foreign adjudication systems like the American, English, and civilian systems.

In India, the accent is more on the statutory interventions combined with decisions interpreting the single cases heavily referring to the English authorities; in Nigeria and Cameroon, it is built along a series of autochthone judgements independent one with the other. These latter two countries exemplify the two main macro phenomena present in the African continent's landscape. On one hand, Nigeria has developed a native system for the creation of its own legal framework which is more akin to the common law tradition and based on a line of autonomous precedents that perhaps highlight its somewhat unsystematic and confused spirit.

On the other hand, although Cameroon operates a mixed legal system characterized by a blend of Germanic-Francophone influences and common law elements, it has notably benefited from an advanced common legal regulation through its association with OHADA, an organization for the harmonization of law comprising of 17 African states[2]. It transposes the institution of garnishment in its French version, so much so that the reference text of OHADA, discussed in the preceding pages, was drafted in French and refers to the *saisie*. Notably, this French-language text is effectively implemented through a series of legal precedents as well.

Regulations concerning garnishment orders are not unknown in the Civil law countries. For instance, in the French legal system were intended to be included in the last portions of the

Code of Civil Procedure. Articles 48 and 49 of the 1955 law addressed preventive measures, including security for the requested relief. These clauses were taken out of the code and added to the *Code des Procédures Civiles d'Exécution* in 2012.

Moveable particular articles and immovable property owned by the debtor may be attached upon a judge's approval or when the law enables the adoption of security measures, according to Article 521-1 of this Code under the heading "security seizures".

This is true even in situations where the asset is being held by a third party or has already been seized as a result of previous security measures. Moreover, the same law's Article 111-1 states that «all creditors may compel their debtors who are at fault to satisfy their obligations». To protect their interests, garnishment is an option available to all debtors. It is not feasible to apply a writ of attachment to someone who is exempt from executive action.

When executing a garnishment, careful consideration needs to be given to the opposing party's rights, particular circumstances, and the timing of the execution. For example, premature execution needs to be prevented.

In general, there are two ways that attachment may be carried out under French law. One is known as the *Saisie Conservatoire*, and it allows a claimant to request a garnishment and seize the debtor's property before the legal process ever starts. This is subject to the following requirements: payment must be in jeopardy, the claim must be legitimate and well-reasoned, and the urgency requirement must be met.

A further format known as *Saisie-Arrêt* allows a creditor to seek and seize specific amounts owed to him that are liquid or convertible into other currencies and do not have a moratorium. Under this second category, judicial recourse is not necessary.

After taking into account the laws pertaining to garnishment, security measures, and quick orders, the following conclusions might be drawn:

1. A timely order is broad and applies to any situations in which immediate action is necessary to address an emergency.

This is particularly valid in situations when there are logistical or administrative challenges.

2. The purpose of a garnishment is to preserve the object of a claim.

3. Prompt orders and precautionary attachments are both instantly and temporarily enforceable.

4. It is possible to obtain prompt directives and precautionary/security measures before to the commencement of the substantive evaluation of the primary claim.

5. The Court may request security from the plaintiff in the form of property, guarantor introduction, or proof of solvency in both rapid orders and preventive measures (Article 489 of the current French Law on Civil Procedure and Article 48 of the previous Law).

6. Neither a timely order nor a preventive step is required in the case of a demand that is mature (that is, exigible).

7. Proof of urgency may occasionally be required in order to get a quick order as well as a preventative measure. Provisions in this respect are found in Articles 48 and 49 of the previous law as well as in Articles 484-ff of the French Law.

The technicality of the garnishment favored the transplant being seen as a mere legal institution, appreciated for its efficiency allowed it to remain even when the colonizing power left the foreign territories.

Even though legal academics differ on whether it is feasible, the "transplantability" of legal institutions within a foreign legal system is an intriguing field of inquiry. Thus, while Kahn-Freund contends that institutions or rules can be transplanted, comparative methodology necessitates that there always be a chance of rejection: «knowledge not only of the foreign law, but also of its social, and above all its political context»[3].

To put it another way, if the legal background is ignored, the purely legal viewpoint runs the risk of misguiding those who rely on comparative law. In particular, according to Kahn-Freund, the degree to which a regulation may be adopted is largely determined by how well it meshes with the foreign political power system[4].

Watson disputes this, arguing that it has frequently been possible to successfully transplant from a quite different legal system, even one that is far more developed and has a distinct political complexion. The Scottish professor continues by saying that a reformer of laws studying other systems has to consider a concept that can be truly modified to suit the legal system of that country. As a result, he believes that a comprehensive understanding of the legislation or the political framework of the donor system was not required, but he does acknowledge that a law reformer with such expertise would be more effective[5].

Stein replies by portraying Watson as «plucking ideas from 'black letter' rules in complete ignorance of how the rules operate as 'living law' and where they fit into the legal system»[6]. This viewpoint is not unique, in fact.

In reality, Schmitthoff said as early as 1939 that laws and customs are products of the legal, political, and social structures of a society rather than existing in a vacuum[7]. This implies that legislators should be mindful of the necessity for ongoing revisions to reflect societal shifts and avoid taking a provincial approach to legislation reform[8].

Stein argues critically that discussions on the safety and simplicity of transplantation are nearly irrelevant if they are conducted «without a tacit assumption that a law maker does in fact use the method and considers foreign law models»[9]. Therefore, the comparative method can help both practitioners and reformers understand complicated legal issues that are now only tackled with firmly held, untested presumptions[10]. This means that the goal is to determine whether an institution, doctrine, practice, or tradition is inevitable and universal or if it is the result of particular social, historical, or geographical conditions. It is also to differentiate between what is intrinsic to a country's institutions, customs, and doctrines and what is accidental in terms of geography and history, all made possible by comparative methodology.

In the «old and philosophically now discredited terms», the goal is to determine «what rules are essential for the purposes of the law and what rules are accidental, products of history and tradition»[11].

As a result, comparative attorneys frequently compare the law not only with other laws but also with institutions that are non-legal or meta-legal in nature and with the requirements that societies share[12].

Naturally, there are many challenges and hazards in terms of legislation and technique in this sensitive and intricate investigation[13]. Therefore, it is not shocking that some comparative analysis has not shown very positive results.

Notes

[1] See, A. WATSON, *Legal transplants: an approach to comparative law*, Athens, 1974.

[2] One problem with adopting a current conception of a "mixed system" (wherein the sole requirement is only the presence or interaction of two or more kinds of laws or legal traditions within each system) is that most of Africa, Asia, India, and the "classical" mixed jurisdictions as well will answer to this description. The category is extremely broad since it is as extensive as the notion of legal pluralism". V.V. PALMER, *Mixed legal systems... and the myth of pure laws*, in *La. L. Rev.* 2007, p. 1205.

[3] O. KAHN-FREUND, *On uses and misuses of comparative law*, in *Mod. L. Rev.*, 1974, p. 27.

[4] *Ibid.*

[5] See, in general, A. WATSON, *Society and legal change*, 1977 (suggesting that the failure of many laws to adequately address the specific demands of society can be largely attributed to transplanting); A. WATSON, *The making of the civil law*, 1981; A. WATSON, *Comparative law and legal change,* in *Cambridge L.J.*, 1978, p. 313 (talking about transplanting from the standpoint of how society and the law interact).

[6] E. STEIN, *Uses, misuses - and nonuses of comparative law,* in *Nw. U. L. Rev.*, 1977, pp. 198-214 (referring to H. E. YNTEMA, *Comparative legal research - Some Remarks on "Looking out of the Cave",* in *Mich. L. Rev.*, 1956, p. 209). It is still true that, with a few notable exceptions, American legal scholars and law reformers have neglected to use the comparative method when analyzing foreign law and practice, regardless of whether factors like the significant amount of American investment overseas have made knowledge of such practices vital to some forms of legal practice here. One notable exception is Roscoe Pound. See R. POUND, *The development of American law and its deviation from English law,* in L*aw q. rev.*, 1951, p. 49.

[7] See M. SCHMITTHOFF, *The science of comparative law*, in *Cambridge L.J.*, 1939, pp. 97-99.

[8] See D. THOMSON, *A view from abroad,* in *U.S. Industrial Relations 1950-1980: A Critical Assessment*, pp. 297-298 and 301; J. STEIBER, R. MCKERSIE, D. MILLS, 1981.

[9] E. STEIN, *cit.*, pp. 209-10. See, generally, H. MAINE, *Village-Communities in the East and West 4*, ed 3., 1913 (sustaining that «the chief function of Comparative Jurisprudence is to facilitate legislation and the practical improvement of law»).
[10] A. BORRONI, *Premise*, in *TSL*, vol. 1, 2018, p. 20.
[11] O. KAHN-FREUND, *Comparative law as an academic subject,* in *L.Q. R.*, 1966, p. 60.
[12] See, generally, O. KAHN-FREUND, *Comparative law*, *cit.* (asserting that it has been molded by institutions, customs, and laws outside of the law and that a comparative lawyer needs to look at these extralegal effects).
[13] Walker has cautioned against using descriptive comparative studies since they just highlight the diversity of practices without shedding any light on the variables that contribute to their differences. He contends that, depending on the practitioner's inclination, these studies are unlikely to accomplish anything more than promote "ritualism" – imitating a foreign practice without taking into account whether it is appropriate for transfer – or "isolationism" – ignoring any experience other than one's own. A. WALKER, *The comparative study of industrial relations*, in *Int'l Inst. for Labour Studies Bull.*, no. 3, 1969, p. 107.

Bibliography

ABBAS M.S., *A practical perspective on garnishment orders*, ed. 3, 2012.

ABDOLLHOSSEIN S., *Introduction to the science of Law*, ed. 1, 2020.

ACHIKE O., *Nigerian law of contract*, Enugu, 1972.

ADAMS M., *The rhetoric of precedent and comparative legal research*, in *Modern law review*, 4, 1999.

ADAMS K.D., *Blaming the mirror: the restatements and the common law*, in *Indiana L. R.*, 2007.

AGHEDO E.F., *Attorney general's consent in garnishee proceedings versus constitutionalism: appraising the status of the central bank of Nigeria*, in *Obafemi Awolowo university L. J.*, vol. 1-2, 2018.

AJANI G., FRANCAVILLA D., PASA B., *Diritto comparato. Lezioni e materiali*, Turin, 2018.

ALLISON J.W.F., *The English historical constitution*, Cambridge, 2007.

ALLOTT A.N. (ed.), *The Future of Law in Africa. Record of proceeding of the London conference 28 december 1959-8 january 1960*, London, 1960.

ALPA G., DELFINO R., *Il contratto nel common law inglese*, ed. 2, Padua, 1997.

AMADEI D., *Tutela esecutiva ed azione inibitoria delle associazioni dei consumatori*, in *Riv. esec. Forz.*, 2003; *La tutela degli interessi collettivi e le modifiche al procedimento d'ingiunzione (seconda parte)*, in *Resp. civ. e prev.*, 2003.

American Law Institute, *Restatement of the law, conflict of law as adopted and promulgated by the American law institute*, Minnesota 1971.

AMIN A. M., HOSSEIN A. N., *Assessing the position and competencies of the Supreme Court and the Court of Administrative Justice*, in *New res. Admin. L. J.*, no. 1, 2016.

AMIRANTE D., *India*, Bologna, 2007.

AMIRI H., *Criminal garnishments and legal supervision in criminal procedure rules*, Tehran, 2013.

ANSANELLI V., *Comparazione e ricomparazione in tema di expert whithes testimony*, in *Riv. dir. Proc.*, n. 3, 2009.

ARNOLD C., *Comparison of civil law and common law*, in *Comm. L. Rev.*, vol. 8, 2007.

ASHLEY M., *England in the seventeenth century*, London, 1974.

ASSEPO ASSI E., *La Cour commune de justice et d'arbitrage de l'OHADA: un troisième degré de jurisdiction?*, in *Rev. I. Dr. Comp.*, 2005.

BABALOLA A., *Enforcement of judgments*, ed. 1, Nigeria, 2003.

BAKER J.H., *An introduction to english legal history*, London, 1990.

BALENA G., *Elementi di diritto processuale civile*, Bari, 2007.

BANERJEE B.N., *Law of civil appeals and revisions*, ed. 2, Allahabad, 1963.

BANIRE M., *Emerging issues in garnishee proceedings in Nigeria,* 2018. Available at https://mabandassociates.com/emerging-issues-in-garnishee-proceedings-in-nigeria/#_ftnref92. (Consulted March 2024).

BARBA M., *Procédure civile*, Paris, 2024

BARSOTTI V., *La tradizione giuridica occidentale. Testo e materiali per un confronto civil law common law*, Turin, 2018.

BATIZA R., *The Verbatim and almost verbatim sources of the Louisiana civil codes of 1808, 1825 and 1870: The Original Text,* New Orleans, 1973.

BELLACE J.R., *A foreign perspective,* in E. Livernash (ed.), *Comparable Worth: Issues and Alternatives*, 1980.

BESSONE M., *Principio di buona fede, disciplina del "common law" e massime di "equity"*, in *Riv. trim. dir. proc. civ.*, 1973.

BLACKSTONE W., *Commentaries on the laws of England*, vol. 1, Philadelphia, 1893.

BLANC E., *Les nouvelles procédures d'exécution: commentaire article par article de la loi n °91-150 du 9 juillet 1991 et du décret n °92-755 du 31 juillet 1992 suivi d'un formulaire,* Paris, 1994.

BONAKI S., C*ivil responsibility regarding the damages of a temporary order and garnishment*, Tehran, 2012.

BORDINO I., A. FERRETTI, F. GULLO, et al., *Garnlp: a natural language processing pipeline for garnishment documents*, in *Inf Syst Front*, 2021.

BORRONI A., FIROUZAN M., GIUGGIOLI P. F., PAPA M., PERIALE F., *Il modello di common law,* Padua, 2023.

BOULARBAH H., *Requête unilatérale et inversion du contentieux,* Bruxelles, 2010.

BRACTON H., *De legibvs et consuetudinibus angliae*, vol. 6, Cambridge, 2012.

BROWN P., *Patterns of authority in west Africa*, in *Africa*, vol. XXI, no. 4, 1951.

BUCKLAND W.W., MC NAIR A.D., *Roman law e common law a comparison in outline*, Cambridge, 1965.

BURKE J., *Osborn's concise law dictionary*, ed. 6, London, 1976.

BURKS M., *Common law and statutory pleading and practice*, ed. 4, Virginia, 1952.

BURNHAM W., *Introduction to the law and legal system of the United State*, Minnesota, 1995.

CAIRNS C., *Australian civil procedure*, ed. 2, Sidney, 1985.

CALABRESI G., MELAMED D., *Property rules, liability rules and inalienability: One view of the cathedral*, in *Harvard Law Review*, vol. 85, 1972; *Regole di proprietà, responsabilità e inalienabilità: un'istantanea della Cattedrale*, in *Riv. dir. civ.*, 2020.

CAPPELLETTI M., PERILLO J.M., *Enforcement proceedings*, in *Civil Procedure in Italy,* Netherlands, 2013.

CAPPELLETTI M., *The judicial process in comparative perspective*, Oxford, 1989.

CARLIN L., *The law of garnishment in West Virginia*, in *West Virginia Law Quaterly*, vol. 48, no. 1, 1941.

CASTRO F., *Il modello Islamico*, ed. 2, G.M. PICCINELLI (edited by), Turin, 2007.

CECIL H., *The english judge*, London, 1970.

CHABAS F., *La pena privata in Francia*, in *Riv. dir. proc.*, 1999.

CHABAS F., *Astreinte*, in *Encyclopédie Dalloz de procédure civile*, 1993.

CHIARLONI S., *Un mito rivisitato: nota comparativa sull'autorità del precedente Giurisprudenziale*, in *Riv. Dir. Proc.*, 2001.

CHITTY J., *On Contracts. Specific contracts*, vol. 2, London, 1983.

CIAN M., *Le antiche leggi del commercio*, Bologna, 2016.

CIPOLLA C.M., *Storia economica dell'Europa pre-industriale*, Bologna, 1974.

COMYNS J., *A digest of the laws of England*, vol. 5, Hampshire, 2010.

CONNOLLY W.B., *Garnishment of corporate stock*, in *Mich. L. Rev.*, vol. 39, no. 3, 1941.

COOTER R., MATTEI U., MONATERI P.G., PARDOLESI R., ULEN T., *Il mercato delle regole: analisi economica del diritto civile*, Milan, 2000.

COUCHEZ G., LEBEAU D., SALATI O., *Procédures civiles d'exécution*, ed. 13, Paris, 2022.

COUCHEZ G., LANGLADE J.P., LEBEAU D., *Procédure civile*, Paris, 1998.

COUCHEZ G., *Procédure civile*, Parigi, 1998.

COUTURE E.J., *Fundamentes del derecho procesal civil*, Buenos Aires, 1958.

CRESPI REGHIZZI G., *Disciplina giuridica degli investimenti stranieri in India* (*Legal regulation of foreign investments in India*), Rome, 2007.

CRISCUOLI G., *Introduzione allo studio del diritto inglese. Le fonti*, ed. 3, Milan, 2000; *Il contratto nel diritto inglese*, Padua, 1990; *Caratteri generali del diritto inglese*, in *Econ. & cred.*, 1973; *Tipologia delle fonti giuridiche inglese*, in *Econ. & cred.*, 1973; *Appunti sulla formazione del "common law"*, in *Econ. & cred.*, 1973.

CRISCUOLI G., *Comparazione e prospettive del diritto*, in *Dir. & giur.*, 1979.

CROSS R., *Precedent in English law*, Oxford, 1977.

CROSS K. A., *Pleading in courts of ordinary jurisdiction*, United States, 1885,

CURRIE B., *Attachment and garnishment in the Federal Courts*, in *Mich. L. Rev.,* vol. 59, no. 3, 1961.

CURRY T., *A new digest of the statute laws of the state of Louisiana: from the change of government to the year 1841*, New Orleans, 1842.

DANE N., *The charters and general laws of the colony and province of Massachusetts Bay*, Detroit, 2012.

DARGO G., *Jefferson's Louisiana: politics and the clash of legal tradition*, Cambridge, 1975.

DAVID R., SPINOSI C. J., *I grandi sistemi giuridici contemporanei*, ed. 5, R. SACCO (edited by), Padua, 2004.

DAVIDSON B., *The disposal of attached or garnished property: a procedural knot*, in *Hastings L. J.*, 1972.

DE BOER M. B., *Osservazioni sull'astreinte nel diritto processuale olandese*, in *Dir. proc. civ.*, 1996.

DE FRANCHIS A., *Doctrine in diritto angloamericano*, in *Dig. civ.*, vol. 7, Turin, 1991.

DE GRAZIA L., *Costituzionalismo ed esperienze costituzionali in Iran,* in *Rivista AIC*, no. 2, 2015; *Il diritto islamico nel sistema delle fonti dell'ordinamento iraniano*, in *DPCE online*, 2011.

DEBROY B., *India's economic liberalization and WTO*, in KARMAKAR S., KUMAR R., DEBROY B. (edited by), *India's liberalization experience: Hostage to the WTO?,* New Delhi, 2007.

DELMAS-GOYON P., *Le juge du 21 siècle-Un citoyen acteur, une équipe de justice*, 2013. Available at http://www.justice.gouv.fr/publication/rapport_dg_2013.pdf.

DEHKHODA A., *Glossary*, Tehran, 1994; *Dehkhoda dictionary,* no. 1, Tehran, 1993.

DIETSCH J., *La procédure de recouvrement simplifié de certaines créances*, in *Thèse*, Paris, 1959.

DISSAKE E.M.K., *Language and legal proceedings. Analysing courtroom discourse in Cameroon,* 2021.

DONDI A., ANSANELLI V., COMOGLIO P., *Processi civili in evoluzione. Una prospettiva comparata*, Milan, 2015.

DRAKE C.D., *A treatise on the law of suits by attachment in the United States*, Boston, 2010.

EHRENZWEIG A., *Treatise on the conflict of law*, Minnesota, 1962.

ELIAS T.O., *The Nigerian legal system*, London, 1963.

ESTES N., *Indian law,* in *N. M. L. Rev.*, 1980.

ESTOUP P., *La pratique des procédures rapides*, Paris, 1990.

FARNSWORTH E.A., *Contracts, cases and materials*, ed. 6, New York, 2001; *Introduzione al sistema giuridico degli Stati Uniti d'America*, Milan, 1979.

FISIY C.F., *Colonial and religious influences on customary law: the Cameroonian experiences*, in *Africa: Riv. trim. stud. & docum. dell'Istituto Italiano per l'Africa e l'Oriente*, no. 2, 1988.

FLANAGAN T.M., SMITH L.G, *Garnishment - State vs. Federal Procedures,* in *Clev. St. L. Rev.*, vol. 20, no. 1, 1971.

FLORIDIA G., *L'invenzione farmaceutica nel sistema italiano dei brevetti,* Milano, 1985.

FOMBAD M.C., *Managing legal diversity: Cameroonian bijuralism at a critical crossroad,* in V.P. VERNON, Y.M. MOHAMED, A. KOPPEL, *Mixed legal systems, east and west*, New York, 2015.

FRANCAVILLA G., *Il diritto nell'India contemporanea. Sistemi tradizionali, modelli occidentali e globalizzazione*, Turin, 2011.

FRANCESCHINI G., MISURACA F., *India: diritto commerciale, doganale e fiscale*, Milan, 2006.

FREEMAN A. C., *A treatise on the law of executions in civil cases: and of proceedings in aid and restraint thereof*, Dretoit, 2010.

FRIGNANI A., *La penalità di mora e le astreintes nei diritti che si ispirano al modello francese*, in *Riv. dir. civ.*, 1981.

FRIGNANI A., *L'injunction nella common law e l'inibitoria nel diritto italiano,* Milan, 1974.

GALGANO F., *Diritto civile e commerciale*, Padua, 2004.

GALLO P., *Introduzione al diritto comparato, Analisi economica del diritto*, vol. 3, Turin, 1998; *Grandi sistemi giuridici,* Torino, 1997; *I rimedi restitutori in diritto comparato, Trattato di diritto comparato*, R. SACCO (edited by), Turin, 1997.

GAMBARO A., *Alcune novità in materia di comparazione giuridica*, in *Riv. dir. comm.*, vol. I, 1980.

GAMBARO A., MONATERI P. G., SACCO R., *Comparazione giuridica*, in *Digesto civ.*, vol. II, Turin, 1988.

GAMBARO A., SACCO R., *Sistemi giuridici comparati*, Turin, 2008.

GARNER B., *Black's law dictionary*, ed. 5., Arizona, 2016.

GAROUPA N., LIGUERRE C. G., *The syndrome of the efficiency of the common law*, in *Boston Univer. Intern. L.J.*, 2011, n. 29.

GATENBY J.K., *Recovery of money*, ed. 7, London, 1989.

GILBERT G., *Law and practice of distress and replevin*, London, 2018.

GILMORE G., BLACK. L., *The law of admiralty*, ed. 2, New York, 1975.

GIUSSANI A., *L'esibizione di documenti situati nello spazio giuridico europeo*, in *Riv. trim. dir. proc. civ.*, no. 3, 2002.

GLENN P., *Legal traditions of the world: sustainable diversity in law*, Oxford, 2014.

GLENN H.P., *Comparative legal families and comparative legal traditions*, in R. ZIMMERMANN, M. REIMANN, *The Oxford handbook of comparative law*, Oxford, 2006.

GOLDFACE-IROKALIBE J., *Law of banking Nigeria*, Lagos, 2007.

GOLDSTEIN L., *Precedent in law*, Oxford, 1987.

GODINEC P.F., *Le droit africain - evolution et sources*, Paris, 1968.

GRADINIER D.E., *Cameroon-United Nations challenge to French policy*, Oxford, 1963.

GRAZIADEI M., MATTEI U., *L'insegnamento del diritto comparato*, in *Riv. trim. dir. e proc. civ.*, 1986.

GRAZIADEI M., *Stili dottrinali nell'aerea angloamericana e modelli di civil law*, in *Quadrimestre*, Milan, 1989.

GRONER S. B., *Louisiana Law: Its Development in the First Quarter-Century of American Rule*, in *La. L. Rev.*, vol. 8 no. 3, 1948.

GUADAGNI G., *Diritto dei paesi africani*, in *Enc. giur.*, vol. XI, 1991.

GUADAGNI M., CASTELLUCCI I., *Classificando i sistemi giuridici africani*, in *Annuario Dir. Comp. Stud. Leg.*, 2013.

GUARNERI A., *Lineamenti di diritto comparato*, ed. 2, Padua, 2004.

GUINAMANT M. L., HAFI S., APARISI S., *La procédure civile et les procédures civiles d'exécution en cas pratiques*, ed. 2, Paris, 2024.

GUINCHARD S., MOUSSA M., *Droit et pratique des voies d'exécution*, Paris, 2009.

GUINCHARD S., *L'ambition raisonnées d'une justice apaisée, della Commission sur la répartition des contentieux,* 2008. Available at : http://www.justice.gouv.fr/publications-10047/rapports-thematiques-10049/commission-sur-la-repartition-des-contentieux-15546.html.

GUINCHARD S., *Prolégomènes pour réformer la procédure civile*, Paris, 2017.

GUINCHARD S., *L'affectation des biens en droit privé français*, Paris, 1976.

GUTTERIDGE H., *Comparative law: an Introduction to the comparative method of legal study and research*, ed. 2, 1971.

HAQANI DEHKORDI K., *A jurisprudential review on garnishment*, Tehran, 2016.

HAMILTON A., *Garnishment,* in *The American Law Register* (1852-1891), vol. 33, no. 10, New Series vol. 24, 1885.

HAAS E. F., *Louisiana's Legal Heritage (Studies in Louisiana culture)*, Louisiana, 1983.

HEBRAUD P., *Le recouvrement des petites créances commerciales, Semaine juridique*, 1938.

HENING W.W., *Statutes at large*, vol. 1. Available at: https://vagenweb.org/hening.

HENDERSON P., *Garnishment and execution of contract rights (Part I)*, in *Idaho Law Review*, 1987.

HOLDSWORTH W. S., *A history of English law*, vol. 3, London, 2012.

HOLMES O.W., *The Common law*, Boston, 1881.

HOLT P., LAMBTON A., LEWIS B., *The Cambridge history of Islam*, vol.

1A, *The central Islamic lands from pre-Islamic times to the first world war*, Cambridge, 1977.

HOOD J.T., *The history and development of the Louisiana civil code,* in *Lou. L. R.*, vol. 19, no. 1, 1958.

HOSSEINI M.R., *The law on civil procedure in judicial precedent*, Tehran, 2002.

IRELAND G., *Louisiana's legal system reappraised*, in *Tul. L. Rev.*, vol. 11, 1973.

IRTI N., *Norma e luoghi. Problemi di geo-diritto*, Rome-Bari, 2006.

JABLONSKI J.A., *Wage garnishment as a collection device*, in *Wis. L. Rev.*, 1967.

JACOB I.H., *The Supreme court practice 1973*, vol. 2, London, 1972.

JACOB H., *Courts, law, and politics in comparative perspective*, Connecticut, 1996.

JACOB H., *Trends in the enforcement of non-money judgments and orders. The first international colloqium on the law of civil procedure,* 1988.

JACKSON R.M., *The machinery of justice in England*, ed. 6, Cambridge, 1972.

JAFARI LANGEROUDI J., *Law schools in Islam*, ed. 2, Tehran, 2001; *Extended law terminology*, 2007.

JAHROMI E., MOSTAFA E., *Civil procedure*, vol. 2, ed. 1, 2018.

JENKS E., *A short history of English law*, London, 1934.

JOHNSON J., *Louisiana history: the journal of the Louisiana historical association*, vol. 30, no. 2, 1989.

JURIDICAL SYMPOSIA, *Issues relevant to civil procedure*, Tehran, 2009.

KAHN-FREUND O., *The European social charter,* in F. JACOBS, *European law and the individual*, Amsterdam, 1976; *The Impact of constitutions on labour law,* in *The Cambridge law journal*, vol. 35, no. 2, 1976; *On uses and misuses of comparative law,* in *Modern L. Rev.*, vol. 37, no. 1, 1974; *Comparative law as an academic subject,* in *L. Q. R.*, 1966.

KANTER K.M., *A changing public policy: garnishment of municipal corporations in Ilinois-Henderson v. Foster*, in *DePaul L. Rev.*, vol. 25, no. 3, 1976.

KASHYAP S.C., *Constitution of India and international law*, in PATEL B.N., *India and International Law*, Leiden, 2005.

KATOOZIAN A., *Definite contract*, Tehran, 2011.

KATOUZIAN N., *Introduction to the science of law*, Tehran, 2018.

KEER M., *Situs of a debt in garnishment proceedings*, in *Central L. J.*, 1901.

KEHINDE O., *The attorney-general's consent in garnishee proceedings: a review of the law*, in *Inter. J. Comp. L. L. Phil.*, vol. 1, no. 2, 2019.

KERAMEUS K.D., *Enforcement proceedings*, in ZWEIGERT K., DROBNIG U., *International encyclopedia of comparative law online*, vol. XVI: Civil Procedure, Leida, 2002.

KILBOURNE R.H., *A History of the Louisiana civil code, The Formative years 1803-1839*, Baton Rouge, 1987.

LANGRUDI J., JAFAR M., *Legal terminology*, Tehran, 1997.

LAPIDUS I.M., *Storia delle società islamiche. I popoli musulmani*, vol. 3, Turin, 2000.

LAWSON J., *Rights, Remedies, and practice, at law, in equity, and under the codes: treatise on american law in civil causes, with digest of illustrative cases*, San Francisco, 1890.

LEBORGNE A., SALATI O., DARGENT L., *Code des procédures civiles d'exécution*, Paris, 2013.

LEBORGNE A., BRENNER C., GIJSBERS C., *Droit de l'exécution. Voies d'exécution et procédures de distribution*, ed. 3, Paris, 2019.

LE COURT B., *La procédure d'injonction de payer,* Paris, 1984.

LEHMAN J., PHELPS S., *West's encyclopedia of American law,* ed. 2, 2005.

LIBBY T., *Province and court records of Maine,* Portland, vol. 1, (1928) and vol. 2, (1931).

LINGAT R., *La tradizione giuridica dell'India*, FRANCAVILLA D. (translated by), Milan, 2003.

LISTER J., *Court rolls of the manor of wakefield*, vol. 4, Cambridge, 2013.

LITVINOFF S., *Materials for an introduction to common law legal methodologies*, Baton Rouge, 2005.

LOGUE T., *Due process, postjudgment garnishment, and "Brutal Need" Exemptions*, in *Duke L. J.*, 1982.

Lord Halshamm of St. Marylebone, *Halsbury's Laws of England*, ed. 4, vol. 17, no. 1, United Kingdom, 2002.

LOUGHLIN P., GERLIS S.M., *Civil procedure,* London, 2004.

LUPOI M., *Sistemi giuridici comparati. Traccia di un corso*, Naples, 2000.

MADANI J.A., *Execution of civil judgments*, Tehran, 2000; *Civil procedure law*, Tehran, 1997.

MANCUSO S., *African law in action*, in *J. African L.,* vol. 58, no. 1, 2014; *Diritto commerciale africano*, Naples, 2009.

MA'LUF L.A.M., *Translated by: Ahmad Bandar Beigi*, Tehran, 2002.

MANN A., *The legal aspects of money*, ed. 2, London, 1953.

MARTIN D., *Recouvrement simplifié des créances commerciales,* in *Rev. trim. dr. comm.*, 1954.

MARTOR B., PILKINGTON N., SELLERS D.S., THOUVENOT S., *Business law in Africa: Ohada and the harmonization process,* London, 2002.

MAS D., *Injonction de payer*, in *Enc. Dalloz, Rép. proc. civ.*, vol. 3, Paris, 1997.

MATTEI U., ARIANO E., MARCHISIO G., *Il modello di common law,* ed. 3, Turin, 2020;

MATTEI U., *Common law. Il diritto anglo-americano*, in SACCO R., *Trattato di Diritto Comparato*, Turin, 1992; *Common law*, in *Trattato di diritto comparato*, SACCO R. (edited by), Turin, 1992.

MATTEI U., MONATERI P.G., *Introduzione breve al diritto comparato*, Padua, 1997.

MCDONALD J. D., CARTER J.B., *Garnishment in Louisiana*, in *L. L. Rev.,* vol. 18, no. 3, 1957.

MCQUILLIN E., *Law of municipal corporations*, ed. 3, 1968.

MENSKI W., *Comparative law in a global context the legal systems of Asia and Africa*, Cambridge, 2006; *Hindu law. beyond tradition and modernity*, Nuova Delhi, 2003.

MESSINEO F., *Manuale di diritto civile e commerciale*, vol. II, Milan, 1965.

MESTRE J., *De quelques difficultés concernant les conditions d'obtention des modes de preuve*, in *Rev. trim. dr. civ.*, 1996.

MEYER P., *La sécurité juridique et judiciaire dans l'espace OHADA*, in *Penant*, vol. 116, No. 855, 2006.

MGBEAHURU U.M., *Interlocutory applications. Trial and appellate practice*, ed. 3, Lagos, 2019.

MICHELIN-BRACHET H., VEYRE L., GUEZ M., SABARD O., *Cours de procédure civile 2024. Modes alternatifs de résolution des différends, voies d'exécution*, ed. 6, Paris, 2024.

MILLAR R.W., *Civil procedure of the trial court in historical perspective*, New Jersey, 1952.

MILSOM S.F.C., *Historical foundation of the common law*, London, 1969.

MIRZAVI F., *Practical registration law*, Tehran, 2005.

MISURACA F., FRANCESCHIN G., *India: diritto commerciale, doganale e fiscale*, Milan, 2006.

MOCCIA L., *Common law*, in *Digesto civ.*, vol. II, Turin, 1988; *Diritto giurisprudenziale, legislazione e principio di legalità nel mondo di "common law"*, in *Riv. Trim. dir. e proc. civ.*, vol. VIII, 1988.

MOEEN M., *Persian dictionary*, Tehran, 1982.

MOINE J.N., *The place of customary law in modern Africa*, in *Annales de la fac. de droit du Cameroun*, no. 3, 1972.

MOORE T. S., PFEIFFER R., *Garnishment in Ohio: where is it now*, in *Ohio St. L.J.*, 1971.

MONATERI P.G., *Il precedente in Inghilterra*, in VACCA M.L., *Lo stile delle sentenze e l'utilizzazione dei precedenti. Profili storico-comparatistici*, Turin, 2000.

MORBIDELLI G., PEGORARO L., REPOSO A., VOLPI M., *Diritto pubblico comparato*, Turin, 2004.

MORETTI F., *La dottrina del precedente giudiziario nel sistema inglese*, in *Contr. e impr.*, 1990.

MORRIS R.B., *Select cases of the mayor's court of New York City 1674-1784*, Washington, 1935.

MOUSAVI BOJNOURDI S.M., *Jurisprudential rules*, 1993.

MUKHERJEE M., *A History of the Present*, in *L. History Rev.*, vol. 23, no. 3, 2005; *Justice, war, and the Imperium: India and Britain in Edmund Burke's prosecutorial speeches in the impeachment trial of Warren Hastings*, in *L. H. Rev.*, vol. 23, no. 3, 2005.

MUSAVI S.A., *Prompt trial; garnishment orders*, vol. 1-2, ed. 2, 2021.

MUSSMAN W.E., RIESENFELD S.A., *Garnishment and bankruptcy*, in *Minn. L. Rev.*, vol. 17, n. 1, 1942.

MWALIMU C., *The Nigerian legal system: public law*, vol. 1, New York, 2005; *The Nigerian legal system: private law*, vol. 2, New York, 2005.

NABIT J., *Garnishment in Virginia*, in *William & Mary L. Rev.*, vol. 21, n. 3, 1980.

NEGRI A., *Sistemi giuridici nel mondo,* Turin, 2010.

NICOD B., *Les voies d'exécution*, deuxieme partie, ch. 4, partie 2, Paris, 1994.

NICHOLS F.M., *Britton*, vol. 1, London, 2016.

NJOYA N.T., *OHADA treaty-an unruly horse, the impartial judge*, in *Cameroon Comm. L. J.,* 2003.

NNAMDI D., OLAOYE O., ADEROGBA A., OJOGBO O., ONELE J., *Efficacy of garnishee proceedings against closed banks/Nigeria deposit Insurance Corporation (NDIC),* 2015. Available at: http://dx.doi.org/10.2139/ssrn.2651075.

NWABUOKU M.O.I, MRABURE K.O., *Garnishee proceeding and enforcement in Nigeria. The jurisprudence of a new wine in an old bottle*, in *Unimaid J. Private and Prop. L.*, vol. 5, no. 2, 2020.

NWAEZE G., *Garnishee proceedings in Nigeria: the effects of order absolute*, 2022. Available at: HTTP://DX.DOI.ORG/10.2139/SSRN.4175690.

NWADIALO F., *Civil procedure in Nigeria*, ed. 2, Lagos, 2000.

NWAMARA T.A., *The law of execution of judgments*, ed. 1, Nigeria, 2007.

OBALOLUWA N., *The Nigerian legal system I,* 2023. Available at: https://www.academia.edu/91390000/JIL_201_The_Nigerian_Legal_System_I?email_work_card=view-paper.

OBI-OKOYE, *Essays on civil proceedings*, Anambra, 1997.

OGBONNA N., NWABACHILI O.C., *A critical analysis of garnishee proceedings in Nigeria*, in *J. Comm. and Prop. L.*, 2023.

OLONG A.M., *The Nigerian legal system: an introduction*, Lagos, 2007.

O' HARE J., R. N. HILL, *Civil litigation*, ed. 5, London, 1990.

OLAWUNMI I., *A judgment debtor in garnishee proceedings in Nigeria: To Be Seen or to Be Heard?,* 2021. Available at: https://ssrn.com/abstract=4012038.

OLUWATOSIN S., *The efficacy of garnishee proceedings in the enforcement of judgement debt.* Available at: https://www.oakwoodlegalng.com/assets/files/Ganishee-Proceedings.pdf. (Consulted March 2024).

OJUKWU C.N., *Introduction to civil procedure*, Nigeria, 2002.

OKANY M.C., *Nigerian commercial law*, Nigeria, 2009.

ONUZULIKE O., *An analysis of the consent requirement of section 84 of the sheriff and civil process act 2004 and the judgment enforcement powers of courts*, 2020. Available at: https://ssrn.com/abstract=3662960

OPRINA E., *Are there any intervening creditors involved in garnishment?*, 2021.

ÖRUCU E., *Mixed and mixing systems: a conceptual search*, in ÖRUCU E.,

ATTWOOLL E., COYLE S. (edited by), *Studies in legal systems: mixed and mixing*, The Hague, London, Boston, 1996.

OSBORNE C., *Civil litigation*, ed. 8, London, 2000.

OTU ENYIA J., *The law of banking in Nigeria: principles, statutes and guidelines*, Lagos, 2018.

PALMER V.V., *Mixed legal systems... and the myth of pure laws*, in *Lou. L. Rev.*, n. 67, 2007.

PAPA M., *Introduzione al codice civile iraniano*, in *Iranian Code Civil*, MAURIELLO R. (Italian translation edited by), Rome, 2015.

PARK A.E.W., *Sources of Nigerian law,* London, 1963.

PASCAL R.A., *Louisiana's Mixed Legal System*, in *Revue générale de droit*, vol. 15, no. 2, 1984; *Sources of the Digest of 1808: A Reply to Professor Batiza*, in *Tul. L. Rev*., vol. 46, no. 4, 1972; *Of the Civil Code and Us*, in *Lou. L. Rev.,* vol. 59, 1998.

PASSANANTE L., *La riforma del processo civile inglese: principi generali e fase introduttiva*, in *Riv. trim. dir. proc. civ*., 2000, pp. 1363 ss.

PEJOVIC C., *Civil law and common law: two different paths leading to the same goal*, in *Victoria university of wellington law review*, n. 32, 2011.

PERROT R., *L'inversion du contentieux ou les prouesses de l'ordonnance sur requête, ds Justice et droits fondamentaux, Mélanges offerts à Jacques Normand*, Paris, 2003; *Il procedimento di ingiunzione (studio di diritto comparato)*, in *Riv. dir. proc.*, 1986,

PETRILLLO P., *Iran*, Bologna, 2008.

PICCINELLI G.M., *Le codificazioni nell'era moderna*, in OLIVIERO M., PAPA M., PICCINELLI G.M., *Introduzione al diritto comparato dei paesi islamici*, 2021; *Il diritto agli interessi nei paesi arabi, in diritto del commercio internazionale*, 1996.

PICOD Y., VILLACEQUE J., *Les Rapports Guinchard et Magendie: vers quelle réforme de la procédure civile?,* in *Rev. huissiers,* no.6, 2010.

PIZZORUSSO A., *Sistemi giuridici comparati*, Milan, 1998

PLUCKNETT T.F.T., *A concise history of the common law*, Boston, 1956.

PHELPS A. W., *Handbook of Virginia rules of procedure in actions at law,* in *Wm & Mary L. Rev.,* vol. 2, no. 2, 1960.

POUND R., *The development of American law and its deviation from English law,* in *The law quarterly review*, vol. 67, no.1, 1951; *Common law and legislation*, in *Harv. L. Rev.*, vol. 3, 1908.

POSTEMA G.J., *Common law e sistema*, Naples, 2019.

PRESSER S.B., ZAINALDIN J., *Law and jurisprudence in American legal history. Cases and materials*, St. Paul, 2009.

PROTO PISANI A., *L'attuazione dei provvedimenti di condanna*, in *Foro Italiano*, vol. 111, 1988.

SUBASH RAJ, *Power of Indian courts to issue garnishee order*, in *Inter. J. R. A. Rev.*, vol. 4, no. 4, 2017.

RAJORA V., *Power of Indian courts to issue garnishee order*, 2010. Available at: HTTPS://SSRN.COM/ABSTRACT=1539347.

RAMANATHA AIYAR P., *Advanced law lexicon. The encyclopaedic law dictionary with legal maxims, latin terms,* in Words & Phrases, ed. 6, vol. 4, Nagpur, 2019.

RASTELL J., *Termes de la ley: certain difficult and obscure words and terms of the common and statute laws of this realm, now in use, Expounded and explained*, New Jersey, 2012.

RAVÀ T., *Un'esperienza di interpretazione comparativa: origini e struttura delle fonti nella "common law" inglese*, in *Riv. dir. civ.*, vol. I., 1974.

REID K.G.C., *The idea of mixed legal systems*, in *Tulane L. R.*, n. 78, 2003.

REIMANN M, ZIMMERMANN R., *The Oxford handbook of comparative law*, Oxford, 2006.

RENÉ D., SPINOSI J., *I grandi sistemi giuridici contemporanei*, Padua, 2004, R. SACCO (italian edited by).

RAJANI R., *Execution of civil judgments*, Tehran, 2007.

RESCIGNO F., *Le "Mille e una notte" del costituzionalismo iraniano. Metodo comparato, Teocrazia Islamica e Diritti delle donne quali Diritti Universali*, in *Federalismi.it*, 2023.

RIESENFELD S.A., PAKTER W.J., *Comparative law casebook*, vol. 4, Leida, 2001.

RÖDER T.J., *The separation of powers in Muslim countries. Historical and comparative perspectives*, in GROTER R., RODER T.J., (edited by), *Constitutionalism in Islamic countries. Between upheaval and continuity*, Oxford - New York, 2012.

ROESLER S.M., *Modern legal reform in Egypt: shifting claims to legal authority*, in *Cardozo J. Int'l & Comp. L.*, vol. 14, 2006.

ROMEO G., *L'argomentazione costituzionale di common law*, Turin, 2020.

ROOD J., *Treatise on the law of garnishment*, Minnesota, 1896.

RUSSO A., MOUSAVI S.A., *Funzioni e obiettivi del pignoramento nel diritto iraniani: un'analisi comparativa*, in BORRONI A., FIROUZAN A. M., GIUGGIOLI P.F., PAPA M., PERIALE F., *Il modello di common law,* Padua, 2023.

RUBIN N.N., *Cameroun: an African federation*, London, 1971.

RUDIN H.R., *The Germans in the Cameroons 1884-1913: a case study in modern imperialism*, New Haven, 1938.

SABAHI F., *Storia dell'Iran*, Milan, 2006.

SACCO R., *Diversity and uniformity in the law*, in *The A. J. C. L.,* vol. 49, no. 2, 2001; *One hundred years of comparative law,* in *Tulane L. Rev.*, vol. 75, no. 4, 2001; *Il diritto Africano*, (coll.) GUADAGNI M., ALUFFI BECK-PECCOZ R., CASTELLANI L., Turin, 1995; *Legal formants: A dynamic approach to comparative law (Installment I of II)*, in *The A. J. C. L.*, vol. 39, no. 1, 1991

SACCO R., MONATERI P.G., *Legal formants*, in *2 The new palgrave dictionary of Economics and the Law*, 1998.

SACCO R., GAMBARO A., *Sistemi giuridici comparati*, Turin, 2008.

SACCO R., GUADAGNI M., ALUFFI BECK-PECCOZ R., CASTELLANI L., *Diritto africano*, in *Rev. Inter. Dr. Comp.*, vol. 49, no. 3, 1997.

SADRZADEH AFSHAR M., *Code de procédure civile et commerciale*, Tehran, 2006.

SALACUSE J.W., *An Introduction to the law in French-speaking Africa, volume 1 - South of the Sahara*, Charlottesville, 1969.

SALEH S.S., *Garnishment order*, in *Legal coll. J.*, no. 113, 1994.

SALETTI A., *Cumulo ed eccesso dei mezzi di espropriazione forzata*, in *Riv. dir. proc.*, 1984.

SANI ABADI Z.N., JAFARI HARANDI M., DADASHNEJAD D., *A review on garnishments from legal and juridical perspectives*, in *Inter. J.M.M.U.,* vol. 6, no. 1, 2019.

SATTA S., *Diritto processuale civile*, ed. 9, Padua, 1981.

SATTA S., PUNZI C., *Diritto processuale civile*, Milan, 2000.

SATTARI A., *A comparative study on criminal garnishments in the new bill of criminal procedure rules and in the old rules*, Qom, 2013.

SAUNDERS J.B., *Words and phrases legally defined,* ed. 3, vol. 2, London, 1989.

SCHAUER F., *Civil Law, Common Law, and the data of Jurisprudence*, in BERSIER N., BEZZEMEK C., SCHAUER F. (edited by), *Common law-civil law,* Berlin, 2022.

SCHLESINGER R., *Comparative law 24-25*, ed. 4, New York, 1980.

SCHLESINGER R.B., BAADE H.W., HERZOG P.E., WISE E.M., *Comparative law. cases-text-materials,* New York, 1998.

SCHMITTHOFF M., *The Science of comparative law,* in *The Cambridge L.J.*, vol. 7, no. 1, 1939.

SCHMITTHOFF C.M., *The English conflict of laws*, London, 1954.

SCYBOZ G., GILLIÉRON P.R., *Code civil suisse et code des obligations annotés*, Lausanne, 2016.

SERTORIO G., *L'applicazione del diritto consuetudinario nella regione delle Nigeria occidentale con particolare riguardo alle customary courts*, in *Riv. trim. stud. Doc. dell'Istituto italiano per l'Africa e l'Oriente*, no. 4, 1966.

SHAHRI G.R., *Law of registration of deeds and estates*, Tehran, 2005.

SHAMS A., *Civil procedure rules*, vol. 3, ed. 6, Tehran, 2006.

SHAMS A., *Security in a garnishment order*, in *J.L.R.*, no. 16-17, 1996.

SHAMS A., *Civil Procedure; elementary course*, vol. 1, ed. 26, 2015.

SILVESTRI C., *Il foro lavoristico nell'Unione Europea*, Naples, 2016.

SIME S., *A practical approach to civil procedure*, New York, 2007.

SIMPSON W., *The common law and legal theory*, in *A. W. Simpson*, *Oxford Essays in Jurisprudence*, Oxford, 1973.

SMITH T.B., *Studies critical and comparative*, Edinburgh, 1962.

STEIN E., *Uses, misuses and non-uses of comparative law*, in *Northwestern U.L.R.*, vol. 72, no. 2, 1977.

SUBRIN B., *How equity conquered common law: the federal rules of civil procedure in historical perspective*, in *U. Pa.L.Rev.*, 1987.

SUGG R.P., *Writ of garnishment*, in *Mississippi L. J.*, vol. 24, no. 1, 1952.

SWENSON W., *Conflict of laws problems under the iowa garnishment statutes*, in *Iowa L. Rev.*, 1948.

TAISNE J., *La réforme de la procédure d'injonction de payer*, Paris, 1981.

TAKWANI C.K., *Civil procedure*, Lucknow, 2003.

TARIOL V., *L'Evaluation des dommages-intérêts en contrefaçon de marques*, Paris, 1990.

TARUFFO M., *Il processo civile di «civil law» e di «common law»: aspetti fondamentali*, in *Il Foro Italiano*, vol. 124, no. 11, 2001; *Precedente e giurisprudenza*, in *Riv. trim. dir. proc. civ.*, 2007; *Diritto processuale civile dei paesi anglosassoni*, in *Dig. disc. priv. Sez. civ.*, VI, Turin, 1990.

TARUFFO M., *L'attuazione esecutiva dei diritti: profili comparatistici*, in *Riv. Trim. dir. proc. civ.*, 1988.

TATSI M.T.T., *The Uniform act on arbitration as a simplified debt recovery procedure within the Ohada zone: a critical appraisal,* in *J. Corp. Gover. Inter. Bus. L.,* vol. 4. no. 1, 2021.

THAKKER C.K., *Code of civil procedure*, Lucknow, 2009.

THERY P., PERROT R., *Procédures civiles d'exécution*, ed. 3, Paris, 2013,

THODAY J., *Imprisonment by justices for nonpayment of money*, London, 1936.

TORRI M., *Storia dell'India*, Milano, 2004.

TUMNDE M. S., *Harmonization of business law in Cameroon: issues, challenges and prospects*, in *Tulane Europ. Civ. L. for.*, vol. 25, 2010.

TWIBELL T. S., *Implementation of the United Nations Convention on contracts for the international sale of goods (CISG) under shari'a (Islamic law): will article 78 of the CISG be enforced when the forum is in an Islamic state?,* in *Inter. legal persp.*, 1997.

UDIM E., *Principles of Garnishee proceedings in Nigeria*, Princeton, 2015.

VAN CAENEGEM R. C., *History of European civil procedure*, Tubinga, 1973.

VANDERLINDEN J., *Africa*, in *Digesto civ.*, vol. I, Turin, 1987.

VAN HECKE G., *Currency*, in ZWEIGERT K., DROBNIG U., *International encyclopedia of comparative law online,* vol. 3, ch. 36, 1972.

VASSALLI F., *Il diritto alla libertà morale*, in *Stud. Giur. in memoria di F. Vassalli*, vol. 2, Torino, 1960.

VEHKO J. F., *Enforcement of Family Support Obligations in Virginia*, in *Wm. & Mary L. Rev.*, vol. 21, no. 3, 1980.

VINCENT J., GUINCHARD S., *Procédure civile,* Paris, 1994.

VUITTON J., VUITTON X., *Les référés*, Paris, 2018.

WADE P., *A treatise on the law of attachment and garnishment: with an appendix containing a compilation of the statutes of the different states and territories... governing suits by attachment.*, vol. 1 of 2, London, 2010.

WALKER R.J., *English legal system*, ed. 5, London, 1980.

WAPLES R., *A treatise on attachment and garnishment*, United States, 2010.

WATSON A., *The evolution of law*, Baltimore, 1985; *The Making of the civil law*, 1981; *Society and legal change*, Edinburgh, 1978;

Comparative law and legal change, in *Cambridge L. J.*, vol. 37, no. 2, 1978; *Legal Transplants and Law Reform,* in *L. Quarterly Rev.*, vol. 94, 1976.

WEIR T., *An introduction to comparative law*, ed. 2, Clarendon, 1987.

WEISS M., *The future of comparative labour law as an academic discipline and as a practical tool*, in *Comp. labor l. and policy j.*, vol. 25, 2003.

WODI A., *Garnishment law and practice in Nigeria, UK and U.S.*, Nigeria, 2023; *Jurisdiction in garnishee proceedings: the Nigerian position*, 2022. Available at: https://ssrn.com/abstract=4397466.

WOLF L.L., MICHAEL R.O., *Property interests subject to attachment and garnishment for constructive service in Ohio*, in *U. Cin. L. Rev.* 125, 1952.

WOOD RENTON, *Encyclopaedia of the laws of England*, ed. 3, vol. 5, London, 1940.

YIANNOPOULOS A.N., *Louisiana civil code*, vol. 1, 2006; *Requiem for a civil code: a commemorative essay,* in *Tulane L. Rew.*, vol.78, 2004; *The early sources of Louisiana law: critical appraisal of a controversy*, in *Stud. Lou. Cul.*, 1983.

YANOU M.A., *Practice and procedure in civil matters in the courts of records in anglophone Cameroon*, Cameroon, 2015.

YILDRIM S., *Expanding secularism's scope: an Indian case study*, in *The American J. Comp. L.*, 2004.

YNTEMA H.E., *Comparative legal research - some remarks on "looking out of the cave",* in *Michigan L. Rev.*, vol. 54, no. 7, 1956.

ZIMMERMANN R., *Roman law, contemporary law, european law*, Oxford, 2001.

ZWEIFEL P., *Getting out of debt: garnishment of wage in whose interest?*, in *European J.L. Eco.*, 1999.

ZWEIGERT K., KOTZ H., *Introduzione al diritto comparato*, vol. 1, Milan, 1992.

www.ingramcontent.com/pod-product-compliance
Lightning Source LLC
Chambersburg PA
CBHW071430230926
51846CB00001B/178
9782336460857